Workers' Compensation

Benefits, Costs, and Safety under Alternative Insurance Arrangements

Terry Thomason
Timothy P. Schmidle
John F. Burton, Jr.

2001

W.E. Upjohn Institute for Employment Research
Kalamazoo, Michigan

Dedication

To Julie, my mother, and the memory of my father
T.T.

To Deb Joseph and my parents
T.P.S.

To the memory of C. Arthur Williams, Jr.,
workers' compensation scholar and gentleman,
and
to Janet, Rebecca, John, and Scott
J.F.B., Jr.

Contents

List of Figures

List of Tables

Acknowledgments

This volume reflects the confluence of each of our research interests. Burton's 1965 dissertation analyzed the causes and significance of interstate variations in workers' compensation costs. Over the last three decades, he has refined the methodology he developed in that study and has carried out legal and economic analyses on numerous other topics in the workers' compensation field. This book provides a further extension of the cost methodology that, of necessity, has had to become increasingly sophisticated to account for a variety of state-specific developments that affect the employers' costs of workers' compensation insurance.

Thomason has also written widely on workers' compensation. His prior research that is germane to this volume includes analyses of workers' compensation benefits, claims frequency, costs, experience rating, dispute resolution in workers' compensation programs, and safety regulation.

Schmidle's 1994 dissertation evaluated the impact of deregulation on interstate differences in market structure and the employers' costs of workers' compensation insurance. He also empirically tested the potential determinants of enactment of deregulatory legislation. Schmidle's study, which produced some provocative results with a smaller data set, provided the immediate impetus for this research volume.

This book was more than five years in the making, in large part because the very detailed, state-specific cost and statutory benefit index measures took a long time to compute. The book (and the authors) survived a Canadian postal strike, a "100-years" ice storm, Hurricane Floyd, and a variety of other minor challenges. We think that the cost and benefit index data reported in this volume will be of particular interest to workers' compensation practitioners. We also trust that our empirical analyses of the impact of deregulation on several of the principal objectives of workers' compensation (benefits adequacy, affordability, delivery system efficiency, and injury prevention) make a contribution to the literature that is of benefit to both the practitioner and academic communities.

Given the length and comprehensiveness of this research effort, the assistance of numerous individuals was instrumental to the completion of this volume. Unfortunately, space constraints preclude us from thanking everyone by specific reference. The fact that our acknowledgments are thus selective does not temper our appreciation of those who are not specifically named.

We thank H. Allan Hunt, Assistant Executive Director of the W.E. Upjohn Institute, who initially encouraged us to undertake this effort, patiently supported our efforts, and provided useful comments. Kevin Hollenbeck of the Upjohn Institute, who was appointed Director of Publications in 1999 and assumed direct oversight responsibility as this study neared completion, also provided helpful guidance. David E. Nadziejka was the technical editor for this volume; with great patience and good humor, he carefully and thoroughly edited our manuscript and is responsible for greatly improving the final product. We also appreciate the suggestions of the two anonymous referees who commented on the first draft of this book.

Florence Blum provided invaluable administrative assistance, conscientiously coded and computed manual rates, prepared many of the tables and figures reported in this volume, gathered the various chapters and appendices prepared by the coauthors into a comprehensive manuscript, and otherwise greatly facilitated the completion of the study.

Barry I. Llewellyn, Senior Divisional Executive for Cost Analysis Services at the National Council on Compensation Insurance (NCCI), helped educate us, throughout the entire course of this study, on the finer points of workers' compensation insurance pricing. Our cost methodology benefited greatly from his advice and assistance, and he provided crucial data needed to implement the methodology. We also received assistance from Debra Charlop and Krista Casey, who are Actuarial Associates at the NCCI.

Professor Robert W. Klein of Georgia State University provided valuable advice concerning the system we used to categorize states in terms of the extent of deregulation of their workers' compensation insurance markets.

Numerous officials in a variety of state agencies and other organizations provided data, documentation, and advice that were also of crucial importance to this study. The long list of individuals and groups that we thank includes (but is not limited to) Mark Miller at the California Workers' Compensation Institute; David M. Bellusci at the Workers' Compensation Insurance Rating Bureau of California; Jon D. Heikkinen at the Compensation Advisory Organization of Michigan; Frederick A. Huber at the Compensation Rating and Inspection Bureau for the state of New Jersey; Martin G. Heagen at the New York Compensation Insurance Rating Board; Sharon M. Bye and Craig Anderson at the Minnesota Workers' Compensation Insurers Association, Inc.; William E. Darlage at the Ohio Bureau of Workers' Compensation; Fran Barton and Joe Walter Rutkowski at the Pennsylvania Compensation Rating Bureau; Catherine A. Morse and Ling-Ling Liu of the Workers' Compensation Rating and Inspection Bureau of Massachusetts; Bill Vasek at the Department of Labor and Industries of the state of Washington; and Judith Greenwood of the

West Virginia Bureau of Employment Programs. We also appreciate the time and effort of those state officials who responded to our surveys.

Though we have strenuously attempted, through extensive consultations and a system of cross-checks, to avoid errors in our research, we assume sole responsibility for any mistakes that we inadvertently may have made.

Lastly, as indicated by our dedications, we acknowledge the assistance of several other individuals, who have enriched our lives in a variety of ways.

Terry Thomason
Timothy P. Schmidle
John F. Burton, Jr.

The Authors

Dr. Terry Thomason was appointed Director of the Charles T. Schmidt, Jr. Labor Research Center at the University of Rhode Island in 1999. He had previously taught for 11 years at the Faculty of Management of McGill University in Montreal, Canada. He received his Ph.D. from the New York State School of Industrial and Labor Relations at Cornell University in 1988. Dr. Thomason has authored or coauthored reports on workers' compensation commissioned by the state of New York, the state of Washington, the state of Oregon, the Workers' Compensation Board of Nova Scotia, and the Royal Commission on Workers' Compensation in British Columbia. He is co-editor of *Research in Canadian Workers' Compensation* (IRC Press, 1995) and *New Approaches to Disability in the Workplace* (Industrial Relations Research Association, 1998), and he coauthored a volume of essays published by the C.D. Howe Institute in 1995 entitled *Chronic Stress: Workers' Compensation in the 1990s.*

Timothy P. Schmidle is a Senior Research Associate at the School of Industrial and Labor Relations, Cornell University, where he serves as a principal co-investigator of an evaluation of New York State's alternative dispute resolution pilot program for workers' compensation. He received his B.A. from Georgetown University, a Masters degree in public administration from Syracuse University, and his M.S. and Ph.D. from Cornell's ILR School. His dissertation was entitled "The Impact of Insurance Pricing Deregulation on the Employers' Costs of Workers' Compensation Insurance." Schmidle's current research interests include workers' compensation and educational policy and human resources issues in primary, secondary, and higher education. He previously served as Associate Editor of John Burton's *Workers' Compensation Monitor.*

John F. Burton, Jr. is a Professor in the School of Management and Labor Relations at Rutgers: The State University of New Jersey. He previously was the Dean of the School. He has also been a Professor at Cornell University and at the University of Chicago. He has written on public sector bargaining and workers' compensation, including co-authoring (with Monroe Berkowitz) Permanent Disability Benefits in Workers Compensation, which was published by the W.E. Upjohn Institute. He served as Chair of the National Commission on State Workmen's Compensation Laws, which submitted its report to the President and Congress in 1972. Burton holds an undergraduate degree from Cornell University, and an LL.B. and Ph.D. in Economics from the University of Michigan.

1
Introduction

On October 1, 1992, Harold Werner, owner of the Potter Clothing Company of Newport, Rhode Island, received the first workers' compensation insurance policy issued by the Beacon Mutual Insurance Company. Beacon Mutual had been established as a publicly owned workers' compensation carrier by the Rhode Island state legislature two years earlier—using $5 million in seed money borrowed from the state pension fund—as a means of coping with a workers' compensation insurance system that seemed to be out of control in the late 1980s and early 1990s.[1]

Indeed, it was exceedingly difficult to find anyone who was happy with Rhode Island's program in that period. Insurers were rapidly abandoning the Rhode Island market, claiming that premium rates, which were regulated by the state Department of Business Regulation, were inadequate. In 1988, the incurred losses were in excess of revenues by $56.2 million, and Peter Burton, a director of the National Council on Compensation Insurance (NCCI), declared that "[t]he Rhode Island workers' compensation program is probably the most out-of-balance system in the United States."

Private carriers were not the only discontented participants in the Rhode Island workers' compensation program. Rhode Island employers, 90 percent of whom had been forced into the state's assigned-risk pool, were dissatisfied with the high costs of workers' compensation insurance. Skyrocketing compensation costs had been held responsible for some highly publicized departures of business from the state, including a 90-year-old truck body manufacturer that expected to save $500,000 in compensation costs by moving to Pennsylvania. This dissatisfaction led to a protest march on the statehouse reminiscent of civil rights demonstrations from a bygone era. The march was organized by the Rhode Island Chamber of Commerce and featured businessmen and businesswomen carrying banners and wearing buttons that read, "Everybody out of the [assigned-risk] pool."

When the state legislature responded to the crisis initially by trimming benefits to workers with permanent partial disabilities, organized labor responded with its own brand of hyperbole. "We are adamantly opposed to any reductions in benefits. We do not see the benefits being received as the problem in this system," stated George Nee, secretary-treasurer of the state AFL-CIO. Rather, Nee saw the insurance industry as "the root of problem," claiming that insurers were "making money off the backs of employers and employees in this state."

In 1989, the insurance industry sought a 139 percent increase in rates for the state's assigned-risk pool. At the time of the increase, over 90 percent of Rhode Island employers were in the pool. The Department of Business Regulation approved an increase of 32 percent. Not surprisingly, insurers were back within six months, asking for a 129 percent increase. The department delayed action on this request while state policymakers scrambled. Two legislative initiatives were enacted: creation of Beacon Mutual as a means for beleaguered employers to escape the dreaded assigned-risk pool, and a reduction of benefits paid to injured workers with a permanent partial disability.

In September 1991, nearly two years after the initial request, the Department of Business Regulation recommended that insurers receive a 55 percent rate increase. However, that next February, the increase was overturned by Rhode Island's Democratic governor, Bruce Sundlun, who accused insurers of collusion in the rate-setting process and expressed skepticism about industry claims that rates were inadequate. At the same time that he froze rates, the governor proposed legislation intended to reduce program costs and obviate the need for a rate increase. Perhaps even more significantly, Sundlun also administratively streamlined the appeals process of the Workers' Compensation Court.

Among other things, the governor's proposed legislation called for a further reduction of benefits for permanently and partially disabled workers, establishment of a fraud prevention unit, and restrictions on medical expenditures. Labor received a guarantee that employers must rehire injured workers whose benefits had expired, as well as provide greater dependency benefits for totally disabled workers and the families of fatally injured workers. Finally, the legislation offered incentives to insurers to remain in or return to the state's insurance market in the form of a "Fresh Start" provision, which required employers to assume 90 percent of the losses sustained by insurers in 1992 and 75 percent of the losses sustained in 1993.

While carefully crafted to offer something to everyone—except, perhaps, claimant attorneys, who were all but driven out of the system by the changes to the Workers' Compensation Court—these reforms seemed to have been surprisingly successful. Within two years, injury rates and severity dropped dramatically, which resulted in the NCCI requesting a 7 percent rate decrease in 1996. By that time, several large insurers, including Liberty Mutual and ITT Hartford, had returned to the state after leaving it during the fiscal crisis of 1989–1990. In 1998, Rhode Island experienced its third straight rate reduction.

Yet not all Rhode Islanders were rejoicing. Although it had supported the overall goals of the process and ultimately the final package, organized labor had reluctantly acquiesced to some of the reforms of 1990 and 1992. By 1998, labor began to argue that it was time to return some of the cost savings to injured workers. A spokesman was quoted as saying that the labor movement would like to "begin a new dialogue" on workers' compensation and that "[u]p until now, the dialogue has been very much one-sided. It's been very much about cutting costs."

While it remains to be seen whether labor's dissatisfaction will eventually lead to future reforms that restore benefits and thus increase costs once again, the Rhode Island experience illustrates the tensions that exist among the interests of different stakeholders in the workers' compensation program. It also shows how these various interests, which are translated into program objectives by policymakers, are reconciled in the legislative process. Finally, Rhode Island serves a microcosm illustrating the confluence of forces that have buffeted compensation programs nationwide in recent decades.

As we shall describe in this volume, the workers' compensation program has undergone significant changes in recent decades. Benefits paid to workers and the costs of the program to employers were significantly higher in the early 1990s than at any other time during the last 40 years, although both have declined during the 1990s. These changes in benefit payments and costs were accompanied by fundamental alterations in the insurance arrangements used to finance workers' compensation programs. Most of the 45 jurisdictions (including the District of Columbia) that allow private carriers to sell workers' compensation insurance deregulated the workers' compensation insurance market in the last 20 years. Furthermore, several states established public insurance funds to compete with private insurers, while a few states passed laws expanding the role of private insurers by eliminating state funds or making them compete with private carriers.

These changes in public policy may have a direct bearing on important aspects of the workers' compensation system, including the adequacy of workers' compensation benefits, the affordability of workers' compensation insurance, the efficiency of the workers' compensation benefits delivery system, and the prevention of workplace injuries and diseases. Clearly, workers, employers, insurance carriers, state officials, and other parties to workers' compensation want to know the impact of such statutory revisions.

Remarkably, researchers have paid little attention to the effects of deregulation and other changes in workers' compensation insurance pricing arrangements. In this volume, we address this deficiency through various empirical analyses that use state-specific cost, benefit, and injury data from 48 states for 1975 to 1995. We examine these developments over recent decades in terms of four objectives. First, are the benefits provided by the state workers' compensation programs adequate? Second, are the costs of the program to employers affordable? Third, do the insurance arrangements used to provide the benefits help achieve delivery system efficiency? Fourth, do the insurance arrangements encourage prevention of work-place injuries and diseases? While these are not the only objectives for a workers' compensation program, they are fairly comprehensive and also are particularly relevant for the developments examined in this study.[2]

We will discuss these objectives in greater detail after providing some background information on the workers' compensation system. We will also describe several federal and state policies that have been proposed to achieve these objectives and that will be examined in this study.

AN OVERVIEW OF WORKERS' COMPENSATION

Workers' compensation statutes in every state require employers to provide cash benefits, medical care, and rehabilitation services to workers who experience work-related injuries and diseases. In this section, we provide a brief overview of the history of workers' compensation in this country. We also highlight salient features of workers' compensation programs.

Historical Origins

Prior to the passage of workers' compensation laws, injured employees' only recourse was to sue their employer for negligence when disabled by work-related injuries or diseases. However, workers seldom won these lawsuits because of the legal doctrines that were prevalent in the 19th and early 20th centuries. On those infrequent occasions when employees did win these lawsuits, employers sometimes had to pay substantial cash awards. The result was unsatisfactory for everyone: employers confronted potentially large and uncertain financial risks, while, at the same time, many workers faced destitution as a result of occupational injuries.

State governments established workers' compensation programs to overcome these deficiencies of the common law. The programs were based on two principles that continue to the present day. First, benefits are provided to injured workers without regard to fault. To qualify for benefits under this no-fault approach, the worker only has to show that the injury is work-related, not that the employer was negligent. Second, the program provides limited liability for employers. Employers are required to pay for the benefits prescribed by the workers' compensation statute, but they are insulated from negligence suits. Furthermore, workers' compensation systems were also intended to make employers' costs of providing benefits predictable, manageable, and insurable and to curtail the delays and expenses of lawsuits.

Workers' compensation laws were established early in the 20th century by state governments rather than by the federal government, because at that time the Supreme Court's interpretation of the U.S. Constitution precluded broad federal legislation for private-sector workers. Most states established workers' compensation programs in the decade after Wisconsin's workers' compensation program went into effect in 1911. This pattern of state control has persisted, with minor exceptions, to the present day. Employees throughout the United States are, for the most part, covered by a state workers' compensation program; federal government involvement is limited to a few programs pertaining to federal employees and longshore workers.[3]

Coverage

Today, most workers—about 97 percent of all workers covered by the state unemployment insurance programs (Mont, Burton, and Reno 2000, pp. 14–15)—are covered by workers' compensation programs.[4] However, even when employed in industries or occupations covered by workers' compensation statutes, workers in most states must also meet four legal tests in order to receive benefits: 1) there must be a <u>personal injury</u>, which in some jurisdictions is interpreted to exclude mental disorders; 2) that results from an <u>accident,</u> which historically was interpreted by many states to exclude injuries that develop over a long period of time, as opposed to injuries resulting from a single traumatic incident; 3) that must <u>arise out of employment</u>, which means that the source of the injury must be related to the job (if you have a personal quarrel with a neighbor who stalks you to the job and shoots you there, this is unlikely to meet the "arising out of employment" test); and 4) that must <u>occur during the course of employment</u>, which normally requires that the injury occur on the employer's premises and during working hours. Most work-related injuries can meet these four tests, although there are numerous exceptions.[5]

Benefits

Injured workers who meet the four-part legal test will receive workers' compensation benefits prescribed by state law. State workers' compensation programs provide three types of benefits to injured workers. First, medical benefits, including medical rehabilitation, are provided for all injured workers, and in most states there are no statutory limits (such as deductibles or co-payments) on appropriate medical care. Second, some states provide vocational rehabilitation services that must be provided to an injured worker seeking reemployment. Third, cash benefits must be paid to disabled workers who satisfy certain criteria, or to their survivors if the worker was fatally injured.

The statutorily prescribed cash benefits for disabled workers vary by the extent of disability (that is, whether the worker is totally or partially disabled) and by the duration of the disability (whether the consequences of the injury are temporary or permanent). The most common type is temporary total disability (TTD) benefits, which are paid to someone who is completely unable to work but whose injury is of a temporary nature. The weekly TTD benefit is two-thirds of the pre-injury wage in most states, subject to maximum and minimum amounts that vary considerably among states.

Permanent partial disability (PPD) benefits account for the greatest share of benefits payments in states' workers' compensation programs (based on the cost of awards). PPD benefits are paid to injured workers who have permanent consequences of their work-related injury or disease. There are two general approaches to PPD benefits: scheduled benefits (paid for injuries listed in the workers' compensation statute, such as loss of an arm) and nonscheduled benefits (paid for permanent injuries that are not on the schedule, such as a back injury). The method of determining weekly benefits for a PPD case is less uniform and more complicated than that for TTD cases.

Permanent total disability (PTD) benefits are paid to an injured worker who is completely unable to work for an indefinite period; PTD cases are not very common. Finally, death benefits are paid to the survivor(s) of a worker killed on the job; these types of workers' compensation cases are also not very common.[6]

Financing of Benefits

Workers' compensation laws assign the responsibility for providing the benefits to employers, who in turn can provide the benefits by one of three mechanisms (depending on the state in which they are located): 1) by purchasing insurance from a private insurance carrier; 2) by purchasing insurance from a state workers' compensation fund; or 3) by qualifying to be a self-insured employer and paying the employees directly.

Some states, such as New York, have a three-way system in which all three insurance options are available to employers; the state workers' compensation insurance fund in jurisdictions that permit private carriers are referred to as "competitive" state funds. A few states, such as Ohio, restrict insurance coverage options to self-insurance or the state workers' compensation fund. Jurisdictions that do not permit private carriers to provide coverage are referred to as "exclusive" or "monopolistic" state funds.[7] Still other states, such as New Jersey and Wisconsin, restrict the employers' choices to private insurance carriers or self-insurance. In Chapter 2, we discuss in greater detail these workers' compensation insurance coverage options for employers. Specifically, we trace the changes in the relative importance of the three types of insurance (as measured by the relative distribution of benefit payments) and also discuss in detail the deregulation of the insurance provision by private carriers.

OBJECTIVES OF THE WORKERS' COMPENSATION PROGRAMS

In this section, we describe four objectives of workers' compensation programs that guided our research design and some public policies that may help meet these objectives. One of the themes of this study is that achieving these objectives is complex and, in some cases, counterproductive: achieving one objective often interferes with reaching one or more of the remaining goals. Because the various parties to workers' compensation—including, but not limited to injured workers, employers, state officials, insurers, and the medical community—place different emphasis on the relative worth of each objective, conflicts among these parties often arise with respect to what is the "best" public policy for a state's workers' compensation program.

Adequacy

The National Commission on State Workmen's Compensation Laws (National Commission 1972, pp. 36–37) included adequacy of cash benefits as one of its five objectives for a modern workers' compensation program.[8] The general objective, that "workers' compensation should provide substantial protection against interruption of income," was translated by the National Commission into 27 specific recommendations.[9] One use of the specific recommendations was to provide a basis for assessing the adequacy of state workers' compensation benefits as of 1972. For example, recommendation R3.8 stated that the maximum weekly benefits for temporary total disability benefits should be at least 66.67 percent of the state's average weekly wage by 1973 and at least 100 percent of the state's average weekly wage by 1975.

At the time of the National Commission's report in 1972, only 10 of the 50 states had weekly maximums for temporary total disability that were greater than 66.67 percent of the state's average weekly wage. The National Commission characterized as "substandard" the TTD maximums in 32 states that were less than 60 percent of the state's average weekly wage. The National Commission thus concluded "a majority of States have maximum weekly benefits which are inadequate" and added this observation (National Commission 1972, p. 61):

> Our judgment that the maximum weekly benefit levels are generally inadequate is reinforced by comparing the maximum weekly benefit in each State as of January 1, 1972, with the 1971 poverty level for a non-farm family of four persons, which is $79.56 a week. It is distressing that as of January 1, 1972, the maximum weekly benefit for temporary total benefits in more than half the states did not reach this poverty level.

The National Commission standards also allow an ongoing assessment of state workers' compensation programs. The National Commission made 84 recommendations, designating 19 of them as "essential," and recommended that, if necessary, Congress should guarantee compliance with these 19 essential recommendations by federal legislation. Although Congress has never enacted such legislation, the U.S. Department of Labor has monitored the progress of the states in complying with the 19 essential recommendations on a continuing basis.

Nine of these 19 provide quantifiable measures of the adequacy of cash benefits that we rely on in this study. The recommendations can be summarized under three types of benefits:

- Temporary Total Disability Benefits: A worker's weekly benefit should be at least 66.67 percent of the worker's preinjury wage, subject to a maximum of 100 percent of the state's average weekly wage. There should be no limit on the duration or dollar amount of these benefits while the worker is disabled.

- Permanent Total Disability Benefits: A worker's weekly benefit should be at least 66.67 percent of the worker's preinjury wage, subject to a maximum of 100 percent of the state's average weekly wage. There should be no limit on the duration or dollar amount of these benefits while the worker is disabled. These benefits should not be paid to workers who retain substantial earning capacity.

- Death Benefits: A survivor's weekly benefit should be at least 66.67 percent of the worker's preinjury wage, subject to a maximum of 100 percent of the state's average weekly wage. There should be no limit on the duration or dollar amount of these benefits during the statutory period of dependency, which, for example, is for the life of the widow or widower or until remarriage.

There is one major category of cash benefits for which the National Commission was unable to reach a consensus and make recommendations, namely, permanent partial disability benefits. Fortunately, an alternative source that provides an operational measure of adequacy for evaluating permanent partial disability benefits exists in the Workmen's Compensation and Rehabilitation Law, generally known as the "Model Act," published by the Council of State Governments.

The Model Act was originally published in the 1960s and then was revised in 1974 to make the proposed statutory language consistent with the recommendations of the National Commission. The Model Act (revised)[10] will be used in Chapter 4 as the standard of adequacy against which state workers' compensation laws will be evaluated in this study for the period since 1975.[11] We will also examine whether the policy prescription of the National Commission—the enactment of federal standards to ensure compliance with the 19 essential recommendations—is still warranted on the basis of the progress that states have made to improve the adequacy of the cash benefits in their workers' compensation programs.

Affordability

Fulfillment of the adequacy objective may sometimes jeopardize another objective of modern workers' compensation programs, namely, affordability. Affordability is concerned with designing a workers' compensation program that employers, workers, and the public can afford without serious adverse consequences, such as loss of jobs. Although affordability was not specified as one of the objectives of a modern workers' compensation program by the National Commission, the importance of affordability was implicitly recognized in the Commission's report (pp. 124–125):

> The economic system of the United States encourages the forces of efficiency and mobility. These forces tend to drive employers to locate where the environment offers the best prospect for profit . . . Any State which seeks to regulate the by-product of industrialization, such as work accidents, invariably must tax or charge employers to cover the expenses of such regulation. The combination of mobility and regulation poses a dilemma for policymakers in State governments. Each State is forced to consider carefully how it regulates its domestic enterprises because relatively restrictive or costly regulation may precipitate the departure of the employers to be regulated or deter the entry of new enterprises.

When it prepared its report, the National Commission did not feel that the interstate differences in workers' compensation costs were sufficient to induce any rational employer to move to another state in order to reduce costs. The National Commission reached this conclusion because, at the time (1972), interstate differences in workers' compensation costs rarely exceeded 1 percent of payroll, and such differences were relatively insignificant compared to interstate variation in other costs such as wage levels. Despite this reassurance about the implausibility that employers would make relocation decisions based on workers' compensation costs, the National Commission (1972, p. 125) went on to provide a warning:

> While the facts dictate that no State should hesitate to improve its
> workers' compensation program for fear of losing employers,
> unfortunately this appears to be an area where emotion too often
> triumphs over fact . . . whenever a State legislature contemplates
> an improvement in workers' compensation which will increase
> insurance costs, the legislators will hear claims from some
> employers that the increase in costs will force a business exodus.
> It will be virtually impossible for the legislators to know how gen-
> uine are these claims . . .
>
>   When the sum of these inhibiting factors is considered, it seems
> likely that many States have been dissuaded from reform of their
> workers' compensation statutes because of the specter of the van-
> ishing employer, even if that apparition is a product of fancy not
> fact. A few States have achieved genuine reform, but most suffer
> with inadequate laws because of the drag of laws of competing
> states.

In this study, we will examine whether the average cost of workers'
compensation insurance in the United States has increased and, in particular, whether the differences among states in the costs of workers'
compensation insurance have widened since the National Commission's report in 1972. Such developments would mean that the specter
of the vanishing employer is more credible now than it was when the
National Commission characterized the threat as "a product of fancy
not fact."

There is anecdotal evidence that by the early 1990s, workers' compensation costs had become a serious threat to employer viability. A
1992 cover story in *Nation's Business* was entitled "Workers' Comp
Costs: Out of Control." Thompson (1992, p. 22) documented the financial ruin that almost befell a California company run by Robert
Boucher, who stated (perhaps with some hyperbole), "This cancer
[workers' compensation] is killing thousands and thousands of honest
companies." Thompson also reported that the estimated costs of workers' compensation were $62 billion in 1991, nearly triple the amount
spent in 1980, and postulated that "[a]t the present growth rate, costs
will nearly triple again by the year 2000." In retrospect, the concerns
about costs appear exaggerated: we now know that total costs of the
workers' compensation programs were $55.2 billion in 1991 and $52.1
billion in 1998.[12] However, the article was indicative of the general

attitude among employers towards workers' compensation costs in the early 1990s, which, in turn, resulted in statutory benefit reductions and other consequences that will be examined in Chapter 2.

If, as we now know to be the case, average workers' compensation costs have increased since the 1970s, and especially if—as we will attempt to demonstrate in this study—interstate cost differences have widened, there is a strong argument for invoking the policy prescription that the National Commission made in light of fears regarding interstate cost differences. The National Commission (1972, p. 27) called for federal standards for workers' compensation programs, using this rationale:

> We believe that the threat of or, if necessary, the enactment of Federal mandates will remove from each state the main barrier to effective workers' compensation reform: the fear that compensation costs may drive employers to move away to markets where protection for disabled workers is inadequate but less expensive.

This rationale is unassailable—or so it would seem. If there are differences among states in workers' compensation costs as well as in the adequacy of the cash benefits in their workers' compensation statutes, then forcing laggard states to improve their benefits should result in less interstate variation in costs. However, earlier research by Krueger and Burton (1990) raised serious doubts about the assertion that federal standards would reduce the disparity among states in workers' compensation costs. We will revisit this issue in our empirical analysis in Chapter 4.

Delivery System Efficiency

A third objective of a modern workers' compensation program that was articulated by the National Commission (1972, p. 99) was an effective delivery system. This was necessary to ensure that the "other program objectives are met efficiently and comprehensively" (National Commission 1972, p. 39). Responsibility for an effective delivery system lay with a variety of private and public organizations (including insurance carriers, workers' compensation agencies, and courts) and with various individuals who are also involved (including employees, attorneys, physicians, employees, and employers). We translate the effective delivery system objective into an objective of delivery system efficiency, by which we mean that workers' compensation benefits of a particular quality should be provided at the least possible administrative cost.

One of our principal goals in this volume is to evaluate the effect of different insurance arrangements on the employers' costs of workers' compensation insurance. We will thus examine whether, after controlling for factors such as injury rates and benefits levels, particular insurance arrangements are associated with lower workers' compensation insurance rates. If, for example, we find that, after controlling for benefits and other factors, provision of insurance by exclusive state workers' compensation funds is associated with lower workers' compensation insurance rates, then we could conclude that the presence of such a state fund helps achieve delivery system efficiency. Likewise, if strict regulation of rates charged by private carriers results in lower rates than would be achieved with deregulation, then the regulation of rates helps achieve delivery system efficiency.

Determining the net impact of various insurance arrangements on the costs of workers' compensation insurance is a complicated endeavor. There are a variety of factors affecting insurance rates, such as the levels of cash and medical benefits, that must be measured and taken into consideration. Furthermore, there are subtle interrelations between the insurance cycle and the effects of deregulation of private carriers that must also be addressed before any conclusions about delivery system efficiency can be made. Moreover, there are a wide variety of forms of workers' compensation insurance market deregulation that have been adopted by states in recent decades. These permutations must also be taken into consideration when evaluating the delivery system efficiency of state workers' compensation programs. All of these are examined in Chapters 5 to 7.

Prevention

The National Commission (1972, p. 87) also postulated that the encouragement of safety is one of the basic objectives of a modern workers' compensation program. The National Commission noted that the workers' compensation program operates in at least two ways to reduce the frequency and severity of work-related injuries and diseases. First, state agencies and private and public carriers provide employers with preventive services, including safety engineering. Second, the program provides a monetary incentive to employers to improve their safety records.

The monetary (financial) incentive occurs because workers' compensation insurance is experience-rated, which means that the premium charged depends on the level of benefit payments. There are two steps in the experience-rating process, beginning with industry-level (or occupational-level) experience rating.[13] Every employer who purchases insurance is assigned to a particular insurance classification, for which the initial insurance rate can be determined by looking in an insurance manual. In addition, medium or large employers are eligible for firm-level experience rating, which means they pay more or less than the initial rates depending on their own experience relative to other firms in the same insurance classification.

The traditional rationale for experience rating is that it provides an incentive for employers to improve their safety records in order to reduce their insurance premiums. Empirical evidence regarding the success of experience rating as a prevention tool is mixed: some studies suggest that experience rating promotes safety, but others do not.[14]

Our study is concerned with another dimension of the relationship between workers' compensation and safety: namely, the effect of different insurance arrangements on improving workplace safety. One issue is whether competitive and exclusive state funds are more or less likely to promote safety and health than are private insurance carriers. Some have argued, for example, that private carriers are likely to emphasize profits over safety, and therefore that state funds are more likely to be concerned with worker safety and health. Another workplace safety issue is whether the type of regulation of private carriers affects safety incentives. One argument is that administered pricing or other forms of price regulation will distort the financial incentives to improve workplace safety and, therefore, that deregulation is likely to improve workplace safety.

We examine these various possible relationships among workplace safety and insurance arrangements in workers' compensation in Chapter 8. There are obvious policy implications of any finding that the prevention objective is furthered by a state's choices about whether to rely on a state fund or private carriers for workers' compensation coverage, and, if private carriers are allowed, whether the insurance rates charged by those carriers should be regulated.

Relationships among Objectives

We have discussed four objectives for a workers' compensation program that provide the conceptual framework for our study: adequacy of benefits, affordability, delivery system efficiency, and injury prevention. In this volume, we will examine various public policies that states or the federal government could adopt to achieve these objectives. Ideally, policies that help achieve one objective will also facilitate reaching another objective. Thus, if regulation of private carriers both lowers workers' compensation insurance rates and improves workplace safety, a state that uses this approach will foster both the delivery system efficiency and prevention objectives.

Candor compels us to admit, at this point, that some policies that help achieve one objective may actually impede the realization of another objective. Thus, for example, higher levels of benefits may help improve benefit adequacy but may also undermine affordability and contribute to job losses. One contribution we make in this study is to help quantify the tradeoffs between adequacy and affordability that would result from a federal statute requiring adequate benefits. This is one of our tasks in Chapter 4.

Another contribution we make is our analysis of the possible tradeoffs in using different public policies regarding insurance arrangements. We will quantify, for example, the possible savings to employers from deregulation of private insurance carriers. We will then be able to compare these possible savings with the added costs of achieving adequate cash benefits resulting from federal standards. These are some of our tasks in Chapter 9.

The conclusions we reach at this book's end are, of course, the result of the requisite groundwork that we have prepared for the reader as well as for ourselves. The remainder of this volume begins in the next chapter with an overview of salient developments in workers' compensation developments since 1960. We then (in Chapter 3) critique various ways of measuring employers' costs of workers' compensation and explain the relative advantages of our cost methodology. In Chapter 4, we present our basic model for determining costs and *inter alia* use it to examine the possible effects of federal workers' compensation standards on adequacy of benefits and affordability. Chapter 5 compares the costs of workers' compensation insurance provided by state versus private carriers. In the succeeding two chapters, we review economic theory and our empirical findings about the effects of insurance regulation on workers' compensation costs and market structure. The impact on workplace safety of different workers' compensation arrangements is investigated in Chapter 8. Chapter 9 contains our conclusions about the public policy implications of our empirical research, including policy prescriptions.

Notes

1. Information about the recent history of Rhode Island workers' compensation reform came from various issues of the *Providence Journal*. Citations are available from Terry Thomason on request. We are indebted to Matthew Bodah for his assistance in compiling this history.
2. For an alternative version of the objectives of workers' compensation programs, see the National Commission (1972). "Equity" is often used as an additional objective or criterion for the workers' compensation program. The National Commission (p. 137) defined an "equitable" workers' compensation program as one that delivered "benefits and services fairly as judged by the program's consistency in providing equal benefits or services to workers in identical circumstances and its rationality in providing benefits and services in proportion to the impairment or disability for those with different degrees of loss." For an example of the use of the equity criterion to evaluate permanent partial disability benefits in the workers' compensation program, see Berkowitz and Burton (1987).
3. The decentralized nature of workers' compensation in the United States has advantages and disadvantages for researchers. One advantage is that variation among states provides a natural laboratory for evaluating the impact of different public policies. There are considerable variations among the states in many aspects of their workers' compensation programs, with various combinations of the features we are examining. For example, some states that rely solely on private carriers and self-insuring employers to provide workers' compensation coverage have low statutory benefits, while other states with identical insurance arrangements have generous statutory benefits. This interstate variability in combinations of attributes makes it easier to determine the net effect on costs of different insurance pricing arrangements. However, the decentralized nature of workers' compensation in the United States and the lack of a federal presence is also disadvantageous, because it results in a paucity of comparable data. Most of our research effort for this book was devoted to constructing a comparable data set for the 48 jurisdictions in our study.

4. There is less than 100 percent coverage because of exemptions that are permitted by state workers' compensation statutes. These exemptions include 1) employers with few employees (e.g., three or less); 2) exempted industries, such as state and local governments and agriculture; 3) occupational exemptions, such as household workers; and 4) a Texas law that allows employers in the state to elect not to provide coverage. Certain employees—those who are "casual" workers or workers not engaged in the normal trade or business of the employer—may not be protected by a state workers' compensation law, even when their employer is otherwise within the scope of the mandatory coverage specified by the statute. In addition, independent contractors normally are not covered by workers' compensation.

5. The coverage of work-related diseases by workers' compensation has been more problematic, as discussed by Spieler and Burton (1998).

6. Additional information on workers' compensation cash benefits is included in Appendix D.

7. As of 1999, Ohio, Nevada, Washington state, and West Virginia had exclusive state funds and permitted self-insurance; North Dakota and Wyoming had exclusive state funds and did not permit self-insurance.

8. The term *workmen's compensation* was generally used to describe the program as late as 1972, when the National Commission submitted its report. Shortly thereafter, most jurisdictions and commentators adopted *workers' compensation* as the preferred term. We have retained *workmen's compensation* when referring to the name of the National Commission, but have used *workers' compensation* in all references to the contents of the National Commission's report.

9. The National Commission made 84 recommendations in total covering all aspects of workers' compensation programs and designated 19 of them as "essential."

10. The Model Act (revised) is reprinted as Appendix A of Larson and Larson (1999).

11. The procedure used to make the Model Act (revised) an adequacy standard is discussed in Thomason and Burton (2000a).

12. The principle of full disclosure requires an admission: the source of the $62.0 billion estimate for the costs of the workers' compensation program in 1992 cited in Thompson (1992, p. 23) was Burton (1992).

13. Some writers define what we term "industry-level (or occupational-level) experience rating" as *class rating* and would confine the term *experience rating* to what we refer to as "firm-level experience rating." Regardless of differences in terminology, economic theory posits that both levels of what we call "experience rating" promote workplace safety and health.

14. After reviewing all of the available (and conflicting) empirical evidence, Burton and Chelius (1997, p. 266) endorsed a view that experience rating "has had at least some role in improving safety for large firms."

2

Developments in Workers' Compensation since 1960

As the Chapter 1 tale of workers' compensation woes in Rhode Island illustrated, achieving workers' compensation program objectives can sometimes result in sharp conflicts among the various stakeholders. This chapter provides a more general historical perspective of developments in workers' compensation as well as a context for our modeling and empirical analysis in later chapters.

Our historical overview of workers' compensation developments begins with the 1960s, which was a relatively tranquil period in workers' compensation, at least for employers and carriers. However, criticisms of the coverage and benefits of the workers' compensation program were building in the 1960s and early 1970s, culminating in the indictment of the state programs as "in general . . . inadequate and inequitable" by the National Commission on State Workmen's Compensation Laws in 1972. One result was a flurry of activity by the states to update their laws, which resulted in higher benefits (improved adequacy) but also led to higher costs. Workers' compensation costs also increased after the mid 1980s because of the rapid escalation of payments for medical benefits. By the early 1990s, an almost inevitable backlash against higher costs of the program occurred, which resulted in "reforms" that have affected workers' compensation throughout the 1990s.

To be sure, the overview in the preceding paragraph is simplistic, because it ignores such important factors as the role of high interest rates in temporarily suppressing the employers' costs of the program in the early 1980s and the role of private carriers in spearheading the cost-cutting reforms of the early 1990s. That brief history also ignores the changes in workers' compensation insurance arrangements, which were arguably both a cause and a consequence of the changes in workers' compensation costs in recent decades. We attempt to tell the more complex, more accurate—and, we trust, more compelling—story in this chapter.

BENEFITS AND COSTS

The costs to employers and the benefits paid to workers as a percentage of payroll, which are two measures of interest to all aficionados of workers' compensation, fluctuated significantly from 1960 to 1998 (Figure 2.1).[1]   Employers' costs as a percentage of payroll ranged from a low of 0.93 percent in 1960 to a high of 2.17 percent in 1993, followed by a decline to 1.35 percent in 1998. Over the same period, benefits as a percentage of payroll started at 0.59 percent in 1960, climbed to 1.66 percent in 1992, and then dropped to 1.08 percent in 1998.

There were significant variations in the rates of increase or decrease of workers' compensation costs between 1960 and 1996. We have divided the post-1960 experience into subperiods, defined by whether total costs of the program were increasing relatively slowly (defined by those years in which costs increased on average by less than 10 percent a year) or relatively rapidly (defined by those years in which costs increased on average by 10 percent or more a year). Analysis of these subperiods allows us to identify the dynamics of the last 40 years that have affected the benefits, costs, and insurance arrangements in the program.

The Era of Tranquillity: 1960–1971

The era from 1960 through 1971 was relatively tranquil for workers' compensation, at least for employers and insurance carriers. Employers' costs increased from $2.1 billion in 1960 to $5.2 billion in 1971, an 8.8 percent annual rate of increase (Figure 2.2).[2]   The costs grew more rapidly than wages, and thus workers' compensation costs increased from 0.93 percent of payroll in 1960 to 1.11 percent in 1971 (see Figure 2.1). Benefits paid to workers increased from $1.3 billion in 1960 to $3.2 billion in 1971, which represented an annual rate of increase of 8.5 percent (Figure 2.3). Benefits as a percentage of payroll increased from 0.59 percent in 1960 to 0.67 percent in 1971 (see Figure 2.1).

Despite the increase in benefits paid relative to payroll during this period, workers' compensation programs were increasingly criticized for failing to provide adequate benefits and coverage. The statutory

Figure 2.1 Costs and Benefits of Workers' Compensation, 1960–98

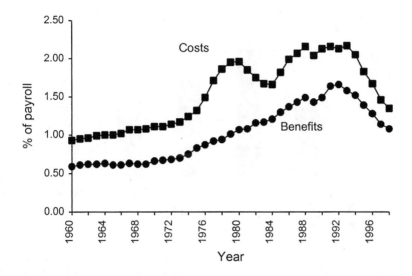

SOURCE: Table A.1, columns 1 and 2.
Note: The apparent drop between 1988 and 1989 is due to a change in methodology
described in Table A.1, note a.

Figure 2.2 Annual increase in Workers' Compensation Costs, 1960–98

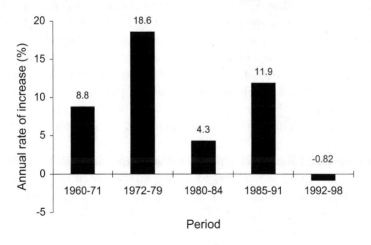

SOURCE: Table A.2.

Figure 2.3 Annual Percentage Increase in Workers' Compensation Benefits, 1960–98

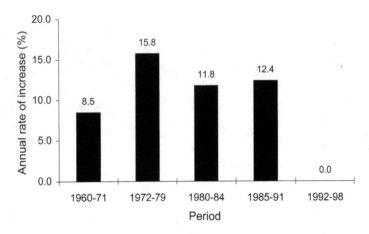

SOURCE: Table A.3.

benefits had not been improved since the beginning of World War II to keep up with increases in the average wage level, and in most jurisdictions the maximum weekly benefits were lower relative to wages in the 1960s than they had been in 1940.[3]   Indeed, as of 1972, the maximum weekly benefit for temporary total disability in more than half the states was less than $79.56, the national poverty level for a nonfarm family of four (National Commission 1972, p. 61). Moreover, the extent of coverage of workers by workers' compensation did not match the extent of coverage by other social insurance programs, such as the Social Security (OASDHI) and unemployment insurance programs.

Other related developments in this era provided the impetus for subsequent changes in state workers' compensation programs. The number of disabling work injuries increased in the 1960s, resulting in more deaths, permanent disabilities, and temporary total disabilities (Williams and Barth 1973, p. 3). A 1968 explosion in a West Virginia coal mine served as the catalyst for the enactment of the federal Coal Mine Health and Safety Act of 1969, which *inter alia* provided benefits to disabled coal miners and their survivors (Barth 1987, p. 12–13). Many viewed this law both as an indicator of increased federal concern regarding the inadequacy of state compensation for occupational diseases and as a harbinger of increased federal involvement in the workers' compensation arena.

The Era of Reform: 1972–1979

Concern about deteriorating workplace safety and the increasing criticisms of the workers' compensation program prompted Congress to create the National Commission on State Workmen's Compensation Laws as part of the Occupational Safety and Health Act of 1970. The National Commission conducted a series of hearings, sponsored extensive research, and intensively deliberated over a 15-month period. The result was a 1972 report that was critical of the state workers' compensation programs and concluded that state laws "in general are inadequate and inequitable" (National Commission, 1972, p. 119). The Commission made its recommendations for state workers' compensation programs and urged Congress to enact federal minimum standards incorporating its "essential" recommendations if the states did not improve their laws by 1975.

Congress did not enact federal standards. One reason was that state laws were significantly improved in the 1970s in response to the threat of federal intrusion into the traditional domain of the states. One way of measuring improvements in states' workers' compensation laws is the extent to which they complied with the Council of State Government's Model Act, which incorporated the recommendations of the National Commission. The cash benefits provided by the state statutes increased on average between 1972 and 1979, from 39.6 percent to 50.4 percent of the benefits prescribed by the Model Act (Figure 2.4).[4] Another example of the rapid improvements in state laws after the submission of the National Commission report is that one of the Commission's recommendations—the maximum weekly benefit for temporary total disability benefits be at least 100 percent of the state's average weekly wage—was complied with by one state in 1972; by 1979, 28 states had complied.

The changes in statutory benefits translated into higher benefit payments to workers.[5] Benefits as a percentage of payroll rose from 0.67 percent to 1.01 percent between 1971 and 1979 (see Figure 2.1); the costs to employers increased from 1.11 percent of payroll in 1971 to 1.95 percent in 1979.

**Figure 2.4 Statutory Cash Benefits Relative to Model Act
           Benefits, 1974–96**

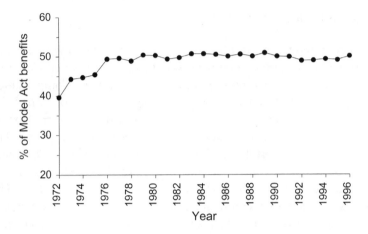

SOURCE: Table A.1, column 3.

Although costs and benefits grew rapidly during this period, private carriers were generally able to increase premiums fast enough to cover the higher benefit payments. Three measures of underwriting experience—the pure loss ratio, the combined ratio, and the overall operating ratio—are shown in Table 2.1 and are explained in Appendix B. Lower levels of each of these measures are preferable for the insurance industry and represent higher profits (or lower losses). The overall operating ratio is the most comprehensive measure of profitability because it includes both underwriting experience and investment income. An overall operating ratio in excess of 100 indicates that the insurance industry is experiencing a net loss on operations.

Underwriting experience in the workers' compensation line from 1973 to 1997 is depicted in Figure 2.5. The data indicate that underwriting experience deteriorated from 1973 to 1976 but then improved from 1976 to 1979. The insurance industry by the end of the 1970s had accommodated to the higher benefit payments of the decade by increasing workers' compensation premiums at a sufficient rate to achieve satisfactory underwriting results.

Table 2.1 Workers' Compensation Underwriting Experience, 1999[a]

Line 1	Pure loss ratio (incurred losses)[b]		65.9
2	Loss adjustment expenses[b]	+	15.8
3	Losses and adjustment expenses incurred (lines 1 + 2)[b]		81.7
4	Underwriting expenses incurred[c]	+	28.0
5	Dividends to policyholders[b]	+	5.6
6	Combined ratio after dividends (lines 3 + 4 + 5)		115.3
7	Net investment gain loss and other income[b]	–	20.5
8	Overall operating ratio (lines 6 – 7)		94.8

SOURCE: From *Best's Aggregates and Averages, Property/Casualty*, 2000 edition and prior editions,© A.M. Best Company, used with permission.
[a] Terms are explained in Appendix B.
[b] Expressed as a percentage of net premiums earned.
[c] Expressed as a percentage of net premiums written.

Figure 2.5 Workers' Compensation Insurance Underwriting Experience, 1973–99

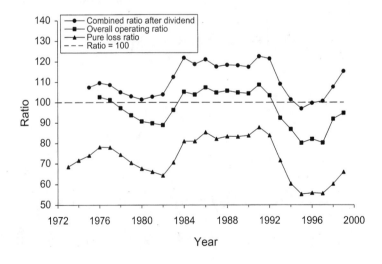

SOURCE: Table A.4.

The Squeeze of Benefits and Costs: 1980–1984

The growth in workers' compensation benefit payments decelerated in the early 1980s, dropping to 11.8 percent a year from the 15.8 percent annual rate of increase in the 1972–1979 period (see Figure 2.3). The slowdown in part reflected the slower pace of state reform as the threat of federal standards for state workers' compensation programs vanished in wake of the 1980 election of President Reagan. Between 1980 and 1984, the expected cash benefits provided by state statutes on average only increased from 50.3 to 50.5 percent of the benefits prescribed by the Model Act (see Figure 2.4). Actual benefits paid as a percentage of payroll nonetheless increased from 1.01 to 1.21 percent of payroll between 1979 and 1984 (see Figure 2.1).

Workers' compensation costs grew at a modest annual rate of 4.3 percent from 1980 to 1984 (see Figure 2.2), not even matching total payroll growth. As a result, costs as a percentage of payroll plummeted from 1.95 percent in 1979 to 1.66 percent in 1984 (see Figure 2.1).

The squeeze between costs and benefits can be explained by macroeconomic developments. Rapid inflation of the late 1970s and early 1980s led to high interest rates and bond yields (Figure 2.6), which resulted in favorable investment opportunities for workers' compensa-

Figure 2.6 Nominal and Real Interest Rates, 1960–99

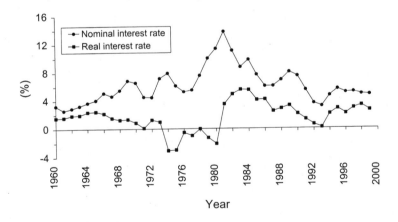

SOURCE: Table A.5.

tion carriers and substantial improvements in net investment income. Investment income increased from 9.2 percent of premiums in 1979 to 16.7 percent in 1984, which is reflected in the increasing spread in Figure 2.5 between the combined ratio (which measures underwriting experience) and the overall operating ratio (which measures overall profitability, including investment income). The higher investment income allowed carriers to compete for business by reducing insurance rates, despite increasing benefit payments. For most of the period, this strategy worked: from 1979 to 1983, the overall operating ratio in workers' compensation insurance ranged from 96.3 to 88.9, indicating industry profitability. However, the loss ratio deteriorated rapidly after 1982, and by 1984 the overall operating ratio exceeded 100 (see Figure 2.5).

Seeds of Neo-Reform: 1985–1991

The falling workers' compensation costs that characterized the early 1980s did not persist through the balance of the decade. There was a rapid escalation in the employers' costs of workers' compensation, increasing from $25.1 billion in 1984 to $55.2 billion in 1991, an average of 11.9 percent a year (see Figure 2.2), which far outpaced payroll growth. As a result, workers' compensation costs as a percentage of payroll increased rapidly, rising from 1.66 percent in 1984 to 2.16 percent in 1991 (see Figure 2.1).

Workers' compensation benefits also increased during this period, from $18.0 billion in 1984 to $40.8 billion in 1991, an average annual increase of 12.4 percent (see Figure 2.3). Payroll grew at a slower rate than benefits, so benefits increased from 1.21 percent of payroll in 1984 to 1.64 percent in 1991 (see Figure 2.1). Medical benefits increased by 14.9 percent per year between 1985 and 1991, more rapidly than both the annual increase of 10.8 percent in cash benefits[6] (Figure 2.7) and the high rate inflation for general health care costs. The sources of the rapid escalation in medical costs in the workers' compensation program included the rapid spread of managed care through the health care system used for non-occupational medical conditions and the resulting cost shifting to the workers' compensation health care system.[7]

**Figure 2.7 Annual Percentage Increase by Type of Workers'
Compensation Benefit, 1960–98**

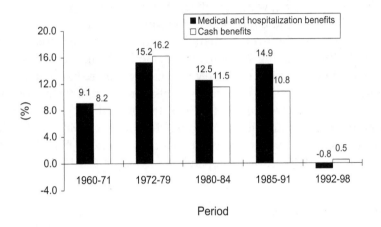

SOURCE: Table A.3.

Throughout the late 1980s and early 1990s, many employers became concerned, if not alarmed, about the increasing costs of the workers' compensation program.[8] In addition to cost increases resulting from higher statutory cash benefits and escalating medical benefits, employers were also concerned about what they perceived to be widespread fraud and rampant litigation, especially involving conditions such as workplace stress, which employers felt were outside the proper domain of the program.

The workers' compensation insurance industry was particularly agitated by the developments concerning the relationships between benefits and costs. Several factors contributed to the industry's problems. Benefit payments reaccelerated during this period, but in many states, carriers were unable to gain approval from regulators for the significant premium increases the industry believed were actuarially justified. As a result, loss ratios, which were always below 71 from 1979 to 1983, were always above 80 from 1984 to 1991 (see Figure 2.5). Furthermore, even though net investment income remained relatively high from 1984 to 1991 (always exceeding 12 percent of premiums), underwriting losses were so substantial that the overall operating ratio was 103.8 or higher in every year between 1984 and 1991. In other words, the workers' compensation insurance industry lost money in every year during this period, even after taking into consideration returns on investments.

The major legacy of the period from 1985 to 1991 was the planting of the seeds for reform that bloomed in the 1990s. Employers were concerned about the increases in the costs of workers' compensation, which (as a percentage of payroll) had more than doubled from the 1960s by 1991 (see Figure 2.1), with much of that increase having occurred since 1984. At the same time, private carriers experienced serious financial difficulties as the workers' compensation line was unprofitable every year between 1984 and 1991.

The Neo-Reform Era: 1992–1998

Escalating costs from 1985 to 1991 galvanized political opposition by employers and insurers to workers' compensation programs that had been liberalized in the wake of the National Commission's report. Opposition to growth in workers' compensation costs led to significant changes in many state programs. Over half of the state legislatures passed major amendments to workers' compensation laws between 1989 and 1996, generally reducing benefits and attempting to contain health care costs.[9] There were five significant developments in workers' compensation related to these efforts, as identified by Spieler and Burton (1998).

First, the statutory level of cash benefits was reduced in a number of jurisdictions, particularly with regard to benefits paid for permanent disabilities. Second, eligibility for workers' compensation benefits was narrowed due to changes in compensability rules. From the perspective of employers and carriers, much of the narrowing of eligibility was justified in order to eliminate fraud and marginally work-related conditions from the program.

Third, the health care delivery system in workers' compensation was transformed, most notably by the introduction of managed care. The fourth development was the rise of disability management by employers and carriers, largely due to unilateral actions by these parties in response to the higher costs of the workers' compensation program, but also in part as a result of inducements provided by state legislation. Finally, in a development that ultimately could result in higher employers' costs outside the workers' compensation program, the exclusive remedy doctrine was challenged by several court decisions, due in part to judicial reactions to the increasing limitations on the availability of workers' compensation benefits.

In addition to these five developments, another factor that may help explain the decline in cash and medical benefits during the 1990s is the apparent drop in the work-related injury rate in the decade[10] (Figure 2.8). This decline in the injury rate may be due to more effective enforcement of the Occupational Safety and Health Act (OSHA), or to the increased effect of the experience rating of workers' compensation premiums as the costs of workplace injuries increased, or to greater accident prevention efforts by employers for reasons other than experience rating, or to a shift in the national economy towards employment in safer industries and occupations.[11]

Favorable conditions in the labor market are another likely reason for the reductions in workers' compensation benefits paid during the 1990s. The sustained economic expansion during the 1990s produced national unemployment rates that dropped every year between 1993 and 1997, a five-year achievement that had not occurred since the 1960s (Figure 2.9). The duration of workers' compensation benefits paid to injured workers typically declines when unemployment rates are low, because employers are more willing to accommodate disabled workers when workers are generally unavailable and because injured employees are more likely to be recalled to work or find alternative jobs in tight labor markets.[12]

As a result of these various factors, workers' compensation benefits increased modestly or even declined in the 1990s, depending on the measure used. Benefits paid to workers increased from $40.8 billion in 1991 to $40.7 billion in 1998, which represented a very small (less than 0.1 percent) annual rate of increase (see Figure 2.3). Benefits as a percentage of payroll peaked at 1.66 percent of payroll in 1992 and then declined to a low of 1.08 percent of payroll in 1998 (see Figure 2.1). The multiyear decline in benefits paid relative to payroll is unprecedented in duration and magnitude since at least 1948, when the annual data were first published for successive years (Burton and Schmidle 1995, p. III-28).

Cash benefits paid to injured workers increased from $24.1 billion in 1991 to $24.9 billion in 1996, which represented a modest 0.5 per-

Figure 2.8 Work-Related Injury and Illness Rates, 1972–98

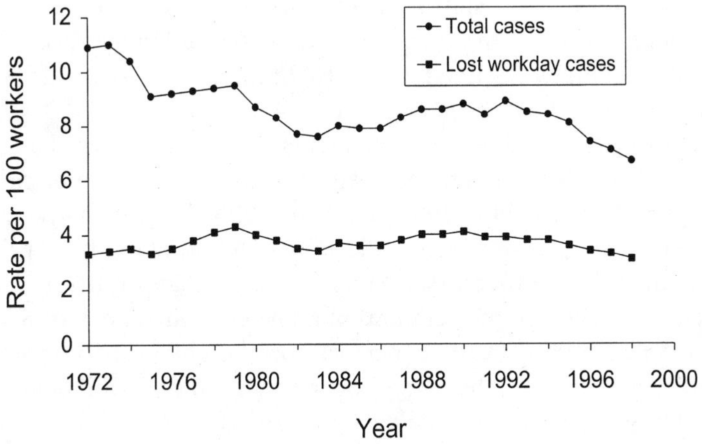

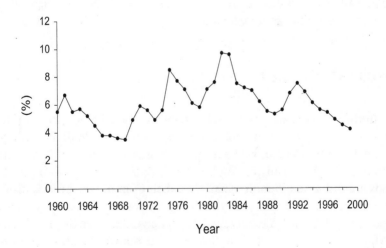

SOURCE: Table A.6.

Figure 2.9 Unemployment Rates, 1960–99

SOURCE: Council of Economic Advisers (2000), Table B-42, "Unemployment Rate for All Civilian Workers," p. 330.

cent annual growth rate (see Figure 2.7). Part of the slowdown in cash benefits was due to the relative stability in statutory benefits during this period, with the average state's benefits increasing from 49.9 percent of the Model Act in 1991 to 50.1 percent in 1996 (see Figure 2.4). Medical benefits actually declined from $16.7 billion in 1991 to $15.8 billion in 1998, which is a drop of 0.8 percent per year.

As a result of the reduced payments of benefits to workers, the employers' costs of workers' compensation as a percentage of payroll (see Figure 2.1) peaked in 1993 and then declined significantly. Also, as benefits and costs declined in the 1990s, the profitability of private carriers quickly improved (see Figure 2.5). The loss ratio (incurred losses as a percentage of premium) plummeted from a peak of 87.8 in 1991 to 55.2 in 1995, and then increased only slightly (to 55.6 percent) in 1997. Furthermore, the overall operating ratio (which includes net investment income) fell from a peak of 108.7 in 1991 to a low of 80.2 in 1995, and then increased slightly (up to 80.3 percent) in 1997. The four years from 1994 to 1997, when the operating ratio was below 90 in every year, represent the most profitable period in at least 20 years for workers' compensation insurance. The rapid increases in the loss ratio and the overall operating ratio in 1998 and 1999 (see Figure 2.5) indicate that profitability of workers' compensation insurance is still cyclical and suggest that some of the stresses the system experienced in the early 1990s may soon reemerge.

INSURANCE ARRANGEMENTS

In this section, we review salient developments since 1960 in the insurance arrangements in workers' compensation.[13] We first examine the relative importance of benefit payments from state funds, private carriers, and self-insuring employers; developments involving state funds are discussed in more detail. We then examine the private insurance market, which evolved from a highly regulated industry in the 1960s and 1970s into a relatively deregulated industry in the 1980s and 1990s.[14] Finally, we review the residual market (also called the assigned-risk market) for workers' compensation insurance.

Shares of Benefits by Type of Insurance Arrangement

The share of benefits paid by private carriers, state and federal funds, and self-insuring employers over the period 1960–1998 is shown in Figure 2.10. Private carriers accounted for the predominant share of benefit payments throughout this period; for example, from 1960 to 1990, private carriers paid for about 60 percent of all benefits. During the 1990s, however, the private carriers' share dropped to about 50 percent, reflecting in part their reluctance to provide coverage during the unprofitable early years of the 1990s.

Another significant development in the workers' compensation insurance market during recent decades is the increasing share of benefits paid by self-insuring employers. The share increased from 1990 to 1998 (from 19.7 percent to 25.0 percent of all benefit payments), continuing a long-term trend (Figure 2.10). The recent increasing importance of self-insurance can be explained by three developments. First, many carriers decided to leave an unprofitable line of business in the early 1990s (which is a development that may be reversed with increased profitability). Second, many employers paid increasing

Figure 2.10 Workers' Compensation Benefits by Type of Insurer, 1960–98

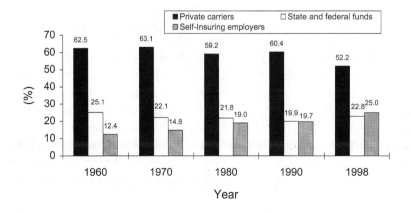

SOURCE: Table A.7.

attention to disability management (including prevention) in response to the higher costs of workers' compensation, which led some employers to self-insure in order to assume greater control over their workers' compensation programs. Finally, some employers decided to self-insure in order to avoid assessments on policies sold in the voluntary market that were used to subsidize losses in the residual market.

The emergence of several new state funds in recent years (discussed below) helps explain why the share of benefits paid by state and federal workers' compensation funds increased from 19.9 percent in 1990 to 22.8 percent in 1998, reversing the downward trend in the share of benefits provided by government funds that occurred between 1960 and 1990 (Figure 2.10).

State Workers' Compensation Funds

From its origin (in most states) between 1910 and 1920, workers' compensation has relied on a mixture of state funds, private carriers, and self-insurance, and from the beginning there were arguments concerning the merits of the various arrangements. State funds were lauded because of lower overhead (notably the absence of a broker's fee) and because proponents thought that profits were inappropriate in a mandatory social insurance program. Private carriers were praised because they promoted efficiency and were considered more compatible with our capitalist society. The arguments that prevailed varied from state to state: some jurisdictions created exclusive state funds, some authorized only private carriers to provide insurance, and some permitted private carriers to compete with state funds.

As shown in Figure 2.11, as of 1960 there were seven exclusive state funds, the youngest of which was the North Dakota fund (established in 1919). There were also 11 competitive state funds (those in competition with private carriers), the youngest of which was the Oklahoma fund (established in 1933). The numbers and types of state funds were relatively constant for half a century. Oregon converted its exclusive state fund into a competitive state fund that began operation in 1966; this represented the only change in state funds between the early 1930s and the early 1980s.

One of the significant developments in the workers' compensation insurance market in the last two decades was the emergence of several

Figure 2.11 Number of State Workers' Compensation Funds, 1960–98

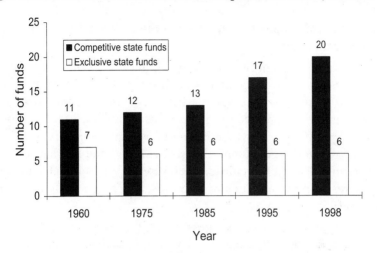

SOURCE: Table A.8. The numbers are determined as of January 1 of each year.

new competitive state funds. The pioneer of the modern movement towards state funds was Minnesota, which established a competitive state fund in 1984. Then, in the 1990s, five new competitive state funds began operation by January 1, 1995, the last date we use in this study for interstate comparisons of the costs of workers' compensation insurance; three more states established state funds by 1998. However, in a contrarian move, the long-existing Michigan competitive state fund was privatized in 1994.[15]

The state legislators' motives for establishing the new state funds were 1) to reduce costs of workers' compensation in the state and/or 2) to provide an alternative source of insurance for employers who could not purchase policies in the voluntary market or who did not like the surcharges or other conditions imposed on policies purchased in the residual (assigned-risk) market, which we discuss below. One of our research objectives is to determine the effects, if any, of state funds (new or old) on the costs of workers' compensation insurance and on workplace safety.

Regulation of the Workers' Compensation Insurance Market

Historical origins of regulation in the property/casualty insurance line

State regulation of insurance pricing in the United States was initially applied to fire and marine insurance and thus predated the establishment of workers' compensation programs. In the early 19th century, insurers were free to charge whatever rate they felt was appropriate or profitable. However, because coverage for a particular company tended to be geographically concentrated due to transportation and communication limitations, fire insurers were vulnerable to insolvency resulting from catastrophic fires. As noted by Kimball and Boyce (1958, p. 547):

> Historically, fire insurance losses seemed to follow cyclical patterns. When the loss ratio was low and profits high, the prospect of large profits attracted newcomers to the insurance business. Companies were easy to start; neither experience nor elaborate physical plant were essential . . . Premium volume might be enormous in relation to capital, and a new company might easily enjoy the illusion of large profits if its accounting practices did not provide for adequate reinsurance reserves . . . Hence overconfident underwriting with rates driven down to uneconomic levels by excessive competition might go undetected until a catastrophic fire wiped weak companies out of existence with great loss to policyholders.

Insurance companies first attempted to resolve these problems through self-regulation, i.e., the establishment of rating boards or professional associations. These rating boards attempted to control rates by providing insurers with better data and underwriting guidance as well as common pricing agreements. However, continuing waves of insolvency among fire insurers demonstrated that these boards, in and of themselves, were ineffective and led to the call for increased state regulation of the insurance industry.

As a consequence, state insurance departments were established in the 1850s. The initial focus of state regulation was on such matters as the licensing of insurers and agents, minimum financial and deposit requirements, reviews of insurance contracts, and reporting requirements, rather than on insurance rates. Licensing and bond deposit requirements mandated by the state of Virginia were challenged in court by New York insurers, but the Supreme Court upheld the regulations in *Paul v. Virginia*, 75 U.S. 168 (1869). The Court concluded that the issuance of an insurance policy was not a transaction of interstate commerce, which arguably would have made insurance subject to federal regulation and thus preempted state regulation.

In part out of a concern with alleged unfair discrimination in insurance rates, states subsequently enacted rate regulatory laws, beginning with Kansas in 1909. New York's statute, for example, prohibited unfair discrimination in rates and allowed fire insurance rates to be set in concert; the rating bureau had to file rates with the state's insurance commissioner, whose approval was required before the rates could be used. Rating bureaus were viewed as way to develop more accurate rates (based on insurers' collective experience rather than on an individual insurer's experience). Regulators believed that competition resulted in below-cost pricing since losses were difficult to predict and tended to be underestimated.

Although the *Paul* decision upheld the general right of states to regulate the insurance industry in the absence of federal regulation, the issues of whether the U.S. Congress could also regulate the insurance industry and, if so, what were the consequences of such federal regulation for state authority, were not clearly resolved until the Supreme Court's decision in *United States v. South-Eastern Underwriters Association (SEUA)*, 322 U.S. 533 (1944). The Court held that the business of insurance was interstate commerce and, as such, price-fixing agreements for insurance rates (including those involving state rating bureaus) were subject to prosecution under the federal Sherman Antitrust Act. In addition, under the preemption doctrine of constitutional law, the presence of a federal statute meant that states were precluded from also regulating rates.

As a result of the *SEUA* decision, Congress in 1945 approved the McCarran-Ferguson Act, which declared in part that the federal antitrust laws would be applicable to the insurance industry only to the degree that the industry was not regulated by state law. Model (or "all-industry" bills), drafted collectively by state insurance commissioners, were subsequently adopted by most states, and administered pricing systems were established for most lines of property/casualty insurance. However, after the initial enactment of the all-industry bills, the traditional administered pricing system for most lines of property/casualty insurance was modified over time in many states in order to allow greater competition among insurers. By the 1970s, a substantial minority of states had deregulated their property/casualty insurance lines other than workers' compensation.

Workers' compensation regulation

In contrast to the deregulation movement that generally occurred in property/casualty insurance in the 1970s, rate setting in workers' compensation insurance continued to be highly regulated until the 1980s. The deregulation of workers' compensation insurance was resisted on several grounds: the distinctive characteristic of workers' compensation as a mandated social insurance program (and the resultant concern with both rate levels for employers and the solvency of carriers); the existence of competitive measures other than price competition for workers' compensation insurance (primarily through dividends); and the need for a comprehensive database (with uniform rate classes and information on the experience of a large number of insurers). These arguments helped delay even partial deregulation of workers' compensation in most states until the 1980s and 1990s, and they still operate to preserve "pure" administered pricing in a few states and vestiges of regulation in most states.

The administered-pricing approach to rate setting for workers' compensation involved several components. A rating organization was selected in each state.[16] The rating organization prescribed standardized reporting forms and established an elaborate system of industrial and occupational insurance classifications. The rating bureau collected detailed information on benefits paid and premiums collected by all private carriers providing workers' compensation insurance in the state.[17] These data were then used to establish *pure premiums* (expected losses) for each insurance classification. The pure premiums were then increased by a loading factor, consisting of an allowance for loss adjustment and other expenses and for profits, to produce *manual rates* for each insurance classification.[18] Manual rates were stated as dollars per $100 of payroll (thus bakeries, Class 2003 in a typical state, might have a manual rate of $2.40 per $100 of payroll).

The rating bureau then filed the manual rates with the state insurance commissioner. The rates could not be used without prior approval of the commissioner, who could reject and/or modify the proposed rates if they were "excessive, inadequate, or unfairly discriminatory." Each carrier was obliged to belong to the rating bureau, to provide data to the bureau, and to adhere to the manual rates approved by the insurance commissioner.

Even in administered-pricing states, the premiums paid by many employers were not simply the product of total payroll times the applicable manual rate, because there were several modifying factors, such as premium discounts for larger employers and experience-rating modifications for a medium or large firm based on the firm's previous experience.[19] The modifying factors were precisely defined in rules established by the rating bureau and approved by the insurance commissioner, and they had to be closely followed by each workers' compensation carrier. One additional feature of the workers' compensation insurance market was that most carriers—including mutual and stock companies—paid dividends to policyholders based on their underwriting experience.

In sum, under the administered-pricing approach to workers' compensation rate setting, all carriers were required to start with the same manual rates, and the various modifications to those rates involved either 1) formulae or constants to which all carriers had to adhere and which modified the manual rates at the beginning of the policy period, or 2) dividends that were paid only after the policy period ended. In short, there was virtually no chance for carriers to compete in terms of price at the <u>beginning</u> of the policy period with any of these modifications.[20]

Deregulation of the Workers' Compensation Insurance Market

The types of deregulation

Administered pricing is no longer the dominant approach to workers' compensation insurance pricing in the United States. A fundamental result of the deregulation of the workers' compensation insurance market that has taken place in the last two decades is that private carriers can now compete for business by varying the insurance rates at the beginning of the policy period. Most jurisdictions now allow deviations and schedule rating, and a number of jurisdictions have moved to more comprehensive forms of deregulation that generally fall under the rubric "open competition" or "competitive rating."

If a state allows *deviations*, individual carriers may deviate from the published manual rates and charge lower (or occasionally higher) rates than those promulgated by the rating organization. The deviations are generally stated as a percentage discount from the manual rates. The magnitude of the deviations will vary among carriers; however, the deviations offered by a particular carrier are uniform for all policyholders in the state. In addition, deviations from bureau rates are generally subject to the approval of the state insurance commissioner.

Schedule rating plans have also been introduced in most jurisdictions. Under these plans, insurers can change (usually decrease) the workers' compensation insurance rate an individual employer would otherwise pay. These changes are made through a system of debits or credits that are based on a subjective evaluation of factors such as the employer's loss control (safety) program. The plans are created by the rating organization and are subject to the approval of the insurance commissioner. As a result, these plans are uniform for all insurers operating in a particular state. However, the application of the plans is based on judgmental factors, and this allows insurers to vary rates paid by policyholders, even among employers in the same classification code.

While deviations and schedule rating constitute widely adopted forms of partial deregulation, even more comprehensive reforms have been adopted in a number of states during the last 20 years. These reforms involve various combinations of three different changes to the regulatory environment. First, some states have dropped the requirement that insurers become members of the rating organization or adhere to bureau rates.

Second, other jurisdictions no longer require insurers to obtain regulatory approval prior to using rates. In place of the prior approval requirement, states have adopted "file-and-use" or "use-and-file" systems. In file-and-use states, insurers must file their rates with the regulatory agency prior to or concurrent with their effective date; no specific approval is required before the rates are used, but the agency retains the right to disapprove the rates at a later date. In use-and-file states, the insurer must still file rates; however, the carrier may use those rates before they are filed with the regulatory agency. Use-and-file systems are obviously the less restrictive of these two alternatives to prior approval.

Third, some states prohibit the rating organization from filing fully developed rates; instead, these organizations file loss costs or pure premiums. Each carrier in these states has to decide what loading factor should be used in conjunction with the pure premiums to produce the equivalent of manual rates.[21]

These three approaches to deregulating workers' compensation insurance rate setting have been adopted by the states in various combinations. Arkansas, for example, in 1981 dropped the requirement that insurers adhere to bureau rates. However, Arkansas continued to require that carriers obtain regulatory approval prior to the implementation of new rates and that the rating bureau file fully developed rates. The South Carolina rating bureau began to file pure premiums rather than fully developed rates in 1990, but insurers were required to rely on bureau estimates of pure premiums in developing their own manual rates and to obtain prior approval before implementing these manual rates. Kentucky, beginning in 1982, dropped prior approval and adherence requirements, and the bureau was prohibited from filing fully developed rates. Despite the differences among the three states in their approach to deregulation, each is described by the National Council on Compensation Insurance in the *Annual Statistical Bulletin* (NCCI 2000) as having adopted "competitive rating" legislation. While the NCCI categorization is sufficient for certain purposes, in this study we use a far more complex classification scheme for deregulation, which also allows us to capture the effects of changes in the various approaches to deregulation.

The initial phase of deregulation

Deregulation of the workers' compensation insurance market began in the early 1980s. One type of deregulation—i.e., "competitive rating," also referred to as "open competition"—was introduced in nine states between 1981 and 1984, according to the NCCI (Figure 2.12).[22]

Several factors help explain the onset of deregulation. First, the overall political climate became more hostile to the notion that "big government" could do a better job than competitive forces in determining prices and allocations of resources, and one consequence was a general move towards deregulation involving industries such as airlines

Figure 2.12 Number of States Enacting Open-Competition Statutes, 1981–99

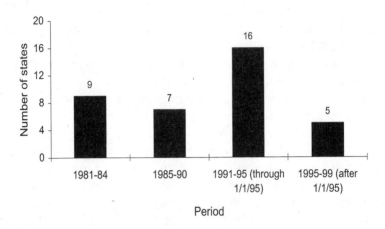

SOURCE: Table A.9.

and trucking, as well as the insurance industry. A second factor, particularly relevant for workers' compensation, was the increasing cost of the program during the 1970s, which concerned employers and state legislators. They hoped that deregulation would reduce the costs of workers' compensation insurance by, for example, promoting efficiency. A third factor was a perception among some legislators, unions, and employers that profits in the workers' compensation insurance line were excessive. Again, the hope was that deregulation would help reduce costs by squeezing out excess profits. Not surprisingly, most workers' compensation insurers resisted deregulation during this period.[23]

Deregulation in the 1990s

After the initial moves to deregulation in the early 1980s, the introduction of open competition slowed in the balance of the 1980s. The reduced pace can perhaps be explained by the general unprofitability of workers' compensation insurance in this period: legislators saw little chance to reduce workers' compensation costs by deregulating an industry in financial distress. However, one consequence of the unprofitability of workers' compensation insurance was the beginning of a change in attitude towards deregulation by many in the insurance industry. Deregulation was now seen as a way to escape from the "onerous" decisions of insurance regulators and to establish rates that would allow carrier profitability. Thus, some of the seven states that adopted open competition between 1985 and 1990 did so with at least the tacit support of the insurance industry.

Deregulation reemerged with vigor during the 1990s: open competition statutes became effective in 16 states between 1991 and January 1, 1995,[24] and in an additional 5 states after that date (Figure 2.12). Deregulation in some of these states—especially those that adopted open competition in the early 1990s when the industry was still experiencing losses—reflected support from the insurance industry, but deregulation in other states (most notably California, where rate filings had generally been approved by the insurance commissioner) was generally resisted by the industry.

While deregulation has been proceeding in recent decades, significant developments that could also affect the employers' workers' compensation premiums were occurring in the assigned-risk (residual) markets for workers' compensation insurance.

Assigned-Risk Markets

Workers' compensation is a mandatory program for employers (with the limited exceptions noted in Chapter 1). A minority of employers (typically large and financially sound) self-insure their workers' compensation obligations with approval of the state. Those employers who do not qualify to self-insure must purchase workers' compensation insurance.

The six exclusive state workers' compensation funds must accept all applicants for insurance, as must most competitive state funds. Private insurers and some competitive state funds, on the other hand, can reject applicants who are considered undesirable. Because the employers whose applications are rejected must have workers' compensation insurance in order to comply with their state's statutory requirements, states that do not have a state fund obligated to accept all employers have established assigned-risk plans.[25]

There are two categories of assigned-risk programs (Williams 1969, pp. 48–49). Under the first approach, applicants who have been unable to secure insurance in the voluntary market are assigned to individual carriers in proportion to the carriers' market shares in the state. Under the second approach, an assigned-risk pool underwrites the insurance. Employers insured by the pool are assigned to one of a limited number of carriers that administer claims on behalf of the pool. All carriers insure the policies written by the pool in proportion to their voluntary market shares.

The traditional reasons why employers were unable to obtain workers' compensation policies in the voluntary market were that the applicant was engaged in some activity that was unusually hazardous relative to the experience of other firms in the appropriate insurance classification, or had a poor loss record, or was so small that the premium did not adequately compensate the insurer for its expenses (Williams 1969, p. 48). In the 1960s, most assigned-risk programs provided for a standard 8 percent surcharge, and the premium was adequate to cover losses and loss adjustment expenses.[26] The assigned-risk market accounted for no more than 3.2 percent of all premiums nationally between 1960 and 1965 (Williams 1969, p. 52).

The assigned-risk share of all premiums accounted for only 4.6 percent of all premiums nationally in 1975, the first year of our study of the determinants of workers' compensation insurance rates (Figure 2.13). However, as the cost of workers' compensation insurance increased after 1975, the assigned-risk market share almost tripled by 1978–1979, when these premiums accounted for 12.7 percent of all premiums nationally. The share then dropped back to 5.5 percent in 1984, reflecting the generally profitable conditions in the workers' compensation insurance market and the declining cost of workers' compensation insurance.

The fiscal stress that the workers' compensation insurance market was under during the years from the mid 1980s to the early 1990s is clearly evident in the explosion of the assigned-risk market share from 5.5 percent of all premiums nationally in 1984 to a peak of 28.5 percent in 1992. In addition to the traditional reasons for applicants being forced to purchase in the assigned-risk market (basically the unattractiveness of individual risks), the dominant factor contributing to assigned-risk market growth in the 1985–1992 period was the general inadequacy of workers' compensation insurance rates because of the reluctance of insurance regulators in many states to approve rate filings

Figure 2.13 Assigned-Risk Market Share, 1975–98

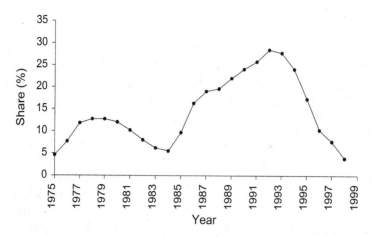

SOURCE: Table A.10.

with substantial rate increases for the voluntary market. Carriers in such jurisdictions became unwilling to write policies in the voluntary market because they could not make an adequate (or in many cases, any) profit.

Several states were particularly noteworthy for the share of workers' compensation insurance provided through the residual market: 79.9 percent of total premiums in 1991 in Louisiana, 88.6 percent of total premiums in 1992 in Rhode Island, and 90.6 percent of 1989 total premiums in Maine. A vicious cycle ensued in some of these states:

- rates were held down in the voluntary market by regulators;

- carriers were unwilling to write policies in the voluntary market at the approved rates, which forced some employers into the assigned-risk market; in addition, regulators sometimes responded to political pressures and held insurance rates in the assigned-risk market well below the levels that were warranted, inducing some employers who were able to purchase policies in the voluntary market to obtain policies in the assigned-risk residual market because the rates were so low;

- the assigned-risk markets ran substantial deficits because of inadequate rates;

- the carriers in the voluntary market were assessed substantial sums to cover the assigned-risk market deficits; and
- when the carriers tried to pass on these assessments to policyholders still in the voluntary market, many employers shifted to the assigned-risk market in order to obtain coverage at the suppressed rates, which only increased the size of the aggregate losses in the assigned-risk market and increased assessments in the voluntary market.

The rapid decline in the national share of total premium accounted for by the assigned-risk market that occurred after 1994 (Figure 2.13) is due to three major factors. First, the overall profitability of the workers' compensation insurance line quickly improved after 1992 (see Figure 2.5). Second, several states established competitive state funds or other special public or quasi-public funds to provide policies to employers who could not find policies in the voluntary market. For example, the Louisiana competitive state fund became operative in 1992; the Maine competitive state fund began payments in 1993; the Kentucky state fund specifically created for assigned-risk policies started operations in 1995; and the Rhode Island competitive state fund became operative in 1996.

Third, a series of changes were made in assigned-risk policies during the last 15 years that made these policies more expensive and reduced the subsidy from the voluntary market. For example, many states introduced separate manual rates for the assigned-risk market that were substantially higher than the rates for the voluntary market. In addition, many states either eliminated premium discounts or introduced special experience-rating plans that tied premiums more closely to each firm's own benefit payments in the assigned-risk markets. We provide more details on these changes in Appendix C.

CONCLUSIONS

Workers' compensation benefit payments increased substantially from the 1970s until the early 1990s, when benefits began to decline. Costs to employers of the program had a more complex history and went through two cycles, increasing from the 1970s until about 1980, then declining for a few years, followed by significant increases until the early 1990s, when costs started to drop rapidly. These benefit and cost developments provide the backdrop for significant changes in the insurance arrangements in workers' compensation, with a number of new state funds emerging in the 1990s and with partial deregulation of private carriers spreading throughout the country beginning in the early 1980s. One of our major tasks in subsequent chapters is to more precisely measure these costs and the various factors that affect costs, such as the level of cash and medical benefits and the nature of the insurance arrangements, in order to allow us to test a model of the determinants of the interstate differences in the employers' costs of workers' compensation insurance.

Notes

1. The data pertain to all states and all types of insurance arrangements, including self-insuring employers.
2. Within the 1960s, there was a subperiod (1965–1969) when costs increased 11.3 percent a year. In order to simplify our analysis, we are including this subperiod with the rest of the years from 1960–1971.
3. In 1940, the maximum weekly benefit for temporary total disability benefits was at least 66.7 percent of the state's average weekly wage in 38 jurisdictions. In 1966, only three jurisdictions met this standard (National Commission 1972, p. 61).
4. The Model Act, which is officially known as the Workmen's Compensation and Rehabilitation Law (Revised), was published by the Council of State Governments in 1972. The Model Act and the methodology we used to measure state workers' compensation statutory provisions relative to the Model Act are discussed in Thomason and Burton (2000a).
5. The change in statutory benefit levels resulted in higher benefit payments in part because of the utilization effect: workers were encouraged to file for benefits and to extend their periods of disability. The utilization effect is further discussed in Chapter 9.
6. Between 1985 and 1991, the cash benefits provided by the average state statute declined slightly from 50.5 to 49.9 percent of the benefits prescribed by the Model Act (see Figure 2.4).
7. Conflicting evidence on the cost-shifting hypothesis and other explanations for the rapid increase in health care costs in the workers' compensation program during the 1985–1991 period are examined in Burton (1997) and Spieler and Burton (1998).
8. Typical employer reactions to the spiraling costs of workers' compensation were provided in Chapter 1.

9. This examination of developments in the 1990s is based in part on Tinsley (1990, 1991), Berreth (1992, 1994, 1996, 1997), and Brown (1993, 1995).

10. Some of the decline in reported injury rates may be due to the indirect consequences of tightened eligibility rules for workers' compensation, which means the apparent decline may exaggerate the actual decline.

11. A more comprehensive examination of the possible explanations of declining injury and fatality rates is provided in Durbin and Butler (1998). They indicate, for example, that the threshold level of premium to qualify for experience rating has increased (which would tend to reduce the impact of experience rating on safety), and that there has been an increasing use of deductibles in workers' compensation policies (which would tend to increase safety incentives for employers).

12. Another factor that may have reduced the costs of workers' compensation insurance in the 1990s was the residual market reforms discussed in the next section.

13. The definitive treatment of insurance arrangements in workers' compensation through the 1960s is Williams (1969).

14. The workers' compensation insurance market has become relatively deregulated in the 1990s compared with its status prior to 1980. We examine the significant movement towards deregulation in this section of Chapter 2 and also in Chapters 5 and 6. Despite this deregulation, the workers' compensation insurance market remains the most heavily regulated commercial insurance line in terms of prices, policy forms, data reporting requirements, and market conduct. Regulators still retain the authority and responsibility to ensure that rates are not excessive, inadequate, or unfairly discriminatory.

15. Other changes in state funds shown in Appendix A, Table A.8, were not effective by 1998.

16. Most states relied on the National Council of Compensation Insurance (NCCI) as the rating organization. Several states instead established "independent" rating bureaus, including California, Delaware, Massachusetts, Minnesota, New York, New Jersey, and Pennsylvania.

17. In some of the states with competitive state workers' compensation funds, the state fund also provided data to the rating bureau.

18. The loading factor was a uniform percentage for all classifications.

19. These and other modifying factors are examined in considerable detail in Chapter 3 and Appendix C.

20. A few states did permit deviations or schedule rating prior to the 1980s, but their use was limited even in these states. These competitive devices are explained in the next section of the text.

21. This three-way characterization of reform is a simplification because there are substantial variations in the configurations of regulation and deregulation. For example, some states permit the rating bureau to file both pure premiums and fully developed rates, and they have one set of rules that apply to the pure premium filing and a different set of rules for the manual rates. Missouri allows downward deviations from bureau rates but not upward deviations. Oklahoma allows insurers to use rates without prior approval as long as the rate increase is

less than 15 percent, but the Insurance Commission must approve higher rate increases.

22. As indicated in the preceding paragraph in the text, the NCCI's "competitive rating" categorization encompasses a variety of forms of deregulation. In Chapter 7, we provide our own historical record of deregulation using a more refined set of categories of deregulation.

23. The states that adopted open competition in the 1980s were rather eclectic (geographically, economically, and politically), and empirical efforts at modeling the determinants of the adoption of open competition have been rather unavailing; see, for example, Schmidle (1994).

24. January 1, 1995, is significant because that is the last comparison date for the insurance rates we analyze in this study.

25. At one time, the competitive state fund in Idaho was not obligated to accept all applicants, but in practice it almost always did so (Williams 1969, p. 48).

26. According to Williams (1969, p. 49), "Losses and loss adjustment expenses have amounted to about 82 percent of the premiums earned during the 11 policy years [from 1955 to 1965]. Since 1961, the trend in the loss and loss adjustment ratio has been downward, and in 1965 was .774."

3
Measuring Employers' Costs

Several significant recent developments in workers' compensation programs were described in Chapter 2. Benefits paid to injured workers relative to payroll increased from the 1970s until the early 1990s and then declined for several years. The employers' costs of workers' compensation had a somewhat more complex history: costs increased in the 1970s, then declined in the early 1980s, only to resume an upward trend in the mid 1980s that peaked in the early 1990s, followed by a period of decline. Workers' compensation insurance arrangements also changed over recent decades: several states established new competitive state insurance funds, and most states with private carriers deregulated their workers' compensation insurance markets.

Our task in this study is to attempt to disentangle these developments in the workers' compensation program. For example, to what extent were the increases in workers' compensation costs due to increased cash benefits as prescribed by state statutes, as opposed to other factors such as changing injury rates and higher payments for medical benefits? One question of particular interest to us is the extent to which the changes in the insurance arrangements affected workers' compensation costs. In order to successfully isolate the effects of the various developments in benefits and insurance arrangements on workers' compensation costs, we must first develop an appropriate measure of these costs.

In this chapter, we discuss several approaches that have been used to measure the employers' costs of workers' compensation. We initially summarize and critique cost measures that are frequently used by practitioners for interstate comparisons or that have been used by academics in empirical studies: these include benefits paid per worker, loss ratios, losses per employee or injury, and average losses per $100 of payroll. We then describe our two measures of employers' costs, namely, premiums paid per $100 of payroll and weekly premiums per worker, as well as our rationale for these measures.

51

ALTERNATIVE MEASURES OF EMPLOYERS' COSTS

Benefits Paid per Worker

Data on workers' compensation benefits paid per worker and on benefits as a percentage of payroll are reported in a widely cited data series published by The National Foundation for Unemployment Compensation and Workers' Compensation, an affiliate of UWC, Inc.[1] The National Foundation uses 1) data on total workers' compensation benefits paid in each state, which are published by the Social Security Administration (SSA) and the National Academy of Social Insurance (NASI); 2) SSA data on the percentage of the workforce covered by the workers' compensation program in each state; and 3) data from state unemployment insurance programs, to produce the estimates of workers' compensation benefit payments per worker and as a percentage of payroll. The most recent version of the report provides data for every state for the period 1986–1995 (National Foundation 1997).

For the 50 states plus the District of Columbia, average benefits paid per covered employee in 1995 ranged from $145 in North Carolina (35.1 percent of the national average, which was $413) to $734 in Hawaii (177.7 percent of the national average). Benefits as a percentage of payroll in 1995 ranged from 0.60 percent (in North Carolina) to 3.87 percent (in West Virginia); the national average was 1.51 percent.

The National Foundation data, and the SSA/NASI data on which the National Foundation figures are largely based, are of considerable value because they represent the only comprehensive data on workers' compensation benefits that apply to all states and to all types of insurance arrangements. There are, however, several limitations that restrict their usefulness. For example, the data are based on current benefits payments (i.e., benefits paid to all claims active during the current calendar year, regardless of the year of injury) rather than on incurred losses (the estimates of benefits that must eventually be paid for injuries occurring during that calendar year). Since workers' compensation benefits are often paid over a period of several years, current benefit payments do not provide an accurate measure of losses for injuries occurring in particular years.

In addition, the National Foundation data are necessarily imprecise in other respects. The SSA data on the extent of each state's workforce covered by the workers' compensation program are only available for a few, nonconsecutive years. As a result, the National Foundation has decided to use changes in the number of workers covered by a state's unemployment insurance program to estimate changes in a state's workers' compensation coverage.[2] The resulting estimates of the proportion of the workforce covered by the workers' compensation program are then used to estimate the proportion of payroll in each state covered by the workers' compensation program. The National Foundation also assumes that the average wage of workers covered by a state's workers' compensation program is the same as that of workers covered by the state's unemployment insurance program. These assumptions are unlikely to hold true for all states and all years, introducing further error into the National Foundation estimates.

Another problem with the National Foundation's benefits data is that they do not control for differences in states' industrial composition. A state with a relatively heavy concentration of industries with inherently dangerous occupations will have higher workers' compensation benefit payments than a state with safer industries, even if the statutory benefit levels and administrative costs are identical in both jurisdictions and even if the benefits per worker in comparable industries are the same. For example, suppose State A has 80 percent of its workforce in coal mining and 20 percent in the financial sector, while State B has 20 percent of its workforce in coal mining and 80 percent in finance. Also assume that in both states, workers' compensation benefits per $100 of payroll are $12.00 for coal mining and $1.00 for finance. This means that the overall average of benefits per $100 of payroll is $9.80 per $100 of payroll in State A and $3.20 in State B, solely because of differences in the industrial composition of the two states.

A final limitation of the National Foundation data as a basis for interstate cost comparisons is that they only measure benefits paid to workers, not the costs of the program to employers, which includes administrative expenses among other things. Because of these limitations, the Foundation's data do not provide an appropriate measure of interstate differences in employers' costs of workers' compensation.

Loss Ratios

The *loss ratio* is the employers' cost measure most frequently utilized in empirical analyses of the impact of insurance regulation. Unfortunately, that term has several alternative definitions. A general guide to workers' compensation underwriting experience is provided in Table 3.1. (An extended discussion of insurance terminology and sources of data is included in Appendix B.)

Table 3.1 is general because it starts with "premium" (although there are actually three different measures of premium defined in Appendix B) and because the table does not specify the method of reporting data (Appendix B provides four methods). Also, Table 3.1 does not specify whether the losses are paid or incurred.[3]

The alternatives in the measure of premiums, in the method of reporting data, and between paid and incurred benefits can be significant, and some will be discussed below. However, knowledge of all these alternatives is not critical to gaining a basic understanding of the

Table 3.1 Workers' Compensation Underwriting Experience: A General Guide

1.		Premium
2.	–	Losses
3.	–	Loss adjustment expenses
4.	–	Underwriting expenses (commissions and brokerage expenses; state and local insurance taxes; department taxes, licenses, and fees; guarantee association assessments; general expenses; and other underwriting expenses)
5.	–	Dividends
6.	=	Underwriting results
7.	+/–	Net investment gain/loss and other income
8.	=	Overall operating results prior to state and federal income taxes

Ratios Used to Evaluate Underwriting Expenses

Loss (or pure loss) ratio = line 2 ÷ line 1

Loss plus loss adjustment expenses ratio = (line 2 + line 3) ÷ line 1

Combined ratio = line 6 ÷ line 1

Overall operating ratio = line 8 ÷ line 1

ratios used to analyze underwriting results in workers' compensation insurance, which is a requisite for our critique of loss ratios as a measure of employers' costs.

Four ratios are used to evaluate underwriting experience listed in Table 3.1.

- The *pure loss ratio* is line 2, losses, divided by line 1, premium. The National Council on Compensation Insurance (NCCI) and A.M. Best refers to this measure as the *loss ratio*.

- The *loss plus loss adjustment expenses ratio* is the sum of line 2, losses, and line 3, loss adjustment expenses, divided by line 1, premium. Neither the NCCI nor Best uses this measure. However, some research studies describe this concept as the "loss ratio," which is obviously inconsistent with the NCCI and Best definitions.

- The *combined ratio after dividends*, the term used by Best, is line 6, underwriting results, divided by line 1, premium. The NCCI refers to this as "underwriting results."

- The *overall operating ratio* is line 8, overall operating results, divided by line 1, premium; this term is used by Best.

The workers' compensation underwriting experience published by A.M. Best shown in Table 2.1 (p. 25) calculates the loss ratio by dividing incurred losses by earned premiums on a calendar-year basis. Calendar-year incurred losses include incurred benefits for accidents that occurred in the calendar year plus changes in reserves for accidents from prior years. However, due to the long-tailed nature of workers' compensation claims, we believe the most appropriate loss ratio for analyzing public policy is the ratio of incurred losses to earned premiums on an accident-year basis, because this ratio accounts for paid benefits plus future losses on claims resulting solely from accidents in a particular year.

Because losses usually are the largest cost component of net premiums (see Table 2.1), the loss ratio is sometimes used as a crude proxy for the inverse of insurer profits; that is, the higher the loss ratio, the smaller the portion of premium that is left for other expenses and profits. Furthermore, the inverse of the loss ratio is sometimes used as a measure of workers' compensation costs in a state. If losses per $100 of payroll are the same in two states, then a relatively higher inverse loss ratio in one state means that premiums per $100 of payroll (which are costs to employers) are also higher in that state.

Using the inverse of the loss ratio on a calendar-year basis as a measure of workers' compensation costs is suspect on two grounds, according to Carroll and Kaestner (1995). First, as we noted above, incurred losses on a calendar-year basis include changes in reserves on prior-year injuries, and insurer reserving practices are subject to random and systematic error. Second, because cash benefits for more-severe work-related injuries are paid out over many years (that is, workers' compensation claims have a long "tail" before they close), the premium component of the loss ratio largely reflects reserves for future payments, while the loss component is largely based on payments made for past claims. If, as can be expected, the premium and loss components vary markedly from one another over time because one is prospective and the other is retrospective, inverse loss ratios derived from calendar year data are measured with error.

In addition to the criticisms of Carroll and Kaestner, there is another flaw in using the inverse of the loss ratio as a proxy for the employers' costs of workers' compensation insurance; this deficiency exists irrespective of whether the loss ratio is based on calendar-year, policy-year, or accident-year data. The inverse loss ratio expresses premiums relative to loss payments, and thus essentially only measures the "loading" that policyholders pay; it does not measure the benefit portion of the premium. Thus, a state could have very high losses per $100 of payroll in conjunction with a high loss ratio. The low inverse loss ratio under these circumstances would indicate that the insurance carriers' profitability in that jurisdiction was low, even though workers' compensation insurance costs paid by employers were high.

Losses per Employee/Injury

Because of the limitations of the inverse loss ratio as a measure of the employers' costs of workers' compensation insurance, Carroll and Kaestner (1995) constructed two alternative cost measures: 1) premiums earned (minus policyholder dividends) relative to the total number of work-related injuries, and 2) premiums earned (minus policyholder dividends) relative to total private, nonagricultural employment. Unfortunately, these measures are also deficient for several reasons.

First, the numerators and denominators of each measure are inconsistent: the premium data in the numerators pertain solely to policies underwritten by private insurance carriers and state insurance funds, but the denominators also include data pertaining to self-insured firms. Because the proportion of self-insured employment varies both over time and among states, these two cost variables are measured with error. In their first cost measure (premiums per employee), Carroll and Kaestner attempt to correct for this problem by using SSA data on the proportion of total workers' compensation benefits paid by self-insured employers in order to adjust the employment data in the denominator. However, this attempted solution is itself flawed, because the SSA estimates of self-insured benefit payments are suspect. Also, because self-insured employers are typically larger than employers that purchase insurance, and because larger firms generally have better safety records than smaller firms, injured employees of self-insured firms will, on average, receive fewer benefits than do injured workers in firms covered by private carriers or state funds.

Another problem with the Carroll and Kaestner cost measures is their failure to adequately address the fact that per-employee costs of workers' compensation insurance will differ among jurisdictions solely because of variations in states' industrial composition.[4] We discuss, in the next section of this chapter, an alternative approach to estimating costs that provides a more refined method for adjusting for the interstate variations in industrial mixes.

Average Losses per $100 of Payroll

In their empirical analysis, Danzon and Harrington (1998) used average losses per $100 of payroll and its growth over time as workers' compensation cost measures. These data are based on NCCI estimates of incurred losses (cash, medical, and total benefits). That is, they are projections of the ultimate cost of claims with accident dates in a policy year, using data from the "first report" of loss experience that, in turn, are extrapolated using historical trends to the "ultimate report" basis. As such, the data that form the basis of Danzon and Harrington's cost measures are subject to error. Projections of the eventual (ultimate) cost of a claim will change as more up-to-date loss data become available. In addition, these data do not include all of the costs of workers' compensation insurance to employers, such as underwriting expenses and carrier profits. Further, as was the case with the cost measures used by Carroll and Kaestner, interstate cost variations may actually be due to differences in industry mix among states and over time; for this reason, interstate cost comparisons may be biased.[5]

We have reviewed four alternative ways of measuring employers' costs: benefits paid per worker, losses per employee (or injury), average losses per $100 of payroll, and loss ratios. There are three principal problems with these measures. First, the first three measures do not reflect all of the costs of employers' workers' compensation insurance; in particular, they do not include the profit and expense loadings charged by insurers. Second, while the loss ratios reflect the loadings charged by insurers (because they are part of premiums), they do not provide an unambiguous measure of employer costs. A high loss ratio could, for example, be due to a relatively small markup by the carrier coupled with very high losses; this combination will result in a low inverse loss ratio but also high costs to employers. Third, these measures ignore or inadequately control for interstate variations in industrial composition, which affect statewide averages of workers' compensation insurance costs for employers. The importance of these variations in industrial composition is discussed in the next section, which provides yet another way—and in our view, a superior way—of measuring the employers' costs of workers' compensation.

COST METHODOLOGY

In the remainder of this chapter, we provide a brief overview of the methodology we used to measure the employers' costs of workers' compensation; a detailed discussion of this methodology is presented in Appendix C. We also indicate why, in our view, this cost measure is better than those critiqued in the preceding section.

The cost methodology used in this volume stems from refinements to the methodology developed by Burton (1965), which was designed to evaluate how plant location decisions are influenced by interstate differences in the employers' costs of workers' compensation insurance. Interstate differences in the average costs of workers' compensation insurance for all employers in each state might appear, on first impression, to be relevant for assessing a state's competitive environment. However, such information on average costs should be irrelevant to rational employers. Employers who are considering relocating facilities to other states should be concerned solely with the insurance rates pertaining to them, rather than with the average costs for all employers in a state.

This point can be illustrated by the following example. Assume that there are only two insurance classifications in states A and B—class 1 and class 2—and that a particular employer would be placed in class 1 in both states. The insurance rates per $100 of payroll for each classification are identical in both states (e.g., class 1 is $0.10 and class 2 is $1.00). Also assume that all employers in states A and B pay their employees $300 per week.[6] Obviously, there is no economic incentive for the employer to move from state A to state B because its insurance costs will be unaffected by the move. However, the average premium as a percentage of payroll for all employers will vary considerably between the two states if the workforce composition differs sharply. If, for example, in state A, 90 percent of the payroll of all employers is in class 2 and 10 percent in class 1, while in State B, 90 percent is in class 1 and 10 percent in class 2, the average premium as a percentage of payroll will be much different in the two states. Specifically, in this example, the average premium in state A will be $0.91 per $100 of payroll (that is, premiums will be 0.91 percent of payroll), and the average premium in state B will be $0.19 per $100 of payroll (that is, premiums will be 0.19 percent of payroll). Nonetheless, there is no incentive in this example for our employer—or any employer—to relocate to state B so long as the employer's workers' compensation insurance classification is not affected by the interstate move.

The purpose of this example is not to argue that a state's competitive environment with respect to workers' compensation insurance costs cannot be assessed. Indeed, the example can be adapted to provide a valid approach to determine interstate variations in employers' workers' compensation costs for purposes of assessing a state's competitive environment. The approach involves using the same distribution of payroll among the various classification codes in both states in order to demonstrate the extent of an employer's incentive to relocate from state A to state B.

For example, the distribution of payroll among workers' compensation insurance classes in state A can be used in conjunction with state B's insurance rates to generate a new average premium as a percentage of payroll for state A's employers; this new premium would be applicable if these employers moved to state B. Obviously, because in this example insurance rates for comparable classifications are identical between states, employers initially located in state A would pay 0.91 percent of their payroll as workers' compensation premium irrespective of whether they remained in state A or moved to state B. Thus, there would be no incentive to change plant locations in order to lower workers' compensation costs.

This two-state example illustrates why using a constant distribution of payroll among the same set of insurance classifications for all states is the most valid approach to comparing employers' costs of workers' compensation insurance among jurisdictions. However, this approach has to be refined. The first step is to increase the number of classifications used to calculate a jurisdiction's average costs of workers' compensation insurance.

Classification Codes

As we indicated in Chapter 2, most employers purchase workers' compensation insurance from private companies or from state insurance funds.[7] The initial step in our methodology for computing the employers' costs of workers' compensation insurance is the assignment of an employer to one or more industrial or occupational categories.[8] In about 40 states where private insurance is available, these categories are prescribed by the classifications published by the National Council on Compensation Insurance. Classification codes currently in use range from 0005 (Nursery Employees) to 9985 (Atomic Energy: Radiation Exposure NOC [not otherwise classified]). Between these two extremities in classification numbers are several thousand other classifications, at least 500 of which are in common use.

Seventy-one employer classes were used for the employers' costs computations in this study, as shown in Appendix Table C.1. We chose these classification codes because of their prevalence throughout many states, their relative importance in terms of the percentage of total payroll they include (they account for over 73 percent of the national payroll covered by workers' compensation insurance), and their representative character in the five industry groups used for workers' compensation insurance classifications: manufacturing; contracting; office and clerical; goods and services; and miscellaneous.[9] The national distribution of payroll among these 71 classes was used to calculate the average cost of workers' compensation insurance in each state, which ensures that our measures of interstate cost differences pertain to a comparable set of employers and are not due to interstate variations in industry mix.

Manual Rates or Pure Premiums

After the carrier assigns the employer to the appropriate insurance classification, the carrier determines an appropriate initial insurance rate.[10] Depending on the regulatory environment of the state, the initial rate may be a manual rate or may be a pure premium. Also, again depending on the regulatory environment, the carrier may be required to use the rates promulgated by the rating bureau or may have discretion in determining the initial insurance rate.[11]

In some states, the rating bureau develops and promulgates loss cost or pure premium rates for each category, which cover payments for cash benefits, medical care, and (in most jurisdictions) loss-adjustment expenses. In these states, the individual carrier will add a *loading factor*, which includes an allowance for other carrier expenses (such as underwriting expenses and commissions) plus an allowance for profits. In other states, the rating bureau prepares fully developed manual rates, which are equal to the sum of the loading factor and the pure premium. Manual rates or pure premiums are specified as a certain number of dollars per $100 of weekly earnings for each employee.

Adjusted Manual Rates

Manual rates or pure premiums do not provide the proper basis for making interstate comparisons that accurately reflect employers' actual costs of workers' compensation insurance. The weekly workers' compensation premium for most employers is not simply the product of their manual rates (or pure premiums) and their weekly payrolls. Rather, their insurance costs are affected by a myriad of modifying factors, including premium discounts for quantity purchases, carrier deviations from the manual rates promulgated by the advisory organization, dividends received from insurance companies, experience-rating modifications due to the employer's own compensable experience compared with that of comparable firms, and other factors. When these modifying factors are taken into consideration, the result is a more accurate measure of the employers' actual costs of workers' compensation insurance. The end result of applying a series of modifying factors to manual rates or pure premiums is what we term *adjusted manual rates*. Adjusted manual rates are measured as a certain number of dollars per $100 of weekly earnings, which represents the percentage of payroll expended by an employer on workers' compensation insurance.[12]

In this study, we use five different models to calculate adjusted manual rates. Though only one model is used to compute the rates in a jurisdiction in a particular year, the model used for each jurisdiction may vary over time, depending upon the changes (if any) that occur in the state's regulatory environment for workers' compensation insurance pricing. The models are mutually exclusive: as of our comparison dates—namely, January 1 for each year between 1975 and 1995—only one of the five models is applicable for a particular state for each date.

The choice of which model to use to compute employers' costs for a particular state and a particular comparison date depends upon the nature of the workers' compensation insurance market at the time. More specifically, it depends upon whether, as of a particular state and date, 1) the state rating bureau publishes manual rates or pure premiums, and 2) the rates in the assigned-risk market differ from those in the voluntary market.

A brief summary of the five models is presented here; a more detailed discussion of each of these models (including the specific steps used in computing adjusted manual rates and an example of the calculations for each model) is presented in Appendix C.

Model I: Voluntary market only with manual rates. This model was used when 1) the rates for the voluntary market contained expense loadings (and thus were manual rates), and 2) there were no separate rates or calculations for the assigned-risk market. The manual rates for the voluntary market may be either mandatory or advisory.[13]

Model II: Voluntary market only with pure premiums. This model was used when 1) the rates for the voluntary market were pure premiums (also known as loss costs), and 2) there were no separate rates or calculations for the assigned-risk market.

Model III: Voluntary market with manual rates and assigned-risk market with identical manual rates. This model was used when 1) the rates for the voluntary market included expense loadings (and thus were manual rates), and 2) there were manual rates for the assigned-risk market that were identical to voluntary market rates. Manual rates for the voluntary market may be mandatory or advisory.

Model IV: Voluntary market with manual rates and assigned-risk market with different manual rates. This model was used when 1) the rates for the voluntary market included expense loadings (and thus were manual rates), and 2) there were manual rates for the assigned-risk market that differed from voluntary market rates. Manual rates for the voluntary market may be mandatory or advisory.

Model V: Voluntary market with pure premiums and assigned-risk market with manual rates. This model was used when 1) the rates for the voluntary market were pure premiums (also known as loss costs), and 2) there were separate manual rates for the assigned-risk market.

Weekly Insurance Premiums

In addition to adjusted manual rates, we also estimated another measure of employers' workers' compensation costs in each state. *Weekly insurance premiums* (net weekly costs) were calculated by multiplying a state's adjusted manual rate by the corresponding average weekly wage for that state. The weekly wage was computed for the period 1965–1975 by multiplying a) a state-specific and year-specific earnings index number that adjusts for interstate variation in wages due to industrial composition by b) a national wage figure (the annual average weekly wage in employment covered by unemployment insurance).[14]

We computed weekly insurance premiums, an additional employers' cost measure, because interstate variations in employee earnings may also influence the relative costs of workers' compensation. Thus, weekly insurance premiums overcome a limitation of adjusted manual rates as a measure of interstate differences in workers' compensation costs.

This point can be illustrated by the use of a hypothetical example. Assume that the adjusted manual rates for an employer's classification in states A and B are identical, e.g., $1.00 per $100 of payroll. Further assume that state A is a northern, industrial, and heavily unionized jurisdiction in which the average weekly earnings of the employer's workforce is $500, and that state B lacks these attributes and has a corresponding earnings figure of $250. As a result, even if adjusted manual rates were equal in states A and B, the weekly insurance premiums (net costs) would be different. The firm's workers' compensation bill is a product of the relevant adjusted manual rate and the employer's payroll. In this example, the employer's insurance cost would be $5.00 per employee per week in state A and $2.50 in state B.

Interstate variations in employee earnings levels can thus influence the relative costs of workers' compensation. Unfortunately, using an unadjusted statewide average wage to compute weekly insurance premiums would introduce a bias to our cost estimates due to interstate variation in the industrial composition of employment. Since there are substantial differences among industries with respect to wage rates, an unadjusted statewide average wage will reflect differences among states in industry mix. States with a high proportion of employment in high-wage sectors will have higher net weekly costs than otherwise, even if underlying insurance costs per $100 of payroll for a particular type of employer are identical among states. We therefore calculated a weekly wage variable for each state and year in our sample that controls for interstate differences in the industrial composition of employment.

COST DATA

Adjusted Manual Rates

Appendix Table C.17 provides the adjusted manual rates averaged over 71 insurance classifications for each of 48 jurisdictions (47 states plus the District of Columbia) in our study[15] for each year with available data during the period 1975–1995. We use a subset of these data (adjusted manual rates for 1995) to rank the states (Figure 3.1). Among the 47 jurisdictions with data in 1995, Montana had the highest adjusted manual rate ($4.94 per $100 of payroll) and Indiana had the lowest ($1.40). Figure 3.1 depicts the substantial variation in adjusted manual rates among states. (As we previously indicated, these results do <u>not</u> stem from differences in the industrial composition of states' economies, but rather reflect a threefold difference in costs for comparable employers in these states.)

More comprehensive—and perhaps, more comprehensible—data (based on the weighted observations in Appendix Table C.18) are presented in Figure 3.2. Here, the average adjusted manual rates for all states with data for each year, as well as the rates that are one standard deviation above or below the national average, are reported for the period 1975–1995.[16] The national average for adjusted manual rates was $0.95 per $100 of payroll in 1975; it then rose to $1.65 in 1980, declined during the early 1980s (for reasons explained in Chapter 2), and reached a trough of $1.47 in 1984. After 1984, the average rate increased sharply, peaking at $3.48 per $100 of payroll in 1993. Rates then declined sharply during the last two years in our study period (1994 and 1995); the national average was $2.97 per $100 of payroll in 1995. The data in Figure 3.2 also indicate that interstate variations in adjusted manual rates increased considerably between 1985 and 1990; thereafter, the variation generally declined.

Weekly Insurance Premiums

Weekly insurance premiums (which are calculated by multiplying a state's adjusted manual rate by the corresponding average weekly wage for that state) constitute another measure of employers' costs used in our study. These costs of workers' compensation insurance

Figure 3.1 Adjusted Manual Rates in 1995, by State

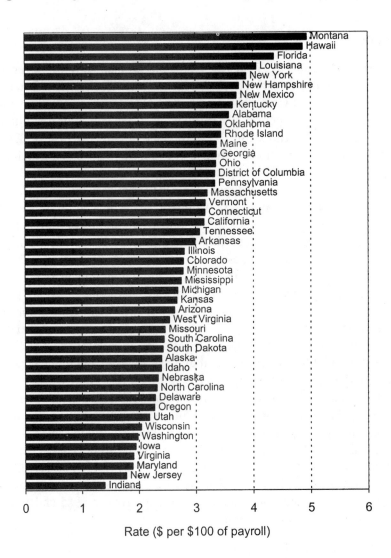

Rate ($ per $100 of payroll)

Figure 3.2 National Average Adjusted Manual Rates (± 1 S.D.), 1975–95

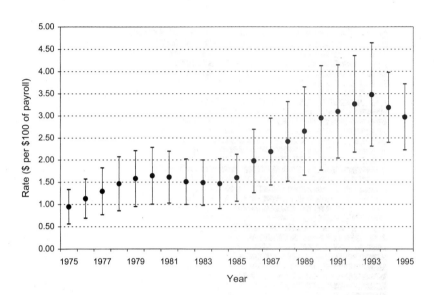

premiums per employee for each of the 48 jurisdictions in our study, for each year over the period 1975–1995 where data are available, are reported in Appendix Table C.21. A ranking by state of net costs (as of 1995) is provided in Figure 3.3. These findings roughly mirror those of adjusted manual rates for 1995: among these 47 jurisdictions with 1995 data, Montana had the highest net weekly costs ($28.59) and Indiana had the lowest ($7.76), once again showing the substantial variation in the cost of workers' compensation insurance among states. However, the findings with respect to net costs in 1995 differ in some instances from those for adjusted manual rates (compare Figures 3.1 and 3.3). Ohio, for example, ranked 14th on the basis of adjusted manual rates, but was the 8th most expensive state using net weekly costs, reflecting the state's relatively high wages.

Figure 3.4 reports the average net weekly costs per employee for all states with data available for each year during the 1975–1995 period, as well as the net costs that are one standard deviation above or below the national average.[17] (The data are from the weighted observations of Appendix Table C.22.) Not surprisingly, the general trend of

Figure 3.3 Net Weekly Costs in 1995, by State

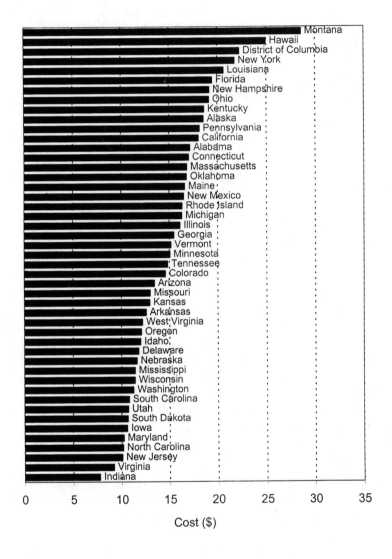

Cost ($)

Figure 3.4 National Average Net Weekly Costs (± 1 S.D.), 1975–95

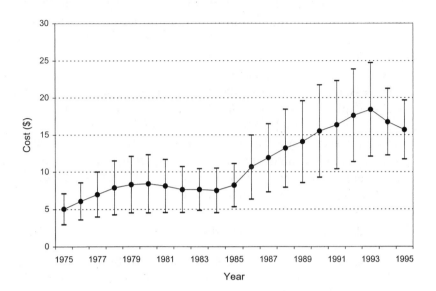

net costs over the period 1975–1995 is similar to the pattern for adjusted manual rates. The national average for net costs was $5.03 per employee per week in 1975. It rose to $8.41 in 1980 and then declined throughout the early 1980s until 1984 (when it was $7.50). Net costs then increased sharply, peaking at $18.40 in 1993, but then fell during the next two years of our study period, reaching $15.69 in 1995.

The data in Figure 3.4 also show that interstate variability in net weekly costs fluctuated between 1975 and 1995, as it increased in the late seventies and declined in the early eighties. From 1985 though 1990, interstate variations in net weekly costs increased substantially, but they then declined significantly during the 1990s.

CONCLUSIONS

In this chapter, we critiqued various workers' compensation cost measures that have been used by practitioners and academics to make interstate comparisons, and we presented what we regard as a more valid approach to computing employers' costs. We also presented state-specific findings and national averages for two cost measures (adjusted manual rates and net weekly costs) for the period 1975–1995. These costs varied significantly over time and also, in any particular year, varied sharply among states.

The essential purposes of the rest of this study are to develop a model to explain the determinants of the intertemporal and interstate variations in these employers' costs and to subject this model to an empirical analysis. We examine, *inter alia*, the impact of deregulation of insurance pricing and the relative generosity of state statutory provisions regarding workers' compensation benefits on the employers' costs of workers' compensation insurance.

Notes

1. UBA, Inc., established the National Foundation in 1984. UBA, Inc. has recently changed its name to UWC, Inc.—Strategic Services for Unemployment and Workers' Compensation.
2. "The Social Security Administration has provided a state-by-state estimate of workers covered by workers' compensation for 1997, 1981, 1984, and 1988. Changes in unemployment compensation coverage are used to develop estimates for other years." (National Foundation 1997, footnote 5, no page number).
3. As further explained in Appendix B, *paid losses* are the benefits that have already been paid for a particular set of injuries as of the evaluation date. *Incurred losses* are the benefits that have been paid for a particular set of injuries as of the evaluation date plus the estimated value of the future benefits for those injuries as of that evaluation date.
4. Carroll and Kaestner (1995) attempt to control for these effects by using state- and industry-mix dummy variables in their statistical analysis. However, these dummy variables measure industry mix at a fairly aggregated level, without recognizing the differences in workers' compensation costs that can occur within industrial categories.
5. Danzon and Harrington's cost growth measure is not subject to these problems to the extent that industry mix remains constant over time within a particular state. Danzon and Harrington also do empirical analyses using loss data for individual rating classification codes; unlike their state-level loss ratio data, these cost measures are not subject to the industry composition problem.
6. This example assumes that the employer's entire payroll is used to calculate premiums. The topic of payroll limitations is discussed in Appendix C.
7. Our discussion of cost methodology does not pertain to the third source of insurance coverage (self-insurance), for which we do not have any cost data.

8. Some of the discussion in this section draws upon Burton and Schmidle (1991, 1992) and Schmidle (1994). See also Kallop (1976); Williams (1986); NCCI (1981); Appel and Borba (1988, pp. 5–9); Webb et al. (1984, pp. 106–112); and Huebner, Black, and Cline (1982, pp. 575–592).

9. The NCCI's *Classification Codes and Statistical Codes for Workers Compensation and Employers Liability Insurance* manual for selected years was the source of the 71 employer categories. Insurance categories in states using other classification systems were "converted" by selecting the classification in that state that was most nearly analogous to the corresponding code among the 71 NCCI employer classes.

10. A particular employer may be assigned to two or more insurance classifications, depending on the industrial or occupational mix of the employer's workforce.

11. When the state regulations allow carriers discretion in determining the initial rates that are used to help determine the premiums actually paid by employers, all carriers are required to report their experience using a set of specified rates for the insurance classifications used by the carrier. These specified rates are known as the "Designated Statistical Reporting (DSR) Level." For example, the policy year 1996 experience in Michigan was reported using the January 1, 1996, pure premiums as the DSR Level.

12. The methodology to compute these "adjusted" manual rates was developed almost 35 years ago by Burton and has been subsequently refined and modified. Substantial refinements and modifications in this methodology were used for this study in order to capture, in a comprehensive manner, all pertinent recent developments affecting workers' compensation insurance pricing. See Burton (1965, 1979); Elson and Burton (1981); Burton, Hunt, and Krueger (1985); and Burton and Schmidle (1992).

13. The distinctions between mandatory and advisory rates were discussed in Chapter 2.

14. A description of the state-specific wage index is provided in Appendix D.

15. The words *state(s)* or *jurisdiction(s)* should be taken as synonyms referring to this study set. Data limitations precluded us from computing employers' costs in three of the six jurisdictions having exclusive state funds (Nevada, North Dakota, and Wyoming).

16. Due to data availability problems, the number of states used to compute these averages is not constant across the entire period from 1975 to 1995. However, as indicated in the discussion of Appendix Table C.18, the results over time are not particularly sensitive to the changing number of observations over time.

17. As was the case with adjusted manual rates, the number of states used to compute these data varies over the period from 1975 to 1995. As was also the case with adjusted manual rates (and once again, as indicated by the discussion of Appendix Table C.22), the results are not particularly sensitive to the changing number of observations over time.

4
Benefit Adequacy
versus Affordability

In the previous chapter, we presented data showing the substantial variations in workers' compensation costs both over time and across states. We now begin a quest to explain these variations. Are they due to differences with respect to the level of benefits provided to injured workers, which may be expected to be a significant driver of compensation costs, or are they due to differences in administrative efficiency or other factors? The answer has obvious implications for public policy issues concerning the efficacy of different insurance arrangements addressed in subsequent chapters. While the affordability criterion suggests that low-cost programs are in some sense superior to high-cost ones, it is important to determine whether low program costs were attained by sacrificing benefit adequacy. Among other things, this suggests that to properly assess the relative efficiency of different insurance arrangements, it is important to control for other variables that affect employer costs.

In this chapter, we explore the relationship between workers' compensation costs and factors such as benefit generosity and the underlying risk of workplace injury or disease. We initially describe an accounting model of insurance prices that is the foundation for our empirical investigation of employers' costs. We then provide a detailed account of the variables and data set used in the cost models, including identification of the data sources and methodology used to construct variables for the analyses. In the third section, we report the results of regression analyses in which the dependent variables are adjusted manual rates and net weekly costs. We then present the results of simulations in which we estimate the cost increase that would result if all states were to adopt workers' compensation statutes that meet alternative definitions of benefit adequacy.

AN ACCOUNTING MODEL OF EMPLOYER COSTS

A simple accounting model of workers' compensation insurance costs indicates that insurer profits are equal to the premiums collected from policyholders plus earnings on reserves minus losses paid, dividends to policyholders, and administrative expenses, which include marketing, underwriting, and claims adjustment costs. If we initially ignore administrative expenses, we can represent expected per-claim insurer profits as follows:

Eq. 4.1 $E[\Pi] = (1 - p)C + p(C - B),$

where Π is insurer profits, p is the probability of injury per covered worker, C is insurer premiums, and B is the average benefit payment per claim. If insurance is actuarially fair, then $C = pB$.

Administrative expenses and profits may be incorporated into the model by allowing for a loading factor that is proportional to premiums, so that $C = \phi C + pB$ where ϕ is the loading factor. This implies that $C = pB/(1 - \phi)$. Taking the natural logarithm of this cost function, we find that

Eq. 4.2 $\ln C = -\ln(1 - \phi) + \ln p + \ln B$.

This result suggests that a regression specification that estimates the employers' cost of workers compensation insurance should 1) include measures of the probability of injury and the average benefits paid to compensation claimants and 2) assume a log-log form. Also, note that the relationship between the expense loading (a component of ϕ) and insurance premiums (or loss costs) may be nonlinear. This is evident from the existence of fixed expense components built into insurer rate filings, such as expense or loss constants or premium discounts.

This result also suggests that interstate differences with respect to the effect of insurance arrangements—including the regulatory regime—will be included in the intercept of the regression model (or $-\ln(1 - \phi)$ of Eq. 4.2), as will temporal variation in rates attributable to the insurance cycle. In other words, holding pure premiums or loss costs constant, the effects of insurance arrangements will manifest themselves through a change in the loading factor and will appear as a lower or higher intercept in an estimated regression equation. We discuss the details of the regression specifications used to estimate costs in the following section.

COST REGRESSION MODEL

As indicated, this simple accounting model suggests that employer costs are a function of the average benefit paid to compensation claimants and the claim rate. Consequently, our empirical specification includes both variables. Unfortunately, these measures are imperfect in that they do not control for interstate differences in administration. There are also other variables included as explanatory factors in our regression model that control for administrative and other differences.[1] The full set of regressors includes estimates of the number of permanent partial disability claims as a proportion of total indemnity claims, the unionization rate, and the extent of workers' compensation coverage. Many of our analyses also include time and state dummies to capture the influence of unobserved, time- and state-specific effects. In particular, we use year dummies in order to control for insurance cycle effects that could influence costs. In the rest of this section, we discuss in detail each of the variables in our regression model, as well as our hypothesis concerning the relationships of these variables to employer costs.

Benefits

As we indicated in Chapter 1, workers who suffer disability or death as the result of a work-related injury or disease are eligible to receive two types of benefits: medical treatment and, if their disabilities are severe enough, cash benefits. Our regression analyses utilize three variables to capture the effect of the relative benefit generosity of each state's workers' compensation law: expected cash benefits, a variable estimating the relative cost of medical and rehabilitation expenses, and a combined (or total) benefit measure. In most of our model specifications, cash and medical benefit variables are entered as separate regressors. However, Eq. 4.2 in the previous section suggests that the coefficient of the logarithm of this combined benefit measure will provide a useful estimate of the cost-benefit elasticity.

Elasticity estimates are interesting in their own right. While our simple accounting model predicts a one-to-one relationship between benefits and costs—that is, a cost-benefit elasticity of 1—economic theory hypothesizes that because benefits affect employer and worker behavior, the value of this elasticity may be more or less than 1. To examine this issue, we estimate a subset of cost regressions using the total benefit variable.

Cash benefits

National trend data on average per claim cash benefits in constant 1995 dollars for our study period (1975–1995) are shown in Figure 4.1. These data depict our estimates of the expected cash benefits that the average compensation claimant will receive during this period,[2] plus or minus one standard deviation. As is evident from this figure, the generosity of workers' compensation benefits did not fluctuate much over the period 1975–1995; however, interstate variability in the generosity of statutory benefits (as measured by the standard deviation) declined over this period.[3]

**Figure 4.1 Real Per-Claim Expected Cash Benefits, 1975–95
         (1995 $; mean ± 1 S.D.)**

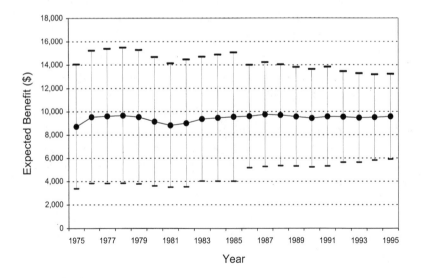

The expected cash benefit from workers' compensation in each of the 48 jurisdictions in our study is shown for 1995 in Figure 4.2. There was substantial variation among the states in benefit levels: the average cash benefit payment was almost $23,000 in the District of Columbia, but little more than $4,300 in Louisiana.

The data in Figures 4.1 and 4.2 are based on an index of cash benefit generosity of each state's workers' compensation statute that we constructed for each jurisdiction and each year in our sample. For a

Figure 4.2 Expected Cash Benefits by State, 1995

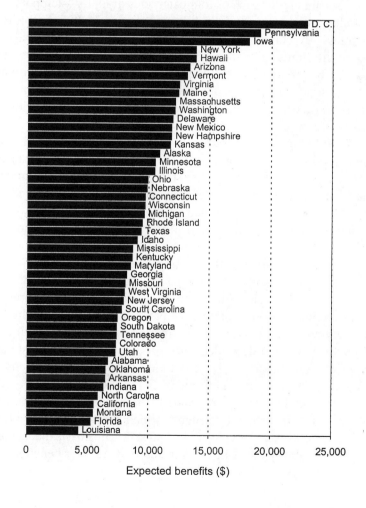

comprehensive discussion of the methodology, see Appendix D. A brief summary of this methodology follows.

The method recognizes that benefit levels are set by each state's workers' compensation statute and depend on factors specific to each claim, including the type and severity of the claimant's injury as well as the claimant's pre-injury wage, age, and, family status.[4] More specifically, a weekly benefit, which typically varies according to the claimant's wage, is paid to claimants over a time period that varies depending on the severity of the claimant's injury. We generated the benefit index by estimating the weekly benefit and the duration of payments separately for each of four categories of injury—temporary total disability, permanent total disability, permanent partial disability, and fatalities—for claimants with various characteristics, e.g., wage, age, and family status. The index for each of these disability categories is equal to the product of the duration and weekly benefits. To obtain an index of total cash benefit generosity, we combined benefit measures for each of these four injury categories using the relative national frequency of injury type as weights.

Weekly benefits. To compute the weekly benefit for the average compensation claimant for a particular state and year, we constructed a wage distribution specific to that state and year. The distribution was based on a national wage distribution centered on an "adjusted" average weekly wage for each state and year.[5] Weekly benefits were then computed for each claimant in the distribution, based on statutory benefit parameters.[6]

Average benefit duration. The average benefit duration for each injury type was calculated using the relevant national distributions for each claim type: a disability duration distribution for temporary total claims, a distribution of permanent partial disability claims by nature of injury and severity,[7] an age distribution for permanent total claims, and a distribution of dependent survivors, by age and family status, for fatalities. Since states limit the duration of benefits in different ways, the actual duration of benefit payments was calculated by applying these statutory limits to the appropriate distribution. In the case of permanent disability or fatality benefits, which are paid out over a lengthy period, benefits were calculated on a present-value basis that accounted for the probability of death or, in the case of survivor benefits, remarriage.

Medical benefits

Although most workers' compensation claimants have relatively minor injuries and thus do not qualify for cash benefits, nearly all claimants receive some sort of medical care. Unlike cash benefits, there is no easy way to construct an index of expected medical costs; as a result, we were forced to rely on measures of actual benefits paid. The average cost of medical benefits for all claims in each jurisdiction was used as the basic measure of medical benefits.

National trend data on per claim medical benefits payments in constant 1995 dollars for our study period (1975–1995) are shown in Figure 4.3.[8] As is evident, there was considerable variation over time in the average real cost of medical benefits. This pattern is also markedly different from that in Figure 4.1, which showed that cash benefits did not change much over the 1975–1995 period. Specifically, the data in Figure 4.3 show that the average real cost of medical benefits more than tripled over this period, from $698 in 1975 to $2,528 in 1995. Average medical benefits grew consistently between 1975 and 1994 and then fell by about 10 percent in 1995.

Figure 4.3 Real Per-Claim Medical Benefits, 1975–95 (mean ± 1 S.D.)

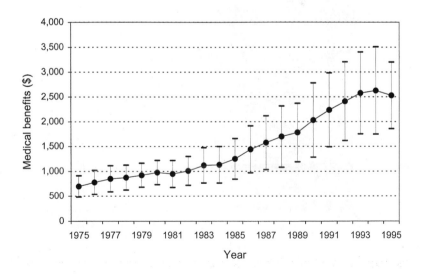

Furthermore, interstate variability in medical benefits also increased substantially between 1975 and 1995. There was more than a fourfold increase in the dollar amount of one standard deviation between 1975 and 1994, from $214 to $882, although the standard deviation then declined to $673 in 1995.

The considerable variability in medical expenses among states is illustrated by the 1995 medical benefits cost data (Figure 4.4).[9] The average workers' compensation medical expenses ranged from a high

Figure 4.4 Average Medical Benefits for 1995 (for those jurisdictions having data for 1995)

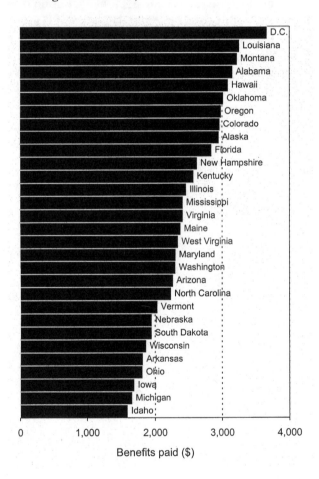

of $3,673 in the District of Columbia to a low of $1,598 in Idaho, a spread of more than $2,000.

During our study period, most state workers' compensation programs paid 100 percent of the claimant's medical expenses. Consequently, the variation in medical benefit costs was primarily attributable to differences in the cost of health care services, the utilization of medical services, or both. The dramatic rise in medical benefit payments evident in Figure 4.3 corresponds with a more general rise in health care costs in the United States during this period. However, the increasing variability suggests that interstate differences in charges for health care or in the utilization of services were widening among states during the study period.[10]

Total benefits

The coefficient on a measure of total benefits may provide important information about the relationship between benefits and costs (see Eq. 4.2, p. 62). A coefficient of 1 for the "total benefit" variable implies that a 10 percent increase in benefits paid per claim results in a 10 percent increase in employer compensation costs: either the behavior of the parties to the workers' compensation claim (the worker, employer, and insurer) is unaffected by changes in benefit levels or the parties' responses to an increase in benefits offset one another.

However, the coefficient will be greater than 1 if higher benefit levels lead to increased benefit utilization by workers, induce riskier behavior on the part of workers, increase the frequency of claims reporting or claims duration, or any combination of the above. On the other hand, we would expect the coefficient on the total benefit variable to be less than 1 if higher benefit levels cause experience-rated employers to improve workplace health and safety or to manage claims more intensively.

Krueger and Burton (1990) used a data set and methodology similar to our own and found a cost-benefit elasticity of 1 for most of their model specifications. However, their study differed from ours in two important ways. First, their data set contained substantially fewer observations— 109, compared with over 900 in the current study—using data from 29 states for four nonconsecutive years (1972, 1975, 1978, and 1983). Second, their model specifications included separate cash and medical benefit variables as regressors rather than a total benefit measure. They interpreted the coefficient on the cash benefit variable as being equivalent to the cost-benefit elasticity. However, since the logarithm of a sum is not equal to the sum of two logarithms, their specification may not provide an appropriate estimate of this elasticity.[11]

In the later section on regression results, we estimate cost–benefit elasticities using a data set that includes more states and a substantially longer period than did the Krueger and Burton study. Even more importantly, our estimates are based on a measure of total expected benefits, including both medical and cash benefits, paid to the average compensation claim in each state. To compute this measure, we inflated the expected cash benefit variable (described previously) by a factor equal to the state-specific and year-specific ratio of the total (cash plus medical) benefits paid to cash benefits paid.[12] Data for this inflation factor were taken from the NCCI "first-to-ultimate" report exhibits described in note 10.[13]

This expected total benefit measure (in 1995 dollars) for the period 1975–1995 is shown in Figure 4.5. There has been considerable growth in total benefits over this period: the national average increased by nearly 60 percent, from $12,450 in 1975 to $19,612 in 1995. The expected total benefit costs for individual states in 1995 are presented

Figure 4.5 Per-Claim Expected Total Benefits, 1975–95 (mean ± 1 S.D.)

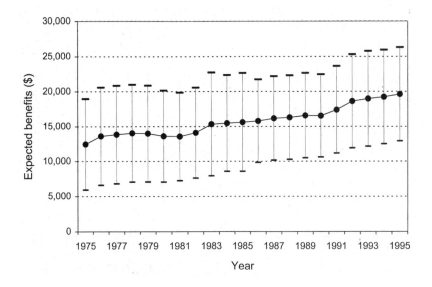

in Figure 4.6. The relative position of states with respect to this total benefit measure is remarkably similar to their position vis-à-vis expected cash benefits. The District of Columbia continues to be the most generous jurisdiction in the nation, paying an average total benefit in excess of $41,500, while Louisiana is the most penurious, averaging less than $9,100 per claimant in total compensation benefit payments.

Figure 4.6 Expected Total Benefits, 1995 (for those jurisdictions having data for 1995)

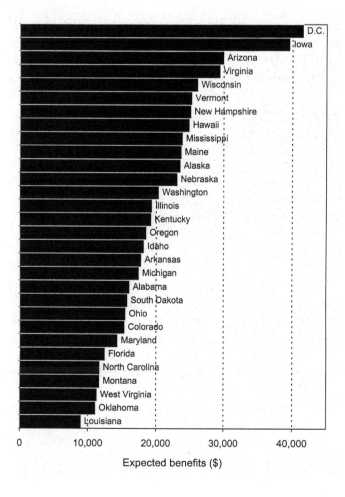

Injury Rate

We also use an injury rate measure as an explanatory variable in our employer costs model. We expect that higher injury rates will, in general, lead to higher benefit payments and to higher insurance costs. Injury rates vary systematically among industries, and so states in which the dominant industry is coal mining will have an higher injury rate for all workers than a state where most workers are in the service sector. Interstate variations in costs solely due to differences in industrial mix among states are accounted for through our construction of the cost variable. As we noted in Chapter 2, the cost variable is based on a homogeneous set of manual rate classification codes, so we statistically control for interstate differences in insurance costs that are due to variations in industrial composition.

However, while our construction of the dependent variable controls for interindustry differences in the probability of injury, there are other potential sources of variation in injury rates. Specifically, there are variations in the injury rate within rate classes, both over time and among jurisdictions. To control for these variations, we included a special measure of the statewide injury rate in our regression analyses.

The special statewide injury rates were calculated using unpublished data obtained from the U.S. Department of Labor. Since the cost variables are based on a homogeneous set of rate groups, our injury rate measure also had to be independent of interstate differences in industrial composition. Consequently, we computed weighted average injury rates for each state and year in our sample by combining injury rate data for the major industrial divisions with national employment by industry division as the weights.[14] That is, injury rates for each major industry division were first collected for each state and year in our sample. These state- and year-specific, major division rates were then aggregated into a state/year average by using a national distribution of employment by industry division. Missing data were imputed in a manner identical to that which we described for missing medical benefits data (see note 10).

The trend in annual occupational injuries per 100 workers in the United States (1975–1995) is shown in Figure 4.7.[15] Overall, these data suggest that there has been a long-term decline in the injury rate. The average annual injury rate dropped from about 8.7 injuries per 100

Figure 4.7 Injury Rate, 1975–95 (mean ± 1 S.D.)

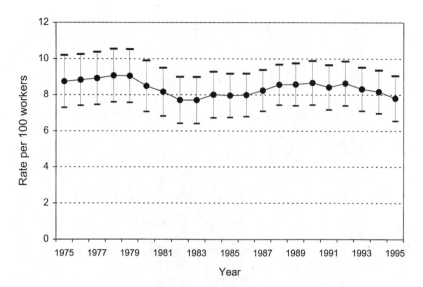

workers in the 1970s to less than 8 injuries per 100 workers by 1995. A cyclical relationship for work injury rates has been reported by a number of studies, including Chelius (1977), Smith (1992), Thomason and Hyatt (1997), and Durbin and Butler (1998). We also find some evidence of this, as the data exhibit a relatively strong cyclical pattern that is consistent with the business cycle, at least during the early part of this period.

The injury rate declined sharply during the recessionary period of the early 1980s, only to rise steadily for the remainder of that decade, when there was relatively strong economic growth. A slight decline in the injury rate occurred in 1991, contemporaneous with another recession. However, since 1992, the injury rate has declined steadily despite a relatively robust economy.

Interstate variations in the annual injury rate per 100 workers for 1995 are shown in Figure 4.8 for the last year in our study. Injury rates range from a high of some 11 injuries per 100 workers in Montana to a low of slightly more than 5 injuries per 100 workers in New York.[16]

Figure 4.8 Injury Rate, 1995 (for states with no missing data for 1995)

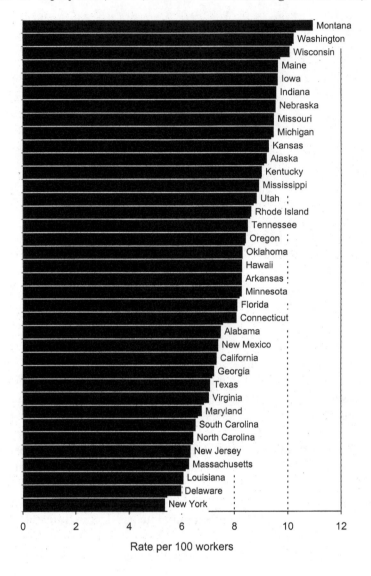

Rate per 100 workers

Permanent Partial Disability Claims as a Proportion of Total Claims

A permanent partial disability (PPD) claims measure is another explanatory variable in our employer costs model. The expected cash benefit index described previously measures benefit generosity as determined by a state's workers' compensation statutory parameters. However, actual benefit payments are also affected by the nature of program administration. States with identical statutory parameters may pay benefits that are substantially different due to interstate variations in administrative rules. This is particularly true for permanent partial disability awards, where there are substantial variations in the methods and criteria used to determine compensation (Berkowitz and Burton 1987).

For example, in some states, compensation for PPD claims is based on the extent of the claimant's impairment, while in others, benefits depend on the extent of the claimant's lost wage-earning capacity. Adjudicators are called upon to make decisions that often involve a substantial element of subjective judgment. The distinction between a claimant who is suffering a 50 percent loss of use of an arm and a claimant who is "merely" suffering a 40 percent loss lacks the kind of clear distinction that is easily incorporated into statutory language or administrative regulations. Since benefits paid to PPD claims account for over 70 percent of total indemnity benefit costs nationwide, interstate differences in PPD claims administration could significantly affect the level of claim benefits.[17]

To account for interstate variation in claims administration, we include in our empirical specification a variable measuring the proportion of total workers' compensation indemnity claims that involve permanent partial disability benefits. These data were taken from the NCCI's *Countrywide Workers Compensation Exhibits* for various years. These exhibits do not include data for all NCCI jurisdictions for some years and do not include data for exclusive-state-fund jurisdictions in any year. We assigned values for missing data from the NCCI states and for Washington state using a procedure identical to the one we used for medical benefits payments. We assigned the other two exclusive-state-fund jurisdictions in our study (West Virginia and Ohio) the national average for the PPD proportion variable.

National data on PPD cases as a proportion of total indemnity claims for the period 1975–1995 are shown in Figure 4.9.[18] This proportion was relatively stable at about 23 percent of total claims from 1975 to 1984, rose to a little more than 35 percent in 1992, and then declined slightly to about 32.5 percent by 1995, the last year of our study. There is considerable interstate variation in the PPD proportion, as illustrated by the 1995 data in Figure 4.10. The PPD proportion ranged from about 10 percent in Maine to nearly 50 percent of total claims in Montana.

Previous studies of compensation costs have found that the PPD proportion is strongly and positively related to compensation costs (Krueger and Burton 1990; Schmidle 1994). We similarly expect a positive relationship between the PPD proportion and employer costs.

Union Density

Union membership also appears to affect the compensation claim process. Hirsch, Macpherson, and Dumond (1997) found that unionized workers are more likely to receive workers' compensation benefits

**Figure 4.9 PPD Cases as Share of Total Indemnity Claims
(mean ± 1 S.D.)**

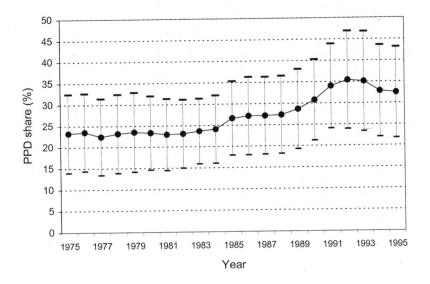

Figure 4.10 PPD Claims as a Share of Total Claims by State, 1995

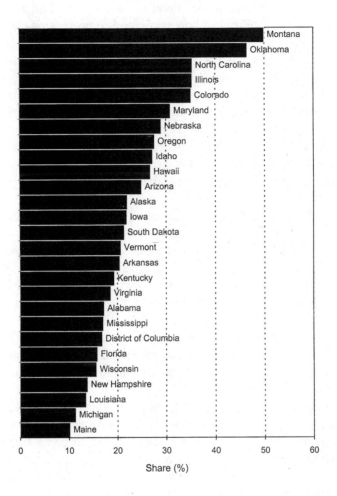

than are comparable nonunion workers. There are at least two possible explanations for this. First, unionized employees may have more information about their rights to workers' compensation benefits. Second, because of due process guarantees contained in collective bargaining agreements, union members may have less reason to fear employer reprisals as a result of filing workers' compensation claims.

In either event, we expect that the extent of union membership in a state is positively related to employer costs; i.e., it will be associated with a greater probability of filing a workers' compensation claim and, possibly, higher benefits per claim. Of course, while unions may increase the probability of a workers' compensation claim being filed, unions are also likely to improve the conditions affecting workplace safety. Weil (1991) found that labor unions aid the implementation of Occupational Safety and Health Act regulations in the workplace, while Thomason and Pozzebon (1999) found that unions have a direct impact on firm safety practices. Nonetheless, to date the evidence indicates that the impact of unions on increasing the likelihood of a workers' compensation claim is greater than their effect on reducing the probability of injury.

To measure the impact of unions, we use the proportion of workers who are union members in a state—that is, union density—as an explanatory variable. Three sources, all of which derive estimates from the Current Population Survey (CPS), were used for our union density measure. Data for the period between 1975 and 1982 (inclusive) were taken from Kokkelenberg and Sockell (1985), and estimates from Hirsch and Macpherson (1996) were used for 1994 and 1995. We estimated union density data for the remaining years (1983–1993) using CPS data files. Missing values for particular states and years were imputed using the same procedure we employed for the medical benefit variable.

Average union density throughout the United States in the 1975–1995 period is presented in Figure 4.11. These data show the well-known decline in unionization that occurred during this period. In 1975, almost one-quarter of the workforce were union members. By 1995, the proportion had dropped to close to 15 percent. The distribution of union density by state for 1995 is shown in Figure 4.12. Union density ranged from a low of 3.3 percent in South Carolina to a high of 27.7 percent in New York.

Covered Employment

Workers' compensation programs do not cover all workers. Historically, state workers' compensation statutes have exempted from coverage such occupational groups as farmworkers and household

Figure 4.11 Union Density, 1975–95 (mean ± 1 S.D.)

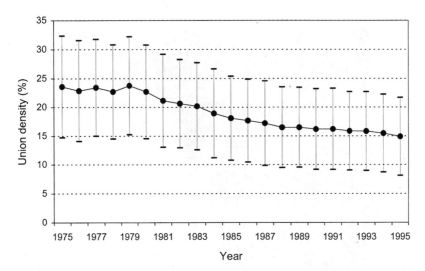

workers. In addition, these statutes often excluded small firms with fewer than a specified number of workers. In a few states, workers' compensation insurance is not compulsory, so individual employers may opt out of the compensation program.[19]

The extent of workers' compensation coverage may affect employer costs, although the nature of its influence is uncertain and depends on the occupational groups that are included or excluded as coverage expands or shrinks. If statutory coverage provisions tend to exempt high-risk employment, then the extent of workers' compensation coverage will be negatively related to employers' workers' compensation insurance costs; the opposite result is expected if low-risk groups are exempt. Thus, in order to predict, *a priori*, the relationship between coverage and costs, it is necessary to examine changes in employment composition that accompany changes in covered employment.

Unfortunately, there are no state-level data on workers' compensation coverage by occupational or industrial class. However, many of the principal statutory changes in coverage that occurred between 1975 and 1995 are reflected in the recommendations of the National Commission of State Workmen's Compensation Laws (National Commis-

Figure 4.12 Union Density by State, 1995

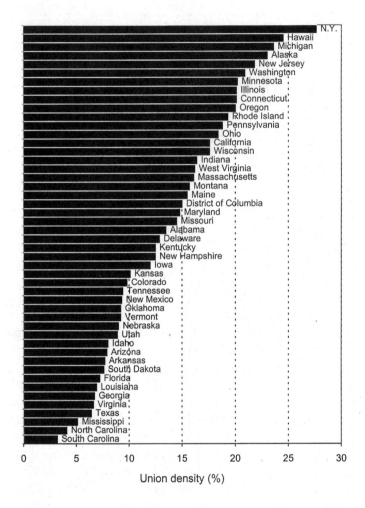

Union density (%)

sion 1972). These recommendations addressed major gaps in workers' compensation coverage that existed in the early 1970s, and the U.S. Department of Labor has tracked compliance with 19 of the recommendations that the National Commission designated as "essential" in subsequent years.

The National Commission made six essential recommendations relating to coverage of workers or employers. Three recommendations involved specific employment classes not covered by many compensation statutes (farmworkers, household and casual workers, and government employees). In addition, the National Commission recommended that workers' compensation be compulsory for private employment, that no waivers be permitted, and that there be no exemption for any class of employee, such as professional athletes or the employees of charitable organizations. Since many states exempted from coverage those employers with few employees, the National Commission also recommended that employers not be exempted because of their size.

We have no *a priori* expectations about the relationship among the general recommendations and employer costs. Unless there are substantial cross-subsidies between occupational classes, the employment-specific recommendations should not have any impact on our measures of employer compensation costs, since exempted groups are not among the 71 occupational classification codes used to compute our employer cost measures.[20] The mandatory inclusion of small employers may increase workers' compensation costs. Small employers generally have higher injury rates relative to large employers due to economies of scale in the development of workplace safety programs and due to differences in the extent to which small and large firms are experience-rated.

U.S. Department of Labor data on the number of states in compliance with the various National Commission recommendations related to covered employment for the 48 jurisdictions in our sample during the 1975–1995 period are shown in Figure 4.13. For the most part, these data indicate that state compliance with these recommendations did not change substantially.

We have empirically tested whether there is any correlation between covered employment and the National Commission's recommendations. These results are presented in Table 4.1, which reports Pearson correlation coefficients for covered employment and for dummy variables representing the National Commission recommendations.[21] Data in parentheses show the *p*-value for each correlation. The results reported in the "Covered employment" row indicate that, as expected, all National Commission recommendations are positively

Figure 4.13 Compliance with Coverage Recommendations .

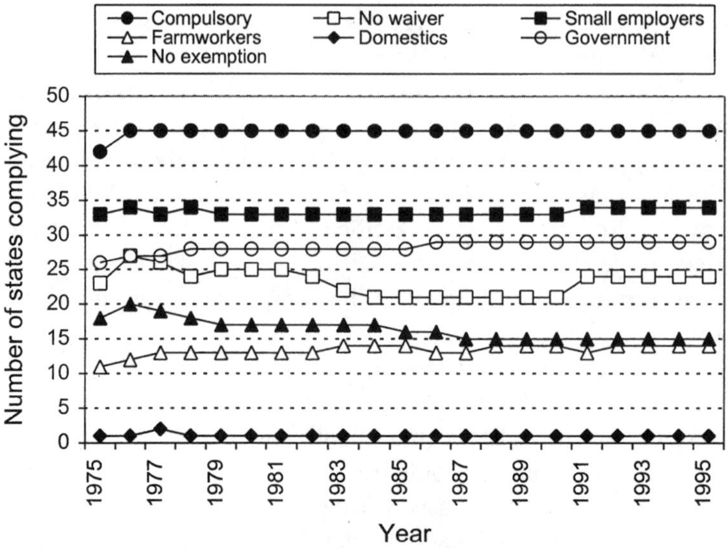

related to covered employment. In particular, the recommendation concerning small employers had a relatively strong relationship with coverage, as indicated by a statistically significant correlation coefficient of 0.2003. This finding provides further support for a hypothesized positive relationship between coverage and costs, since small employers may be expected to have higher costs than larger firms. However, this is only one recommendation, and it is possible that changes in other rules affecting coverage, such as the prohibition of waivers, have the opposite effect, increasing average compensation costs. Thus, it is difficult to make *a priori* predictions concerning the relationship between covered employment and costs.

Nonetheless, it is possible that the extent of covered employment could affect workers' compensation costs for the average employer. Consequently, we include estimates of the statewide proportion of employment covered by workers' compensation as a control variable in our model specifications. This variable was computed by dividing estimates of the average number of workers covered by workers' compensation programs (as reported in various issues of the *Social Security*

Table 4.1 Pearson Correlation Matrix—National Commission Recommendations and Covered Employment

Variable	Compulsory coverage	No waivers permitted	Small employers	Farm workers	Domestics	Government employees	No class exempt.	Covered employment
Compulsory coverage	1.0000							
No waivers permitted	-0.0701 (0.02)[a]	1.0000						
Small employers	0.0182 (0.53)	0.2293 (0.00)	1.0000					
Farm workers	-0.0336 (0.25)	0.0491 (0.09)	0.3309 (0.00)	1.0000				
Domestics	0.0370 (0.21)	0.1280 (0.00)	0.0918 (0.00)	0.2427 (0.00)	1.0000			
Government	0.1359 (0.00)	0.0434 (0.14)	0.1544 (0.00)	0.2314 (0.00)	0.1194 (0.00)	1.0000		
No class exemption	-0.0003 (0.99)	0.0736 (0.01)	-0.1033 (0.00)	0.0088 (0.76)	0.2112 (0.00)	0.2189 (0.00)	1.0000	
Covered employment	0.1323 (0.02)	0.1139 (0.05)	0.2003 (0.00)	0.1202 (0.04)	0.1089 (0.06)	0.3831 (0.00)	0.2647 (0.00)	1.0000

[a] p-values in parentheses.

Bulletin [Price 1979, 1983; Nelson 1988, 1992a]) by total employment in the state.[22]

Unfortunately, the accuracy of these data is suspect. Schmulowitz (1997) concluded that Social Security Administration data on workers' compensation coverage substantially underestimate the extent of coverage. His conclusion is based on a review of recently collected establishment survey data from the Bureau of Labor Statistics, which revealed that 98.6 percent of private-sector employees and 99.8 percent of state and local government employees are covered by workers' compensation programs. These BLS figures are approximately 10 percent higher than the previous Social Security estimates that we rely upon.

Furthermore, the Social Security Administration only estimated workers' compensation coverage for a few years (1973, 1976, 1977, 1980, 1981, 1984, and 1988), so we had to impute workers' compensation coverage values for other years. This was done by means of regression equations that predicted coverage as a function of state compliance with the National Commission recommendations.[23]

Figure 4.14 depicts the proportion of employment covered by workers' compensation insurance nationwide for the 1975–1995

**Figure 4.14 Share of the Workforce Covered by Workers'
Compensation Insurance, 1975–95 (mean ± 1 S.D.)**

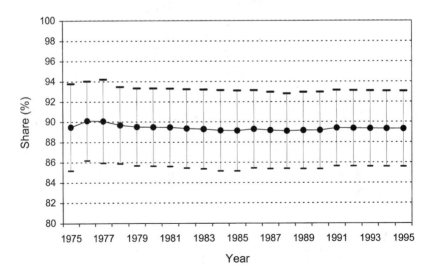

period. The figure shows that coverage remained relatively stable during the period; it rose slightly at the beginning of the period followed by a similarly slight decline, so that coverage in 1995 was approximately equal to that in 1975. There is little interstate variation in the proportion of workers covered by state workers' compensation programs, even among the states in which coverage is not mandatory (Figure 4.15). In 1988, this proportion varied from a low of 80 percent of

Figure 4.15 Covered Employment by State, 1988

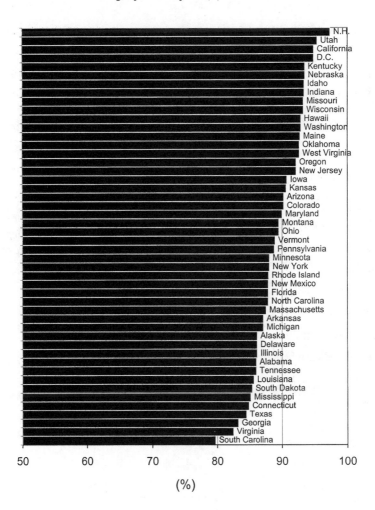

(%)

total employment in South Carolina to a high of 97 percent in New Hampshire.

Summary of the Cost Regression Model

The means and standard deviations of the two dependent variables, as well as the regressors, are reported in Table 4.2. This table also provides a summary of the hypothesized relationship between the regressors and our dependent cost measures.

REGRESSION RESULTS

The results of our regressions estimating the employers' cost of workers' compensation insurance for our entire study period are presented in Table 4.3. These equations include the natural log of the "total benefit" measure (the ln[Benefits] row in Table 4.3) as a regres-

Table 4.2 Means, Standard Deviations, and Hypotheses—Cost Regression Models

Variable	Mean	Standard deviation	Hypothesized relationship to costs
Cost measures			
Adjusted manual rates ($)	2.25	1.12	
Net weekly costs ($)	11.87	6.16	
Control variables			
Expected cash benefits ($)	10,354.23	9,502.29	+
Average medical benefits ($)	1,587.09	857.78	+
Expected total benefits ($)	16,140.31	6,780.70	+
Injury rate (per 100 workers)	8.26	1.32	+
Proportion of PPD claims (%)	27.72	10.23	+
Union density (%)	18.09	7.86	+
Covered employment (%)	89.65	3.88	+

Table 4.3 Regression Equations Predicting Employer Costs, Weighted Least Squares Estimates[a]

Variable	Spec. 1	2	3	4	5	6	7
Adjusted manual rates							
ln(Benefits)	0.3981***	0.4007***	1.3383***	0.0754*	0.5588***	0.4794***	0.0499
	(8.87)	(9.00)	(24.25)	(1.64)	(13.88)	(9.19)	(1.15)
ln(Injury)	—[b]	0.3878***	0.3915***	0.6124***	0.4958***	0.3620***	0.6830***
		(3.82)	(3.14)	(6.60)	(4.78)	(3.91)	(7.61)
PPD percentage	—	—	—	—	0.0222***	0.0282***	0.0132***
					(14.96)	(17.79)	(8.44)
Union density	—	—	—	—	-0.0106***	-0.0517***	0.0049
					(5.17)	(14.92)	(1.22)
Covered employment	—	—	—	—	0.0130***	0.0218**	0.0200***
					(2.77)	(2.56)	(3.13)
State dummies	No	No	Yes	Yes	No	Yes	Yes
Year dummies	No	No	No	Yes	No	No	Yes
Adjusted R^2	0.0765	0.0904	0.6815	0.8972	0.3030	0.8268	0.9079

(continued)

Table 4.3 (continued)

Variable	Spec. 1	2	3	4	5	6	7
Net weekly costs							
ln(Benefits)	0.4305***	0.4334***	1.3558***	0.1006**	0.5919***	0.5026***	0.0731*
	(9.14)	(9.27)	(24.48)	(2.14)	(14.02)	(9.60)	(1.65)
ln(Injury)	—	0.4259***	0.4400***	0.5424***	0.5446***	0.3993***	0.6234***
		(4.00)	(3.52)	(5.70)	(5.01)	(4.29)	(6.82)
PPD percentage	—	—	—	—	0.0244***	0.0289***	0.0134***
					(15.66)	(18.11)	(8.44)
Union density	—	—	—	—	-0.0032	-0.0501***	0.0079*
					(1.47)	(14.41)	(1.94)
Covered employment	—	—	—	—	0.0185***	0.0278***	0.0249***
					(3.75)	(3.26)	(3.82)
State dummies	No	No	Yes	Yes	No	Yes	Yes
Year dummies	No	No	No	Yes	No	No	Yes
Adjusted R^2	0.0808	0.0960	0.7104	0.9022	0.3074	0.8422	0.9136

[a] Values in parentheses are absolute value t-ratios. *** = significant at the 1% level; ** = significant at the 5% level; * = significant at the 10% level.

[b] A dash (—) = coefficient not estimated.

sor. Several sets of estimates are reported, each of which includes a different set of independent variables (such as ln[Injury] and state and year dummies). Given are the results of equations predicting adjusted manual rates, and those predicting net weekly costs.[24] Because Cook-Weisberg tests indicated that ordinary least squares (OLS) estimates suffered from heteroscedastic error variance, the regression equations reported in this table were estimated using weighted least squares; average nonfarm employment, by state and year, served as weights.[25] All regressions were based on the full data set of 953 observations, including observations from exclusive-state-fund jurisdictions.

The results presented in Table 4.3 provide substantial support for the accounting model of employer costs described on pp. 62–63. The statutory benefits index is positively and significantly related to employer compensation costs in all specifications except that using the full set of control variables, including year dummies (specification 7).[26] The coefficient for the injury rate variable (ln[Injury]) is positive and is statistically significant in all models. The percentage of benefits paid for permanent partial disability (PPD) claims is also directly related to compensation costs, indicating that there is a positive relationship between "liberal" claims administration—particularly as it relates to PPD claims—and employer costs. The results indicate that these variables in combination are relatively good predictors of employer costs.

Further confirmation for these results is provided by the fact that our findings are similar to those found by most previous studies. Krueger and Burton (1990) and Schmidle (1994) also found that expected cash benefit levels, the injury rate, and the proportion of PPD claims were positively related to both adjusted manual rates and net weekly costs. Positive and statistically significant relationships between adjusted manual rates and the proportion of PPD cases were also reported by Appel, McMurray, and Mulvaney (1992). Likewise, Danzon and Harrington (1998) found that expected growth in statutory benefit levels was positively related to cost growth. On the other hand, Carroll and Kaestner (1995) reported mixed results for several benefit proxies: as expected, the benefit maximum was positively related and the waiting period was negatively related to the price of compensation per injury and per employee. However, they also found a negative and statistically significant relationship between these price measures and two other regressors: the ratio of the benefit maximum to the state average weekly wage and a measure of scheduled benefit generosity.

Our empirical results for the union density variable are mixed. Union density is negatively related to costs and rates in four out of six equations, and this relationship is statistically significant at the 5 percent level in three of these four models. Only in the model that includes the full set of regressors—specification 7—does the union variable have the expected positive sign, although it is only statistically significant in the net weekly cost equation. These results suggest that, with the exception of the full model, the union density variable is picking up the effects of other, unobserved variables that affect employer costs. Union density has a relatively consistent downward trend for all states during our study period. This variable may be picking up unobserved trends in the injury distribution or some other time-related, unmeasured factor that drives up costs in equations that do not include year dummies. These mixed results for the union variable are similar to those of Krueger and Burton (1990) and Schmidle (1994), who found a negative relationship between union density and costs in equations that included state dummies and a positive relationship between these two variables in equations that did not.

Lastly, our results in Table 4.3 indicate that a higher proportion of covered employment during our study period is associated with higher compensation costs. We did not have strong prior expectations for this variable, since its impact on compensation costs depends on whether coverage is, on balance, extended to relatively high- or relatively low-risk occupations. Examining one set of changes in covered employment during this period—i.e., compliance with the recommendations of the National Commission on State Workmen's Compensation Laws—we hypothesized that increased coverage of small employers, who generally have inferior safety records relative to larger firms, may increase costs. Our conclusion was tempered by the realization that there were several other, concurrent changes in workers' compensation coverage that could have unpredictable effects on costs. Nevertheless, our results provide some tenuous support for this hypothesis. In previous research, both Krueger and Burton (1990) and Schmidle (1994) obtained mixed results for covered employment; while these studies found that the relationship was positive in most equations, it was significantly different from zero at conventional levels in only a few regressions.

F-tests reveal that the state dummies, considered collectively, are significant, suggesting that these variables, which are used in specifications 6 and 7 in Table 4.3, account for unobserved, state-specific variation in employer costs. Similarly, F-tests reveal statistically significant year effects, suggesting that costs are subject to unobserved, time-dependent effects.

Cost–Benefit Elasticity

As we indicated on p. 64, the coefficient associated with the natural log of the benefit variable provides a measure of cost–benefit elasticity. As such, we expect that this coefficient will be positively signed and will have a value close to 1. However, the data in Table 4.3 indicate that the size of these estimates vary considerably depending on model specification, although in each model the coefficient is positively signed and (in all but one) it is significantly different from zero. These results differ from those obtained by Krueger and Burton (1990), who used a similar methodology with a much smaller data set.[27] Save for specifications 4 and 7 in Table 4.3, Krueger and Burton estimated equations identical to ours and reported cost–benefit elasticity estimates that ranged from 0.954 to 1.083 in their adjusted manual rate regressions and from 0.812 to 1.218 in their net weekly cost regressions.

Our results in Table 4.3 present coefficients for the benefits variable that, in general, are significantly less than 1.0, which suggests that our benefit coefficient estimates may be subject to two forms of bias. Comparing the results from specifications 1 and 2 with those for specification 3 implies that the first two equations suffer from omitted-variable bias. Specifically, the results suggest that models using specifications 1 and 2 fail to capture variations among states in benefit administration that affect employer costs, and that this omitted "benefit administration" variable is negatively correlated with our total benefit measure, resulting in a reduction in coefficient values from their true levels. Comparing results from specification 3 with those from specifications 4 through 7 further suggests that the benefit variable is subject to measurement error, which results in an attenuation in the coefficient estimates, as other control variables and the year dummies absorb some variation in "true" benefits.

To examine potential effects of measurement error, we reestimated the equations reported in Table 4.3 after instrumenting the benefit variable. Similar to the approach used by Krueger and Burton, our instruments included the statutory maximum benefit for TTD claims, the minimum benefit for TTD, the waiting period, and the retroactive period.[28] The results of these regression analyses are reported in Table 4.4.

The instrumental variable regression equations reported in Table 4.4 are closer to our *a priori* expectations. They confirm our hypothesis that error in the benefit variable led to an attenuation of the benefit coefficients (as reported in Table 4.3). Additionally, the Table 4.4 results are much closer to the estimates reported by Krueger and Burton. This can be seen most clearly in Table 4.5, which compares our results with those of Krueger and Burton for the four regression models that are common to both studies. (The top row of Table 4.5 lists the particular specification per the numbered regression equations from Tables 4.3 and 4.4.) However, as is evident in Table 4.5, some discrepancies remain, even after we control for measurement error. Overall, the results indicate that our regressions are more susceptible to this measurement error problem than were those of Krueger and Burton. There are two possible explanations for this.

First, the expected cash benefit measures in both studies were based on an injury distribution taken from a single point in time. However, some workers' compensation experts believe that the underlying injury distribution has changed—that, for example, the average duration of temporary total disabilities (TTDs) has increased (Butler 1994). In addition, data in Figure 4.9 show that the number of PPD claims has increased as a proportion of total indemnity claims over the 1975–1995 period. Neither our study nor Krueger and Burton's fully accounted for possible temporal shifts in the injury distribution.[29] However, the Krueger and Burton data came from a much shorter period (1972–1983) than the data used in our analyses (1975–1995), during which time the injury distribution—at least as measured by PPD claims as a proportion of total claims (see Figure 4.9)—appear to have changed very little. For these reasons, it is likely that our benefit measure is subject to greater error.

Table 4.4 Employer Costs Regression using Combined Benefit Measures, Instrumental Variable Estimates[a]

Variable	Spec. 1	2	3	4	5	6	7
Adjusted manual rates							
ln(Benefits)	1.1779***	1.1880***	2.4824***	0.2634	1.0161***	1.9240***	0.4315**
	(12.43)	(12.59)	(25.21)	(1.32)	(14.09)	(10.70)	(2.27)
ln(Injury)	—	0.4157***	0.4034***	0.5507***	0.4862***	0.3515***	0.5541***
		(3.55)	(2.66)	(4.86)	(4.40)	(2.79)	(4.93)
PPD percentage	—	—	—	—	0.0251***	0.0166***	0.0125***
					(15.47)	(6.56)	(7.52)
Covered employment	—	—	—	—	-0.0133***	-0.0072	0.0045
					(6.00)	(1.04)	(1.09)
Union density	—	—	—	—	0.0185***	0.0089	0.0193***
					(3.66)	(0.77)	(2.89)
State dummies	No	No	Yes	Yes	No	Yes	Yes
Year dummies	No	No	No	Yes	No	No	Yes

(continued)

Table 4.4 (continued)

Variable	Spec. 1	2	3	4	5	6	7
Net weekly costs							
ln(Benefits)	1.2726***	1.2827***	2.4855***	0.2324	1.1079***	1.9203***	0.4068**
	(12.70)	(12.86)	(25.29)	(1.14)	(14.51)	(10.74)	(2.12)
ln(Injury)	—	0.4560***	0.4518***	0.4992***	0.5338***	0.3891***	0.5107***
		(3.69)	(2.99)	(4.31)	(4.56)	(3.10)	(4.50)
PPD percentage	—	—	—	—	0.0277***	0.0175***	0.0128***
					(16.10)	(6.96)	(7.66)
Covered employment	—	—	—	—	-0.0062***	-0.0065	0.0076*
					(2.63)	(0.94)	(1.81)
Union density	—	—	—	—	0.0247***	0.0152	0.0242***
					(4.61)	(1.31)	(3.60)
State dummies	No	No	Yes	Yes	No	Yes	Yes
Year dummies	No	No	No	Yes	No	No	Yes

[a] Values in parentheses are absolute value t-ratios. *** = significant at the 1% level; ** = significant at the 5% level; * = significant at the 10% level.

[b] A dash (—) = coefficient not estimated.

Table 4.5 Comparisons of Estimates in Tables 4.3 and 4.4 with Krueger and Burton Estimates

Estimate	Spec. 1[a]	2	5	6
Adjusted manual rates				
Ordinary least squares				
Table 4.3	0.398	0.401	0.559	0.479
Krueger & Burton	1.083	1.023	1.000	0.954
Instrumental variables				
Table 4.4	1.178	1.119	1.061	1.924
Krueger & Burton	1.303	—[b]	1.445	1.087
Net weekly costs				
Ordinary least squares				
Table 4.3	0.431	0.433	0.592	0.503
Krueger & Burton	1.218	1.105	1.050	0.831
Instrumental variables				
Table 4.4	1.273	1.283	1.108	1.920
Krueger & Burton	1.345	—	1.375	0.905

[a] The specification numbers in the column headings match those used in Tables 4.3 and 4.4.

[b] A dash (—) = did not estimate.

Second, in recent years, several states have sought to reduce compensation costs not by reducing the statutory generosity of cash benefits, but through statutory changes in eligibility requirements or in the method of assessing permanent partial disability.[30] These changes are not reflected in our statutory benefit index. Since we include data from this period while Krueger and Burton do not, our benefit variable is likely to be subject to greater measurement error.

After we correct for potential measurement error, substantial differences still remain among the estimates produced by the different model specifications reported in Table 4.4. For example, the cost–benefit elasticity is about 1.92 in model 6 but shrinks to between 0.41 and 0.43 when year dummies are added in model 7. The difference between these estimates is likely due to a combination of omitted variable bias and measurement error. Model 7 is our preferred specification, suggesting that the cost–benefit elasticity is less than 1. An F-test rejects the null hypothesis—that the benefit coefficient is equal to 1—at the 0.05 significance level for the model 7 adjusted manual rate equation, but fails to reject this hypothesis for the comparable net weekly cost regression.

This result suggests that a 10 percent increase in benefits results in a 4 percent increase in costs, a surprising finding that is inconsistent with a large number of previous empirical studies that concluded that higher benefits are associated with disproportionately higher claim rates and benefit payments. For these reasons, we are hesitant to accept our cost–benefit elasticity at face value, and we are inclined to believe that the variables used to instrument benefits in the instrumental variable regressions are imperfect. Specifically, these instruments are limited to parameters affecting benefit generosity for TTD claims only, and they would therefore fail to account for measurement error in the other components of the benefit index, such as PPD benefits, or for changes in the injury distribution.

Separate Medical and Cash Benefit Regressors

Table 4.6 reports the result of regression analyses estimating employer costs as a function of separate medical and cash benefit variables. Similar to the regressions reported in Table 4.4, the cash benefit measure was instrumented using the TTD minimum and maximum weekly benefits as well as the waiting and retrospective periods for benefit eligibility.

From Table 4.6, it is apparent that the coefficient estimates for the cash benefit variable are highly sensitive to specification. The cash benefit coefficient in the adjusted manual rate varies from a low of 0.0844 in specification 4 to a high of 0.5983 in specification 6; in the net weekly cost regressions, the cash benefit coefficient ranges from 0.0546 to 0.4922. The coefficient for the medical benefit measure also varies substantially across specifications, although not quite as dramatically as cash benefits. Once again, the year dummies seem to substantially reduce the magnitude of both benefit coefficients.

Table 4.6 Employer Costs Regression using Separate Benefit Measures, Instrumental Variable Estimates[a]

Variable	Spec. 1	2	3	4	5	6	7
Adjusted manual rates							
ln(Cash benefits)	0.1955***	0.2051***	0.4842***	0.0844	0.1016**	0.5983***	0.2746*
	(4.99)	(5.26)	(2.58)	(0.48)	(2.19)	(3.23)	(1.69)
ln(Medical benefits)	0.8678***	0.8638***	0.7808***	0.4880***	0.9126***	0.6974***	0.3607***
	(55.40)	(55.57)	(38.27)	(10.82)	(46.93)	(22.33)	(7.38)
ln(Injury)	—	0.2044***	0.5674***	0.6939***	0.4120***	0.5135***	0.6508***
		(4.01)	(6.55)	(6.79)	(7.24)	(5.84)	(6.38)
PPD percentage	—	—	—	—	0.0026***	0.0053***	0.0077***
					(2.59)	(3.16)	(4.39)
Union density	—	—	—	—	0.0132***	−0.0048	0.0024
					(8.02)	(1.33)	(0.61)
Covered employment	—	—	—	—	−0.0163***	−0.0051	0.0092
					(5.27)	(0.70)	(1.43)
State dummies	No	No	Yes	Yes	No	Yes	Yes
Year dummies	No	No	No	Yes	No	No	Yes

(continued)

Table 4.6 (continued)

Variable	Spec. 1	2	3	4	5	6	7
Net weekly costs							
ln(Cash benefits)	0.2994***	0.3141***	0.3465*	0.0546	0.1575***	0.4922***	0.2537
	(6.79)	(7.16)	(1.93)	(0.31)	(3.30)	(2.78)	(1.56)
ln(Medical benefits)	0.8894***	0.8845***	0.8022***	0.5492***	0.9527***	0.7300***	0.4111***
	(50.40)	(50.52)	(41.08)	(12.03)	(47.53)	(24.47)	(8.37)
ln(Injury)	—	0.2546***	0.6498***	0.6516***	0.4516***	0.5834***	0.6116***
		(4.43)	(7.84)	(6.30)	(7.70)	(6.94)	(5.97)
PPD percentage	—	—	—	—	0.0042***	0.0054***	0.0075***
					(4.12)	(3.35)	(4.24)
Union density	—	—	—	—	0.0208***	-0.0019	0.0052
					(12.20)	(0.56)	(1.31)
Covered employment	—	—	—	—	-0.0107***	-0.0002	0.0126*
					(3.34)	(0.03)	(1.94)
State dummies	No	No	Yes	Yes	No	Yes	Yes
Year dummies	No	No	No	Yes	No	No	Yes

[a] Values in parentheses are absolute value t-ratios. *** = significant at the 1% level; ** = significant at the 5% level; * = significant at the 10% level.

[b] A dash (—) = coefficient not estimated.

BENEFIT ADEQUACY VERSUS AFFORDABILITY

The empirical results discussed in the previous section document a positive relationship between workers' compensation benefits and the cost of the program to employers. In all of the regressions reported there, higher cash or medical benefits are associated with higher costs of workers' compensation insurance. These results illustrate a potential tradeoff between the benefit adequacy and affordability objectives discussed in Chapter 1. The purpose of this section is to provide a more refined analysis of the conflict between these objectives, which must first be operationally defined. We begin by identifying two standards against which we may evaluate benefit adequacy: the National Commission on State Workmen's Compensation laws and the Model Act promulgated by the Council of State Governments.

The National Commission on State Workmen's Compensation Laws

The Report of the National Commission on State Workmen's Compensation Laws (1972) was discussed in Chapter 1. One of the fundamental features of the report was support for federal standards for workers' compensation programs if states did not voluntarily improve their laws by 1975. An implicit assumption underlying the recommendation for federal standards was that states with low levels of statutory benefits also had low compensation costs. The assumption was challenged shortly after the National Commission issued its report by skeptics who argued that some high-cost states had statutes that provided relatively low benefits. In the 1970s, Michigan was often cited as an example of such a state, in which low statutory benefits in conjunction with liberal rules for determining compensability and awarding permanent disability benefits resulted in high insurance costs. The skeptics argued that imposing benefit standards on states like Michigan would only further widen the differences in workers' compensation costs among the states.

Federal standards for the state workers' compensation programs have never been enacted, and so we have no direct evidence about the effect of such standards on program costs. However, as a "second-best" approximation, Krueger and Burton (1990) simulated the effects on the costs of workers' compensation insurance of federal standards.[31] Specifically, they first estimated regressions predicting actual statewide average employer costs as a function of expected cash benefits under existing state statutory provision.[32] (Similar to our analyses, Krueger and Burton estimated several different model specifications, which yielded somewhat different results.) They then derived estimates of expected benefits for each state, assuming that the state had adopted these essential recommendations of the National Commission.[33] Next, these "expected benefits under the federal standards" estimates were used in combination with the coefficient on the expected cash benefit variable from the regression equation to forecast employer costs, which were then compared with actual costs to determine the impact of federal standards.

The mean, standard deviation, and coefficient of variation for the simulated and actual costs are presented in Table 4.7 (which was Table 5 in Krueger and Burton 1990). The simulated costs were estimated under two extreme assumptions, which were represented by models 1 and 6 of the Krueger and Burton study.

The 1972 entry for adjusted manual rates can be used to illustrate the findings of the simulation. The average (mean) actual costs of workers' compensation insurance for the 29 states in the study was 0.699 percent of payroll in 1972. The actual dispersion of costs among these 29 states, as measured by the standard deviation, was 0.270 percent of payroll. The coefficient of variation, which is an alternative measure of dispersion calculated by dividing the standard deviation by the mean, was 0.386 for the actual adjusted manual rates in 1972.

The model 1 and model 6 results for 1972 provide alternative estimates of the effects of enforcing national standards that overrode inadequate state statutory provisions: compared with the actual costs, the average (mean) costs nationally increased to 0.971 percent or 0.932 percent of payroll, and the standard deviation increased to 0.343 or 0.329 percent of payroll. However, the coefficient of variation declined to 0.353 for both models.

Based on the results in Table 4.7, Krueger and Burton (1990, p. 239) concluded:

> Finally, our simulations indicate that the federal minimum standards proposed by the National Commission on State Workmen's

**Table 4.7 Simulation for National Standards and Actual Workers'
Compensation Costs, Summary Statistics by Year**[a]

Year		Mean	Standard deviation	Coefficient of variation
Adjusted manual rates				
1972,	Actual	0.699	0.270	0.386
	Model 1	0.971	0.343	0.353
	Model 6	0.932	0.329	0.353
1975,	Actual	0.935	0.436	0.466
	Model 1	1.078	0.456	0.423
	Model 6	1.059	0.451	0.426
1978,	Actual	1.232	0.560	0.455
	Model 1	1.322	0.579	0.438
	Model 6	1.310	0.574	0.438
1983,	Actual	1.194	0.621	0.520
	Model 1	1.345	0.607	0.451
	Model 6	1.325	0.608	0.459
All,	Actual	1.015	0.530	0.522
	Model 1	1.179	0.525	0.445
	Model 6	1.157	0.524	0.453
Net costs[b]				
1972,	Actual	2.287	1.001	0.438
	Model 1	3.296	1.282	0.389
	Model 6	2.926	1.157	0.395
1975,	Actual	2.929	1.534	0.524
	Model 1	3.429	1.606	0.468
	Model 6	3.254	1.563	0.480
1978,	Actual	3.679	1.919	0.522
	Model 1	3.989	2.013	0.505
	Model 6	3.875	1.966	0.507

(continued)

Table 4.7 (continued)

Year		Mean	Standard deviation	Coefficient of variation
1983,	Actual	3.429	1.865	0.544
	Model 1	3.914	1.818	0.464
	Model 6	3.746	1.831	0.489
All,	Actual	3.081	1.688	0.548
	Model 1	3.655	1.705	0.466
	Model 6	3.450	1.681	0.487

SOURCE: This table is a reprint of Table 5 from Krueger and Burton (1990).
[a] Sample size is 29 states each year. Estimates for model 1 assume the cost-benefit elasticities estimated in the first column of Tables 3 and 4 in Krueger and Burton (1990), and estimates for model 6 assume the elasticity estimated in column 6 of Tables 3 and 4 from the same article.
[b] In 1983 dollars.

Compensation Laws would increase the average cost of workers' compensation insurance, and decrease the coefficient of variation among the states in all time periods. The impact of the minimum standard on the standard deviation of costs is mixed; for 1983 and for the four years combined the standard deviation for either cost measure would be decreased by the standards, but in the three other years studied the standard deviations would increase. As a result, the success or failure of the National Commission's prescription to narrow the dispersion in workers' compensation costs among the states by requiring minimum federal standards appears dependent on the time period of interest and on the measure of dispersion used.

This passage provides *inter alia* three measures of affordability that we will also use: 1) the national average of workers' compensation insurance costs; 2) the dispersion of insurance costs among states as measured by the standard deviation; and 3) the dispersion of insurance costs among states as measured by the coefficient of determination, which is the standard deviation divided by the average.

These measures represent alternative views about which measure of input costs is relevant for an employer. If all of a firm's competitors pay the same rate for an input (such as wages or any element of remuneration for workers), then the average cost of that input does not affect the firm's competitive position and the firm is relatively unconcerned about the average level of the costs.[34] This is consistent with the traditional trade union goal of "taking wages out of competition"; by forcing all the employers in the relevant product market to pay the same wage, the union is able to raise wages without substantially affecting employment for union members. Of course, as U.S. employers increasingly compete in a global economy, identical workers' compensation costs within the United States may be little comfort if overseas employers have lower workers' compensation costs.

The standard deviation measures the dispersion among states in workers' compensation costs measured in dollars per $100 of payroll: statistically, two-thirds of the states fall in the range of the mean plus or minus one standard deviation. If the standard deviation increases due to the enactment of federal standards, then the spread between low- and high-cost states increases. In 1972, imposition of federal standards would have increased the spread (measured by the standard deviation) from an actual dispersion of $0.270 per $100 of payroll to a maximum dispersion (in model 1) of $0.343 per $100 of payroll. If employers within the United States react to the absolute differences among states in the costs of workers' compensation insurance, imposition of federal standards in 1972 would have increased competitive pressures among states.

The coefficient of variation measures the dispersion of workers' compensation costs among states relative to the average cost of the program. In 1972, imposition of federal standards would have increased the spread in employer costs among states (as measured by the standard deviation, as described in the preceding paragraph) but would have increased average costs at a faster rate, so that the ratio of the standard deviation to the mean (i.e., the coefficient of variation) would have declined. Do employers care less about a standard deviation of $0.30 per $100 of payroll when the mean cost of workers' compensation insurance for the United States is $2.00 per $100 of payroll (a coefficient of variation of 0.15) than when the standard deviation is $0.30 per $100 of payroll and the mean cost is $1.00 per $100 of payroll (a coefficient of variation of 0.30)? If employers care less about the absolute value of the spread among states as the average costs in all states increase, then the standard of deviation is the better measure of dispersion.

We do not think that there is a clear advantage to using any of these three measures of affordability. However, since the United States is still largely a domestic economy, we are less concerned about the average level of workers' compensation costs than about the dispersion among states in these costs. Among the competing definitions of dispersion, we prefer the standard deviation as the most relevant for assessing competitive conditions, because employer location decisions are likely to be based on absolute (as opposed to relative) costs. If a firm can save $2.00 per $100 of payroll by moving from Indiana to California, that savings is important whether the average costs of workers' compensation nationally is $1.00 per $100 of payroll or $3.00 per $100 of payroll.

Our conclusions with respect to the relationship between benefit adequacy and affordability are subject to two important qualifications. First, thus far we have focused on employer costs and have assumed that employers' actual costs are equivalent to the premium charged by the insurance carrier. In fact, while the employer may initially pay the insurance premium and bear the costs of workers' compensation in the short run, in the long run these costs are shared three ways: by the employer, the worker, and the consumer (Spieler and Burton 1998). That is, part of the costs of workers' compensation is ultimately borne by the consumer in the form of higher prices for goods and services and by the worker in the form of lower wages. Most of the empirical evidence suggests that workers bear the largest share of the costs of workers' compensation (Chelius and Burton 1994) and that workers pay for higher benefit levels with reduced wage rates. To the extent that this is true, there is no trade-off between benefit adequacy and affordability; adequate benefits are no less affordable (at least for employers) than inadequate benefits.

Second, while our discussion of interstate cost differences has been in terms of statewide averages, it is important to recognize that there are vast differences in rates among different employer classes within a particular jurisdiction. A particular percentage cost difference between states will have greater impact on employers in relatively more hazardous classes than on employers in safer classes. For example, assume that the average cost of workers' compensation paid by employers in state A is $2 per $100 of payroll while the average rate for employers in neighboring state B is $2.20, a 10 percent differential. Yet, employers in some high-risk industries in state B may be paying as much as $2 per $100 of payroll more than their counterparts in state A. Critics may argue that the plant location decisions of these high-risk employers are affected by such differences in compensation costs.

Does this example eviscerate our analysis? The National Commission (1972, pp. 124–125) suggested a response to this criticism:

> There are, to be sure, a small minority of employers for whom workers' compensation costs are significant because of their adverse loss experience, but it seems folly for a State to contrive a cheap workers' compensation program in order to keep these employers from moving elsewhere. In any event, the incentive to relocate is dampened because the Federal corporate profits tax would substantially reduce the benefit an employer would gain by moving to a State with low workers' compensation costs.

In addition, it is worth also noting that many employers have costs that are less than the state's average, and for these employers the interstate differences are of even less importance in determining location decisions than for an employer with average workers' compensation costs.

Using the essential recommendations of the National Commission on State Workmen's Compensation Laws as an operational definition of benefit adequacy, the simulation results for 1983 in Table 4.7 indicate that federal standards mandating this level of adequacy would have these consequences for the three measures of affordability: 1) the national average of adjusted manual rates would increase by 11.0–12.6 percent, and the national average of net weekly costs of workers' compensation would increase by 9.2–14.1 percent; 2) the dispersion of costs among states as measured by the standard deviation would decrease by 0.9–1.1 percent for adjusted manual rates and by 1.8–2.5 percent for the net weekly costs; and 3) the dispersion of costs among states as measured by the coefficient of variation would decrease by 13.2–14.7 percent for adjusted manual rates and by 10.5–14.7 percent for the net costs of insurance.

We focus on 1983 because that is the latest year included in the Krueger and Burton study. However, the results for all years shown in Table 4.7 are similar: 1) average workers' compensation costs increased (by 11.8–18.6 percent, depending on the measure used); 2) in most years, dispersion as measured by the standard deviation declined; and 3) in every year, dispersion as measured by the coefficient of variation declined. Since the all-years results include 1972 and 1975, before the point at which the states had responded to the National Commission's recommendations by raising benefit levels,[35] we believe the 1983 results concerning the impact of federal standards on the average costs of workers' compensation insurance are more indicative of the consequences if the 19 essential recommendations had been imposed on the states during our study period.

The Model Act

In this section, we further examine the relationship between adequate workers' compensation benefits and affordable employer costs by exploring the cost impact resulting from the adoption of the Model Act promulgated by the Council of State Governments. The Model Act was revised in 1974 to incorporate the National Commission's 84 recommendations, some of which were more generous than the benefits provided by the National Commission's 19 essential recommendations.[36] One important difference between the Model Act and the National Commission's recommendations was that the National Commission made no recommendations concerning the adequacy of permanent partial disability (PPD) benefits, while the Model Act contains detailed statutory provisions pertaining to both the durations and the weekly benefit amounts for PPD benefits.

Table 4.8 presents data on the average expected cash benefits paid to injured workers in the United States due to actual statutory provisions as well as the average cash benefits that would be paid to those workers if all states adopted the Model Act. Actual average cash bene-

Table 4.8 Actual and Simulated Cash Benefits, Means and Standard Deviations

	Actual	Model Act
Mean ($)	9,502.29	20,856.08
Standard deviation ($)	4,771.61	1,949.91
% difference from actual		119.48

fits are based on the actuarial assessments of the actual statutes in effect in each state as of January 1 of each year, as described in the cost regression model description (pp. 75–98) and Appendix D. Simulated Model Act benefits were calculated using the same actuarial procedure, except that rather than using the actual statutory parameters—for example, the weekly benefit maximum and minimum, the waiting period, and the PPD schedule—in effect in a particular state during a particular year, we substituted the recommended statutory parameters contained in the Model Act. In some instances, simulated benefits under the Model Act were actually lower than the actual benefits specified by the state workers' compensation statute.

Adoption of the Model Act by all states would have resulted in a substantial increase in statutory workers' compensation benefits, as shown by Table 4.9. In 1975, our estimate of the average benefits paid to workers' compensation claimants under actual state laws was $8,794, while the Model Act statutory language would have provided $21,039 in benefits, an amount that is almost 140 percent higher than actual expected benefits. Since adopting the Model Act means that states pay similar benefits—the benefits would vary among jurisdictions primarily because of interstate differences in average wages—the variance in simulated benefits ($2,205) is quite a bit less in 1975 than the variance in actual benefits ($5,614).[37]

The data in Table 4.9 indicate that differences in average benefits between actual and simulated cash benefits vary over time. Thus, while the ratio of mean actual benefits to mean Model Act benefits was about 0.42 in 1975, the ratio climbed substantially over the next 10 years, reaching 0.48 in 1985. Since that time, the ratio has dropped back to about 0.45. Similarly, there is some intertemporal variation in the difference in the standard deviation between actual and simulated benefits. In 1975, the standard deviation for Model Act benefits was nearly 60 percent less than the standard deviation for actual benefits.

Adjusted manual rates and net weekly costs resulting from the adoption of the Model Act were simulated by multiplying the cash benefit coefficient from the instrumental variable regressions (depicted in Table 4.6) by the change in benefit levels due to the adoption of the Model Act for each state and year in our data set. This product was then added to the actual adjusted manual rate for that state and year to

**Table 4.9 Actual and Simulated Cash Benefits by Year, 1975–95:
Means and Standard Deviations**

Year	Actual		Model Act		Actual mean as a % of Model Act mean
	Mean ($)	Std. dev. ($)	Mean ($)	Std. dev. ($)	
1975	8,794	5,614	21,039	2,205	41.80
1976	9,506	5,736	21,261	2,340	44.71
1977	9,593	5,860	21,318	2,383	45.00
1978	9,741	5,901	21,116	2,278	46.13
1979	9,682	5,832	20,650	2,141	46.89
1980	9,302	5,599	20,027	1,909	46.45
1981	8,942	5,343	19,734	1,873	45.31
1982	9,195	5,497	19,882	1,903	46.25
1983	9,354	5,239	20,296	1,942	46.09
1984	9,429	5,364	20,274	1,914	46.51
1985	9,680	5,596	20,346	1,899	47.58
1986	9,692	4,500	21,200	1,889	45.72
1987	9,765	4,474	21,406	1,784	45.62
1988	9,711	4,345	21,506	1,833	45.15
1989	9,577	4,250	20,973	1,745	45.67
1990	9,448	4,198	20,840	1,757	45.33
1991	9,582	4,256	20,854	1,694	45.95
1992	9,540	4,041	21,333	1,732	44.72
1993	9,454	3,954	21,035	1,741	44.94
1994	9,510	3,810	20,877	1,730	45.55
1995	9,580	3,790	21,103	1,929	45.40

arrive at the simulated adjusted manual rate. The actual calculations may be represented as follows:

Eq. 4.3 $R_{Sit} = \exp\{\ln(R_{Ait}) + \beta[\ln(B_{Sit}) - \ln(B_{Ait})]\}$,

where R_{Sit} is the simulated adjusted manual rate (or net weekly cost) for the ith state and tth year, R_{Ait} is the actual rate (or net weekly cost), B_{Ait} is the actual expected benefit, B_{Sit} is the Model Act benefit, and β is the coefficient on the cash benefits variable from the instrumental variable equation.[38]

The results of this exercise are reported in Table 4.10, which presents the average actual and expected adjusted manual rates and net weekly costs, as well as the associated standard deviation and coefficient of variation for each regression equation reported in Table 4.6. The row labeled "Diff. from actual (%)" in Table 4.10 shows the difference in means, in percentage terms, between the actual and predicted costs using the various models. As expected, there is considerable variation in the impact of the change in benefits on costs, depending on the specification. For reasons explained in the previous section, model 6 is our preferred specification. Predictions based on this model indicate that the Model Act would have increased adjusted manual rates by nearly 75 percent and weekly costs by nearly 60 percent.

Tables 4.11 and 4.12 present the means, standard deviations, and coefficients of variation for a) actual and predicted adjusted manual rates and b) actual and predicted net weekly costs, respectively, using the regression coefficient for our preferred specification, model 6. The right-most columns of these tables show the differentials for the means between predicted and actual costs.

Adoption of the Model Act would have increased adjusted manual rates by 57 to 75 percent and net costs of workers' compensation by 45 to 57 percent depending on the years used for the comparisons. Replacing actual statutes with the Model Act would also have increased the standard deviations for adjusted manual rates for every year and the coefficient of variation for most years (Table 4.11). Similarly, replacing actual statutes with the Model Act would have increased the standard deviations for net weekly costs for every year and the coefficient of variation for most years (Table 4.12).

Table 4.10 Actual and Predicted Employer Costs

	Actual	Spec. 1	2	3	4	5	6	7
Adjusted manual rates								
Mean ($)	2.249	2.676	2.700	3.501	2.422	2.460	3.907	2.877
Diff. from actual (%)		19.02	20.06	55.69	7.72	9.39	73.75	27.94
Std. dev ($)	1.114	1.389	1.405	2.031	1.220	1.244	2.387	1.533
Coeff. var.	0.495	0.519	0.520	0.580	0.504	0.506	0.611	0.533
Net weekly costs								
Mean ($)	11.89	15.57	15.79	16.27	12.47	13.68	18.68	14.93
Diff. from actual (%)		31.02	32.81	36.89	4.94	15.06	57.13	25.60
Std. dev ($)	6.14	8.75	8.92	9.31	6.51	7.33	11.38	8.25
Coeff. var.	0.517	0.562	0.565	0.572	0.522	0.536	0.609	0.553

Table 4.11 Actual and Predicted Adjusted Manual Rates, 1975–95

	Actual			Predicted			
Year	Mean ($)	Std. dev. ($)	Coeff. var.	Mean ($)	Std. dev. ($)	Coeff. var.	% change[a]
1975	0.949	0.387	0.408	1.648	0.789	0.479	73.69
1976	1.130	0.441	0.390	1.889	0.900	0.477	67.16
1977	1.294	0.528	0.408	2.153	1.024	0.476	66.36
1978	1.466	0.608	0.415	2.396	1.122	0.468	63.44
1979	1.582	0.628	0.397	2.525	1.038	0.411	59.60
1980	1.645	0.640	0.389	2.627	1.012	0.385	59.65
1981	1.613	0.584	0.362	2.586	0.908	0.351	60.30
1982	1.511	0.511	0.338	2.398	0.785	0.327	58.76
1983	1.490	0.510	0.342	2.358	0.795	0.337	58.26
1984	1.504	0.521	0.347	2.383	0.831	0.349	58.48
1985	1.599	0.529	0.331	2.498	0.819	0.328	56.27
1986	2.014	0.685	0.340	3.342	1.574	0.471	65.96
1987	2.189	0.756	0.346	3.655	1.810	0.495	66.99
1988	2.420	0.901	0.372	4.075	2.110	0.518	68.37
1989	2.653	0.997	0.376	4.424	2.235	0.505	66.75
1990	2.951	1.181	0.400	4.914	2.445	0.497	66.54
1991	3.096	1.054	0.340	5.098	2.266	0.445	64.66
1992	3.267	1.091	0.334	5.542	2.779	0.502	69.63
1993	3.478	1.166	0.335	5.865	2.953	0.503	68.65
1994	3.188	0.791	0.248	5.220	1.901	0.364	63.75
1995	2.973	0.747	0.251	4.843	1.680	0.347	62.91

[a] Percentage change between actual and predicted means. The "% change" values shown may not be exact due to rounding error.

Table 4.12 Actual and Predicted Net Weekly Costs, 1975–95

	Actual			Predicted			
Year	Mean ($)	Std. dev. ($)	Coeff. var.	Mean ($)	Std. dev. ($)	Coeff. var.	% change[a]
1975	5.029	2.079	0.413	7.883	3.513	0.446	56.76
1976	6.073	2.484	0.409	9.226	4.118	0.446	51.92
1977	6.986	3.006	0.430	10.578	4.796	0.453	51.42
1978	7.875	3.618	0.459	11.758	5.505	0.468	49.31
1979	8.306	3.782	0.455	12.180	5.160	0.424	46.64
1980	8.409	3.898	0.464	12.335	5.177	0.420	46.69
1981	8.109	3.562	0.439	11.936	4.752	0.398	47.19
1982	7.631	3.076	0.403	11.153	4.090	0.367	46.15
1983	7.634	2.789	0.365	11.152	3.906	0.350	46.08
1984	7.701	2.799	0.363	11.256	3.990	0.354	46.16
1985	8.222	2.880	0.350	11.872	3.916	0.330	44.39
1986	10.866	4.156	0.382	16.507	8.081	0.490	51.91
1987	11.901	4.590	0.386	18.134	9.153	0.505	52.38
1988	13.184	5.265	0.399	20.184	10.456	0.518	53.10
1989	14.058	5.527	0.393	21.362	10.694	0.501	51.95
1990	15.500	6.230	0.402	23.512	11.331	0.482	51.69
1991	16.339	5.956	0.365	24.517	10.682	0.436	50.05
1992	17.602	6.259	0.356	27.028	12.846	0.475	53.54
1993	18.401	6.328	0.344	28.113	12.991	0.462	52.78
1994	16.741	4.502	0.269	25.054	8.770	0.350	49.66
1995	15.691	3.980	0.254	23.347	7.210	0.309	48.79

[a] Percentage change between actual and predicted means. The "% change" values shown may not be exact due to rounding error.

The finding that substituting the Model Act provisions for cash benefits for the actual benefits provided by state workers' compensation statutes would lead to a general widening of interstate differences in the employers' costs of workers' compensation insurance seems anomalous. It is perplexing because—as shown in Table 4.9—replacing actual workers' compensation provisions with the Model Act reduces interstate variation in statutory cash benefits (as measured by the standard deviation).

Table 4.13 illustrates how this can happen, i.e., how reducing the disparity in the statutory level of benefits among states can lead to greater variation in employer costs. In this table, states are rank-ordered by level of actual adjusted manual rates in 1995 (as shown in the first data column), ranging from 4.937 percent of payroll in Montana to 1.397 percent of payroll in Indiana. Estimates of the benefits that would be paid by states if they adopted the Model Act provisions are shown in the second data column and range from $30,177 in Alaska to $16,821 in Arkansas. As indicated, since the statutory provisions are identical—with the exception of the weekly benefit minimums and maximums, which are tied to the state average weekly wage under the Model Act—cost differences are due to interstate variation in wages.

Estimates of actual benefits provided by the states in 1995 according to existing statutory law range from $22,941 in the District of Columbia to $4,310 in Louisiana. The differences between the benefits required by the Model Act and the actual benefit required by the state's workers' compensation statute in 1995 are also shown. For example, in Montana, the Model Act would have resulted in average benefits of $22,983, while the actual 1995 statute in Montana only provided $5,522 of benefits, a difference of $17,461. The range in the differences was from $19,233 in Alaska to $2,517 in Pennsylvania.

The predicted adjusted manual rates (Table 4.13, right-most column) were calculated by use of Eq. 4.3, which

a) begins with the actual rates in Table 4.13;
b) adds the product of (the differences between the Model Act and actual benefits from the "Difference" column of Table 4.13 × the benefits coefficient for adjusted manual rates from model 6 of Table 4.6); resulting in
c) the predicted adjusted manual rates.

Table 4.13 1995 Actual and Predicted Adjusted Manual Rates, and Model and Actual Benefits, by State ($)

State[a]	Actual rates	Model Act benefits	Actual benefits	Difference[b]	Predicted rates
Montana	4.937	22,983	5,522	17,461	10.819
Hawaii	4.867	20,932	13,912	7,020	6.093
Florida	4.366	18,301	5,323	12,978	8.612
Louisiana	4.059	20,162	4,310	15,853	9.486
New York	3.883	22,277	13,923	8,354	5.029
New Hampshire	3.757	20,086	11,919	8,167	5.006
New Mexico	3.713	17,835	11,925	5,910	4.634
Kentucky	3.650	20,323	8,708	11,615	5.819
Alabama	3.585	19,129	6,728	12,401	6.371
Oklahoma	3.456	19,359	6,532	12,827	6.283
Rhode Island	3.448	18,945	9,536	9,408	5.030
Maine	3.373	19,589	12,492	7,097	4.320
Georgia	3.370	18,518	8,266	10,251	5.252
Ohio	3.358	22,946	9,988	12,958	5.307
District of Columbia	3.341	26,275	22,941	3,334	3.600
Pennsylvania	3.340	21,642	19,125	2,517	3.575
Massachusetts	3.207	20,839	12,234	8,605	4.299
Vermont	3.171	19,098	13,205	5,892	3.884
Connecticut	3.167	21,185	9,762	11,423	4.850
California	3.150	22,880	5,573	17,307	6.851
Tennessee	3.071	19,254	7,434	11,820	5.183
Arkansas	2.993	16,821	6,512	10,309	5.045
Illinois	2.803	22,824	10,547	12,277	4.286
Colorado	2.788	20,786	7,374	13,412	4.931
Minnesota	2.782	21,600	10,580	11,019	4.120
Mississippi	2.750	17,049	8,742	8,307	3.971

State[a]	Actual rates	Model Act benefits	Actual benefits	Difference[b]	Predicted rates
Michigan	2.689	23,806	9,694	14,112	4.408
Kansas	2.673	19,497	11,828	7,670	3.519
Arizona	2.630	20,408	13,401	7,007	3.315
West Virginia	2.540	19,185	8,085	11,100	4.086
Missouri	2.463	21,170	8,137	13,033	4.168
South Carolina	2.445	17,773	7,854	9,919	3.832
South Dakota	2.425	17,155	7,446	9,709	3.838
Alaska	2.400	30,177	10,944	19,233	4.193
Idaho	2.394	19,928	9,121	10,807	3.680
Nebraska	2.338	19,616	9,918	9,697	3.403
North Carolina	2.316	17,997	5,907	12,090	4.276
Delaware	2.288	20,680	12,024	8,656	3.083
Oregon	2.275	20,857	7,505	13,353	3.992
Utah	2.186	19,279	7,339	11,940	3.719
Wisconsin	2.044	21,934	9,754	12,180	3.193
Washington	1.981	22,432	12,195	10,237	2.771
Iowa	1.946	21,508	18,230	3,278	2.131
Virginia	1.907	19,295	12,554	6,741	2.415
Maryland	1.891	21,394	8,573	12,821	3.128
New Jersey	1.777	22,286	7,999	14,286	3.123
Indiana	1.397	22,022	6,367	15,655	2.766
Mean	2.973	21,103	9,580	11,522	4.869
Standard deviation	0.747	1,929	3,790	3,794	1.698

[a] States ordered from highest actual rate to lowest.
[b] Difference = "Model Act benefits" value minus "Actual benefits" value.

Consider the calculations for Montana as a clue to the solution to our anomaly of widening interstate cost differences as the result of the imposition of federal standards. Montana had adjusted manual rates in 1995 that were 4.937 percent of payroll, well above the national average of 2.973 for adjusted manual rates. At the same time, Montana had a workers' compensation statute that provided limited workers' compensation cash benefits; indeed, the difference between the actual statutory benefits and the benefits prescribed by the Model Act in Montana in 1995 was $17,461, which was second only to Alaska in the gap between the Model Act and the actual statutory provisions. Multiplying our estimates for the relationship between statutory benefits and insurance costs (shown in model 6 in Table 4.6) times the difference in the log value of the Montana adequate benefits and the log value of the Montana actual benefits results in a predicted adjusted manual rate of 10.891 percent of payroll devoted to workers' compensation premiums by Montana employers if only the state had the Model Act provisions.

This result for Montana is interesting and instructive. The actual adjusted manual rate in 1995 of 4.937 percent of payroll was 67 percent above the national average of adjusted manual rates of 2.973 percent of payroll. If Montana had substituted the Model Act for its actual workers' compensation statute, we estimate that adjusted manual rates would have been 10.819 percent of payroll, or 222 percent above the national average of 4.869 percent of payroll if all states had adopted the Model Act. In short, the Model Act would have widened the difference in workers' compensation costs between Montana and the national average.

The combination of high actual workers' compensation rates and substandard workers' compensation statutory provisions, which explains the Montana results, is not unique to that state. Indeed, 6 of the 10 most expensive states for workers' compensation insurance shown in Table 4.13—Montana, Florida, Louisiana, Kentucky, Alabama, and Oklahoma—had adequacy gaps in their workers' compensation statutes that exceeded the national average of $11,522 for the difference between the Model Act and actual benefits. For each of these states, we estimate that substituting the Model Act for the state's actual workers' compensation statute would have increased the gap between their costs and the national average, while at the same time it would have reduced the gap between national average benefits and benefits paid by the state.[39]

What accounts for these results? The likely explanation is that other factors are driving up costs in these low-benefit states. For example, medical costs may be substantially higher, or the administration of the program—e.g., the determination of which claimants are eligible for PPD benefits—may be more liberal in these high-cost, low-benefit states.

In this regard, we note that Durbin and Kish (1998), using individual workers' compensation claim data, found that weekly PPD benefit levels were negatively related to the adjudicator's assessment of the extent of the claimant's disability. They interpreted this result as evidence that adjudicators "redistribute" income to "poorer" workers, i.e., workers whose compensation benefits are relatively low.[40] It is possible that in some states with low statutory benefit levels, the claims administration process has been liberalized to "compensate" for less generous benefits, and vice versa (i.e., high-benefit states have stricter administration).

Our results suggest that superimposing the Model Act on states without regard to these other factors will not only lead to a substantial increase in the average costs of workers' compensation insurance (in the range of 60–75 percent of actual costs), but will also widen the gap among states in the costs of workers' compensation insurance. However, it is important to note that our simulation holds constant the other factors in our equation, including those unobserved variables such as the liberality of the claims administration process. If Durbin and Kish are correct, high-cost, low-benefit states like Montana may more strictly administer the workers' compensation claims process following the imposition of federal standards in an effort to control costs. Nevertheless, the results provide evidence supporting the hypothesis that the imposition of federal standards incorporating the Model Act would adversely affect affordability by increasing differences in employer costs among states.

CONCLUSIONS

In this chapter, we have explored the relationship between employer costs and several variables thought to influence costs. We were particularly interested in the relationship between cash benefit generosity and two conflicting objectives of workers' compensation programs: benefit adequacy and affordability. Among other things, our investigation involved estimating regression equations to measure the effect of benefits and other variables on our cost measure. We described the data set, variables, and statistical methods used to estimate these relationships. The regression equation described in this chapter is the basic model employed to determine the impact of insurance arrangements on employer costs discussed in Chapters 5 and 8.

To examine the relationship between the adequacy and affordability objectives, it was first necessary to choose standards by which we could evaluate system performance toward these objectives. Two operational standards were used to evaluate cash benefit adequacy: the recommendations of the National Commission on State Workmen's Compensation Laws and the Model Act promulgated by the Council of State Governments as revised in 1974. Both standards represent a consensus among policymakers and experts in the field of workers' compensation.

Three measures of affordability were used in this chapter: the average cost of workers' compensation insurance nationally, and two measures of dispersion among states in workers' compensation costs, the standard deviation and the coefficient of variation. Because workers' compensation costs are tied to payroll, as these costs rise, so does the price of labor. Thus, the primary danger of high workers' compensation benefits is the loss of employment. Employment loss can occur for two reasons. First, economic theory tells us that as the price of an input to the production process rises, employers use less of that input, substituting other factors of production such as machinery and other capital equipment for labor. Second, to the extent there is variation in costs among different jurisdictions, then employers will move from high-cost jurisdictions to low-cost ones.

Two of our affordability measures—the standard deviation and coefficient of variation—are meant to address the latter problem, i.e., the effect of workers' compensation costs on employer decisions about plant location. Both provide a sense of the degree to which there is significant interstate variation in costs among states. Increased cost dispersion signifies a growing gap between high- and low-cost states, as well as greater problems with respect to firm relocation decisions adversely affecting employment. Both measures assume that relocation to foreign soil, where workers' compensation costs may be lower, is not a significant problem. This would appear to be a valid assumption given that the United States continues to be largely a domestic economy.

The national average of workers' compensation costs provides a measure of the first problem, the potential impact of a general rise in workers' compensation costs on employment due to the substitution of capital and other inputs for labor. Unfortunately, it is difficult to identify a standard of affordability based on any of our measures that is similar to the adequacy standards based on the National Commission recommendations or the Model Act. There is no level of national average costs or coefficient of variation that marks the dividing point between "affordable" and "not affordable." However, we are able to observe the effect of changes in program parameters on our operational measures of adequacy so that we can judge whether the change has made the program more or less affordable.

Specifically, we used the results of regressions predicting the costs of workers' compensation insurance as a function of cash benefits and other variables to simulate the effect of benefit adequacy on affordability. The adequacy standard used in these simulations is that defined by the Model Act. These simulation estimates are compared with similar ones derived by Krueger and Burton (1990), who used the National Commission recommendations as an adequacy benchmark.

We find that adoption of the Model Act substantially increased both the average national cost of workers' compensation as well as cost dispersion among states. In contrast, the Krueger and Burton results indicated that federal standards incorporating the essential recommendations of the National Commission would have had a modest impact on average costs and, based on the 1983 and overall results, would have narrowed the cost dispersion. The difference between our results with respect to dispersion and those of Krueger and Burton is probably due to the fact that the Model Act is more comprehensive than the essential recommendations and thus had a greater effect on costs overall. Specifically, unlike the essential recommendations of the National Commission, the Model Act included specific recommendations for PPD benefits, which account for a substantial proportion of total cash benefits paid to injured workers. Among other things, this means that the Model Act had a greater impact on the cost of low-benefit, high-cost states than the essential recommendations.

Two potential policy implications flow from our analysis. First, we may conclude that less federal intervention (rather than more) is desirable in terms of reducing dispersion in costs among states, assuming that states retain basic control over workers' compensation. Alternatively, if adequacy is the primary objective (but if policymakers are also concerned with affordability and the potential adverse effects of plant relocation), then a federal program—as opposed to federal standards—is the logical policy prescription. Of course, the savings from proper policies for the insurance arrangements in workers' compensation may produce savings that will make adequate benefits in conjunction with affordable insurance rates feasible in the context of the present system of state-run workers' compensation programs. We return to this issue in Chapter 9.

A final word of caution: our conclusions and policy prescriptions assume that the measured costs of workers' compensation are identical to the employer's actual costs. However, there is substantial evidence that employees pay for the cost of increased workers' compensation benefits through a reduction in their wage rates. To the extent that this is true, then the supposed conflict between adequacy and affordability is a chimera, and policymakers need not be concerned with raising benefits to adequate levels.

Notes

1. There may also be uncontrolled differences in eligibility criteria or program administration, so that identical injuries are compensable in one jurisdiction but not in another. These differences may be controlled using state dummies, presuming that this variation is time-invariant.

2. All of the national averages reported in this chapter are weighted averages; each state's nonfarm employment is used as the weight.

3. Specifically, the data in Figure 4.1 show that, in real terms, average expected cash benefits remained relatively static over the 1975–1995 period: they increased

slightly from 1975 to 1976, declined somewhat between 1978 and 1981, and then increased to pre-1978 levels in the rest of the study period. Interstate variability in benefit generosity first increased slightly, rising from $5,300 to $5,800 between 1975 and 1978, remained relatively static between 1979 and 1985, and then declined, first sharply and then steadily, from about $5,500 in 1985 to approximately $3,700 in 1995.

4. Type of injury refers to whether the injury resulted in a fatality or disability and, if the latter, whether the disability is temporary or permanent and total or partial. Family status refers to whether the claimant is married or single and whether the claimant has dependent minor children.

5. The wage distribution we used did not vary across time, although the state average weekly wage did.

6. In some instances, weekly benefits were adjusted to account for Social Security offsets or for the fact that benefits are computed on the basis of spendable (i.e., after-tax) rather than gross earnings. For further details, see Appendix D.

7. The nature of injury refers to the body part injured; whether the injury involved amputation or loss of use; and the extent of the loss of functional impairment.

8. Unfortunately, our measure of medical benefits does not account for changes in the injury distribution, since it is a measure of benefits paid for all claims. In other regressions (not reported here), we attempted to control for injury distribution by using, as a measure of medical benefits, the average medical costs of temporary total disabilities. We obtained essentially identical results. (We did not have data on average TTD medical costs for exclusive-state-fund jurisdictions, which led us to use average total medical costs.)

9. The data in Figure 4.3 include imputations where data were missing for individual states. Figure 4.4 only includes states with data for 1995.

10. Data for states with private carriers were obtained from the National Council on Compensation Insurance's *Countrywide Workers' Compensation Experience* exhibit for the years 1979–1998. These data were reported on a "fifth report" basis in the 1979–1983 exhibits and on an "ultimate" report basis for the years 1984–1998. It was necessary to obtain benefit data on both cash and medical benefits for our regression analysis, as explained in the next section. Data for exclusive state fund states (other than Washington) were obtained from the "Workers' Compensation Agency Information" exhibit contained in various issues of *State Workers' Compensation Administrative Profiles* published by the U.S. Department of Labor. There was one exception: data for Washington state were obtained from actuaries at Washington's Department of Labor and Industries; these data are comparable to the data provided by the NCCI.

   Neither data source had comprehensive information for all years in our study; missing data were particularly a problem in the latter years of our study when a larger number of states no longer used the NCCI to set rates. Consequently, we imputed values for these missing observations. If data were missing between two years for which data were available, then missing values were imputed using interpolation. For other years, an index was constructed by taking the ratio of the state benefit to the average national benefit. Missing values were imputed as equal to the product of this index and the national average benefit for the missing year.

Unfortunately, the NCCI data and the U.S. Department of Labor data series are not equivalent. The NCCI data are "first report" estimates of incurred benefits that have been developed to "ultimate." This means that the NCCI data are based on insurers' reports of the number and cost of claims that occurred during the policy period as evaluated at a point 18 months after the beginning of each policy period. The NCCI "developed" these reported claims and costs on the basis of past trends to estimate the "ultimate" frequency and dollar amount of claims for each policy period. These claim costs are reported on an incurred basis; that is, reported costs include an actuarial estimate of future payments that the insurer expects as well as the benefits actually paid by the date of the first report. It is not possible to determine whether the U.S. Department of Labor costs were reported on an incurred or paid basis, at what point claim costs were evaluated, or whether these costs were developed to the "ultimate" basis. Because of possible discrepancies in the two medical benefits data series, we use multiple model specifications in the exclusive-state-fund regressions that include and exclude the medical benefits variable.

11. However, we note that the Krueger and Burton data pertain to a time during which there was less or limited variability (either over time or among jurisdictions), in the medical benefit payments measure, so their cash benefit variable may have explained all of the associated variation in costs. See Figure 4.3.

12. We begin with the assumption that the expected total benefit is equal to the expected cash benefit multiplied by an adjustment factor:

$$\mathrm{E}[c_t] = \mathrm{E}[c_c] \times X,$$

where $\mathrm{E}[c_t]$ is the expected total benefit, X is the inflation factor, and $\mathrm{E}[c_c]$ is the expected per-claim cash benefit. We then assume that the actual per-claim benefits paid are an unbiased estimate of expected benefits, so that

$$c_t = c_c \times X$$

where c_t is equal to the average per-claim benefit paid for all claims and c_c is the average actual cash benefit paid in lost time claims. Rearranging terms, we have

$$X = c_t \div c_c.$$

This inflation factor is described in the main body of the text of this chapter.

13. An illustration of our computation of the "total benefits" figure is as follows. Using data from the NCCI *Countrywide Workers' Compensation Experience* exhibit dated March 1997, we determined that in the 1995 policy period, the total and cash benefits <u>actually</u> paid by Alabama insurers was $311,258,996 and $129,973,586, respectively. The <u>expected</u> cash benefit to Alabama workers' compensation claimants in 1995, per our estimates of the generosity of Alabama's workers' compensation statute that year, was $6,728. To obtain expected total benefits, we multiplied expected cash benefits ($6,728) by the ratio of actual total benefits paid ($311,250,996) to cash benefits paid ($129,973,586). This calculation yields a total expected benefit per claimant of $16,113 for Alabama in 1995.

14. We used the following industry divisions: agriculture, forestry, and fishing; mining; manufacturing; construction; transportation and public utilities; wholesale and retail trade; finance, insurance, and real estate; and services.

15. The data in this figure are adjusted for industrial composition, as described in the previous paragraph.

16. The national averages in Figure 4.7 were calculated using imputed values for states with missing data. However, only states with no missing data are reported in Figure 4.8.

17. Durbin and Kish (1998) provided evidence that there is substantial interstate variation with respect to average impairment ratings, the final disability rating, and the difference between the two. The 70 percent figure cited in the text is from this data source as well.

18. These data include imputed values for missing data.

19. Although workers' compensation coverage is not mandatory in three states (New Jersey, South Carolina, and Texas), employer opt-outs are widespread in Texas and rare in the other two jurisdictions.

20. However, regulatory agencies sometime revise the relativities (cost differences) between rate groups established by rating bureaus. This suggests that cross-subsidies may exist, so that differences in coverage may affect costs. On the other hand, insurers try to circumvent this problem by targeting rate groups or by negotiating rates with individual employers.

21. Data on state compliance with National Commission recommendations were obtained from various issues of a biannual report by the U.S. Department of Labor.

22. Employment data were obtained from various issues of *Employment and Wages, Annual Averages* (U.S. Department of Labor).

23. We used in these regressions not only compliance with the National Commission recommendation regarding covered employment, but also compliance with two other coverage recommendations not specifically relating to employment coverage. These are the recommendation that workers be given a choice of filing a claim either in the jurisdiction in which they were injured or in the state in which the employee was hired and the recommendation that occupational disease be fully covered by a state's workers' compensation statute. In addition, because the Department of Labor publishes separate compliance scores for 1) states that have compulsory workers' compensation and 2) states that do not permit waivers from coverage, we treated this recommendation as two separate variables.

24. As we noted in Chapter 3, our adjusted manual rates measure is computed by modifying manual rates or pure premiums by a variety of factors (including premium discounts for quantity purchases, dividends received from insurance companies, manual rate modifications due to the employer's own compensable experience, and other variables). The resultant adjusted manual rate, which constitutes an accurate measure of employers' actual costs of workers' compensation insurance, represents the percentage of payroll expended by an employer on workers' compensation insurance. Net weekly costs (or net weekly insurance

premiums) were calculated by multiplying a state's adjusted manual rate by the corresponding average weekly wage for that state.

25. Cook-Weisberg tests revealed that these weighted least squares estimates did not suffer from heteroscedasticity.

26. Krueger and Burton (1990) did not include year dummies in their regression equations.

27. As we indicated in the previous chapter, the Krueger and Burton benefit variable only measured the variation in expected cash benefits, although in some specifications they included a separate medical benefit payments variable. In contrast, the benefit variable we used in Table 4.1 combines both medical and cash benefits. We also estimated models with separate cash and medical benefit measures. The results using separate measures do not explain the discrepancy between our findings in Table 4.1 and those of Krueger and Burton.

28. *Minimum* and *maximum* here refer to the weekly benefit payment. In most states, an injured worker may not begin to collect disability benefits immediately upon the onset of disability, but must wait a minimum period (typically three or seven days) before he or she becomes eligible for indemnity benefits; this is known as the *waiting period*. Claimants who are disabled for a certain period—typically 14 or 21 days—following the waiting period may receive, retroactively, cash benefits for the waiting period; this is known as the *retroactive period*.

29. PPD claims as a proportion of total lost-time claims partially account for this change in injury distribution. However, it does not, for example, account for changes in severity among PPD claims or changes in the duration of TTD claims.

30. This is discussed in greater detail in Chapter 2.

31. Krueger and Burton (1990) did not attempt to quantify recommendation R3.11 of the National Commission, which states

> We recommend that the definition of permanent total disability used in most states be retained. However, in those few States which permit the payment of permanent total disability benefits to workers who retain substantial earning capacity, we recommend that our benefit proposals be applicable only to those cases which meet the test of permanent total disability used in most States.

32. The Krueger and Burton model of the determinants of the costs of workers' compensation insurance was similar to the one that we used, which is discussed in the "Cost Regression Model" section of this chapter. They estimated this model using data on adjusted manual rates and net weekly costs of workers' compensation insurance from 29 states for four years (1972, 1975, 1978, and 1983). Adjusted manual rates and net weekly costs were calculated using methodology similar to that used in the present study, which is described in Chapter 3 and Appendix C. One difference is that the Krueger and Burton used only 45 insurance classifications, while the present study relied on 71 classifications. In addition, our study used more state-specific data for the adjustment factors than did Krueger and Burton to calculate adjusted manual rates; those state-specific adjustment factors reflect increasing variation among states in the pricing arrangements

permitted or required in the voluntary market in recent years. We also calculated, for many states and years, separate adjusted manual rates for the voluntary and residual markets, and then blended these rates to obtain a state-wide average; Krueger and Burton only calculated adjusted manual rates for the voluntary market. As a result, our measures of employers costs are not directly comparable with those of Krueger and Burton.

33. This hypothetical variable was an actuarial measure that replaced the state's actual level of benefits with any higher level of benefits included in the essential recommendations of the National Commission for each state in each year in their sample. Thus, if the actual state law had a maximum weekly benefit that was only 82 percent of the state's average weekly wage, Krueger and Burton calculated the benefits that would be paid after substituting a maximum weekly benefit of 100 percent of the state's average weekly wage as prescribed by the National Commission. If a provision of the state's actual workers' compensation law prescribed more generous compensation benefits than the recommendations of the National Commission, the state's benefit was not changed. Thus, if a state had a maximum weekly benefit for temporary total disability benefits that was 130 percent of the state's average weekly wage, that provision was not changed in calculating the hypothetical measure of adequate benefits.

34. However, such a cost increase would likely result in a reduction in consumer demand and thus employment.

35. The only year between 1975 and 1995 in which our actuarial assessment of actual cash benefits in 1995 dollars was below $9,000 was 1975, as shown in Table 4.9. The 1972 actual levels of benefits were probably below those in 1975 since they predated by seven months the submission of *The Report of the National Commission on State Workmen's Compensation Laws* (National Commission 1972), which triggered a period of rapid improvements in state workers' compensation laws.

36. One of the 19 essential recommendations of the National Commission was that each state's maximum weekly benefit for temporary total disability should be at least 100 percent of the state's average weekly wage. One of the 84 recommendations of the National Commission was that each state's maximum weekly benefit for temporary total disability should be at least 200 percent of the state's average weekly wage.

37. Under the Model Act, the weekly maximum and minimum benefits are equal to 200 percent and 20 percent of the state's average weekly wage, so that the dollar values of these limits on benefits will vary among states.

38. We relied on basically the same formula and procedure as Krueger and Burton (1990) to derive the simulated adjusted manual rates.

39. There are also states with low workers' compensation costs for which the use of our simulation procedure for the effect of substituting the Model Act for the state's actual workers' compensation provisions increases the cost dispersion among states. Iowa, as shown in column 1 of Table 4.13, had actual adjusted manual rates that were 1.946 percent of payroll, which was 35 percent below the

national average of adjusted manual rates of 2.973 percent of payroll in 1995. Iowa also had a statute with relatively generous statutory benefits, so that the difference between the benefits required by the Model Act and the actual Iowa statute was only $3,278. As a result, following the imposition of the Model Act, Iowa has a predicted adjusted manual rate of 2.131 percent of payroll, which is 56 percent below the national average of 4.869 percent. Thus, imposition of the Model Act would have widened the cost difference between Iowa and the national average. Four of the 10 least costly workers' compensation programs states—namely, Delaware, Washington, Iowa, and Virginia—had adequacy gaps that were less than the national average. For each of these states, we estimate that substituting the Model Act for the state's actual workers' compensation statute would have increased interstate cost variation.

40. An alternative explanation of these results offered by Thomason, Hyatt, and Roberts (1998, note 23) is that higher weekly benefits may lead claimants to pursue marginal claims.

5
Employer Costs
Public versus Private Provision of Insurance

As indicated in Chapters 1 and 2, three fundamentally different approaches are used to finance workers' compensation benefits in the United States. In some states, workers' compensation insurance is only offered by a state agency, typically called a state insurance fund. In other states, workers' compensation insurance is only available from private insurance companies. In the third group of states, employers may purchase insurance from private carriers or a state insurance fund.[1]

The decisions concerning which of these three approaches would be adopted were, in general, made at the time that workers' compensation laws were first enacted. Fishback and Kantor (1996) argued that these decisions were the outcome of a political process in which agricultural interests and the insurance industry were aligned against a coalition of labor unions and social reformers.[2] The insurance industry feared losing a potentially lucrative market, while farmers, who had successfully exempted themselves from coverage by workers' compensation laws, were concerned that they would be forced to help bail out an under-reserved state fund.[3] On the other hand, adverse experience under the negligence system that preceded workers' compensation caused unions to be leery of insurance companies, and both unions and social reformers believed that state insurance could reduce workers' compensation costs by eliminating insurer profit and overhead. As history has shown, agricultural interests and insurers were triumphant in all but a handful of states, although a few jurisdictions established competitive state funds as a compromise.[4]

These divergent approaches to insurance arrangements invite evaluation using the delivery system efficiency objective of workers' compensation programs. Is workers' compensation in exclusive-state-fund jurisdictions more or less costly than in states that permit private insurers to provide compensation insurance? That is, do private systems deliver benefits to injured workers more or less efficiently than public ones? Are competitive state funds more or less costly than monopolistic funds, and do they affect overall market costs in states where they operate?

In this chapter, we address these questions by first considering relevant economic theory and the empirical literature. We then estimate cost differentials among these different insurance arrangements using the data set described in Chapter 4.

THEORETICAL CONSIDERATIONS

As previously indicated, workers' compensation programs fall into one of three categories: exclusive-state-fund jurisdictions (type E); states where only private companies provide insurance coverage (type P); and states where private insurers compete with state funds (type C). In this study, we examine market outcomes under all three types of insurance arrangements. Among other things, we are interested in the relative performance of public versus private provision of compensation insurance. However, it is recognized that the effect of public provision may be very different with an exclusive, as opposed to a competitive, state fund.

There are many reasons to believe that a monopolistic state insurance fund should be able to deliver workers' compensation insurance coverage to employers at a lower cost than private-sector insurance carriers. Private-sector insurance rates incorporate both marketing expenses and profit loadings, which are not included in monopolistic state funds' rates. In addition, exclusive state funds may be able to capture economies of scale that are not available in a competitive, private-sector insurance market.

On the other hand, the lack of a profit motive means that both exclusive and competitive state funds could be subject to administrative and allocative inefficiencies. Arguably, since public-sector managers do not face competitive market pressures, they lack incentives to adopt cost-efficient technologies, policies, and practices. This is especially true for monopolistic state funds; because competitive funds must contend for business with private carriers, they are not completely insulated from market forces. In general, we expect that decision making in state funds is more influenced by political considerations, which may further distort incentives for efficiency.

Additionally, due to the taxing power of the state, both types of state funds have less to fear from insolvency than do their private-sector counterparts;[5] as such, they have a weaker incentive to maintain sufficient reserves. Combined with a decision-making process guided by political rather than economic considerations, state funds may be subject to under-reserving problems that could lead to inequitable and inefficient transfers, either among industrial sectors or between different generations of employers.

Economies of Scale in Insurance Markets

Unfortunately, there is little research examining most of these issues. A number of studies have addressed one issue: whether there are economies of scale in workers' compensation or other property/casualty lines; that is, whether there is evidence that the insurer's cost of underwriting additional compensation coverage declines as the amount of coverage that the insurer writes increases. For the most part, this research uses data limited to the insurance costs for private carriers and does not compare private and public insurers.[6] Overall, it has produced conflicting results. Some studies have found that costs are lower as size increases, using various measures of scale (Doherty 1981; Hammond, Melander, and Shilling 1971; Skogh 1982; and Cho 1988). Other studies have found either significant diseconomies (Allen 1974)—that is, that costs are greater for larger insurers—or mixed results (Johnson, Flanigan, and Weisbart 1981). More recently, researchers have found economies of scale for small firms (Cummins and Weiss 1993; Hanweck and Hogan 1996) but significant diseconomies for large firms (Hanweck and Hogan 1996).

While recent research is divided on the question of whether there are significant economies of scale in property/liability insurance, the reality is that insurers of various sizes seem to prosper in this market generally and in the workers' compensation market in particular. One reason may be that in certain commercial lines, such as workers' compensation, insurers are able to pursue a "niche marketing" strategy. That is, by concentrating on the risk characteristics and needs of a particular type of employer, small insurers are able to gain a significant informational and service advantage.

Butler and Worrall (1986) argued that there is little evidence of economies of scale in the workers' compensation insurance market. More specifically, they claimed that if there were such economies in this market, "then a large private carrier ought to be able to drive other carriers out of the market . . . but we do not see this happening" (p. 331). As noted by Klein, Nordman, and Fritz (1993), under guidelines established by the Antitrust Division of the Department of Justice to evaluate the competitive effects of a proposed merger, workers' compensation insurance markets in most states would be considered relatively competitive.[7] However, these data come from a period during which the industry was highly regulated (or had only recently deregulated) in many states, so that market structure may reflect the effects of rate regulation.

Butler and Worrall (1986) explored the issue of the relative efficiency of public or private provision of compensation insurance by estimating separate regression equations that predict insurer costs as a function of premiums charged by private insurers and competitive state funds, respectively. They estimated "total cost" equations as well as equations estimating separate cost components, such as incurred loss adjustment expenses, general expenses, commissions and brokerage fees expenses, other acquisition expenses, and incurred taxes, licenses, and fees expenditures. Their observations consisted of statewide aggregates for private insurers as well as financial data for individual state funds.

Butler and Worrall argued there are potentially three factors that could account for cost differences between private insurers and competitive funds. First, because state funds are typically much larger than private insurers, they may enjoy economies of scale. Second, some costs incurred by private insurers, such as taxes and marketing expenses, are "hidden" in state funds because they are not reflected in state fund accounts; that is, state funds either do not pay these costs (taxes) or do not fully record them as operating costs. Finally, there may be differences in the efficiency of private versus public sector providers irrespective of their size.

Their regression estimates for the total cost equations suggest that private insurers enjoy some economies of scale: that is, total costs increase more slowly than premiums in regression equations that use only private insurance carrier data. However, their statistical results in the state fund regressions indicate constant returns to scale. Thus, taken together, these data fail to clearly support the hypothesis that there are economies of scale in the property/casualty insurance industry.

Furthermore, when examining the private/state fund differential in scale effects, they found that state funds enjoy a cost advantage vis-à-vis private carriers, although they were unable to determine from these estimates whether this advantage is due to hidden costs or greater efficiency. However, after isolating the scale effects for the various subcomponents of total costs, they found that this cost advantage is primarily attributable to components in which the problem of hidden costs in state funds is most likely to be significant: incurred taxes and licensing fees and brokerage fees and commissions. On balance, they concluded that, "[a]t this point, it seems premature to claim (and certainly unwarranted by our study) that the state or private carriers are more efficient" (Butler and Worrall 1986, p. 345).

While there is no clear evidence of economies of scale in workers' compensation, it is also possible that there are economies of scope. Economies of scope occur where a cost advantage is realized when the producer markets more than one product. In the insurance industry, these economies may be realized where insurers sell a package of coverage: for example, health insurance, general liability, and workers' compensation coverage. To the extent that economies of scope exist in the insurance industry, state funds would be at a relative disadvantage.

To date there is little empirical research examining this issue. While economies of scope have been found in other financial service industries—and, in particular, banking—one study of the property/casualty insurance industry concluded that "economies of scope do not appear to be important" (Hanweck and Hogan 1996, p. 141).

Costs and Competitive State Funds

Two studies (Krueger and Burton 1990; Schmidle 1994) have investigated the effect of competitive state funds on statewide estimates of the employers' costs of workers' compensation insurance. Their "adjusted manual rates" and "net weekly cost" measures of employer costs were constructed using a methodology similar to that described in Chapter 3. The impact of competitive funds was measured by the coefficient on the state fund dummy variable. The dependent variables were state averages of workers' compensation costs. The Krueger/Burton and Schmidle studies found that the presence of a competitive state fund was, per the coefficient on a state fund dummy variable, associated with higher employer costs for workers' compensation insurance.

The Krueger/Burton and Schmidle results suggest that the public provision of workers' compensation insurance is less efficient and therefore more costly than the private provision of insurance. However, there are deficiencies in these analyses, and thus any generalizations about the relative merits of public provision have to be accompanied by several caveats. Both studies only examined competitive state funds. A market in which a competitive state fund competes with private insurers is likely to be very different than one in which an exclusive state fund is the sole provider of compensation insurance; for example, a competitive state fund is unable to take full advantage of economies of scale.

There is an additional reason for caution in using the Krueger/Burton and Schmidle findings to draw conclusions about the relative cost of the public provision of workers' compensation insurance: there was no variation in the value of the state fund variable during the Krueger/Burton study period, making it difficult to disentangle the effects of competitive state funds from unobserved variables that are associated with these funds. Although the Schmidle study used data from a period in which there was some intrastate variation in the state fund variable, the change only applied to two states.[8]

The Krueger/Burton and Schmidle findings were contradicted by Klein, Nordman, and Fritz (1993), who found that compensation costs may be lower in states with a competitive fund. They investigated the impact of different insurance arrangements, including the presence or absence of a competitive state fund, on loss ratios of private insurance carriers for the period 1986–1991.[9] The impact of competitive state funds on loss ratios depended upon the specification of their regression models. In their regressions that included a measure of the relative size of the residual market, the loss ratio was negatively related to the state fund dummy and this relationship was statistically significant. In equations that did not include this variable, coefficients for the state fund dummy were positive but not statistically significant. Taken together, these results reflect a negative correlation between the size of the residual market and the presence of a competitive state fund, which possibly reflects the state fund's role as an insurer of last resort. The Krueger/ Burton and Schmidle studies had not controlled for the size of the residual market, which may explain differences in results.

Costs and Exclusive State Funds

In one of the few studies that include exclusive-state-fund jurisdictions in employer costs analyses, Thomason and Burton (2000a) compared compensation costs for employers in Canada and the United States for the period 1975–1995.[10] Unlike in the United States, workers' compensation benefits in all Canadian provinces are financed by exclusive provincial funds. Thomason and Burton used cost data from two Canadian provinces (Ontario and British Columbia) and data from the 45 jurisdictions in the United States that permit private insurance. After controlling for a number of factors that could influence costs, Thomason and Burton found that compensation costs were lower in both Canadian provinces than in the average private insurance jurisdiction in the United States, although the results for Ontario were not statistically significant. While these results suggest that the public provision of workers' compensation insurance is less costly than private provision, the authors were nonetheless cautious in their interpretation of these findings. They noted that their analyses employed only a small number of exclusive-state-fund jurisdictions and that there were other data comparability problems between U.S. and Canadian jurisdictions that could affect the results.

Thus, theoretical arguments may be marshaled on both sides of the issue of the relative costs of private versus public insurance. Theory is also inconclusive about the relative merits of competitive versus exclusive state funds. Furthermore, the limited empirical research directly examining either issue is inconclusive. One study provides some evidence that two Canadian publicly funded programs enjoy a cost advantage relative to insurance offered through private markets in the United States. On the other hand, previous research investigating compensation costs has found that costs were significantly higher in competitive-fund states than in purely private markets.

REGRESSION ANALYSES

In this section, we examine the issue of the relative efficiency of public versus private workers' compensation insurance providers through two comparisons: 1) the cost of workers' compensation insurance in three exclusive-state-fund jurisdictions (Washington, West Virginia, and Ohio) relative to the cost in jurisdictions in which private carriers offer insurance coverage, and 2) the cost of compensation insurance in states with a state insurance fund that competes with private carriers relative to insurance costs in private-carrier states that do not have a competitive state fund.

Model Specification

We estimated regression equations predicting two annual, state-specific measures of the employers' cost of workers' compensation—adjusted manual rates and net weekly costs—as a function of a set of control variables including state and year dummies. This general regression model may be represented as follows:

Eq. 5.1 $\ln(C_{it}) = \beta X_{it} + \alpha S_{it} + \delta_i d_i + \delta_t d_t + \varepsilon_{it},$

where C_{it} is the dependent cost measure for the ith state and tth year; X_{it} is a vector of control variables, such as the level of cash and medical benefits and the injury rate; S_{it} is a dummy variable indicating whether the jurisdiction had a competitive or exclusive state fund in effect in the ith state and tth year; d_i and d_t are vectors of state and year dummies, respectively; β, α, δ_i, and δ_t are associated coefficients; and ε_{it} is an error term.

In these equations, control variables are designed to capture variation in insurance costs due to underlying differences in losses. We use two dummy variables to test the cost impact of public provision of workers' compensation insurance. One dummy denotes whether compensation insurance is provided solely by an exclusive state insurance fund (that is, either of three jurisdictions in our data where private insurers are not permitted to offer workers' compensation insurance). The other dummy variable indicates whether the state has a state fund that competes with private insurers. The set of regressions with the exclusive-state-fund variable includes states that permit private insurance carriers for workers' compensation; exclusive-state-fund jurisdictions are excluded from the set of regressions that include the competitive state fund.

Results: Exclusive State Funds

Weighted means and standard deviations of employer costs in private-carrier and exclusive-fund states are presented in Table 5.1. The data in the table suggest that, for the entire period of our study, compensation insurance offered by an exclusive state fund is somewhat more expensive than the insurance sold in states that allow private carriers. However, this simple comparison is misleading, because cost data for two of the three exclusive-state-fund jurisdictions in our data set—Washington state and Ohio—are not available for the early (and less costly) years in the study period.

The difference in relative costs between privately and publicly provided workers' compensation insurance is further illustrated in Figures 5.1 and 5.2, which depict the annual, weighted means of adjusted manual rates and net weekly costs, respectively, for 1975–1995. These data show that, except for 1983–1986, employers in exclusive-state-fund jurisdictions experienced costs that, on average, were noticeably lower than those of employers in private-carrier states. This was particularly true for years prior to 1983. Interestingly, the data in the figures also show that workers' compensation costs in exclusive-state-fund jurisdictions do not exhibit the same degree of cyclicality found in non-exclusive fund states. This suggests that exclusive-state-fund insurance

Table 5.1 Mean Adjusted Manual Rates and Net Weekly Costs: Private Insurance versus Exclusive State Funds[a]

Variable	Private insurance	Exclusive state fund
Adjusted manual rate ($)	2.24	2.43
	(1.13)	(0.81)
Net weekly costs ($)	11.81	13.25
	(6.21)	(4.45)
Number of observations	908	45

[a] Means are followed by standard deviations in parentheses.

Figure 5.1 Adjusted Manual Rates, Private Insurance and Exclusive State Funds, 1975–95

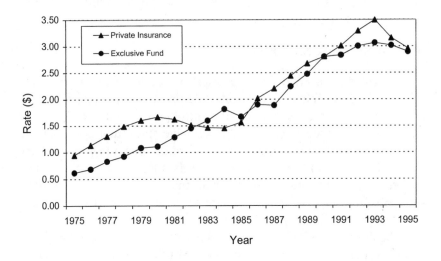

Figure 5.2 Net Weekly Costs, Private Insurance and Exclusive State Funds, 1975–95

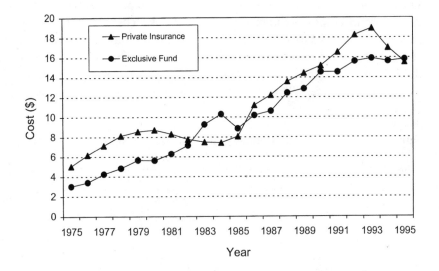

prices are not as responsive to changes in the real interest rate or whatever factors are inducing the cost cycle.

Of course, such comparisons of summary data are problematic for two reasons. First, they do not account for interstate variability within these two broad categories of jurisdictions. Second and more importantly, they do not control for other factors (such as benefit generosity) that affect employer costs. To overcome these limitations, we used multiple regression analysis, a statistical procedure that allows us to empirically control for the influence of various factors on interstate variation in workers' compensation costs. Specifically, a dummy variable indicating whether the data come from an exclusive-state-fund jurisdiction is added to our basic regression model of employers' cost.

Because no state either adopted or abandoned an exclusive state fund during our study period and because there is an insurmountable statistical problem (namely, it is impossible to identify the state-fund variable when state dummies are included as regressors), we did not include state dummies in any regressions in which the exclusive-state-fund dummy was a regressor (explanatory variable). In addition, since data for the permanent partial disability (PPD) and medical benefit variables for the exclusive-state-fund jurisdictions come from different sources and may not be comparable with those for private insurers, we estimated two specifications, one that included the PPD and medical variables and one that did not. Finally, the data set includes all states, so that the sample size is 953 observations.

The results of the cost models that include the exclusive-state-fund dummy variable are presented in Table 5.2. Findings from equations predicting adjusted manual rates are displayed in columns 1 and 2, while equations predicting net weekly costs are shown in columns 3 and 4. Columns 1 and 3 contain the results of equations that include the medical benefit and PPD share variables, while the equations in columns 2 and 4 exclude these variables. These equations were estimated using weighted least squares to control for potential effects of heteroscedasticity. Finally, the values of the coefficients on the exclusive state fund dummy have been transformed into their elasticity equivalents.[11]

Table 5.2 Regression Equation Coefficients Predicting Employer Costs: Private Insurance versus Exclusive State Funds[a]

Variable	Adjusted manual rates		Net weekly costs	
	Col. 1[b]	2[c]	3[b]	4[c]
ln(Cash benefits)	0.2994*** (12.39)	0.1332*** (4.09)	0.3136*** (12.31)	0.1333*** (3.88)
Medical benefits	0.0005*** (28.38)	—	0.0005*** (28.05)	—
ln(Injury)	0.5440*** (8.10)	0.2648*** (2.91)	0.5865*** (8.28)	0.2747*** (2.86)
PPD percentage	0.0067*** (6.74)	—	0.0080*** (7.68)	—
Union density	0.0090*** (6.20)	0.0010 (0.50)	0.0177*** (11.51)	0.0093*** (4.40)
Covered employment	−0.0141*** (4.67)	−0.0011 (0.26)	−0.0101*** (3.18)	0.0037 (0.82)
Exclusive state fund	0.0678 (1.63)	−0.0633 (1.16)	0.0541 (1.24)	−0.0823 (1.44)
State dummies	Yes	Yes	Yes	Yes
Year dummies	No	No	No	No
Adjusted R^2	0.7627	0.5244	0.7612	0.5209

[a] Coefficients are followed by t-ratios in parentheses. *** = significant at the 1% level.
[b] Equations include medical benefit and PPD share variables.
[c] Equations exclude medical benefit and PPD share variables.
[d] A dash (—) means the variable is not included in the specification.

These regression results indicate that after controlling for other factors that influence employer costs, there are no apparent, reliable differences in the price of workers' compensation insurance between exclusive-state-fund jurisdictions and states that allow private carriers. The elasticity for the exclusive-state-fund dummy variable is negative in equations that do not include the medical benefit and PPD proportion variables and is positive in equations that include the full set of regressors. However, these coefficients are not statistically different from zero at conventional levels in any equation.

Overall, these results are inconclusive concerning the relative cost-liness of public versus private provision of workers' compensation insurance. However, it is important to remember that at least two of the exclusive state funds in our database, West Virginia and Ohio, experi-enced substantial and persistent deficits during much of the study period. Since private insurers are unable to sustain such deficits in the long run, this suggests that our measures of compensation cost may underestimate the "true" employers' costs for these exclusive state fund jurisdictions. If so, average compensation costs for these three exclusive-state-fund jurisdictions are probably either equal to or greater than average costs in states that permit private carriers to under-write workers' compensation insurance.

In some ways, this is a surprising result. Our cost measure controls for interstate variation in the loss component of costs, so that the state fund dummy is a measure of the profit and expense loading described in Chapter 4 (pp. 74–75). As we indicated previously, exclusive state funds—unlike private carriers—do not incur marketing expenses, and there is no allowance for profits. This implies that administrative inef-ficiencies must increase the costs of compensation policies provided by exclusive state funds relative to insurance provided by private carriers. That is, lacking a profit motive, state fund managers are less aggressive than their private sector counterparts in rooting out inefficient policies and practices. Rather, state fund decisions may be based in part on a political calculus that is only tangentially related to cost consider-ations.

Three further caveats with respect to our exclusive-state-fund find-ings are in order. First, the results for exclusive state funds are based on a small number of observations that come from only three states. Furthermore, for two of those jurisdictions, we lack data for the entire study period (the Ohio data only include observations going back to 1983, while the earliest Washington data are from 1985). As a result, it is possible that these results are peculiar to our sample or to a subset thereof. Simply put, one state fund outlier—a data point where costs are extraordinarily high relative to the rest of the data set—could bias our results substantially.

Second, since no state either abandoned or adopted the exclusive state fund model during the study period, we are unable to control for unobservable state-specific effects that could bias estimates of costs for exclusive state funds. In other words, these results may be peculiar to the characteristics of the particular state-fund jurisdictions used in the analysis.

Third, these results contradict those of Thomason and Burton (2000a), who found that two monopolistic-state-fund jurisdictions in Canada (British Columbia and Ontario) experienced lower costs than did U.S. states that permit private insurance.[12] Importantly, the exclusive-state-fund cost estimates reported by the authors of this earlier study were adjusted for state fund deficits, so that they represent a more comparable cost comparison. The Thomason and Burton results further suggest that our analyses are sensitive to the particular jurisdictions used for comparison and to possible problems regarding data comparability. In this context, it is important to recognize that state funds may be administered either well or poorly, and that the quality of administration will obviously affect performance.

Results: Competitive State Funds

Weighted means and standard deviations of employer costs in private-carrier and competitive-state-fund jurisdictions are presented in Table 5.3. (These data exclude jurisdictions with exclusive state funds.) As can be seen, competitive-state-fund jurisdictions have substantially higher costs with respect to both adjusted manual rates and net weekly costs. This difference is also found when average costs for individual years are considered.

Table 5.3 Mean Adjusted Manual Rates and Net Weekly Costs: Private Insurance versus Competitive State Funds[a]

Variable	Private insurance	Competitive state fund
Adjusted manual rate ($)	2.01	2.65
	(1.11)	(1.04)
Net weekly costs ($)	10.19	14.77
	(5.67)	(6.08)
Number of observations	655	253

[a] Means are followed by standard deviations in parentheses.

Figures 5.3 and 5.4 show that compensation premiums were greater in states with competitive state funds. It is also notable that costs in competitive-state-fund jurisdictions exhibit greater cyclicality than costs in private-carrier states that do not have competitive state funds. Thus, the cost gap between private-carrier states with and without competitive funds widens and narrows as the market for compensation insurance hardens and softens, respectively.[13]

It should be recalled that, in many states, the competitive fund is the insurer of last resort, so that as the market hardens, it is likely that private carriers are increasingly reluctant to insure high-risk employers, who are then required to turn to the competitive fund. Thus, the market share of the competitive fund increases during a hard market. If competitive funds incur higher costs than private carriers, we would expect to see greater cost swings in competitive-fund states relative to states where only private carriers underwrite insurance.

To control for other factors that might influence employer costs, we estimated regression equations using a dummy variable to indicate whether a state had a competitive fund. Unlike exclusive-state-fund jurisdictions, five states either adopted or abandoned state funds during our study period; because of these changes, we were thus able to include state dummies in our regression model when the competitive state fund was included as a regressor.[14] The regressions only use observations from states where private insurers operate, so that the sample size is 908 observations. The regression results are reported in Table 5.4.

The empirical results in Table 5.4 suggest that states with competitive funds have higher costs than private-carrier jurisdictions without competitive state funds. Specifically, the elasticity estimates for the competitive-state-fund variable indicate that adjusted manual rates are nearly 18 percent higher in competitive-fund jurisdictions than in states without state funds, while net weekly costs are nearly 19 percent higher. Although these results are consistent with prior research (see Krueger and Burton 1990; Schmidle 1994), they are nevertheless surprising, since a primary impetus for creating these funds was to reduce employer costs by providing competition for private carriers.

At face value, these results suggest that public programs are less efficient than private carriers. The fact that the cost differential for competitive state funds is much larger than the differential for exclu-

Figure 5.3 Adjusted Manual Rates, Private Insurance and Competitive State Funds, 1975–95

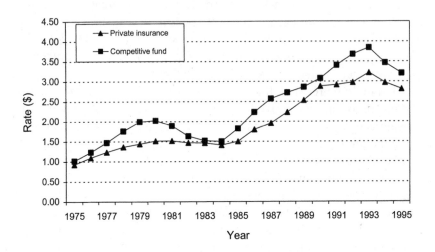

Figure 5.4 Net Weekly Costs, Private Insurance and Competitive State Funds, 1975–95

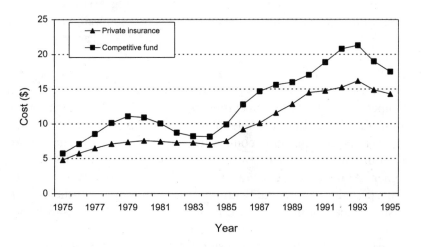

Table 5.4 Regression Equations Predicting Employer Costs, Competitive State Funds[a]

Variable	Adjusted manual rates	Net weekly costs
ln(Cash benefits)	0.1163***	0.1478***
	(2.75)	(3.44)
Medical benefits	0.0001***	0.0001***
	(4.66)	(5.03)
ln(Injury)	0.8832***	0.8367***
	(9.34)	(8.74)
Union density	0.0105***	0.0104***
	(6.40)	(6.26)
PPD percentage	0.0017	0.0046
	(0.42)	(1.08)
Covered employment	0.0193***	0.0237***
	(2.96)	(3.59)
Competitive state fund	0.1780***	0.1870***
	(3.34)	(3.44)
State dummies	Yes	Yes
Year dummies	Yes	Yes
Adjusted R^2	0.9135	0.9197

[a] Coefficients are followed by t-ratios in parentheses. *** = significant at the 1% level; ** = significant at the 5% level; * = significant at the 10% level.

sive funds is also noteworthy. A possible explanation is that, unlike monopolistic state funds, the competitive state funds incur marketing expenses in addition to bearing higher administrative costs resulting from inefficient public administration.

While these results provide some evidence that public provision of insurance is less efficient than private provision, there are at least two or three reasonable alternative explanations. First, it is possible that the causal arrow is reversed: high costs are causing states to create competitive funds rather than competitive funds leading to high costs. Unfortunately, we are unable to identify a system of equations to control for this possibility. However, it is important to note that Krueger and Burton's (1990) analysis produced a nearly identical result even though their data set was less likely to suffer from endogeneity problems. Specifically, their data came from a period that had not seen the creation of a competitive state fund for several decades, so that it is unlikely that many factors that possibly led to the creation of the existing state funds were still in effect during their study period.

Finally, higher employers' costs in competitive-state-fund jurisdictions may be attributable to the competitive state fund's role as the insurer of last resort. In many states with a competitive state fund, a firm that is unable to obtain insurance from a private carrier will be assigned to the state fund. In states without a competitive state fund, these employers are placed in an assigned-risk pool in which each carrier shares a part of the cost of providing coverage to these firms. Before an employer may be assigned to an assigned-risk market pool in a state without a competitive fund, the employer must show that it has been denied coverage in the private market. However, employers may typically apply to the competitive fund directly without evidence of refusal by private insurers. For these reasons, a high-risk employer may find it easier to get a subsidized market rate in states with state funds than in states without them. As Danzon and Harrington (1998) argued, the incentive effects of this cross-subsidization eventually results in higher costs for the market as a whole.[15]

SUMMARY AND CONCLUSIONS

As indicated in Chapter 1, one objective of the workers' compensation program is delivery system efficiency, i.e., the extent to which a program is able to minimize administrative costs associated with the delivery of benefits. In this chapter, we have examined the relative costs of public versus private provision of compensation insurance and have obtained decidedly mixed results. It is unclear whether exclusive state funds are more or less costly than the average jurisdiction in which private carriers provide insurance. On the other hand, states with competitive funds apparently experience costs that are significantly greater than jurisdictions in which only private insurers offer workers' compensation insurance. As measured by the delivery efficiency criterion, exclusive state funds and private-carrier-only systems would seem to be superior to "blended" systems.

However, it is important to note that these analyses suffer from methodological problems that must temper our conclusions. We have only a handful of observations involving three states on exclusive state-fund costs, and we are unable to control for potential endogeneity in the competitive fund equations.

Notes

1. In most states, regardless of approach, employers also have the option of self-insuring.

2. Fishback and Kantor (1996) provided evidence indicating that employers were generally split over this issue. Some were convinced by the arguments of social reformers who believed that employer costs would be lower with a monopolistic state fund. Others saw the state fund as the thin end of the wedge of creeping socialism.

3. Williams (1969) argued that, due to the small size of the market and its hazardous nature, the insurance industry was simply not interested in underwriting workers' compensation insurance in some states that established an exclusive state fund.

4. Of interest, at about the same point in time, Canadian jurisdictions uniformly established monopolistic provincial funds.

5. The term *taxing power* refers to the fact that the state insurance fund is free to establish assessment rates that are necessary to cover deficits and that employers can be required to purchase insurance that includes assessments to cover prior deficits. It does not mean that states will use general revenues to bail out insolvent state funds.

6. An exception is Butler and Worrall (1986), which is discussed in the text below.

7. The Department of Justice guidelines specify that a market is considered to be highly concentrated if it has a Herfindahl-Hirschman Index (HHI) in excess of 1,800; moderately concentrated if it has an HHI between 1,000 and 1,800; and unconcentrated if the index if less than 1,000. (The HHI is the sum of the squares of the percentage market shares of each firm in the market.) Klein, Nordman, and Fritz (1993) reported that in 1991 there were only four states whose compensation insurance markets had an HHI in excess of 1000.

8. The Krueger and Burton study used data from 1972, 1975, 1978, and 1983; the Schmidle study used data from 1975, 1978, 1983, and 1986–1989.

9. Loss ratios can be considered as either a measure of insurance price or as an inverse measure of insurer profitability. Their use for either purpose was critiqued in Chapter 3.

10. We are unaware of any study other than Burton (1965) that examines the employers' cost of workers' compensation insurance for exclusive-state-fund jurisdictions relative to jurisdictions in which private insurance carriers offer compensation insurance.

11. This was done using the equation: $\eta = \exp(\beta) - 1$, where β is the coefficient on the exclusive-state-fund dummy.

12. However, Canadian workers' compensation programs differ from their U.S. counterparts in several respects, so that a simple comparison, without further analysis, may not be appropriate.

13. A *soft market* is one in which market supply is greater than demand, so that prices are declining. A *hard market* is the opposite: demand exceeds supply and prices rise.

14. Four states (Maine, Minnesota, Louisiana, and Texas) introduced a competitive state fund during this period, while one (Michigan) privatized its fund.

15. See Chapter 8 for a more extensive discussion of the Danzon and Harrington hypothesis.

6
The Effect of
Workers' Compensation
Insurance Regulation

Theory and Prior Research

As indicated in Chapter 2, the market for compensation in those states that permit private workers' compensation insurance has traditionally been highly regulated. Prices have been largely administered by a state agency rather than determined by competitive forces. However, since the 1980s, state workers' compensation markets have been deregulated to varying degrees. In the political debate surrounding these efforts, contradictory claims are made regarding the effect of deregulation on employer costs and other market outcomes. In this chapter and the next two, we will address two questions relevant to this debate:

Does the regulation of the insurance market raise or lower the costs of workers' compensation insurance for employers?

Is the quality of the product offered by compensation insurers affected by regulation?

This chapter examines the economic theory of rate regulation as well as previous empirical research addressing this issue. In the following chapter, we present the results of regression analyses predicting employer costs and the extent of concentration in the workers' compensation insurance market.

ECONOMIC THEORY OF RATE REGULATION

In this section, we discuss economic theory concerning the effect of insurance regulation on market outcomes. Specifically, we summarize economic theory relating to the effect of regulation on the price and availability of compensation insurance.

Theoretical Considerations: Costs and Availability

According to economic theory, two factors determine the effect of rate regulation (or deregulation) on the workers' compensation insurance market: 1) the goals and strategy of the regulatory agency and 2) the structure of the unregulated market. In this context, the terms *regulated* and *unregulated* refer to price regulation and not other forms of regulation, such as minimal capital requirements or exit barriers (including advance notice provisions). *Market structure* refers to the characteristics of the organization of the market, such as the relations of the present sellers to each other and to potential sellers. The element of market structure most commonly emphasized is the degree of concentration, which measures the number and size distribution of sellers in the market.[1] Other elements of market structure include the degree of product differentiation among the outputs of firms in the industry and the relative ease or difficulty that new firms have trying to enter the market.

Market structure

The structural characteristics of the workers' compensation insurance market suggest a competitive market. There are a large number of firms that sell a homogeneous product. Capital requirements are relatively modest (even including legislatively imposed requirements) and there are no significant technological barriers to entry. Using U.S. Department of Justice criteria, the workers' compensation insurance market in most states would be judged competitive as of the early 1990s.[2] Nonetheless, it is possible that in the absence of regulation, large firms could take advantage of economies of scale to set prices at levels that drive smaller carriers out of the market, i.e., rates that are below the firms' short-run average costs. After purging small competitors from the market, these large firms could then raise rates to supra-competitive levels—rates at which the large firm is able to earn excess profits, but not so high as to attract new entrants, who would be at a disadvantage due to their smaller size.[3] Furthermore, other aspects of the rate-setting process, such as possible collusion between insurers and the rating organization, may enable these large carriers to effectively "cartelize" the industry.

In the next sections, we discuss economic theory regarding various aspects of market structure, including price setting in unregulated competitive or monopolistic markets and the impact of rate regulation in competitive or monopolistic markets.

Price setting in an unregulated, competitive market. In a competitive market, insurance rates are determined by the levels of supply and demand in the market. The relationships among supply, demand, and rates are illustrated in Figure 6.1; the insurance rate (or price) is measured on the vertical axis, while the quantity of insurance offered by carriers or demanded by employers at various rates is measured on the horizontal axis.

Figure 6.1 shows that at higher rates, more insurance coverage is offered to employers by carriers.[4]   At the same time, however, employer demand for coverage declines as the price increases. In the context of mandatory workers' compensation insurance, insurance demand may vary in three ways. First, employers who are sufficiently large may choose to self-insure as prices rise. Alternatively, employers facing higher labor costs due to higher insurance prices will substitute

Figure 6.1 Price Setting in a Competitive Insurance Market

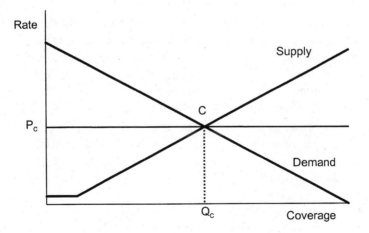

capital and other inputs to the production process, including employ-ment in low-risk occupations, for high-risk labor.[5] This reduces the payroll covered by workers' compensation insurance or the average rate at which payroll is taxed. Finally, firms may choose to terminate or restrict operations.

The lines labeled "Supply" and "Demand" in Figure 6.1 represent levels of potential supply and demand at different price levels. The actual price and quantity of insurance sold in the market is determined by the intersection of supply and demand, which occurs at point C. This is the point at which demand is equal to supply, so that at price P_c, employers are willing buy and insurers are willing to provide coverage equal to Q_c.

The competitive market price is significant for policymakers because, under standard economic assumptions, it represents the point at which there is an efficient allocation of resources. That is, at com-petitive rates, insurers will offer and employers will purchase a socially optimal amount of insurance coverage.

Individual insurance carriers determine the extent of insurance coverage that they are willing to offer based on reviews of market price and the firms' cost structure. Specifically, insurers will underwrite additional coverage up to the point where the marginal cost of includ-ing an additional insurance policy is equal to the additional revenue that the policy generates.

In a competitive market, the individual carrier faces a level of demand that is perfectly elastic with respect to price; that is, the indi-vidual insurer may expect to be able to sell an unlimited amount of coverage at this price. However, the individual carrier is unable to raise rates above this level, as it will lose business to competitors. Impor-tantly, since demand is perfectly elastic, the insurer's marginal revenue in a competitive market is equal to the competitive price, P_c. In other words, the additional revenue generated by underwriting an additional policy is the same as the revenue generated by all other policies sold. Under these circumstances, the level of coverage that maximizes prof-its occurs at the point where the insurer's marginal cost (i.e., the cost of offering an additional unit of coverage) is equal to the price of that additional coverage.

Price setting in an unregulated, monopolistic market. If we assume that the unregulated insurance market is not competitive, then different results are reached in the market. For convenient exposition, the following analysis assumes that the unregulated insurance market is a monopoly. While this is unlikely for the insurance industry, the results from this analysis approximate those for an oligopoly, a more realistic possibility.[6]

Demand for a monopolistic firm is identical to market demand. As a result, the monopolist faces a demand curve that is downwardly sloping. Furthermore, the slope of the marginal revenue curve (MR) is also downwardly sloping and is steeper than the slope of the demand curve, because the firm may only increase coverage by reducing price. That is, unless the insurer can price-discriminate, it must reduce the rate for all policies in order to sell an additional policy. This means that the added revenue from each additional policy sold is not only less than the revenue added from the sale of the previous policy, but it is also less than the price of the additional policy.

Figure 6.2 illustrates the monopoly insurer's decision-making process about price setting, assuming that there are constant returns to scale (that is, that costs do not increase or decrease with additional sales), so that the marginal cost curve (MC) is horizontal. The profit-maximizing monopolist will select a level of coverage that equates the marginal cost and marginal revenue curves, which occurs at the intersection of these two curves (point A). As a result, the insurance carrier will offer coverage equal to Q_m at price P_m. Note that this price is higher than the competitive rate, which is equal to the firm's long-run average (or marginal) cost curve. At price P_m, the quantity of coverage purchased in the market is less than that which would be purchased in a competitive market.

Effect of rate regulation on a competitive market. If the regulatory agency sets prices above the competitive level and forces all transactions to take place at this price, then the amount of coverage will shrink relative to its preregulatory level. Figure 6.3 illustrates this point. The unregulated supply curve is depicted as the line S_2S_1, while, presuming that the regulated price is set at P_r, the line P_rBS_1 depicts the regulated supply curve. The demand curve is represented by the line D_2D_1.

As can be seen, the regulated supply curve intersects demand at point A. As a result, coverage falls from Q_c (the quantity of coverage underwritten in an unregulated market, determined by the intersection

Figure 6.2 Price Setting in a Monopoly Market

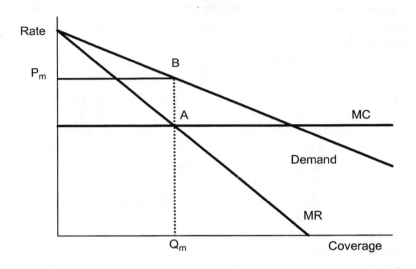

**Figure 6.3 Price Setting above P$_c$ in a Regulated Competitive
         Insurance Market**

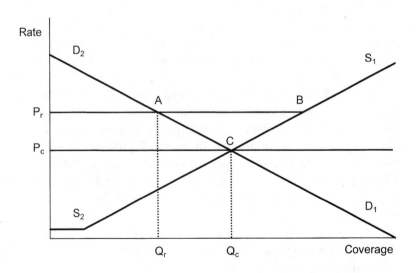

of demand and supply at point C) to Q_r. Importantly, this level of coverage is suboptimal, since there are consumers who are willing to pay for coverage at the competitive market rate but not at the regulated price. If the insurance market is deregulated at some later point, then rates will decline to competitive levels and coverage will increase.

On the other hand, if the regulatory agency sets rates below the competitive price P_c, the market will collapse in the long run, because insurers, who are unable to recoup their costs, will be unwilling to offer coverage at the regulated rate. However, insurers may remain in the market as long as the regulated rate covers the carriers' short-term variable costs. They do so because they are reluctant to abandon their previous investments in marketing, underwriting, and claims adjustment infrastructure, because they anticipate a return to more profitable rates, and because of fears associated with the cessation of writing multistate and multiline accounts.[7] Insurance industry analysts often point to experience in Maine in the 1980s, where insurers remained in the market despite an inability to earn what they considered to be a fair return on investment.

Figure 6.4 depicts the unregulated supply curve as S_2S_1 and the regulated supply curve as the line S_2A. This figure shows that, at best,

Figure 6.4 Price Setting below P_c in a Regulated Competitive Insurance Market

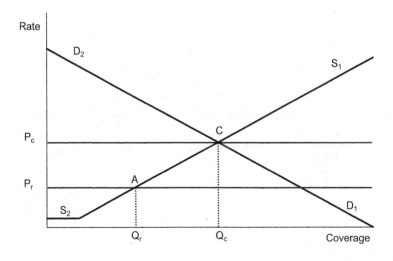

insurance carriers will be willing to offer coverage equal to Q_R, so that once again rate regulation results in reduced coverage, and demand greatly exceeds supply. The amount of coverage underwritten by insurers falls in the short run from Q_c to Q_R. If insureds are heterogeneous with respect to underlying risk, insurers will refuse to extend coverage to high-risk employers, forcing them into the residual market.[8]

In addition, in the face of below-market rates due to regulatory rate suppression, less efficient firms will exit the market and the market will thus become increasingly concentrated. If the market is deregulated at some later point, then we would find that coverage increases concurrently with rising prices. In addition, new carriers would enter an increasingly less concentrated market.

Effect of rate regulation on a monopolistic market. As we previously indicated, the monopolistic insurance carrier will set rates above competitive levels. As a result, if the regulatory agency sets rates below the market rate but equal to or above the competitive market rate, the firm will underwrite a greater level of insurance coverage at this lower price. This is illustrated in Figure 6.5.

Figure 6.5 Price Setting in a Regulated Monopoly Market

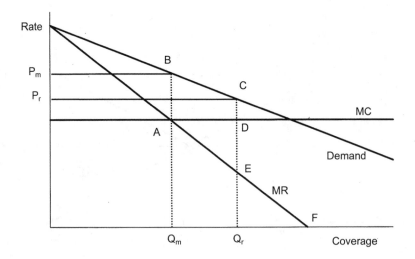

As was the case in an unregulated market, the carrier will select a level of coverage, Q_m, at which marginal costs equal marginal benefits; this occurs at point A. However, assuming that the regulated price is set at P_r, the marginal revenue curve is now depicted by the lines, P_rC and EF. The firm's marginal revenue is now perfectly elastic up to the point where P_r intersects the demand curve. As can be seen, the marginal revenue curve now intersects marginal costs (MC) at point D, so that coverage will increase to Q_r. In other words, rate regulation in this instance results in a reduction in price and in greater coverage. Note that this is the opposite effect from that in a competitive market. Of course, if the regulatory agency were to set a price below the competitive level, then a market failure similar to that depicted in Figure 6.4 will result.

Behavior of the regulatory agency

As indicated by the preceding discussion, the price-setting strategy of the regulatory agency has a bearing on the actual effect of insurance pricing deregulation. Unfortunately, economic theories of rate regulation are not well developed; due to a lack of agreement concerning the nature of the regulatory process, economic theory about the impact of deregulation is inconclusive. At one time, economists assumed that regulatory bodies acted solely in the public interest. According to this view, regulation was a response by legislators to citizen demands for a political solution to a specific problem. This response typically included the formation of a government agency with a mandate to address legislative will and citizens' concerns. According to this view of the regulatory process, we would generally expect that state insurance commissions would thus be expected to set rates at competitive levels.

Of course, the economic effect of any regulatory strategy depends on the structure of the market in the absence of regulation. Assuming that the state insurance commission is able to accurately determine the competitive rate, then we would expect that a regulatory agency that implements a public interest strategy would not affect prices or coverage in a competitive market, but would reduce prices and increase coverage if the market was oligopolistic. However, this outcome is critically dependent on the regulatory agency's ability to accurately determine the competitive rate.

Stigler (1971) challenged the long-standing assumption that regulatory agencies act in the public interest. He noted that regulation affects firms in the regulated industry and that these corporate interests are particularly well-placed to influence legislative and regulatory processes. Relative to consumers (or even small firms in the industry), large corporations' have greater incentives to influence the political process because their financial stake is large and because they can exert greater political pressure on legislators (or regulators). In addition, because large corporations are fewer in number, more homogeneous, and more likely to already be organized, organizational costs for lobbying purposes are less significant, as are potential free-riding problems. As a result, "regulation is acquired by the industry and is designed and operated, primarily for its benefit" (Stigler 1971, p. 3). In Stigler's view, corporate interests, after "capturing" the regulatory process, promote industry interests in two ways: through direct money subsidies and through the control of entry of new firms.

Presumably, with respect to insurance rate regulation, Stigler would argue that since insurance carriers are fewer in number and more homogeneous than policyholders, and since their benefits (or costs) of regulation are potentially greater, insurers have greater incentives to influence the regulatory process. If this is true, these insurers' efforts will lead to a cartelization of the insurance markets, and, presumably, rate regulation will produce supracompetitive rates (i.e., rates that are higher than the competitive market rate and that therefore yield excess or above-normal profits) and a restriction of coverage through carrier-imposed barriers to market entry.

Peltzman (1976) both formalized and modified Stigler's model. Specifically, he hypothesized that legislative regulators (i.e., legislatures that regulate the market or delegate that responsibility to a government agency) seek to maximize a net vote margin or majority in their favor. In other words, the regulator's problem is to maximize the following objective function (in which the net vote margin is represented as M):

$$M = (nf) - [(N - n)h]$$

where N is the total number of voters, n is the number who benefit from the proposed regulation, f is the probability that these beneficiaries will provide political and financial support to the regulator, and h is the probability that nonbeneficiaries will oppose the regulator.

The probability that beneficiaries will provide financial or political support for regulation is a function of the per-capita net benefit received by those interest groups. This benefit is equivalent to the wealth that is transferred to beneficiaries as a result of the regulatory process less the dollar amount spent in efforts to support legislators and less the costs associated with organizing and delivering support (including the costs of overcoming free-rider problems). Monies spent to support legislators include, for example, mass media advertising, direct mail campaigns, or other "voter education" efforts. The probability of political opposition is positively related to the net tax imposed on nonbeneficiary groups to pay for the wealth transfer to beneficiaries and is negatively related to voter education expenditures by regulation supporters.

Importantly, Peltzman departs from Stigler by acknowledging that consumers as well as producer interests may affect the legislative regulatory process. As we have indicated, the relative influence of interest groups that support or oppose regulation depends on the relative size of the affected groups, the per-capita costs and benefits of wealth transfer, the cost of organizing for the purpose of delivering political support, and the cost and effectiveness of voter education efforts.

With respect to insurance regulation, it is difficult to determine *a priori* whether consumers or producers have the advantage vis-à-vis political influence. On the one hand, the probability of insurance industry support for favorable rate regulation likely exceeds the probability of consumer (i.e., employer or worker) opposition for at least two reasons. First, organizing costs for insurers are relatively low, and, second, their financial stakes are relatively great. On the other hand, consumers of workers' compensation insurance are much more numerous than producers (insurance carriers), and workers' compensation policyholders are sophisticated consumers who are also easily organized.

Thus, it is possible that consumer groups (or trade associations of employers) could capture the regulatory process, which would result in regulatory rate suppression relative to the unregulated market.[9] Under this scenario, consumer groups will pressure regulators to set prices below market levels. If they succeed, then the extent of coverage will decline, and subsequent deregulation will result in both higher prices and increased coverage.

However, this possibility raises the issue of whether, even if possible, rational employers would want to suppress insurance rates, since in the long run, rate suppression results in the unavailability of insurance, as insurers who are unable to earn normal profits abandon the market. This hypothesis assumes that employers are unable to foresee the inevitable consequences of such a strategy. If employers do not suffer from this form of myopia, then we could predict that rate regulation will either result in competitive prices or a cartelization of the industry and supranormal prices.

Regulatory lag

If the regulatory agency lacks accurate and timely information on market conditions or if the agency is unable to react quickly to changing market conditions, a different result occurs. For example, assume that the insurers' cost structure fluctuates over time, so the regulatory agency in a regulated market and/or the carrier in an unregulated market must periodically adjust rates. In general, rate adjustments in reaction to changing market conditions will probably occur more slowly in regulated environments than in unregulated ones. There is an obvious delay in the receipt of market information, since the agency receives its information from insurers. In addition, the regulatory process of filing and review itself imposes a delay. The lag between changing market conditions and rate adjustment implies that, at times, the regulated rate will be above or below the competitive level. Specifically, we expect that under conditions of declining costs (due, for example, to rising interest rates), the regulated rate will be higher than the competitive one. The opposite will be true during a period of rising costs.

Expected Results of Deregulation

Economic theory provides ambiguous predictions concerning the effect of deregulation, because the effect differs depending on the nature of the unregulated market and on the behavior of the regulatory agency. Our predictions, which are based on the preceding analysis, are presented in Table 6.1. We make predictions about three market outcomes upon deregulation from different scenarios: the cost of workers' compensation insurance ("Rates"), the extent of coverage in the

Table 6.1 Predictions of the Impact of Deregulation on Market Outcomes[a]

Scenario	Rates	Availability	Market concentration
Competitive market			
Public interest regulation	0	0	0
Regulator captured by insurers	−	+	+
Regulator captured by employers	+	+	−
Oligopoly			
Public interest regulation	+	−	+
Regulator captured by insurers	0	0	0
Regulator captured by employers	+	?	?

[a] + = positive relationship.
 − = negative relationship.
 0 = no relationship.
 ? = ambiguous relationship.

voluntary market ("Availability"), and market concentration. A "+" indicates that there is a positive relationship between deregulation and the outcome variable; a "−", a negative relationship; a "0", no relationship; and a "?", an ambiguous relationship.

For example, assume that we have a competitive market and the regulatory agency has been captured by insurers. In this situation, we would expect that the regulatory agency, responding to the wishes of the insurance industry, would have increased workers' compensation rates above the competitive market level; some employers would no longer be able to afford the premiums, so coverage would have decreased. Increased prices under regulation would attract marginal insurers into the market, reducing market concentration. If the market were then deregulated, insurance prices would return to competitive levels (i.e., rates would decline) and more employers would be able to afford a workers' compensation policy, increasing levels of coverage. Finally, market structure will become more concentrated as marginal insurers leave the market

Predictions as to whether the regulatory agency will represent the public interest or become captured by the insurance industry or employer groups require the analysis of a number of factors, including the concentration of economic interests, transaction costs, information, ideology, and the saliency and complexity of regulatory issues (see Meier 1988; Klein 1995). Unfortunately, we lack good information on these variables. In addition, the predictions reported in Table 6.1 assume that regulatory agencies are able to respond instantaneously to changing market conditions. However, due to delays inherent in the regulatory process as well as the fact the agency is one step removed from market information, it is likely that there is a lag between a market change and the regulatory response (Klein 1995; White 1996). As a result, an agency that pursues a public interest strategy is likely to suppress rates when costs are increasing and to set rates above market levels in periods of falling costs.

EMPIRICAL RESEARCH ON RATE REGULATION[10]

Most empirical research on the impact of the regulatory environment on market outcomes in the property/casualty insurance industry has ignored workers' compensation. We will initially summarize research on the regulatory environment and outcomes for property and casualty insurance lines, principally, automobile insurance, the line most often studied because it is believed that the politically sensitive nature of automobile insurance pricing leads regulators to set prices below competitive rates. We then summarize studies assessing the impact of the regulatory environment on market outcomes for workers' compensation insurance.

Evidence from Other Property/Casualty Insurance Lines

Early studies investigated whether and to what extent regulatory legislation affects insurers' propensity to deviate from bureau rates. These studies typically found that deregulation was associated with increased rate variation among insurers relative to the regulated market, which implies that the deregulated insurance market is competitive.

For example, Joskow (1973) found that the proportion of premiums written at rates different from those promulgated by the rating bureau (off-bureau rates) was much larger in an "open competition" state that did not require prior approval (California) than in a state that did (New York).[11] In addition, his comparison of New York rates before and after enactment of open competition legislation revealed that the proportion of premiums sold at off-bureau rates increased following enactment.[12] Williams and Whitman (1973) examined variation in automobile insurance and homeowners' insurance rates in Minnesota and found that rate variation in both lines increased following the adoption of open competiton.[13] Finally, assessing experience in three insurance lines, the Virginia Bureau of Insurance (1978) found that the number of carriers that charged bureau rates and the relative market share of these companies fell sharply after the competitive rating law went into effect.[14]

Rate levels

More recently, investigators have attempted to determine the impact of rate regulation on insurance prices. Since price data were not readily available, these studies almost uniformly examined loss ratios as the dependent variable.[15] Most found that, contrary to predictions, deregulation is associated with lower loss ratios and thus, inferentially, with higher rates (although there are exceptions). Studies finding a negative relationship between loss ratios and deregulation include Smallwood (1975),[16] Witt and Miller (1981),[17] Cummins and Harrington (1987),[18] Harrington (1984, 1987),[19] Pauly, Kunreuther, and Kleindorfer (1986),[20] and Grabowski, Viscusi, and Evans (1989).[21] A handful of studies support the opposite point of view (Samprone 1979;[22] Chidambaran, Pugel, and Saunders 1997)[23] or fail to find a statistically significant relationship between the loss ratio and the regulatory environment (Witt and Miller 1980; GAO 1986).[24] However, most research suggests that deregulation is associated with higher insurance rates, implying that regulatory agencies suppress rates.

These results are troubling to students of insurance markets for two reasons. First, assuming a competitive market, as indicated by the research on rate deviations, economic theory predicts that rates should in the long run be higher in a regulated market than in an unregulated one. This is because price distortions create cost-increasing inefficiencies in the long run, including a reduction in insurers' incentives to enhance operational efficiency, and because the cost of compliance and the regulatory bureaucracy is inevitably reflected in market prices. Second, casual observation suggests that insurance premiums are often higher in states that stringently regulate rates.

The anomalous results from these studies may be due to deficiencies in the dependent variables examined. As we pointed out in Chapter 3, the loss ratio is a measure of one component of insurer costs (i.e., losses) to revenue (or premiums written). As such, it is as much a measure of profitability as price. Loss ratios are a reasonable price measure only to the extent that the loading factor is invariant, a condition that may be expected in a competitive market. However, if markets are not competitive or if for institutional reasons insurers are willing to remain in a market where they receive less than a normal return on investment, then the loading factor can vary while price remains constant, and vice versa.

A recent study provides some evidence for this hypothesis. Using auto insurance data, Tennyson (1997) examined the relationship between expense ratios (the ratio of underwriting expenses to premiums written) and rate regulation, and she found that this ratio was positively related to the regulatory stringency.[25] She attributed this result to reduced market shares for large cost-efficient carriers in stringently regulated markets.[26] Interestingly, Tennyson also found that stringent rate regulation reduced the market share of national firms, and especially of those that specialize in auto insurance, more than that of other types of insurance carriers. Since these types of insurers (national firms and auto specialists) tend to be more cost-efficient, Tennyson argued that rate regulation increases consumer costs through a change in market structure, i.e., more efficient insurers leave the market.

Availability of coverage

As we previously indicated, economic theory suggests that rate regulation may also affect the availability of coverage underwritten by insurance carriers. There are a number of studies examining the relationship between rate regulation and the size of the residual market. If regulatory agencies suppress rates, then we would expect to find a positive relationship between the size of the residual market and the degree of rate regulation.

Several studies have found such a positive relationship. Grabowski, Viscusi, and Evans (1989) found that prior approval laws were associated with an increase in the size of the involuntary automobile insurance market and that there was a positive relationship between regulatory stringency and residual market size. Similar results were obtained by Suponcic and Tennyson (1995)[27] and Bouzouita and Bajtelsmit (1997).[28] Blackmon and Zeckhauser (1991) noted that over two-thirds of the drivers in Massachusetts, a jurisdiction with stringent rate regulation, were in the involuntary market. Rates did not differ between involuntary and voluntary markets for drivers in the same rating category. As a result, eight insurers who provided some 25 percent of the automobile insurance coverage in the state had stopped or were attempting to stop writing policies in the state, despite the imposition of high exit fees by the state's insurance commissioner.

The results from these studies suggest that rate regulation reduces profit margins, forcing insurers out of the market. As such, they are inconsistent with most research examining loss ratios, which has found a positive relationship between deregulation and loss ratios, indicating that deregulation reduces insurer profits.

Rate variability over time

Advocates of rate regulation in insurance markets assert that such regulation results in lower price variability. They claim that price coordination under regulation reduces or eliminates cutthroat pricing in a soft market, contributing to greater price stability in insurance markets. In hard markets, regulation limits the size of the price increase. In addition, regulation proponents maintain that cyclical price fluctuations are due to insurer error in loss forecasts and that rate regulation precludes any price variation resulting from these errors. In marked contrast, opponents of rate regulation assert that regulation actually leads to greater price volatility in insurance markets. Tennyson (1991, p. 34) noted that, according to this view, critics allege that "rate regulation restricts adjustment of the industry to changing market conditions, and thereby exacerbates underwriting volatility." This is at least partially due to lags inherent in the regulatory process. In other words, insurers incur additional costs because they are unable to make immediate adjustments in insurance prices. This is essentially a restatement of the regulatory-lag hypothesis that we described earlier in this chapter.

Tennyson (1991) found no evidence that rate regulation influenced the amplitude of the insurance cycle as measured by the absolute difference in loss ratios between the peak and the trough of the insurance cycle. She found, however, that rate regulation was associated with greater variance in loss ratios for automobile liability insurance for some carrier types, although this relationship was only statistically significant for national and regional agency companies.[29] While loss ratio variability was also positively associated with rate regulation for the homeowners multiple-peril line, which is less sensitive to political pressures, this relationship was not statistically significant. Importantly, these results suggest that rate regulation increases carriers' underwriting risk, a result that could partly explain why the residual market is larger under rate regulation.

Overall, these studies suggest that rate regulation has a number of deleterious effects for property/casualty insurance markets. Regulated markets appear to be characterized by rate suppression, which increases the size of the residual market and may increase insurance costs in the long run, and by increased price volatility, increasing underwriting risk and possibly further discouraging competition. However, this research is plagued by methodological problems, leading to inconsistent results and tempering the definitiveness of conclusions that can be drawn.

Research into Workers' Compensation Rate Regulation

In recent years, as a rapidly increasing number of states have deregulated workers' compensation insurance market pricing, a few studies have investigated the impact of this deregulation. Unlike most research examining the impact of regulation on other property/casualty lines, the studies have used dependent variables other than the loss ratio. There remains, however, a paucity of research compared with other property/casualty insurance lines.

Klein, Nordman, and Fritz (1993)

These researchers estimated ordinary least squares regression equations predicting statewide average loss ratios and residual market shares as function of regulatory environment dummy variables indicating whether 1) the state regulatory agency required that insurers obtain prior approval before implementing rates; 2) the agency required adherence to bureau rates; and 3) the rating organization filed fully developed manual rates as opposed to loss costs.[30] A fourth variable, regulatory stringency, attempted to gauge the extent to which the state insurance commission suppressed rates.[31] All four regulatory environment variables were lagged one year.

They found mixed evidence concerning the effect of rate regulation on insurance pricing. Consistent with the rate suppression hypothesis, regulatory stringency was positively related to the loss ratio, implying that stringent regulation reduced prices in regulated markets and led to higher workers' compensation insurance rates. However, the prior-approval dummy was negatively related to the loss ratio, suggesting the opposite, i.e. that prices are higher when insurance carriers must obtain prior approval of rate increases.[32]

Results for the residual market equations were similarly inconsistent. On one hand, the prior-approval dummy and the regulatory stringency ratio were positively related to residual market share, indicating that the residual market shrinks following the elimination of prior approval and that stringent regulation is associated with larger residual markets. On the other hand, the loss-cost coefficient was also positively related to residual market share, suggesting that the residual market increases following the adoption of a loss-cost system.

Klein, Nordman, and Fritz concluded that rate regulation has a significant impact on both profitability and the size of the residual market, although they cautioned that the coefficients on their regulatory environment variables were not robust and were subject to specification error. Interestingly, they also concluded that the effects of regulation vary substantially among states, depending on how statutory provisions regarding insurance rates were actually applied by the regulatory agency.

Carroll and Kaestner (1995)

As in the Klein, Nordman, and Fritz study, Carroll and Kaestner examined the impact of rate regulation on costs and market share for a cross section of states, using two binary measures of the regulatory environment: a "competitive-rating" dummy indicating that the state had adopted an advisory rating or loss cost system and a "partial-competition" dummy indicating whether the state insurance commission permitted deviations from the bureau rates.[33] Two-stage, least-squares regression models were specified, because several variables determining the dependent price measure (including the regulatory environment variable and residual market share) were considered to be endogenous.

The competitive-rating variable was negatively and significantly related to both cost measures (price-per-injury and price-per-employee) compared with states having strict prior approval legislation.[34] The partial-competition variable was also negatively related to costs, but it was only statistically significant in the price-per-employee equation in which the regulatory environment was treated as exogenous.[35] In the residual market share equation, the competitive-rating and deviations variables were statistically significant only when the regulatory environment was treated as exogenous; both variables are inversely related to the size of the residual market. Deregulation (competitive rating) was thus perceived as more closely aligning rates in the voluntary and residual markets.

In sum, as Carroll and Kaestner noted, their results are most straightforward with respect to the competitive-rating variable. The partial-competition variable, on the other hand, was rarely statistically significant. They concluded that insurance regulators "have in the past been more responsive to industry needs, either by tacitly encouraging collusion in the industry or by directly keeping insurance rates high." They also concluded that allowing deviations from bureau rates was an ineffective method for deregulating the insurance market.

Appel, McMurray, and Mulvaney (1992)

Two studies have examined cost measures similar to those used in this book, i.e., adjusted manual rates and weekly insurance premiums. In one, Appel, McMurray, and Mulvaney estimated 12 regression specifications as a function of a competitive-rating dummy variable and a variety of controls. They found that costs were positively related to a competitive-rating dummy in all but one equation, although these relationships were statistically significant at conventional levels in only three of these equations.[36] They concluded (p. 16) that "[w]hile there are indications that the adjusted manual rates are higher in competitive rating states, the evidence is not overwhelming." They also estimated regression models with more refined measures of the regulatory environment, i.e., dummy variables that classified states as falling into one of five different regulatory environments, but the results of these regressions produced no clear pattern of results vis-à-vis the impact of rate regulation.[37]

Schmidle (1994)

This study used data from 47 states for 1975, 1978, 1983, and 1986 to predict employers' costs and market structure. Importantly, Schmidle also attempted to control for the endogeneity of competitive-rating statutes. His regulatory environment variables included binary variables indicating that the state had a competitive rating law (open competition) or that the states had partially deregulated insurance pricing by permitting deviations or scheduled rating (partial competition).[38]

Schmidle's regression models estimated manual rates, adjusted manual rates, weekly insurance premiums, and a "spread" measure to ascertain the impact of deregulation on employers' costs. The spread measure, which attempted to gauge the extent of workers' compensation price discounting (and competitiveness) in a state, was computed by dividing the adjusted manual rates average by the corresponding manual rates average; this quotient was then subtracted from 1.

Overall, these analyses produced mixed results. In many regression equations, particularly those that employed the full set of explanatory variables, the coefficients for the two regulatory environment variables were not different from zero at conventional levels of statistical significance. As a result, Schmidle concluded that most of the evidence from these analyses suggested that deregulation had no effect on the price of workers' compensation insurance, but there was some support for the hypothesis that deregulation increased insurance prices.

However, results for the regulatory environment variables that were statistically significant indicated that open competition was associated with higher adjusted manual rates, higher manual rates (although manual rates typically increased more than adjusted manual rates with the introduction of open competition), and higher weekly insurance premiums. Several regressions also suggested that open competition was associated with greater price discounting (as represented by the spread between manual rates and adjusted manual rates). None of these regressions supported the hypothesis that deregulation (open competition or partial competition) was associated with lower manual rates, lower adjusted manual rates, or a decline in the spread between manual rates and adjusted manual rates. All of this evidence is indicative of rate suppression in administered-pricing states prior to the adoption of open competition laws.

Schmidle also attempted to examine the impact of insurance pricing deregulation on market structure, a topic that has not received much attention in the research literature. His dependent measures were concentration ratios (top four and top eight firms) and proxy measures for exit/entry patterns (number of direct writers, state agency companies, national agency companies, and all workers' compensation private insurance carriers). He found some evidence that open competition influenced market structure, but his conclusions were circumscribed due to the paucity of control variables with available data.

Schmidle's model of the factors contributing to enactment of open competition statutes had little explanatory power. Most notably, neither cost measures (adjusted manual rates) nor insurers' previous loss experience (loss ratios) were associated with passage of open competition legislation and thus apparently were not an impetus to adopting such legislation.

Summary

In summary, the research examining the impact of rate regulation on various outcomes for the workers' compensation line has produced mixed results. In particular, research investigating the impact of regulation on insurance pricing has produced very inconsistent results; some of these studies have found that regulation is associated with lower prices, while other studies have found the opposite. While the topic of rate variability has received less attention, research on this topic has likewise failed to produce uniform findings. On the other hand, existing research tends to show that rate regulation is associated with a reduction in insurance availability and less competitive markets, i.e., a less concentrated market with fewer insurance providers.

There are at least two possible explanations for the lack of consistent results. First, in the absence of effective measures of regulatory behavior, these results may reflect variation in regulatory strategy among states and over time. In other words, insurance regulators may be suppressing rates in a particular jurisdiction at a particular point in time while they set prices above competitive market levels at other times or in other jurisdictions. Second, these studies suffer from methodological problems that potentially affect the results. Most cost studies fail to utilize direct measures of costs, relying primarily on loss ratios (which, as discussed in Chapter 3, are questionable measures of costs). In addition, there is a conspicuous lack of agreement among studies, particularly those examining workers' compensation insurance markets, on the definition and measurement of the regulatory environment variables.

CONCLUSIONS

Economic theory fails to offer unambiguous predictions with respect to the impact of the regulation of rates in private insurance markets. Instead, theory holds that the effect of rate regulation depends on the underlying market structure in the absence of regulation and on the behavior of the regulatory agency. Existing evidence suggests that, in the absence of regulation, the workers' compensation market is competitive; thus, the impact of deregulation depends primarily on the regulatory agency's behavior (or strategy). Agency strategy depends on the relative political influence of the various actors in the workers' compensation system. If employers have more political power and thus greater influence over the agency's decisions, deregulation should result in rate hikes; if insurers have more political power, deregulation should result in a rate reduction; and if neither group predominates, then there should be no systematic effect. Consequently, regulation (or deregulation) could have different effects in different jurisdictions and at different periods in time, depending on which group has the greater political influence.

Empirical research on the effects of rate regulation supplies some support for the latter "contingency" view, in that, in general, there is a lack of consistent results across studies. That is, the effect of rate regulation (or deregulation) depends on the interaction of the statutory framework, regulatory behavior, insurer behavior, and market conditions. However, it is also possible that these divergent results are due to methodological inconsistencies. Most previous research has relied on proxy measures of insurance costs—typically, loss ratios—that are only indirectly related to the underlying variable that they seek to measure. Many fail to control for important variables that influence costs (or other market outcomes)—aside from some rudimentary measures of the regulatory environment—and often use a relatively short time series that fails to span the insurance cycle. Finally, this research has typically employed relatively simple constructions of the insurance regulatory environment.

Notes

1. Market concentration is usually measured in terms of the value of sales in a particular industry accounted for by the four largest or the eight largest companies.
2. See Klein, Nordman, and Fritz (1993). For additional evidence indicating that the workers' compensation insurance market is competitive, see Schmidle (1994) and Appel and Gerofsky (1985).
3. Importantly, if there are economies of scale in workers' compensation insurance, then large size provides firms with market power due to their size. This topic is discussed in greater detail in Chapter 4.
4. Increased coverage is made possible in two ways. Either more carriers are willing to offer coverage or each carrier is willing to offer additional coverage. The former implies variation in cost structure among insurers (so that some carriers are able to offer coverage at lower rates than others). It should be recalled that while the law mandates that employers purchase compensation insurance (or demonstrate that they have sufficient financial resources to self-insure), there is no requirement that insurers offer coverage to employers in the voluntary market; thus, it is possible that the extent of coverage offered by private carriers will, in fact, vary depending on the state of the market.
5. For example, the employer could choose to automate production lines substituting a programmable robot (operated by a computer technician) for one or more semi-skilled machine operators.
6. An oligopoly is a market in which there are only a small number of sellers who are able to collude in setting prices and are thus, in effect, able to act like a monopolist.
7. Insurers may also be reluctant to abandon a market because of state regulations that increase the cost of exit.
8. However, it is important to note that unless regulators establish differential rates for the voluntary and residual markets, expansion of the residual market will lead to higher rates in the voluntary segment, as employers purchasing policies in the voluntary market are taxed to pay for shortfalls in the residual market. (Recall that residual market losses are tied to the insurer's share of the voluntary market.) This will, in turn, cause insurers to further reduce available voluntary market coverage, which will cause the residual market to expand further, leading to even greater costs. The insurance literature refers to this process as the "death spiral."

9. Peltzman's model did not allow for the regulatory suppression of rates below the competitive price. However, both Harrington (1992) and Klein (1995) have offered reasonable explanations for why this might occur in insurance rate regulation.

10. The discussion in this section draws upon and updates the literature review in Schmidle (1994).

11. Similarly, the U.S. Department of Justice (1977) compared automobile insurance prices as of January 1, 1976, under regulatory regimes that required prior approval of rates (Pennsylvania and New Jersey) with those in California. The Department found that a larger proportion of the insurance market in California used off-bureau rates and that these rates tended to be 10 percent or more below bureau rates. In a critique of this research, Danzon (1983) noted that the percentage of deviations above bureau rates was greater in the prior-approval states than in California. She hypothesized that "prior approval regulation may be used to hold down [bureau] rates below the level desired by the bureau and possibly below the competitive level" (p. 379; emphasis in the original.) She also noted that average loss ratios tended to be higher in prior-approval states, indicating that insurers in these states were less profitable.

12. New York adopted an "open competition" law for various property/casualty insurance lines that went into effect on January 1, 1970. This law was modeled on California's open competition law, which had been in effect since 1947.

13. Williams and Whitman (1973) attributed the greater variation to a "greater willingness of insurers to compete on price following the enactment of the new law," although they also counseled that "if the variation persists, it may indicate inadequate consumer knowledge and hence ineffective competition" (p. 490).

14. These lines were homeowners, private passenger physical damage, and private passenger auto liability.

15. See Chapter 3 for a critique of these measures. However, an earlier exception to this generalization was a study by the Virginia Bureau of Insurance (1978), which examined statewide average rates. This study found that prior to competitive rating, the average statewide rate increase closely mirrored several large increases in bureau rates; afterwards, the average statewide rate increases were considerably lower than rate increases promulgated by the rating bureau.

16. Smallwood predicted average loss ratios (private passenger and commercial automobile insurance) of the top 36 firms as a function of five dummy variables representing the regulatory environment. These variables placed states into one of five categories: open competition, file and use, prior approval, mandatory bureau rates, or "regulatory stringency." The last are states in which the insurance commissioner "had disapproved a rate filing as excessive or had otherwise intervened in a case significant enough to generate prominent discussion in the trade press" (p. 271). He estimated separate regressions for each of five classes of carriers (all insurance carriers, direct writers, national agency companies, liability insurance line, and physical damage insurance line). Of the regulatory environment variables, only the regulatory stringency measure was statistically significant; it was

positively associated with loss ratios in all regressions and had the largest coefficient in the liability insurance model, suggesting that prices are lower in regulated environments. With respect to the result regarding the magnitude of the coefficient, Smallwood concluded that because automobile liability insurance was compulsory (or essentially compulsory), regulators felt obliged to keep prices low.

17. They examined disaggregated loss ratios by insurer type (direct writers, national agency companies, and regional specialty companies) and found statistically significant and lower average loss ratios for national agency companies and regional companies in competitive rating states, suggesting that deregulation increased consumer costs and insurer profits for those companies.

18. Cummins and Harrington found that loss ratios for private passenger automobile, commercial automobile, and homeowners' lines were lower in competitive states than in noncompetitive ones. They used two competitive-rating dummy variables (one indicating that the state had a file-and-use law, the other indicating a no-file or a use-and-file state) in multiple regression analyses predicting average loss ratios for each of four insurance lines.

19. Harrington found that the regression coefficient for the prior-approval dummy variable (states with mandatory bureau rates, state-made rates, or prior-approval laws) was statistically significant and positively associated with average loss ratios for private passenger automobile liability for the 1976–1981 period. When significant, the coefficient was also positively associated with average loss ratios in the regressions for individual years.

20. They estimated three-year moving averages of statewide loss ratios for private passenger collision and liability insurance coverage by insurer type (direct writers and independent agency firms). The coefficient for their prior-approval dummy variable was statistically significant and positively associated with loss ratios in all of the agency firms regressions and in most of the direct writers regressions. They concluded that rate regulation increased loss ratios and therefore reduced insurance prices.

21. Grabowski, Viscusi, and Evans found that rate regulation reduced automobile insurance rates, particularly in states with stringent regulation, and increased the size of the involuntary market (assigned-risk pool). Their dependent variable was the inverse of the loss ratio for automobile liability (bodily injury) and property insurance in the 30 largest states for the period 1974–1981. They used two measures of the regulatory environment: 1) a prior-approval dummy variable and 2) a dummy variable that identified three states with particularly stringent regulatory environments. The prior-approval regression coefficient was statistically significant in all the automobile liability insurance regressions (direct writers; agency companies; and both insurers combined) and negatively associated with unit prices. The stringent-regulation coefficient was significant in two of the liability regressions (agency companies and the combination of insurer types), had a negative sign, and suggested "an impact on prices more than twice that in other regulated states" (p. 284).

22. Samprone found that the inverse of the loss ratio automobile liability insurance, averaged over a three-year period (1973–1975), was higher in regulated states, suggesting that rates were also higher. However, he failed to find a similar relationship for another auto insurance line, physical damage. He concluded that higher rates in regulated states did not result in higher profits. He noted that if above-normal profits were present in the regulated sector, there should be a greater influx of new firms into that sector than into the competitive sector, assuming no barriers to entry. The absence of an influx suggested that excess profits were not being realized in regulated states. In his view, insurers in states with rate regulation incurred additional expenses because they were engaged in "nonprice" competition (by offering more services than they otherwise would have). In a later study, Frech and Samprone (1980) hypothesized that independent agents, who provide more services than direct writers, should, in regulated states, have a higher average market share than that of direct writers. They found this to be the case for two lines of automobile insurance, thus supporting Samprone's hypothesis.

23. Chidambaran, Pugel, and Saunders used data from 18 property/liability insurance lines for 1984–1993 to assess the determinants of an economic loss ratio equal to the sum of the present value of expected losses on insurance policies in year t, divided by the sum of premiums in year t, less costs and expenses. Their "regulatory scrutiny" measure was a binary variable indicating whether the loss ratio was for the automobile or workers' compensation insurance lines (the authors asserted that these two lines were subject to more intense regulatory attention than were others). They found that loss ratios were negatively related to both the extent of regulatory scrutiny and the degree of industry concentration. They attributed the latter result to a reduction in price rivalry. The authors claimed that this reduction resulted from historical cooperation in price setting among insurers, coupled with broad exemptions from antitrust legislation.

24. The GAO classified prior-approval states and used data from 44 states for a period (1975–1982) that overlapped most of the years used by Pauly, Kunreuther, and Kleindorfer (1986). Unlike in the latter study, the GAO regression coefficient for the prior-approval dummy variable was not statistically significant in the model estimating the determinants of the inverse loss ratio of automobile liability insurance.

25. Tennyson used 1992 data from all 50 states to investigate the impact of rate regulation on expense ratios and state-specific 1992 data from 64 national insurance groups to examine its effect on market share. As a measure of regulation, she used a dummy variable that indicated whether states had prior-approval regulation, state-made rates, or mandatory bureau rates; she also used three dummies that identified subsets of states with particularly stringent regulatory environments. The regulatory-environment dummy variable was not statistically significant in the regression models estimating either liability or physical damage expense ratios for private passenger automobile insurance; however the stringency variable was significant and positively related to the expense ratio.

26. A potential explanation for these findings is that stringent rate regulation allowed more inefficient carriers to survive in a less competitive market.

27. Suponcic and Tennyson (1995) investigated the relationship between rate regulation and the market structure for automobile insurance markets, using state-level data for the period 1987–1992. Regression analyses estimated two dependent variables: the total number of insurers in each jurisdiction and in various subgroups (direct writers, national direct writers, national auto specialists, national firms in total, and auto producers), and the market share. Three variables were used to measure the impact of the regulatory environment: a dummy for states with prior-approval regulation, state-made rates, or mandatory bureau rates for automobile insurance; a stringent-regulation dummy, which indicated that the state's residual market accounted for more than 20 percent of the total insurance market; and a regulatory stringency index based on the results of a survey of insurance industry executives, who were asked to rate the states' regulatory environments.

28. Bouzouita and Bajtelsmit examined the relationship between automobile insurance rate regulation and the size of assigned-risk market using state-specific data for 1984–1992. They hypothesized that noncompetitive rating in the voluntary market would lead, in turn, to inadequate rates, higher loss ratios, restricted availability, and increases in the percentage of drivers in the assigned-risk market. Bouzouita and Bajtelsmit categorized states as either noncompetitive (they required prior approval of rates, modified prior approval, and file-and-use with bureau adherence) or competitive (they had file-and-use or use-and-file provisions or did not regulate insurance prices). They found that rate regulation (that is, noncompetitive rating) was statistically significant and positively associated with the percentage of drivers in the assigned-risk market. Interestingly, the coefficient on the size of the assigned-risk market was statistically significant and inversely related to market concentration, suggesting that the size of that market increased as the voluntary market became more concentrated.

29. She estimated regressions predicting the variance in loss ratios (automobile liability and homeowners multiple-peril insurance) in 48 states and for three different types of insurance carriers (direct writers, national agency companies, regional companies) for the period 1972–1986.

30. They used data from all non-exclusive state fund jurisdictions for the period 1986–1991.

31. This variable was equal to the ratio of the percentage advisory rate change filed by the rating bureau to the percentage rate change approved by regulators, minus 1.

32. Specifically, Klein, Nordman, and Fritz found that nonstringent prior-approval regulation (where the regulatory agency approved the full rate request of the rating bureau) reduces the loss ratio by 13.9 percent, while more stringent prior-approval regulation (where the agency approves only one-half of the bureau's rate request) reduces the loss ratio by 11.3 percent.

33. Specifically, they estimated equations predicting price and residual market share using a pooled, cross-sectional, fixed-effects model and data from 43 jurisdictions

for the period 1980–1987. They used two price measures: 1) the ratio of workers' compensation premiums earned (adjusted for policyholder dividends) to the total number of work-related injuries in the state, which they termed *average price per injury*, and 2) the ratio of compensation premiums to the total number of private nonagricultural employees in the states, or the *average price per employee*. The merits of these variables as cost measures were reviewed in Chapter 3. Competitive-rating states included states that did not require prior approval of rates by the state insurance commission.

34. In the price-per-injury equations (in which the regulatory environment was treated as either exogenous or endogenous), the competitive-rating variable was statistically significant and associated with a 14–29 percent price reduction relative to states with strict prior approval legislation. In the price-per-employee equations, the competitive-rating variable was either statistically significant and associated with a 25 percent decrease in the average price-per-employee of workers' compensation, or it was not statistically significant.

35. In that equation, the partial-competition variable was associated with a 13 percent drop in the price per employee.

36. Using data from 47 jurisdictions for the years 1983 and 1986–1989, Appel, McMurray, and Mulvaney estimated 12 regression specifications predicting the natural logarithm of adjusted manual rates.

37. These researchers also compared means of these cost measures for competitive and noncompetitive jurisdictions for individual years—except, for weekly premiums, 1986 and 1989—and for the entire period. Adjusted manual rates in competitive-rating states exceeded those in noncompetitive-rating states for all comparison years except 1983, but the difference in means for adjusted manual rates was only statistically significant when the individual-year data were aggregated. The average weekly insurance premium in competitive-rating states was greater than that in noncompetitive states for three of the four periods examined (1987, 1988, and all years combined, but not in 1983), but the difference was never statistically significant.

38. Three basic variants (six permutations) of the open-competition variable were also used. These variants were designed to measure time-dependent effects of competitive rating legislation. However, regressions using these variables produced inconclusive results.

7

The Effect of
Workers' Compensation
Insurance Regulation

Evidence

Our review of relevant economic theory in the previous chapter indicated that insurance rate regulation potentially affects workers' compensation insurance pricing and, consequently, delivery system efficiency. However, theory fails to yield unambiguous predictions about the nature of these effects. To date, the empirical literature has similarly failed to yield consistent results, which may be due to methodological problems (including difficulties associated with the dependent measure, the characterization of the regulatory environment, and a failure to capture insurance cycle effects due to a short time series).

In this chapter, we present the results of regression analyses predicting the employers' cost of workers compensation and the extent of market concentration as a function of the state regulatory environment. We believe that we are able to overcome many of the methodological difficulties encountered by prior research. Specifically, we think that we have a superior dependent measure, that we capture many of the complexities in the nature of the regulatory environment, and that our time series is long enough to control for insurance cycle effects.

EMPLOYER COST SPECIFICATION

As we indicated in Chapter 4, employers' workers' compensation costs are determined by a number of factors, including statutory benefit levels, the liberality of claims administration, and the underlying injury rate, as well as the state regulatory environment. Thus, the estimating equation for predicting employer costs as a function of the regulatory environment takes the following form:

Eq. 7.1 $\ln(C_{it}) = \beta X_{it} + \alpha A_{it} + \delta_i d_i + \delta_t d_t + \varepsilon_{it}$,

where C_{it} is the dependent cost measure for the ith state and tth year; X_{it} is a vector of control variables, such as the level of cash and medical benefits and the injury rate; A_{it} is a vector of variables indicating the insurance arrangement in effect in the ith state and tth year; d_i and d_t are vectors of state and year dummies, respectively; β, α, δ_i, and δ_t are associated coefficients; and ε_{it} is an error term. More specifically, A_{it} consists of a set of dummy variables, each of which designates either a particular regulatory rule or regulatory regime that is in effect in a particular state and year.   In some analyses, two other variables are included as supplements to the regulatory regime variables: a "hard-market" dummy and an estimate of regulatory stringency. In these equations, the hard-market and regulatory-stringency variables are interacted with the regulatory-regime dummies. These variables are described in greater detail in the following section.

Regulatory Environment Variables

Insurance rate regulation is a complex phenomenon, not easily modeled by a single binary variable indicating whether or not the market is regulated. Our analyses use five classification categories or rules to characterize the regulatory environment for workers' compensation insurance pricing in a particular state. These decision rules are as follows:

1) *Prior approval rule*: The insurer may implement a rate adjustment without prior approval from the state insurance commission.

2) *Advisory rate rule*: The insurer may use rates or loss costs different from those filed by the rating organization (bureau rates). Unlike deviations, rates can vary among insureds for a particular carrier.

3) *Loss cost rule*: The rating organization files loss costs.

4) *Deviations rule*: Deviations from bureau rates are permitted. For a particular carrier, deviations must be uniform for all insureds.

5) *Schedule rating rule*: The insurer may use schedule rating.

Significantly, the cost impact of these rules may vary depending upon the particular configuration of rules in a state. For example, a market that permits deviations (rule 4) but requires the prior approval of rates (rule 1 is violated) may be either more or less regulated (i.e., may constrain insurer behavior to a greater or lesser extent) than a market that does not permit deviations but that also does not require prior approval (that is, allows insurers to "file and use" rates). Thus, the particular configuration of rules may be as important in determining insurance costs as the individual rules themselves. In our subsequent analyses, we have attempted to measure not only the effects of the individual regulatory rules on costs but also the effects of particular combinations or configurations of those rules, which we term *regulatory regimes*.

As indicated, we measured the effects associated with these rules or regulatory regimes by using a series of dummy variables. A value of 1 was assigned to jurisdictions that are less regulated (or more deregulated), according to the rule. For example, jurisdictions in which the insurers could either "use and file" or "file and use" rates without first obtaining the prior approval of the state regulatory agency (rule 1) were assigned a value of 1 for the without-prior-approval variable. Jurisdictions in which the insurer was required to first obtain prior approval before implementing new rates were assigned a value of zero.

Unfortunately, economic theory and the rate regulation literature offer little guidance as to the appropriate schema for classifying regulatory regimes in order to assess their potential effect on insurance market outcomes. Consequently, our first step was simply to identify which of the five rules described in the previous paragraph applied to each of the states in our study for each year in the study period. We did this, in part, through a survey of state insurance commissioners, which is described in Appendix F. Commissioners were asked to characterize the actual practice of the insurance commission relative to these rules, as opposed to the "letter of the law" contained in the statute.

We then examined the resultant distribution of jurisdictions with respect to the various configurations of the five regulatory rules (i.e., the regulatory regimes). Those regimes that included only a small number of observations were combined into larger categories that made sense conceptually. This produced a set of seven regimes that represent an overwhelming majority of regulatory environments in effect during the study period. We term this set our full-set regulatory environment model, and it includes the following categories: pure administered pricing, administered pricing with deviations, administered pricing with schedule rating, advisory rates with prior approval, advisory rates without prior approval, loss costs with prior approval, and loss costs without prior approval. We then identified six additional regulatory environment models, which are subsets of the full-set model and which were created by collapsing categories of the full set. Some of these subset models correspond to those used in prior research, and these are identified in our discussion of the results. F-tests were used to select a preferred specification from this group of regulatory environment models.

The seven regulatory environment models are shown in Table 7.1, versus the five regulatory rules. Model 1 represents the full-set model, while models 2 through 7 are subsets. For statistical reasons, one category in each regime has to be omitted from our regression analysis; these omitted categories are identified in Table 7.1 as well.

For model 1, the table indicates that prior approval of rates is required in all regimes except advisory rates without prior approval and loss costs without prior approval. The table also indicates that states must adhere to bureau rates under pure administered pricing and in regimes of administered pricing with deviations or with scheduled rating; however, rates are advisory in the next two regimes (advisory rates with prior approval and advisory rates without prior approval). Under the two loss-cost regimes, adherence to bureau loss-cost filings may or may not be required.

The change in the number of jurisdictions for which each of the five regulatory rules were in effect over the 1975–1995 period is illustrated in Figure 7.1. These data show that workers' compensation insurance markets in the United States have become more deregulated over time, as indicated by the increasing number of states with no prior approval, advisory rates, loss costs, and schedule rating. The sole exception to this deregulatory trend is the decline in the number of states that permit deviations. This anomaly can be explained by the

Table 7.1 Relationship between the Regulatory Environment Models and the Regulatory Rules[a]

Regulatory environment models	Rule: Without prior approval	Advisory rates	Loss costs	Deviations	Schedule rating
Model 1 (omitted category, pure administered pricing)	No	No	No	No	No
Administered pricing with deviations	No	No	No	Yes	No
Administered pricing with schedule rating	No	No	No	—	Yes
Advisory rates with prior approval	No	Yes	No	—	—
Advisory rates without prior approval	Yes	Yes	No	—	—
Loss costs with prior approval	No	—	Yes	—	—
Loss costs without prior approval	Yes	—	Yes	—	—
Model 2 (omitted category, non–loss cost systems)	—	—	No	—	—
Loss costs with prior approval	No	—	Yes	—	—
Loss costs without prior approval	Yes	—	Yes	—	—
Model 3 (omitted category, pure administered pricing)	No	No	No	No	No
Partial competition	No	—	No	—	—
Open competition	Yes	—	—	—	—
Model 4 (omitted category, pure administered pricing)	No	No	No	No	No
Administered pricing with deviations or schedule rating	No	No	No	—	—
Advisory rates	—	Yes	No	—	—
Loss costs	—	—	Yes	—	—

(continued)

Table 7.1 (continued)

Regulatory environment models	Rule: Without prior approval	Advisory rates	Loss costs	Deviations	Schedule rating
Model 5 (omitted category, pure administered pricing)	No	No	No	No	No
Variation from bureau rates with prior approval	No	—	No	—	—
Advisory rates without prior approval	—	Yes	No	—	—
Loss costs with prior approval	No	—	Yes	—	—
Loss costs without prior approval	Yes	—	Yes	—	—
Model 6 (omitted category, pure administered pricing)	No	No	No	No	No
Administered pricing with deviations or schedule rating	No	No	No	—	—
Advisory rates or loss costs	—	—	—	—	—
Model 7 (omitted category, pure administered pricing)	No	No	No	No	No
Administered pricing with deviations	No	No	No	Yes	No
Administered pricing with schedule rating	No	No	No	—	Yes
Advisory rates with prior approval	—	Yes	No	—	—
Loss costs	—	—	Yes	—	—

[a] A "yes" in a table cell indicates that the rule listed in the table heading applies in the particular regime listed in the left-most column; a "no" indicates the rule does not apply. (For example, a "yes" under the "without prior approval" heading indicates that the regime does not require the prior approval of rates [per rule 1] by the state regulatory agency, while a "no" denotes that it does.) A dash (—) indicates that either interpretation of the rule may apply; for example, a dash under the "deviations" column indicates that the regime may or may not permit deviations from bureau rates.

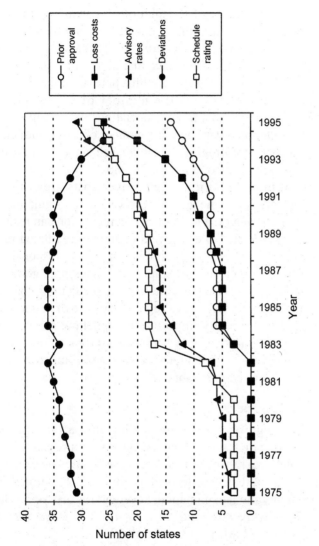

Figure 7.1 Regulatory Rules, 1975–95

fact that deviations are superfluous in those states that have adopted other components of workers' compensation insurance pricing deregulation.

The change in the number of jurisdictions for which each of the seven regulatory regimes in the full-set model were in effect over the 1975–1995 period is illustrated in Figure 7.2. These data also show that the workers' compensation insurance market has become increasingly deregulated. The number of states with a pure-administered-pricing regime has declined, as has the number of states with an administered-pricing regime that permits deviations (but requires prior approval of rates). On the other hand, the number of states with either form of loss-cost regulatory regime has increased since the loss-cost approach was first implemented in the early 1980s.

The effects of rate regulation on employer costs are critically dependent on the behavior of the agency responsible for regulating the insurance industry. As we noted in Table 6.1, deregulation can result in either higher or lower costs for employers relative to regulated rates, depending on whether the insurance commission is more responsive to the concerns of insurance carriers or employers. Lacking a good theory of regulatory behavior, we are unable to make predictions concerning the relationship between these regulatory rules/regimes and employer costs. It is critically important to somehow measure the extent to which the regulatory agency suppresses insurance rates or, on the other hand, the extent to which rates may exceed competitive market levels due to industry cartelization.

Regulatory stringency

In some of our regression equations we included a variable measuring the degree to which the regulatory agency suppresses (or elevates) rates. This variable, which we have termed *regulatory stringency*, is an index that was derived by dividing the lagged loss ratio for each state by the lagged national average for that year. State average loss ratios were obtained from *Best's DataBase Service, P/C/State/Line Report* (A.M. Best Company 1997 [and other years]). Recall that the inverse of the loss ratio is a rough measure of employer profitability; the higher the loss ratio, the less profitable the insurer. Lagged values measure profitability in the previous year.

197

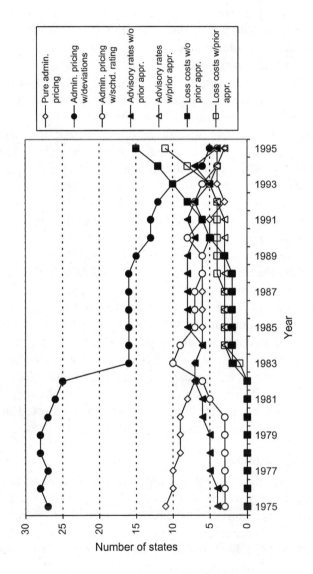

Figure 7.2 Regulatory Regimes, 1975–95

Because this index was calculated separately for each year in our study period and because it compares the loss ratio for each state to the national average, it is independent of the insurance cycle to the extent that the insurance cycle is nationally based. A high value for the regulatory stringency variable means that the state's loss ratio is above the national average. The interpretation of this variable differs between regulated and deregulated markets. In a regulated market (for example, an administered pricing environment), the loss ratio is a measure of the degree of rate suppression: the greater the extent of rate suppression, the higher the relative loss ratio. In addition, in the year in which a market is deregulated, this variable measures the degree of stringency in the regulated market in the year immediately prior to deregulation. For both reasons, we expect a negative relationship between regulatory stringency and employer costs in pure-administered-pricing jurisdictions.

Similar measures have been used in other studies of workers' compensation insurance rate regulation. Klein, Nordman, and Fritz (1993) and Danzon and Harrington (1998) used measures that combine the rate requested by the rating organization and the rate granted by the state insurance commission. Both sets of authors hypothesized that as the difference between these two rates increased, the more stringently the insurance commission suppressed rates. However, as Klein, Nordman, and Fritz pointed out, rate filings are often made strategically. In other words, the rate request is not necessarily equal to the rate the rating organization believes will yield the desired level of profitability, but instead reflects other factors such as the likelihood that the regulatory agency will grant the request. The stringency measure used in this study does not suffer from this weakness.

Hard-market dummy

In order to examine the relationship between the insurance cycle and the effect of deregulation on employer costs, we also included a dummy variable that identifies the existence of a "hard" insurance market nationally in our regression equations. For the purpose of our regression analyses, a *hard market* is defined as one in which the national combined ratio for the workers' compensation insurance line exceeded 100.[1] We thus concluded that the years 1975–1977 (inclusive) and 1984–1992 (inclusive) were hard-market periods. Our hard-market variable was assigned a value of 1 during these years and a value of 0 for all other years in our study.

By definition, a hard market is one in which insurers are, on average, experiencing losses. Recall from the discussion of the accounting model in Chapter 4 that, in our regression equations, dummy variables measure cost differences attributable to differences in profit and expense loadings. As such, we expect that the hard-market dummy variable will be negatively related to employer compensation costs, reflecting the reduction in insurers' profits. If the effects of a hard market are somehow exacerbated by rate regulation—if, for example, a regulatory lag in approving rates retards the insurers' price adjustments in response to changing market conditions—then we expect to find that cost reductions associated with a hard market will be greater in a regulated market than in an unregulated one.

EMPLOYER COSTS: REGRESSION RESULTS

As indicated, state regulatory environments are multidimensional, so that it is inappropriate to code regulatory approaches using a single binary variable to denote the presence or absence of "regulation." In addition, while regulatory rules may have different effects in different configurations, both economic theory and prior research offer little guidance concerning the expected impact of regulation or deregulation on employer costs generally or the relative impact of different regulatory regimes specifically. Consequently, our empirical strategy is to let the data guide our choice of regulatory model.[2]

The means and standard deviations of adjusted manual rates and net weekly costs in different regulatory environments (using our detailed rule/regime scheme described earlier) are shown in Table 7.2 for the different regulatory rules and for the full set of regulatory regimes. The data for rules suggest that, in general, the greater the extent of regulation, the lower the employers' costs. Specifically, the means of both adjusted manual rates and net weekly costs are lower when prior approval is required, when adherence to bureau rates or loss costs is required, when the bureau files fully developed rates rather than loss costs, and when schedule rating is not permitted. The devia-

Table 7.2 Employer Costs by Regulatory Environment[a]

Rule or regime	N	Adjusted manual rates ($/$100 payroll)	Net weekly costs ($ per employee)
Regulatory rule			
Prior approval required	813	2.1893 (1.176)	11.4916 (6.468)
No prior approval required	95	2.5389 (0.703)	13.7519 (3.850)
Adherence to bureau rates required	616	2.2061 (1.204)	11.6693 (6.628)
Advisory rates (adherence not required)	292	2.3213 (0.906)	12.1710 (5.017)
Bureau submits fully developed rates	780	2.1466 (1.150)	11.2816 (6.325)
Bureau submits loss costs only	128	2.8572 (0.704)	15.3685 (3.845)
Deviations not permitted	233	2.4475 (1.293)	13.2620 (7.315)
Deviations permitted	675	2.1231 (1.008)	11.0074 (5.348)
Schedule rating not permitted	617	2.1910 (1.206)	11.5459 (6.629)
Schedule rating permitted	291	2.3667 (0.875)	12.5224 (4.877)
Regulatory regime[b]			
Pure administered pricing	129	2.4128 (1.393)	13.1340 (7.919)
Administered pricing with deviations	364	2.0779 (1.089)	10.7008 (5.600)
Administered pricing with schedule rating	116	1.9739 (0.913)	10.5487 (5.275)
Advisory rates with prior approval	133	1.6754 (0.777)	8.2456 (4.071)
Advisory rates without prior approval	38	2.3964 (0.731)	12.5903 (3.680)

(continued)

Table 7.2 (continued)

Rule or regime	N	Adjusted manual rates ($/$100 payroll)	Net weekly costs ($ per employee)
Loss costs with prior approval	71	3.1918 (0.636)	16.5239 (3.720)
Loss costs without prior approval	57	2.6491 (0.667)	14.6478 (3.769)

[a] Values are means, with standard deviations in parentheses.

[b] The regulatory regimes in this panel are listed from top to bottom in order of our *a priori* expectations regarding the degree to which the statute provides for greater regulatory control, so that pure administered pricing is the most regulated statutory environment, while a loss-cost system that does not require prior approval is the most deregulated environment.

tions rule is the sole exception; that is, mean adjusted manual rates and net weekly costs are slightly lower in states that permit deviations from bureau rates than in states that do not.

Data for the regulatory regimes are less straightforward. The lowest costs are found in states where rating bureaus promulgate advisory rates and where insurers must obtain approval before implementing new rates. In these jurisdictions, the adjusted manual rate averages $1.68 per $100 of payroll and the net weekly costs are $8.25 per employee. The highest costs were found in loss-cost jurisdictions that require the prior approval of rates; in these states, adjusted manual rates per $100 of payroll and net weekly costs are $3.19 and $16.52, respectively.

It is difficult to draw conclusions from this simple comparison of means, because the incidence of these different regulatory environments has varied considerably over time. Administered pricing was more prevalent in the early years of our study period, when costs were generally lower, whereas loss-cost systems are a much more recent phenomenon. Taken at face value, these results imply that the decision making of state regulatory agencies about rate levels is more likely to be influenced by insurance consumers (i.e., employers) than by providers (i.e., insurers), since rates tend to be lower in more regulated environments.

Figures 7.3 and 7.4 display average adjusted manual rates and average net weekly costs, by year, for different regulatory regimes. The

Figure 7.3 Adjusted Manual Rates under Different Regulatory Regimes, 1975–95

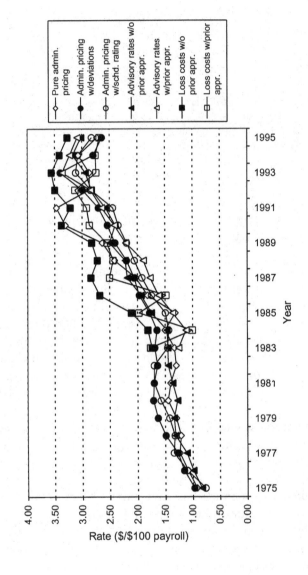

Figure 7.4 Net Weekly Costs under Different Regulatory Regimes, 1975–95

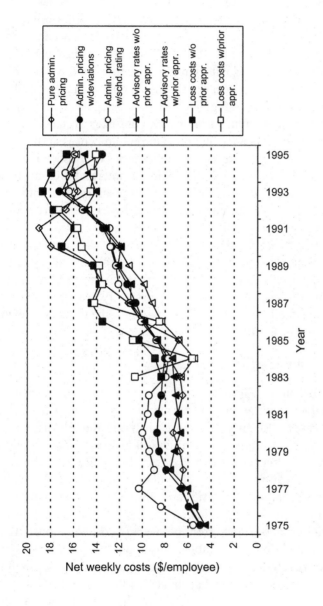

principal empirical regularity emerging from the data in these figures is that employers' relative costs associated with these regimes shift over time. For example, while loss-cost systems that do not require prior approval were relatively costly during the period between 1985 and 1990, costs in these states by 1995 (the end of the study period) were lower than in all other regulatory regimes as measured by the adjusted manual rate. Part of this cost differential is due to changes in the mix of states that fall into each regulatory regime category in any particular year. Due to the small number of observations in each category (particularly with respect to some categories in more recent years), there is a great deal of variability in these individual series over time. For similar reasons, it is important to be cautious in our interpretation of the relationship between employers' costs and the regulatory environment.

The fact that costs in one of the most highly regulated regimes (administered pricing with deviations) are approximately equal to those under the least regulated regime (loss-cost systems that do not require prior approval of rates) suggests that the regulatory environment does not affect costs or that other variables are equally important determinants. To control for the latter possibility, we estimated regression equations predicting costs as a function of the regulatory environment.

Regulatory Rules

As we previously indicated, we use variables representing five rules to characterize the regulatory environment for workers' compensation insurance. Results from eight different models are reported, each offering a different characterization of the regulatory environment. Data with respect to the impact of these rules on employer costs are presented under the heading "Regulatory Rules" in Tables 7.3 and 7.4. Table 7.3 reports elasticities and the associated absolute t-ratios from equations predicting adjusted manual rates, and Table 7.4 displays elasticities and t-ratios from net weekly cost equations. To simplify the presentation, these tables only report the coefficients and t-ratios for the regulatory-environment variables. (Results for the full set of regressors are presented in Appendix G, Tables G.1 and G.2. Unlike the data reported in Tables 7.3 and 7.4, which are estimated elasticities, the data in Tables G.1 and G.2, as well as the other appendix tables, are the untransformed regression coefficients.)

All models were estimated using data from the 45 jurisdictions that permit the private provision of compensation insurance, so that the sample size is 908 observations. All models were estimated using weighted least squares to control for problems arising from heteroscedasticity.

Each regulatory rule variable is coded so that the elasticity has a negative sign if deregulation results in reduced employer costs. As can be seen, the results are mixed, although the signs are relatively consistent between Tables 7.3 and 7.4.

The elasticities for the loss-cost variable in both the adjusted manual rates and net weekly costs equations are negative and statistically significant. Together, the loss-cost results in these two tables suggest that employer costs are around 11 percent lower in a more deregulated environment where the rating organization files loss costs rather than fully developed rates. This result is similar to that reported by Klein, Nordman, and Fritz (1993), who also found a negative (although statistically insignificant) relationship between loss-cost filing and the statewide loss ratio. On the other hand, Appel, McMurray, and Mulvaney (1992) found an insignificant positive relationship between loss-cost filing and adjusted manual rates for their sample.

Likewise, the data indicate that employer costs in jurisdictions that do not require prior approval of rates are around 5 percent lower than costs in states that require approval, indicating once again that deregulation reduces costs. This finding is also similar to the results of Klein, Nordman, and Fritz (1993), who found a significant negative relationship between prior approval and average loss ratios. On the other hand, Tables 7.3 and 7.4 show that the elasticities for the schedule-rating variable are statistically significant and positive, suggesting that employer costs are higher where insurance carriers are permitted to use schedule-rating plans for individual carriers. Specifically, costs are 8–9 percent higher in those jurisdictions that permit schedule rating. Finally, the results for deviations and advisory rates are generally unreliable (that is, the estimates are not statistically different from zero at conventional levels), implying that these variables have little effect on employer costs.

As we previously indicated, the regulatory rules specification ignores interaction effects among various combinations of these regu-

Table 7.3 Regression Coefficients for Adjusted Manual Rates under Different Regulatory Rules and Regimes[a]

Regulatory rules		Model 1[b]		Model 2		Model 3	
W/o prior approval	-0.0521* (1.71)	Admin. pricing w/dev.	0.0608* (1.90)	Loss costs w/prior appr.	-0.0193 (0.59)	Partial compet.	-0.0069 (0.20)
Adv. rates	0.0357 (1.18)	Admin. pricing w/sched. rating	0.0826** (2.05)	Loss costs w/o prior appr.	-0.1644*** (5.75)	Open compet.	0.0441 (1.51)
Loss costs	-0.1112*** (3.83)	Adv. rates w/prior appr.	0.0860** (2.22)				
Deviations	-0.002 (0.11)	Adv. rates w/o prior appr.	0.1825*** (3.23)				
Sched. rating	0.0790*** (2.89)	Loss costs w/prior appr.	0.0552 (1.26)				
		Loss costs w/o prior appr.	-0.1041*** (2.82)				

(continued)

Table 7.3 (continued)

Model 4		Model 5		Model 6		Model 7	
Admin. pricing w/dev. or sched. rating	0.041 (1.38)	Var. from bur. rates w/prior appr.	0.0714** (2.44)	Admin. pricing w/dev. or sched. rating	0.043 (1.43)	Admin. pricing w/dev.	0.047 (1.48)
Adv. rates	0.1024*** (2.74)	Adv. rates w/o prior appr.	0.1657*** (3.25)	Adv. rates or loss costs	0.023 (0.71)	Admin. pricing w/sched. rating	0.010 (0.27)
Loss costs	−0.045 (1.32)	Loss costs w/prior appr.	0.056 (1.27)			Adv. rates w/prior appr.	0.0680* (1.74)
		Loss costs w/o prior appr.	−0.1081*** (2.98)			Loss costs w/o prior appr.	−0.009 (0.25)

[a] Coefficients are followed by t-ratios in parentheses. *** = significant at the 1% level; ** = significant at the 5% level; * = significant at the 10% level.

[b] Model numbers correspond to those in Table 7.1.

208

Table 7.4 Regressions Predicting Net Weekly Costs under Different Regulatory Rules and Regimes[a]

Regulatory rules		Model 1[b]		Model 2		Model 3	
W/o prior appr.	−0.0557* (1.81)	Admin. pricing w/dev.	0.0796** (2.44)	Loss costs w/prior appr.	−0.0167 (0.51)	Partial compet.	0.0065 (0.19)
Advisory rates	0.0196 (0.65)	Admin. pricing w/sched. rating	0.1165*** (2.81)	Loss costs w/o prior appr.	−0.1639*** (5.66)	Open compet.	0.0620** (2.09)
Loss costs	−0.0100*** (3.38)	Adv. rates, w/prior appr.	0.0926** (2.36)				
Deviations	0.0093 (0.45)	Adv. rates w/o prior appr.	0.1992*** (3.46)				
Sched. rating	0.0903*** 3.25	Loss costs w/prior appr.	0.0739* (1.65)				
		Loss costs w/o prior appr.	−0.0942** (2.51)				

(continued)
(continued)

Table 7.4 (continued)

	Model 4		Model 5		Model 6		Model 7	
Admin. pricing w/dev. or sched. rating	0.0624**	(2.05)	Var. from bur. rates w/prior appr.	0.0899*** (3.01)	Admin. pricing w/dev. or sched. rating	0.0644** (2.08)	Admin. pricing w/dev.	0.0648** (1.99)
Adv. rates	0.1082***	(2.85)	Advisory rates w/o prior appr.	0.1747*** (3.37)	Adv. rates or loss costs	−0.0330 (0.99)	Admin. pricing w/sched. rating	0.0413 (1.08)
Loss costs	−0.0326	(0.93)	Loss costs w/prior appr.	0.0752* (1.68)			Adv. rates w/prior appr.	0.0744* (1.88)
			Loss costs w/o prior appr.	−0.0967*** (2.61)			Loss costs w/o prior appr.	0.0050 (0.14)

[a] Coefficients are followed by *t*-ratios in parentheses. *** = significant at the 1% level; ** = significant at the 5% level; * = significant at the 10% level.

[b] Model numbers correspond to those in Table 7.1.

latory rules. It is likely that these rules have different effects when they appear in different combinations with other rules. For instance, requiring an insurer to adhere to fully developed rates may very well have a different impact on employer costs than requiring adherence to the rating organization's loss-cost estimates. To examine these potential interaction effects, we estimated additional regression equations, using dummies to represent various regulatory rule configurations or regimes.

Regulatory Regimes

Seven additional specifications (summarized in Table 7.1) were estimated using different combinations of the regulatory rules, and these regression results are presented in Tables 7.3 and 7.4. If deregulation is associated with a reduction in employer costs, we would expect the elasticities associated with each regime to be negatively signed. Moreover, the regime categories in these tables are ordered, according to our *a priori* expectations, from "least deregulated" to "most deregulated" (from top to bottom), so that we would also expect to find an ordered relationship for the associated elasticities.

Cox tests (data not shown) comparing the regulatory-rules specifications with model 1 in Tables 7.3 and 7.4 reveal that the latter are preferred for both the net cost and adjusted manual rate regressions (Greene 1993, pp. 223–225).[3] In other words, regression specifications with the full set of regulatory regime dummies are superior to the equation including regulatory rule dummies. This suggests that there are significant interaction effects among regulatory rules. This is also evident from a comparison of coefficients for loss-cost regimes in models 1 through 7 with the coefficient for the loss costs in the regulatory rule specification. As previously noted, costs are negatively related to the loss-cost rule, while in most of the regulatory regime models, adjusted manual rates and net weekly costs under loss-cost regimes that require prior approval are not significantly different from those under a pure-administered-pricing regime.

A comparison of the results for the different regulatory regimes paints a mixed picture of the impact of deregulation on employer costs. The data indicate that employers in loss-cost-without-prior-approval jurisdictions experience costs that are 10–16 percent lower than those in pure-administered-pricing jurisdictions. However, other forms of deregulation apparently either do not affect or actually increase employer costs.

Our regression results suggest that inconsistent findings among studies examining the effects of workers' compensation insurance deregulation are, at least partially, due to differences in the characterization of the regulatory environment in these studies. For example, model 2, which finds that deregulation reduces employer costs, is similar to that used by Barkume and Ruser (1997) and Carroll and Kaestner (1995), each of whom also found that deregulation was associated with lower injury rates and costs. On the other hand, the regulatory environment simulated by model 3 is similar to that employed by Schmidle (1994), who failed to find a consistent, statistically significant relationship between costs and his open competition and partial competition measures.

Models 2 through 7 are restricted versions of the more general model 1. For example, model 2 assumes that coefficients on the dummies representing the first four regimes of model 1 are equal. As such, hypothesis tests of these linear restrictions may be used to select a preferred model. These tests reveal that there are no significant differences between administered-pricing jurisdictions that permit deviations and administered-pricing regimes that permit schedule rating. They further reveal no significant differences between states that do not permit deviations or schedule rating and states that require prior approval of advisory rates. Consequently, model 5 was chosen as the preferred specification. Subsequent analyses will examine the effects of regulation using this model exclusively.

The results for model 5 suggest that there are differences between the effects of a partial deregulation of the workers' compensation insurance market (such as the adoption of deviations or schedule rating) and more comprehensive reform (such as the adoption of loss-cost filing). Specifically, partial deregulation—at least in the form of advisory rates and no prior approval—is apparently associated with higher employer costs, while the adoption of a loss-cost system that does not require prior approval of rates substantially reduces employer costs. This is a puzzling result. If partial deregulation increases costs relative to a regulated market, why would more comprehensive deregulation have the opposite effect?

As we have seen, these two forms of deregulation (partial and comprehensive) were generally adopted at different points in the insurance cycle. It is possible that insurance cycle effects may explain these anomalous results. Specifically, price deregulation during a hard market when rates are likely to be suppressed by the state insurance commission may be associated with higher employer costs, while deregulation in a soft market may be associated with a cost reduction. Accordingly, in the next section we examine whether there is variation in the effects of deregulation on employer costs at different stages of the insurance cycle.

Employer Costs and the Insurance Cycle

We used the national average of a loss ratio measure to examine the relationship between the insurance cycle and the effect of deregulation on employer costs, using a dummy variable that is coded as 1 when the combined ratio for workers' compensation insurance in the United States is greater than 100, and as 0 otherwise. By this definition, the years 1975–1977 (inclusive) and 1984–1992 (inclusive) were designated as hard-market periods. This variable was used as a regressor and was also interacted with the regulatory regime dummies.

If rate suppression by regulatory agencies is greater during a hard market than during a soft one, we expect that when entered separately, the dummy variable indicating the hard stage of the insurance cycle will be negatively related to costs. (The noninteracted dummy captures the effect of a hard market under a pure-administered-pricing regime.) In addition, since insurers should be more responsive to market forces in a deregulated environment and since a hard market is one in which demand exceeds supply, then we expect that interaction terms representing various deregulated regimes in a hard market will also be positively related to employer costs.

The results of the regression equations that predict costs as a function of the regulatory environment and of the stage of the insurance market are presented in Table 7.5. Because the insurance cycle stage is defined by time, the hard-market variable is perfectly collinear with the year dummies; thus, the time dummies had to be dropped from these regression equations.

Table 7.5 Regression Coefficients for Predicting Costs as a Function of Regulatory Environment and Stage of the Insurance Cycle[a]

Variable	Adjusted manual rates	Net weekly costs
ln(Cash benefits)	0.1900***	0.2240***
	(4.07)	(4.79)
Medical benefits	0.0003***	0.0003***
	(17.56)	(18.62)
ln(Injury)	0.8982***	0.9318***
	(11.02)	(11.41)
Union density	−0.0425***	−0.0388***
	(12.94)	(11.80)
PPD percentage	0.0108***	0.0104***
	(6.33)	(6.06)
Covered employment	0.0140*	0.0189**
	(1.83)	(2.46)
Competitive state fund	0.2094***	0.2215***
	(3.62)	(3.82)
Hard market	−0.0597**	−0.0323
	(2.33)	(1.26)
Var. from bureau rates w/prior appr.	0.1793***	0.1950***
	(5.02)	(5.45)
Var. from bureau rates w/prior appr. × hard market	−0.1365***	−0.1413***
	(4.43)	(4.58)
Adv. rates w/o prior appr.	0.2145***	0.2165***
	(3.19)	(3.21)
Adv. rates w/o prior appr. × hard market	0.0602	0.0659
	(0.99)	(1.08)
Loss costs w/prior appr.	0.0549	0.0808
	(0.99)	(1.46)
Loss costs w/prior appr. × hard market	0.0618	0.0410
	(0.95)	(0.63)
Loss costs w/o prior appr.	−0.1482***	−0.1265***
	(3.02)	(2.57)
Loss costs w/o prior appr. × hard market	0.1538***	0.1372**
	(2.86)	(2.55)

(continued)

Table 7.5 (continued)

Variable	Adjusted manual rates	Net weekly costs
State dummies	Yes	Yes
Year dummies	No	No
Adjusted R^2	0.8892	0.8993

[a] Coefficients are followed by t-ratios in parentheses. *** = significant at the 1% level; ** = significant at the 5% level; * = significant at the 10% level.

The regression results reported in this table are partially consistent with our prior expectations. The hard-market dummy has a negative sign (which is statistically significant at the 5 percent level in the adjusted manual rate equation), indicating that employer costs are lower during a hard market. This may seem to be a surprising result, since a hard market is characterized by excessive demand relative to supply, which tends to drive up prices. However, recall that these regression estimates control for loss costs, so the hard-market dummy measures the extent to which the loading factor—which includes the insurer's profit margin as well as marketing and underwriting expenses—is affected by the hard market. Because expenses are relatively fixed, these results suggest that insurer's profits shrink during the hard stage of an insurance cycle, which would occur if regulators suppressed rates below competitive levels.

The results in Table 7.5 show that one of the interaction terms (hard market in states that allow variations from bureau rates) is significantly different from zero. This indicates that the effect of this type of deregulation partially depends on the stage of the insurance cycle. Consequently, separate estimates of regulation effects were made for both hard and soft markets.[4] These estimates, which are equivalent to the cost difference between the associated regulatory regime and pure administered pricing in a hard versus a soft market, are reported in Table 7.6. The results indicate that in a soft market, adjusted manual rates are 19.64 percent higher under a regime that allows variation from bureau rates (deviations, schedule rating, or advisory rates) subject to prior approval than they are under a pure-administered-pricing system. However, in a hard market, rates under this form of deregulation are not statistically different from rates under pure administered pric-

Table 7.6 Effects of Regulatory Regimes and the Insurance Cycle[a]

Regulatory regime	Adjusted manual rates	Net weekly costs
Regulatory regime effects in a hard market		
Var. from bureau rates w/prior appr.	0.0437 (1.19)	0.0552 (1.49)
Adv. rates w/o prior appr.	0.3161*** (4.82)	0.3263*** (4.94)
Loss costs w/prior appr.	0.1238* (1.87)	0.1296* (1.95)
Loss costs w/o prior appr.	0.0056 (0.10)	0.0108 (0.20)
Regulatory regime effects in a soft market		
Var. from bureau rates w/prior appr.	0.1964*** (5.02)	0.2153*** (5.45)
Adv. rates w/o prior appr.	0.2392*** (3.19)	0.2417*** (3.21)
Loss costs w/prior appr.	0.0564 (0.99)	0.0842 (1.46)
Loss costs w/o prior appr.	–0.1377*** (3.02)	–0.1188*** (2.57)
Effects of a hard market under different regulatory regimes		
Pure admin. pricing	–0.0579*** (2.33)	–0.0317 (1.26)
Var. from bureau rates w/prior appr.	–0.1782*** (11.04)	–0.1593*** (9.75)
Adv. rates w/o prior appr.	0.0006 (0.01)	0.0342 (0.60)
Loss costs w/prior appr.	0.0022 (0.04)	0.0088 (0.15)
Loss costs w/o prior appr.	0.0987** (1.99)	0.1107** (2.21)

[a] Coefficients are followed by t-ratios in parentheses. *** = significant at the 1% level; ** = significant at the 5% level; * = significant at the 10% level.

ing. A possible explanation for this difference is that under the variations-from-bureau rates-without-prior-approval regime, the regulatory agency continues to hold rates down during a hard market but allows the insurer to increase rates relative to pure administered pricing during the soft phase of the cycle.

Similar to our previous results, the data on regime effects show that more moderate forms of deregulation tend to have a positive impact on employer costs, suggesting once again that partial deregulation is associated with higher insurance prices. The coefficient on the loss-cost-with-prior-approval variable indicates that the adoption of this type of deregulation has little or no effect on employer costs relative to pure-administered-pricing regimes, while loss-cost systems with prior approval tend to reduce costs in the soft (but not the hard) phase of the insurance cycle. Once again, we are left with the anomalous result that the most unregulated regime has lower compensation insurance prices relative to pure administered pricing, while costs are higher under some milder forms of deregulation.

Table 7.6 also reports estimates of the effect of a hard market on employer costs under different regulatory regimes, i.e., the cost differential between a hard and a soft market under each regime (although the net weekly cost result is not statistically significant). These data show that adjusted manual rates and net weekly costs per employee are 5.79 percent and 3.17 percent lower, respectively, during a hard market than during a soft one under a system of pure administered pricing (although the net weekly cost result is not statistically significant). This difference is even more marked for regimes that allow variation from bureau rates but still require prior approval. For these regimes, costs are 16 to 18 percent lower under a hard market than under a soft one. These results are consistent with the hypothesis that regulatory agencies are more likely to suppress rates during a hard market, while during a soft market, regulatory rate suppression is not binding because insurers are likely to cut rates in the face of reduced demand. The data simply indicate that cuts are less dramatic in less-regulated environments.

In more-deregulated environments (i.e., lost-cost systems without prior approval), a hard market actually leads to higher rates. This result is consistent with the idea that in a deregulated regime, insurers more readily respond to market forces. Recall that in a hard market, the demand for insurance outstrips the supply, a condition that should be associated with higher prices.

Nonetheless, this analysis fails to explain why partial deregulation appears to have a greater impact on insurance prices than more radical reform; we continue to find this result after controlling for the stage of the insurance cycle.

Employer Costs and Regulatory Stringency

As we noted in Chapter 6, the impact of deregulation will vary depending on the behavior of the state agency responsible for regulating the workers' compensation insurance market. If the agency follows a rate suppression strategy, then deregulation will result in higher employer costs for workers' compensation insurance. On the other hand, if the agency effectively creates a cartel in which insurers are permitted to pursue oligopolistic pricing policies, then premium rates will drop following deregulation. Thus, differences in regulatory strategies among state insurance commissions may explain the inconsistent results obtained in our previous analyses.

To control for potential variation in regulatory strategy across jurisdictions and over time, we reestimated our regression models after including a measure of rate suppression, a variable we termed *regulatory stringency*. Recall that this variable is an index of the size of the state's lagged loss ratio relative to the national average.

Under pure administered pricing, the regulatory-stringency variable measures the extent to which the state insurance commission suppresses rates. As such, higher values of this variable indicate greater rate suppression, so it should be negatively related to employer costs. However, in states where the insurance market has been truly deregulated, the regulatory-stringency variable reflects the impact of prior regulation (since it is lagged one year). Alternatively, the regulatory-stringency variable reflects underlying differences in costs among states that are uncontrolled by other variables in the regression equation and that are necessarily unrelated to any regulatory rate suppression.

In other words, the value for the stringency variable for a state in which the insurance market was deregulated during the previous year indicates the extent to which insurers suppressed rates prior to deregulation. The higher the value, the greater the degree of rate suppression, and we expect that the greater the extent of rate suppression during the previous year, the higher that prices will rise following deregulation. Similarly, if insurer costs are high relative to the national average in an unregulated market, insurers are expected to raise prices, a response that is either unavailable or somehow restricted in a regulated environment. For both reasons, we hypothesize that costs will be positively related to the regulatory-stringency variable under deregulated regimes.

As was the case for the hard-market dummy, the regulatory-stringency variable entered each equation separately and was also interacted with the regulatory-environment variables. The results from this regression are reported in Table 7.7. The data indicate that regulatory stringency (as measured by the loss ratio) is negatively related to employer costs, as predicted. In addition, stringency appears to have an important moderating influence on regulatory regime effects. After controlling for stringency, the coefficients for all deregulation dummies are negatively signed and statistically significant, except for "advisory rates without prior approval," which is not statistically different from zero. In other words, the more stringently regulators suppress rates during the previous year, the smaller the subsequent cost reduction due to deregulation. This latter result suggests that the positive relationship between partial deregulation and employer costs reported in Tables 7.3 and 7.4 may be due to differences in the extent of pre-deregulation rate suppression.

Table 7.8 presents estimates of the effects of the different forms of deregulation on employer costs, relative to pure administered pricing, under different severities of regulatory stringency. In other words, these coefficients measure the cost differential, in percentage terms, between the corresponding deregulated environments and pure administered pricing. Low stringency indicates that the lagged loss ratio index is one standard deviation below the mean, medium stringency means that the state-specific lagged loss ratio is equal to the national average, and high stringency denotes a lagged loss ratio that is one standard deviation above the mean. The pattern of these effects is consistent with our expectations: the impact of deregulation depends on the degree of regulatory stringency. Several empirical regularities emerge.

Table 7.7 Regression Coefficients for Costs as a Function of the Regulatory Regime and Regulatory Stringency[a]

Variable	Adjusted manual rates	Net weekly costs
ln(Cash benefits)	0.1223***	0.1489***
	(2.92)	(3.51)
Medical benefits	0.0001***	0.0001***
	(5.10)	(5.38)
ln(Injury)	0.9088***	0.8609***
	(9.83)	(9.19)
Union density	−0.0006	0.0024
	(0.15)	(0.58)
PPD percentage	0.0111***	0.0109***
	(6.79)	(6.56)
Covered employment	0.0100	0.0132**
	(1.51)	(1.96)
Competitive state fund	0.2299***	0.2374***
	(4.39)	(4.47)
Regulatory stringency	−0.3155***	−0.3079***
	(3.88)	(3.74)
Var. from bureau rates w/prior appr.	−0.3512***	−0.3333***
	(3.58)	(3.35)
Var. from bureau rates w/prior appr. × regul. stringency	0.4045***	0.4038***
	(4.48)	(4.41)
Adv. rates w/o prior appr.	0.0921	−0.0273
	(0.41)	(0.12)
Adv. rates w/o prior appr. × regul. stringency	0.0431	0.1744
	(0.19)	(0.76)
Loss costs w/prior appr.	−0.3352**	−0.3337**
	(2.17)	(2.13)
Loss costs w/prior appr. × regul. stringency	0.3637***	0.3792***
	(2.65)	(2.73)
Loss costs w/o prior appr.	−0.5760***	−0.5662***
	(3.61)	(3.50)
Loss costs w/o prior appr. × regul. stringency	0.4524***	0.4536***
	(2.94)	(2.90)
State dummies	Yes	Yes
Year dummies	Yes	Yes
Adj. R^2	0.9202	0.9258

[a] Coefficients are followed by t-ratios in parentheses. *** = significant at the 1% level; ** = significant at the 5% level; * = significant at the 10% level.

Table 7.8 Effects on Employer Costs of Regulatory Regimes under Different Conditions of Regulatory Stringency[a]

Regulatory regime	Regulatory stringency		
	Low	Medium	High
Adjusted manual rates			
Var. from bureau rates w/prior appr.	−0.0272 (0.78)	0.0547* (1.88)	0.1436*** (4.26)
Adv. rates w/o prior appr.	0.1349** (1.99)	0.1447*** (2.85)	0.1546** (2.13)
Loss costs w/prior appr.	−0.0433 (0.77)	0.0289 (0.65)	0.1065** (2.23)
Loss costs w/o prior appr.	−0.1927*** (4.32)	−0.1163*** (3.23)	−0.0326 (0.68)
Net weekly costs			
Var. from bureau rates w/prior appr.	−0.0102 (0.28)	0.0731** (2.45)	0.1633*** (4.74)
Adv. rates w/o prior appr.	0.1187* (1.75)	0.1584*** (3.06)	0.1996*** (2.66)
Loss costs w/prior appr.	−0.0299 (0.52)	0.0466 (1.02)	0.1290*** (2.64)
Loss costs w/o prior appr.	−0.1840*** (4.05)	−0.1065*** (2.90)	−0.0216 (0.44)

[a] Coefficients are followed by t-ratios in parentheses. *** = significant at the 1% level; ** = significant at the 5% level; * = significant at the 10% level.

First, as we found previously, under most regulatory stringency scenarios, employer costs are lower under pure administered pricing than under a deregulated regime, suggesting that regulators are primarily influenced by employers rather than carriers and therefore suppress workers' compensation insurance rates relative to their competitive levels. Second, the impact of deregulation on employer costs is more positive (or less negative) at higher levels of regulatory stringency, implying that regulatory agency behavior is an important cost determinant, as expected. Interestingly, where regulatory stringency is low, insurance costs are reduced under all deregulated regimes relative to pure administered pricing (with the exception of systems where rating bureaus file advisory rates that are not subject to prior approval).

Finally, there is a rough correspondence between our *a priori* ranking of the restrictiveness of the statutory regime and the cost differential under all stringency conditions. With the exception of the advisory-rates-without-prior-approval regime, the regulatory cost differential shrinks as the statute becomes less restrictive until it becomes significantly negative for the most deregulated environment. This suggests that a more restrictive regime can provide the regulatory agency with more effective tools that can be used to suppress rates.

Our estimates of the effect of regulatory stringency on employer costs for different regulatory systems are presented in Table 7.9. The results in this table are also consistent with our hypotheses. The relationship between employer costs and stringency is significantly negative for pure administered pricing, significantly positive for regimes that allow variation from bureau rates subject to prior approval, and not statistically different from zero for other jurisdictions. These results imply that under pure administered pricing, regulators are able to suppress rates. However, when the insurance market is less regulated, insurer pricing is either unaffected by the loss ratio or, in the case of regimes that allow variation from bureau rates subject to prior approval, insurers increase rates subsequent to a drop in profit margins (as measured by the lagged loss ratio).

Importantly, the results in Tables 7.8 and 7.9 offer an explanation for the difference between the effects of partial and comprehensive

Table 7.9 Effects of Regulatory Stringency on Employer Costs under Different Regulatory Regimes[a]

Regulatory regime	Adjusted manual rates	Net weekly costs
Pure admin. pricing	–0.3155***	–0.3079***
	(3.88)	(3.74)
Var. from bureau rates w/prior appr.	0.0889*	0.0959*
	(1.65)	(1.75)
Adv. rates w/o prior appr.	–0.2724	–0.1335
	(1.29)	(0.63)
Loss costs w/prior appr.	0.0482	0.0713
	(0.43)	(0.62)
Loss costs w/o prior appr.	0.1369	0.1457
	(1.01)	(1.06)

[a] Coefficients are followed by t-ratios in parentheses. *** = significant at the 1% level; ** = significant at the 5% level; * = significant at the 10% level.

deregulation on workers' compensation costs. Specifically, these results imply that partial deregulation has asymmetric effects on employer costs, while the impact of comprehensive deregulation is more symmetric. That is, partial deregulation removes price ceilings imposed by regulatory agencies without substantially affecting downward competitive pressure, so that when regulatory restrictions are removed under conditions of low stringency, prices do not fall relative to their levels under pure administered pricing. A possible explanation for this asymmetry is that under partial deregulation, the rating bureau continues to act as a cartelizing force pushing rates up above competitive levels. On the other hand, insurance prices under a loss-costs-without-prior-approval system are much more responsive to market forces.

Employer Costs, the Insurance Cycle, and Regulatory Stringency

The regression results presented in the previous section suggest that the effect of deregulation on employer costs is dependent upon the strategy of the regulatory agency prior to deregulation. Where insurance commissions suppress rates (resulting in high loss ratios), then deregulation is associated with higher costs as insurers raise rates to more profitable levels (or, in the case of loss-cost regimes without prior approval, deregulation leads to smaller rate reductions). The opposite is true if rates are not suppressed under regulation; in this case, insurers will reduce rates following deregulation—at least in the most deregulated environment. Results from Tables 7.5 and 7.6 also suggest that the effect of these regulatory strategies on employer costs may differ depending on the stage of the insurance cycle.

In this section, we examine the effect of the interaction of regulatory stringency and market conditions (stage of the insurance cycle) on the relationship between insurance price regulation and employer costs. Specifically, we present regression results predicting employer costs as a function of a series of terms that interact the hard-market dummy with the regulatory-stringency variable, the hard-market dummy with the regulatory-environment dummies, and all three variables together. These regressions, which are reported in Appendix Table G.3, include the full set of control variables (with the exception of year dummies, which were excluded due to collinearity with the hard-market dummy).

Table 7.10 presents estimates of the effects of regulatory stringency and of the insurance cycle ("Effect of a Hard Market") in different regulatory environments per these regression models. The first data set shows that, in a hard market, the regulatory stringency variable has a consistent (negative) relationship with employer costs under pure administered pricing. There is some suggestion that this reduction in costs associated with stringency is more marked during the soft phase of the insurance cycle than during the hard phase. Interestingly, there is no apparent relationship between stringency and costs in variations-from-bureau-rates-with-prior-approval jurisdictions when these additional controls are introduced, suggesting that the impact of stringency on costs under this regime (see Table 7.9) is solely attributable to cycle effects.

The data also indicate that the insurance cycle has different effects on employer costs under different regulatory regimes. Similar to our previous results, costs are lower in a hard market relative to a soft one in jurisdictions where the statute provides regulators with greater control over rates. However, under more comprehensive deregulation, while these costs appear to be lower in a hard market, the differences are not statistically significant. This provides further evidence that regulatory agencies suppress rates in regulated markets, while prices in a deregulated market environment are more responsive to market forces.

Our estimates of the effects of deregulation relative to pure administered pricing under three conditions of regulatory stringency, during both the hard and soft stages of the insurance cycle, are reported in Table 7.11. The values in this table are estimates of the percentage cost differential between the regulatory regime listed in the row headings and pure administered pricing (under different conditions of regulatory stringency and during different stages of the insurance cycle). For example, these results show that under conditions of low stringency in a hard market, adjusted manual rates in loss-cost systems that do not require prior approval of rates are 31.52 percent lower than adjusted manual rates in pure-administered-pricing jurisdictions.

Overall, the results in Table 7.11 are consistent with prior expectations, as well as with the results of our previous analyses. Once again, the estimates suggest that, under most scenarios, costs are higher in

Table 7.10 Effects of Regulatory Stringency or Hard Markets on Employer Costs under Different Regulatory Regimes[a]

Regulatory regime	Adjusted manual rates	Net weekly costs
Effect of regulatory stringency in a hard market		
Pure admin. pricing	–0.2621**	–0.2086*
	(2.51)	(1.93)
Var. from bureau rates w/prior appr.	–0.0377	–0.0157
	(0.49)	(0.20)
Adv. rates w/o prior appr.	–0.4998***	–0.4780**
	(2.66)	(2.49)
Loss costs w/prior appr.	–0.1627	–0.1333
	(0.80)	(0.64)
Loss costs w/o prior appr.	0.0867	0.0190
	(0.38)	(0.09)
Effect of regulatory stringency in a soft market		
Pure admin. pricing	–0.3805***	–0.3785***
	(3.96)	(3.92)
Var. from bureau rates w/prior appr.	–0.1043	–0.0960
	(1.36)	(1.24)
Adv. rates w/o prior appr.	–0.1055	0.1828
	(0.21)	(0.31)
Loss costs w/prior appr.	–0.2150	–0.2127
	(1.48)	(1.45)
Loss costs w/o prior appr.	0.6500**	0.7199**
	(2.33)	(2.52)
Effect of a hard market		
Pure admin. pricing	–0.0717***	–0.0439*
	(2.90)	(1.74)
Var. from bureau rates w/prior appr.	–0.3082**	–0.3382***
	(2.30)	(2.57)
Adv. rates w/o prior appr.	–0.1661	–0.2021
	(1.08)	(1.33)
Loss costs w/prior appr.	–0.1510	–0.2025
	(0.96)	(1.33)
Loss costs w/o prior appr.	–0.0394	–0.0903
	(0.24)	(0.57)

[a] Coefficients are followed by t-ratios in parentheses. *** = significant at the 1% level; ** = significant at the 5% level; * = significant at the 10% level.

Table 7.11 Effects of Regulatory Stringency and the Insurance Cycle on Employer Costs under Different Regulatory Regimes[a]

Regulatory regime	Regulatory stringency		
	Low	Medium	High
Adj. manual rates in a hard market			
Var. from bureau rates w/prior appr.	0.0813	0.1641***	0.2532***
	(1.55)	(4.13)	(5.41)
Adv. rates w/o prior appr.	0.1078	0.1923**	0.2832*
	(0.88)	(2.47)	(1.72)
Loss costs w/prior appr.	−0.0180	0.0296	0.0796
	(0.24)	(0.51)	(1.24)
Loss costs w/o prior appr.	−0.3152***	−0.1670***	0.0134
	(5.00)	(3.67)	(0.21)
Adj. manual rates in a soft market			
Var. from bureau rates w/prior appr.	−0.0201	0.0333	0.0897*
	(0.45)	(0.89)	(1.80)
Adv. rates w/o prior appr.	0.3789***	0.2757***	0.1803**
	(4.14)	(4.23)	(1.96)
Loss costs w/prior appr.	0.0937	0.1217*	0.1504*
	(0.99)	(1.77)	(1.92)
Loss costs w/o prior appr.	−0.0497	0.0268	0.1095
	(0.73)	(0.48)	(1.35)
Net weekly costs in a hard market			
Var. from bureau rates w/prior appr.	0.0984*	0.1839***	0.2761***
	(1.86)	(4.58)	(5.83)
Adv. rates w/o prior appr.	0.0656	0.2120***	0.3785**
	(0.55)	(2.69)	(2.20)
Loss costs w/prior appr.	0.0108	0.0597	0.1111*
	(0.14)	(1.02)	(1.70)
Loss costs w/o prior appr.	−0.3082***	−0.1520***	0.0395
	(4.85)	(3.30)	(0.62)
Net weekly costs in a soft market			
Var. from bureau rates w/prior appr.	−0.0010	0.0436	0.0901*
	(0.02)	(1.15)	(1.80)
Adv. rates w/o prior appr.	0.3997***	0.2880***	0.1851**
	(4.32)	(4.38)	(2.00)

(continued)

Table 7.11 (continued)

	Regulatory stringency		
Regulatory regime	Low	Medium	High
Loss costs w/prior appr.	0.1053	0.1256*	0.1462*
	(1.10)	(1.82)	(1.87)
Loss costs w/o prior appr.	–0.0232	0.0275	0.0808
	(0.33)	(0.49)	(1.00)

[a] Coefficients are followed by *t*-ratios in parentheses. *** = significant at the 1% level; ** = significant at the 5% level; * = significant at the 10% level.

partially deregulated environments than under pure administered pricing. Similarly, the relationship between regulatory stringency and the regulated/deregulated cost differential is also consistent with prior expectations and previous results. As hypothesized, the cost differential in most instances becomes more positive (less negative) as regulatory stringency increases (as the extent of regulatory rate suppression increases).

Predicted Employer Costs

Table 7.12 presents cost predictions based on the regression results reported in Table 7.7. With the exception of the regulatory regime, all independent variables retained their actual values; that is, the predictions were made assuming that the values of the control variables were identical to their estimated sample values.

The first data column in Table 7.12 reports the actual costs for each regulatory regime listed in the row headings. The remaining columns report predicted costs if the state changed regulatory regimes from that listed in the row heading to that listed in the "New regime" column headings. For example, the table shows that employers under pure-administered-pricing regimes actually paid average adjusted manual rates equal to $1.46 per $100 of payroll or net weekly costs of $7.68 per employee. If these pure-administered-pricing states adopted a regime whereby the regulatory agency permitted variations from bureau rates but continued to require prior approval, employers would pay, on average, an adjusted manual rate of $1.57 per $100 of payroll or net weekly costs equal to $8.25 per employee. This amounts to a

Table 7.12 Predicted Costs under Different Assumed Regulatory Regimes

Current regulatory regime	Actual costs	New regime				
		Pure admin. pricing	Var. from bureau rates w/prior appr.	Adv. rates w/o prior appr.	Loss costs w/prior appr.	Loss costs w/o prior appr.
Adjusted manual rates ($/$100 payroll)						
Pure admin. pricing	1.46	1.51	1.57	1.72	1.54	1.32
Var. from bureau rates w/prior appr.	1.67	1.57	1.65	1.80	1.61	1.39
Adv. rates w/o prior appr.	2.10	2.10	2.20	2.40	2.15	1.84
Loss costs w/prior appr.	3.10	2.98	3.20	3.42	3.12	2.69
Loss costs w/o prior appr.	2.49	2.67	2.87	3.06	2.80	2.41
Net weekly costs ($/employee)						
Pure admin. pricing	7.68	7.72	8.25	8.93	8.05	6.86
Var. from bureau rates w/prior appr.	8.43	7.88	8.44	9.12	8.23	7.03
Adv. rates w/o prior appr.	10.59	9.19	9.85	10.64	9.61	8.20
Loss costs w/prior appr.	15.72	14.81	16.19	17.30	15.77	13.51
Loss costs w/o prior appr.	13.35	14.09	15.46	16.48	15.06	12.91

six-cent cost increase in the adjusted manual rate over the rate predicted under pure administered pricing, an increase of approximately 4 percent. Alternatively, net weekly costs per employee would rise by $0.53, which amounts to a 5 percent increase over the rate paid under pure administered pricing.

The data from this table show that moving from the most regulated regime (pure administered pricing) to the most deregulated (a loss-cost system that does not require prior approval) results in a predicted 19-cent rate reduction, from $1.51 to $1.32 per $100 of payroll, equivalent to a 13 percent drop. However, the adoption of less comprehensive forms of deregulation typically results in higher insurance prices. Pure administered pricing results in costs that are higher than those found in all deregulated environments save the loss-cost regimes without prior approval. Nonetheless, it is important to recall that, in this table, the regulatory stringency is held constant at actual levels.

In Tables 7.13 and 7.14 we present cost predictions at different levels of regulatory stringency based on the regression results reported in Table 7.7. As before, with the exception of the regulatory regime, these predictions are based on the actual values of the independent variables in the equation, including regulatory stringency. Low-stringency predictions were made for states in which the value of the stringency variable was less than 0.8 (one standard deviation below the mean), medium-stringency observations had values between 0.8 and 1.2 (one standard deviation above the mean), and high-stringency observations had values over 1.2.

The data in these tables indicate that under low stringency, the predicted cost of every regulatory regime except advisory rate systems that require prior approval is less than that predicted for the pure-administered-pricing system. Predicted costs for loss-cost regimes that do not require prior approval are substantially less than the costs for pure administered pricing. Under most scenarios, employer costs under comprehensive deregulation are predicted to be 20–25 percent less than costs under pure administered pricing.

Under conditions of average and high stringency, the cost advantage for deregulation (other than loss-cost-without-prior-approval regimes) is eliminated altogether. Under high stringency conditions, moving from a pure-administered-pricing plan to a loss-cost system

Table 7.13 Predicted Adjusted Manual Rates under Different Assumed Regulatory Regimes and Stringency Conditions ($ per $100 of payroll)

Current regulatory regime	Actual costs	New regime				
		Pure admin. pricing	Var. from bureau rates w/prior appr.	Adv. rates w/o prior appr.	Loss costs w/prior appr.	Loss costs w/o prior appr.
Low stringency						
Pure admin. pricing	1.81	1.88	1.79	2.13	1.76	1.48
Var. from bureau rates w/prior appr.	2.00	2.04	1.93	2.31	1.91	1.60
Adv. rates w/o prior appr.	1.17	3.32	3.06	3.74	3.03	2.52
Loss costs w/prior appr.	3.24	4.00	3.56	4.49	3.53	2.92
Loss costs w/o prior appr.	1.93	2.43	2.31	2.75	2.28	1.91
Medium stringency						
Pure admin. pricing	1.29	1.34	1.40	1.53	1.37	1.17
Var. from bureau rates w/prior appr.	1.55	1.47	1.54	1.69	1.51	1.29
Adv. rates w/o prior appr.	2.05	2.01	2.10	2.30	2.05	1.75
Loss costs w/prior appr.	3.11	2.94	3.10	3.36	3.03	2.60
Loss costs w/o prior appr.	2.53	2.76	2.92	3.16	2.85	2.45
High stringency						
Pure admin. pricing	2.67	2.63	3.11	3.05	3.00	2.64
Var. from bureau rates w/prior appr.	2.25	1.84	2.31	2.14	2.21	1.97
Adv. rates w/o prior appr.	3.27	2.72	3.16	3.15	3.05	2.68
Loss costs w/prior appr.	3.00	2.63	3.24	3.06	3.11	2.76
Loss costs w/o prior appr.	2.48	2.32	2.84	2.70	2.73	2.42

Table 7.14 Predicted Net Weekly Costs under Different Assumed Regulatory Regimes and Stringency Conditions ($ per employee)

Current regulatory regime	Actual costs	New regime				
		Pure admin. pricing	Var. from bureau rates w/prior appr.	Adv. rates w/o prior appr.	Loss costs w/prior appr.	Loss costs w/o prior appr.
Low stringency						
Pure admin. pricing	9.80	9.37	9.06	10.38	8.89	7.44
Var. from bureau rates w/prior appr.	10.92	10.99	10.58	12.15	10.39	8.69
Adv. rates w/o prior appr.	5.82	7.28	7.08	8.08	6.95	5.82
Loss costs w/prior appr.	16.26	19.80	17.94	21.32	17.68	14.63
Loss costs w/o prior appr.	10.57	12.84	12.40	14.21	12.17	10.19
Medium stringency						
Pure admin. pricing	6.80	6.90	7.35	7.97	7.17	6.11
Var. from bureau rates w/prior appr.	7.73	7.27	7.75	8.40	7.56	6.45
Adv. rates w/o prior appr.	10.36	8.99	9.58	10.39	9.35	7.97
Loss costs w/prior appr.	15.97	14.81	15.92	17.17	15.53	13.26
Loss costs w/o prior appr.	13.69	14.70	15.86	17.07	15.46	13.21
High stringency						
Pure admin. pricing	13.72	13.55	16.29	16.49	15.78	13.76
Var. from bureau rates w/prior appr.	11.43	9.27	11.85	11.58	11.43	10.08
Adv. rates w/o prior appr.	16.69	12.73	15.06	15.38	14.60	12.69
Loss costs w/prior appr.	14.90	12.71	15.91	15.74	15.37	13.51
Loss costs w/o prior appr.	12.75	11.77	14.64	14.53	14.15	12.42

without prior approval results in a slight increase (about 5 percent) in employer costs.

Overall, the results in this chapter provide evidence consistent with the economic theory outlined in the previous chapter; that is, the strategy of the agency responsible for rate regulation largely determines the effect of deregulation on costs. To the extent that rates are suppressed by the regulatory agency, partial deregulation will be associated with an increase in employer costs. In general, the results for partial deregulation also indicate that, while regulatory strategies appear to vary across state insurance commissions, on average, state commissions are more likely to suppress rates prior to deregulation than act as a cartelizing force that boosts rates above competitive levels. Higher costs are found under all partially deregulated regimes.

On the other hand, under most scenarios, employer costs in loss-cost systems that do not require prior approval, the least regulated market environment, are substantially lower than costs under pure administered pricing. In other words, more comprehensive deregulation has an effect on employer costs that is different from the effect of more moderate forms of deregulation. One possible explanation for these seemingly contradictory results is that partial deregulation has an asymmetric impact on employer costs, i.e., it leads to increased costs under stringent regulation but fails to reduce costs under conditions of low stringency. The reason for this asymmetry is that, under partial deregulation, the rating bureau acts as a cartelizing force blunting the impact of market forces. In addition (or alternatively), insurers in loss-cost systems that do not require prior regulatory approval of rates respond to deregulation by cutting prices in an attempt to gain market share.

MARKET STRUCTURE AND RATE REGULATION

Insurance rate regulation affects market outcomes other than costs. If, for example, the workers' compensation insurance regulatory agency is "captured" by employers, then we would expect that deregulation will increase the number of insurers willing to underwrite workers' compensation policies; as a result, the market should become less concentrated. On the other hand, the market could become more concentrated after deregulation if insurance industry interests dominate the regulatory agency, as marginal insurers who had entered the market attracted by supracompetitive prices are forced to exit following deregulation and consequent rate reductions.

As previously indicated, traditional measures of market structure are four- and eight-firm concentration ratios, which may be defined as the share of the compensation insurance market (in terms of direct premiums written) that is controlled by the largest four and eight insurance carriers in the market, respectively.

National data on four- and eight-firm concentration ratios in the workers' compensation insurance market for the period 1975–1995 are depicted in Figures 7.5 and 7.6, respectively.[5] These data show cyclical variation that is roughly coextensive with the insurance cycle. That is, the average concentration ratio increases during hard market periods (i.e., between 1975 and 1977 and between 1984 and 1992) and declines during the soft market phases (i.e., between 1978 and 1983 and between 1993 and 1995). Interestingly, the variability in these measures shows similar cyclical variation, with a three- to four-year lag. Variability appears to increase from 1988 through 1992 and declines from 1980 through 1985.

The 1995 interstate variation in the four- and eight-firm concentration ratios, respectively, are shown in Figures 7.7 and 7.8. The data in these figures also exhibit substantial variability. The four-firm concentration ratio ranges from 0.685 in Maine to 0.237 in Indiana, and the eight-firm ratio ranges from 0.905 in Maine to 0.393 in Indiana. That is, the four largest groups in Maine account for 68.5 percent of the direct premiums written there, and the eight largest insurer groups account for 90.5 percent of the market.

To determine the effect of rate regulation on workers' compensation market structures, we estimated simple regression equations: four- and eight-firm concentration ratios are predicted as a function of the variables used to characterize the regulatory environment in the cost regression equations, as well as measures of market size and state and year dummies. Data in these regressions are limited to those states that permit private insurance.

Figure 7.5 Four-Firm Concentration Ratio, 1975–95 (mean ± S.D.)

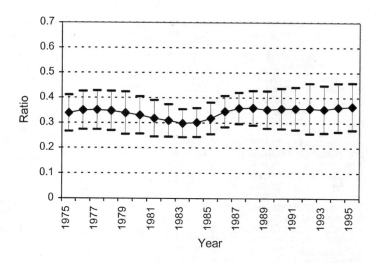

Figure 7.6 Eight-Firm Concentration Ratio, 1975–95 (mean ± S.D.)

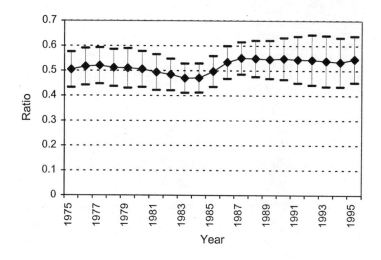

Figure 7.7 Four-Firm Concentration Ratios for 1995, by State

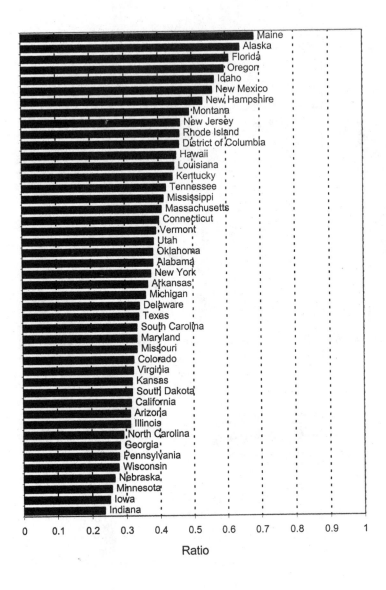

Figure 7.8 Eight-Firm Concentration Ratios for 1995, by State

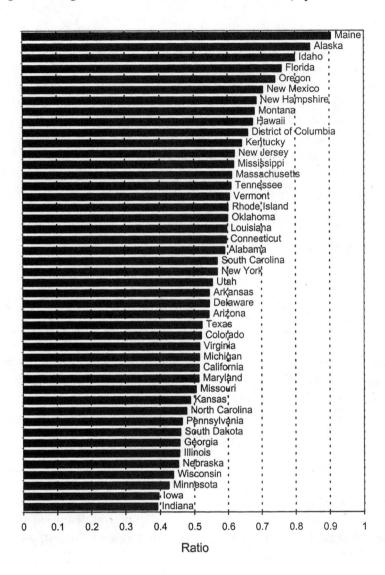

Ratio

MARKET STRUCTURE REGRESSIONS

Assuming that the nearest thing to a competitive market is found in loss-cost systems that do not require prior approval, then our cost results suggest that rates in less deregulated regimes are higher than competitive market levels. The cost results indicate that either there are inefficiencies associated with pure administered pricing or that insurers are able to cartelize the market under administered pricing, at least in the short run. As can be seen from Table 6.1, we are unable to predict the impact of deregulation on market structure if the underlying market, in the absence of regulation, is competitive. However, a finding of a negative relationship (or no relationship) between deregulation and market concentration would provide confirmatory evidence for the economic theory of rate regulation discussed in Chapter 6.

To examine this issue, we estimated regression models predicting statewide four- and eight-firm concentration ratios for the workers' compensation insurance line in states that permit private insurance carriers to offer compensation insurance.[6] These regressions included the regulatory environment variables used in our previous analyses: the stringency variable, the hard-market dummy, and state and year dummies to control for unobserved variation in other factors that could influence market concentration. As controls, we also included the competitive-state-fund dummy, covered employment, and nonfarm employment. These latter variables measure the size of the market and should be negatively related to market concentration. Since the range of the concentration ratio is limited to between zero and one, these market concentration variables were transformed to log-odds ratios. Due to the presence of heteroscedasticity for ordinary least squares regressions, we estimated weighted least squares regressions, using nonfarm employment as weights. Our empirical analysis is similar to that used to estimate the impact of regulation on compensation costs, except that we limit our investigation to our preferred (for purposes of analysis) regulatory regime specification.

Market Structure and Statutory Regulatory Regimes

The results of our market structure regression equations are presented in Table 7.15. As was the case with our previous analyses, the

Table 7.15 Regression Coefficients for Insurance Market Concentration as a Function of the Regulatory Environment[a]

Variable	4-Firm conc. ratio	8-Firm conc. ratio
Covered employment	−0.0306*** (4.09)	−0.0271*** (3.57)
Nonfarm employment × 1000	−0.0374** (2.50)	−0.0418*** (2.76)
Competitive state fund	0.0018 (0.04)	0.0199 (0.39)
Var. from bureau rates w/prior appr.	−0.1902*** (6.28)	−0.1548*** (4.92)
Adv. rates w/o prior appr.	−0.0441 (0.89)	−0.0673 (1.36)
Loss costs w/prior appr.	−0.1321*** (2.62)	−0.1010* (1.94)
Loss costs w/o prior appr.	−0.1396*** (3.18)	−0.1231*** (2.73)
State dummies	Yes	Yes
Year dummies	No	No
Adjusted R^2	0.7165	0.7164

[a] Coefficients are followed by t-ratios in parentheses. *** = significant at the 1% level; ** = significant at the 5% level; * = significant at the 10% level.

reported coefficients measure the effect of the regulatory regime on the dependent variable relative to pure administered pricing. These estimates are generally consistent with the idea that market structure becomes less concentrated following deregulation. On the other hand, an examination of the pattern of coefficients shows that the extent of this reduction in market concentration is apparently unrelated to the extent that the statutory regulatory regime provides regulators with the tools to control rates. In particular, the reduction in market share associated with the most deregulated environment (loss costs without prior approval) is less than the reduction associated with the least deregulated environment (variations from bureau rates with prior approval).

Nonetheless, markets are less concentrated under the loss-costs-without-prior-approval regime than under administered pricing, which is consistent with our cost findings (which were lower also) and with the hypothesis that regulatory agencies are not captured by the insureds. An explanation consistent with both the cost and market concentration results is that this more comprehensive form of deregulation induces smaller insurers to set prices at or below pure premium levels to gain market share. While this hypothesis violates assumptions of economic rationality on the part of insurers, recent anecdotal evidence from California would tend to support it.

Market Structure, Statutory Regimes, and the Insurance Cycle

To determine the effects of the stage of the insurance cycle on market structure, we estimated equations predicting four- and eight-firm concentration ratios as a function of the regulatory regime and the hard-market dummy variable. Regulatory regime/hard market interaction terms were included in these equations, which are reported in Tables 7.16 and 7.17.

Results in the previous section indicated that employer costs under pure administered pricing are lower in a hard market relative to a soft one. We interpret these findings as evidence that rate suppression reduces profit margins in a market where demand outstrips supply. As a result, we expect that under pure administered pricing, markets will be more concentrated in a hard market than in a soft one as marginal insurers leave the market; that is, the reduction in market concentration due to deregulation should be greater in a hard market than in a soft one. Similarly, we expect that deregulation effects will be greater in hard markets relative to soft ones.

The data in Tables 7.16 and 7.17 offer only partial support for this hypothesis. These data indicate that under pure administered pricing, market concentration is reduced during a hard market relative to the soft phase of the cycle, contrary to predictions. However, the interaction terms suggest that the effect of deregulation on market concentration is modified by the phase of the insurance cycle in a way that is consistent with expectations. From Table 7.16, we can see that every regulatory regime dummy is negatively signed, while every interaction term has a positive relationship with market concentration. These

Table 7.16 Regression Coefficients for Insurance Market Concentration as a Function of the Regulatory Environment and Stage of the Insurance Cycle[a]

Variable	4-Firm conc. ratio	8-Firm conc. ratio
Covered employment	–0.0127 (1.62)	–0.0098 (1.22)
Nonfarm employment × 1000	0.0266** (2.32)	0.0564*** (4.82)
Competitive state fund	0.0663 (1.22)	0.0602 (1.07)
Hard market	–0.0619** (2.40)	–0.0568** (2.15)
Var. from bureau rates w/prior appr.	–0.2569*** (7.62)	–0.2158*** 6.09)
Var. from bureau rates w/prior appr. × hard market	0.1480*** (4.56)	0.1620*** (4.88)
Adv. rates w/o prior appr.	–0.1241** (2.12)	–0.1584*** (2.69)
Adv. rates w/o prior appr. × hard market	0.1763*** (2.87)	0.2585*** (4.10)
Loss costs w/prior appr.	–0.1622*** (2.93)	–0.1149** (1.97)
Loss costs w/prior appr. × hard market	0.3597*** (4.85)	0.4068*** (5.35)
Loss costs w/o prior appr.	–0.0844* (1.68)	–0.0738 (1.43)
Loss costs w/o prior appr. × hard market	–0.0008 (0.01)	0.0870 (1.40)
State dummies	Yes	Yes
Year dummies	No	No
Adjusted R^2	0.6727	0.6672

[a] Coefficients are followed by t-ratios in parentheses. *** = significant at the 1% level; ** = significant at the 5% level; * = significant at the 10% level.

Table 7.17 Effects of Regulatory Regimes and the Insurance Cycle on Market Structure[a]

Regulatory regime	4-Firm conc. ratio	8-Firm conc. ratio
Regulatory regime effects in a hard market		
Var. from bureau rates w/prior appr.	−0.1384*** (3.80)	−0.0780** (2.02)
Adv. rates w/o prior appr.	0.0447 (0.75)	0.0898 (1.45)
Loss costs w/prior appr.	0.2004*** (2.63)	0.3295*** (4.00)
Loss costs w/o prior appr.	−0.0852 (1.51)	0.0104 (0.17)
Regulatory regime effects in a soft market		
Var. from bureau rates w/prior appr.	−0.2569*** (7.62)	−0.2158*** (6.09)
Adv. rates w/o prior appr.	−0.1241** (2.12)	−0.1584*** (2.69)
Loss costs w/prior appr.	−0.1622*** (2.93)	−0.1149** (1.97)
Loss costs w/o prior appr.	−0.0844* (1.68)	−0.0738 (1.43)
Effects of a hard market under different regulatory regimes		
Pure admin. pricing	−0.0600** (2.40)	−0.0552** (2.15)
Var. from bureau rates w/prior appr.	0.0899*** (4.40)	0.1109*** (5.25)
Adv. rates w/o prior appr.	0.1212** (2.07)	0.2235*** (3.57)
Loss costs w/prior appr.	0.3468*** (4.27)	0.4192*** (4.90)
Loss costs w/o prior appr.	−0.0608 (1.15)	0.0307 (0.54)

[a] Coefficients are followed by t-ratios in parentheses. *** = significant at the 1% level; ** = significant at the 5% level; * = significant at the 10% level.

results suggest, contrary to predictions, that during the soft phase of the cycle, market concentration is reduced in all deregulated environments relative to its level under pure administered pricing; but, this reduction in the deregulated/administered pricing differential is diminished, eliminated, or even reversed during a hard market. This is confirmed in the bottom data set of Table 7.17, which shows that partially deregulated markets become increasingly concentrated during a hard market and that the market structure is unaffected by the insurance cycle or becomes less concentrated during a hard market in states where prices are administered.

On the other hand, these same data in Table 7.17 also indicate that the insurance cycle has little, if any effect on market structure in states with loss-cost systems that do not require prior approval. Once again, partial deregulation has an effect on market outcomes that is different from the effect of more comprehensive deregulation.

Market Structure, Statutory Regimes, and Regulatory Stringency

The economic theory of rate regulation outlined in the previous chapter predicts that if the underlying market is competitive, markets will become increasingly concentrated as the degree of rate suppression increases. To test this hypothesis, we included the regulatory stringency measure in the regression equation. The results of this analysis are reported in Tables 7.18 and 7.19.

These results substantially support our hypothesis that regulation increases market concentration. Regulatory stringency is positively associated with market concentration in the two most highly regulated environments: pure administered pricing and variations from bureau rates that require prior approval. In addition, this positive relationship between regulatory stringency and market concentration is substantially attenuated in deregulated environments. This is to be expected if the regulatory stringency variable is only meaningful where the statute provides the insurance commission with significant powers to set rates. Finally, the data in the first two data sets of Table 7.19 show that the impact of deregulation on market structure increases as regulators suppress rates. Market concentration ratios under each deregulated regime

**Table 7.18 Regression Coefficients for Insurance Market Concentration
as a Function of the Regulatory Environment and
Regulatory Stringency[a]**

Variable	4-Firm conc. ratio	8-Firm conc. ratio
Covered employment	−0.0290***	−0.0260***
	(3.98)	(3.56)
Nonfarm employment × 1000	−0.0421***	−0.0477***
	(2.88)	(3.25)
Competitive state fund	0.0194	0.0821
	(0.37)	(1.56)
Regulatory stringency	0.6006***	0.6473***
	(6.59)	(7.08)
Var. from bureau rates w/prior appr.	0.2274*	0.2216*
	(1.77)	(1.72)
Var. from bureau rates w/o prior appr. × loss ratio	−0.3981***	−0.3514***
	(3.76)	(3.31)
Adv. rates w/o prior appr.	1.6508***	1.2379***
	(4.38)	(3.57)
Adv. rates w/o prior appr. × loss ratio	−1.0071***	−0.8575***
	(4.45)	(3.73)
Loss costs w/prior appr.	0.4770**	0.1348
	(2.10)	(0.68)
Loss costs w/prior appr. × loss ratio	−0.4977***	−0.2222
	(3.05)	(1.35)
Loss costs w/o prior appr.	0.9930***	1.0055***
	(3.59)	(3.61)
Loss costs w/o prior appr. × loss ratio	−0.8166***	−0.8136***
	(4.42)	(4.39)
State dummies	Yes	Yes
Year dummies	Yes	Yes
Adjusted R^2	0.7340	0.7399

[a] Coefficients are followed by t-ratios in parentheses. *** = significant at the 1% level;
** = significant at the 5% level; * = significant at the 10% level.

Table 7.19 Effects of Regulatory Regimes and Regulatory Stringency on Market Structure[a]

	Regulatory stringency		
Regulatory regime	Low	Medium	High
Four-firm concentration ratios			
Var. from bureau rates w/prior appr.	–0.1023***	–0.1713***	–0.2679***
	(2.57)	(5.65)	(7.32)
Adv. rates w/o prior appr.	0.2045***	–0.0199	–0.2263***
	(3.01)	(0.39)	(3.02)
Loss costs w/prior appr.	0.0050	–0.0934*	–0.2011***
	(0.07)	(1.79)	(3.61)
Loss costs w/o prior appr.	0.0446	–0.1119***	–0.2809***
	(0.73)	(2.58)	(4.85)
Eight-firm concentration ratios			
Var. from bureau rates w/prior appr.	–0.0746*	–0.1373***	–0.2178***
	(1.84)	(4.42)	(5.92)
Adv. rates w/o prior appr.	0.1397**	–0.0433	–0.2192***
	(2.10)	(0.85)	(2.89)
Loss costs w/prior appr.	–0.0423	–0.0859	–0.1365**
	(0.61)	(1.63)	(2.44)
Loss costs w/o prior appr.	0.0524	–0.1051**	–0.2731***
	(0.85)	(2.40)	(4.69)
Stringency effects		4-Firm	8-Firm
Pure administered pricing		0.5989***	0.6448***
		(6.58)	(7.05)
Var. from bureau rates w/prior appr.		0.1990***	0.2940***
		(3.13)	(4.60)
Adv. rates w/o prior appr.		–0.4320**	–0.2302
		(2.14)	(1.12)
Loss costs w/prior appr.		0.0839	0.4116***
		(0.62)	(3.03)
Loss costs w/o prior appr.		–0.2124	–0.1656
		(1.27)	(0.99)

[a] Coefficients are followed by *t*-ratios in parentheses. *** = significant at the 1% level; ** = significant at the 5% level; * = significant at the 10% level.

decline relative to pure administered pricing as the degree of rate regulation intensifies.

The picture that emerges from these data is that deregulation results in increased competition in the workers' compensation market. Furthermore, markets become more concentrated as regulators more stringently suppress rates in more regulated markets. However, unlike the cost analyses, we find only slight evidence that partial deregulation has a different impact on market structure than does more comprehensive deregulation. In addition, the results with respect to the insurance cycle are somewhat difficult to reconcile with similar results from the cost analyses or with the economic theory of rate regulation more generally.

CONCLUSIONS ABOUT THE EFFECT OF DEREGULATION

The important results that emerged from the analyses described in this chapter are as follows. Most forms of partial deregulation are, on average, associated with higher employer costs for workers' compensation. On the other hand, more comprehensive deregulation (e.g., loss-cost systems that do not require prior approval) is, on average, associated with lower employer costs. In addition, the impact of deregulation on costs depends not only on the statutory form of deregulation, but on the behavior of the regulatory agency prior to deregulation; where the regulatory agency has suppressed rates, deregulation is more likely to lead to increased costs. The behavior of the regulatory agency is apparently related to the state of the insurance market; regulatory agencies are more likely to suppress rates during a hard market, when demand exceeds supply, than during a soft one. Consequently, the impact of deregulation varies over the insurance cycle. Finally, all forms of deregulation are likely to lead to an increase in competitiveness, while rate suppression is likely to reduce market competitiveness.

What may we conclude from these results? Given the contradictory findings for partial and comprehensive deregulation, it is difficult to draw clear inferences concerning the nature of regulation (i.e., whether regulatory agencies are more likely to respond to employers and suppress rates or whether they are more likely to help the insurance industry cartelize the market). Our inability to do so leads us to conclude that regulators do neither, at least not consistently. Lags inherent in the regulatory process may be responsible for this inconsistency. However, it may also be due to the ebb and flow of political pressures over the course of the insurance cycle. As the market hardens, political pressures from employers may force regulators to become more concerned with the impact of insurance rates on the state's business climate. As a result, rates are suppressed. When the market softens once again, the political pressures ease and, concomitantly, regulators' concerns over the effect of workers' compensation rates vanish and rates are allowed to rise to competitive (and, perhaps, supracompetitive) levels.

Insurers respond to this pattern of regulatory behavior by increasing prices during the soft phase of the insurance cycle or by not reducing prices as much as would be expected in an unregulated market. This is easier to accomplish where the market has been partially deregulated. Anticipating rate suppression when the market hardens again, insurers in partially deregulated systems are likely to keep market rates higher than the competitive level during the soft phase of the cycle. In a partially deregulated environment, this is facilitated by the rating organization, which promulgates rates that serve as a pricing point for insurance carriers. This accounts for the asymmetry between comprehensive and partial deregulation. Comprehensive deregulation results in lower prices during both phases of the insurance cycle, while insurers take advantage of regulatory indifference to higher rates during the soft phase, in anticipation of the coming crunch when the market hardens once again.

A regulated market is a more risky environment for insurers. Thus, insurers will be attracted to a market that has deregulated, resulting in a less concentrated insurance market. It also seems possible, if not likely, that the influx of insurers into a completely (or near completely) deregulated market results in a price war, as insurers cut rates to gain or maintain market share.

This interpretation of our results leads us to conclude that a completely deregulated market is a more efficient delivery system and is, therefore, preferable to either partial deregulation or administered pricing. The latter two alternatives seem to be associated with inefficiencies resulting from insurer uncertainty over their ability to respond to market changes. Further, anecdotal evidence from states such as Rhode Island (as we described at the beginning of this book) suggest that insurance rate regulation can sometimes have near catastrophic consequences for all of the stakeholders in the workers' compensation program.

Nonetheless, we are cautious in our conclusions for a couple of reasons. First, while we have a relatively long data series spanning at least one complete insurance cycle, most deregulation—and, in particular, most comprehensive deregulation—occurred at the end of study period, so that we were only able to observe the effects of such deregulation for a few years. The evidence suggests that comprehensive deregulation has led to a price war in the workers' compensation insurance market in some states. If so, it is possible that the substantial rate reductions found in those states will be short-lived; as the war for market share is resolved, prices may rise once again. In addition, the latter period (when states moved to open competition) appears to have been a soft phase of the insurance cycle. Despite our best efforts, we may not have adequately controlled for this effect.

Second, while comprehensively deregulated programs seem to perform well relative to the delivery system efficiency objective, their performance on other criteria may be less admirable. As noted in Chapter 2, regulation was first introduced to the insurance industry as a means of preventing insurer insolvency and the concomitant availability problems. In addition, various groups have expressed concerns over quality-of-service problems associated with different insurance arrangements. It is possible that while comprehensive deregulation improves system performance relative to the delivery system efficiency criterion, it diminishes performance relative to other objectives. We are particularly interested in one aspect of service quality as it relates to the injury prevention objective of workers' compensation: workplace health and safety as measured by the lost-time injury rate. We examine this aspect in the next chapter.

Notes

1. We used the combined ratio to distinguish between hard and soft markets because we are interested in the effects of insurance cycles on costs regardless of cause,

that is, whether the cycle is caused by changes in investment returns or other factors.

2. Specifically, a Cox hypothesis test was used to determine whether the regulatory rules model was superior to the full set regulatory regime model. Then, F-tests were used to determine whether the various regimes in the full set regulatory environment model had effects on employer costs that were significantly different from one another.

3. The Cox statistic has a standard normal distribution. Tests comparing the regulatory rules specification predicting adjusted manual rates and net weekly costs with the model 1 regulatory regime specification yielded absolute Cox statistics greater than 6.

4. These values were estimated by adding the coefficient values for the regulatory regime dummy and the associated interaction term.

5. The data in Figures 7.5 and 7.6 are state averages.

6. The Herfindahl-Hirschman Index (HHI), which is the sum of squares of percentage market shares of each firm, is a superior measure of market concentration since it reflects the entire distribution of firms rather than only the largest four or eight firms. However, HHI data were not readily available and resource limitations forced us to rely on the four- and eight-firm concentration ratios. These measures typically are highly correlated with the HHI.

8

Insurance Arrangements and Workplace Safety

Thus far, we have examined two market outcomes potentially affected by workers' compensation insurance arrangements, i.e., employers costs and market structure. Yet, the debate on private versus public provision of insurance or rate regulation frequently centers on another outcome: the quality of services provided to employers and employees covered by workers' compensation programs. Service quality has a number of dimensions, including the accuracy and timeliness of policies issued by the carrier, loss prevention and safety engineering, and carrier claims adjustment efforts. In this chapter, we examine one aspect of this outcome, workplace safety, as it is measured by the lost-time injury rate. We are particularly interested in a hypothesis advanced by Danzon and Harrington postulating that rate suppression by insurance regulators reduces employer and insurer loss control incentives and consequently results in a higher injury rate and greater loss experience more generally.

THE ECONOMIC THEORY OF WORK ACCIDENTS

There is a large theoretical and empirical literature examining the determinants of the incidence of workplace injuries. This literature assumes that while the occurrence of a single work-related accident is, by definition, a random event not within the control of either the worker or the employer, both parties can influence the frequency and severity of injuries in the aggregate: workers can take greater care on the job, and employers can introduce equipment and worksite practices to improve inherent safety in the work environment.

The extent to which both parties adopt practices designed to reduce the probability of a work accident depends on the associated costs and benefits. Accident costs for injured workers include lost income, pain and suffering, and the loss of enjoyment of leisure activities, among other things. The worker must weigh these costs against the burden imposed by taking greater care on the job. This burden may include, for example, the discomfort associated with wearing personal protective equipment, or a potential productivity loss associated with taking additional time to complete a job and the consequent loss of income. For the employer, an accident can result in higher workers' compensation insurance premiums, lost productivity, the associated costs of hiring replacement workers, and damage to property and equipment. The employer must weigh these costs against, for example, the expense of safer machinery and personal protective equipment.

The decision to report a work injury is subject to a similar cost–benefit calculus. Workers who file workers' compensation claims may be subject to sanctions by the employer, including discharge. Moreover, once a claim is initiated, firms must decide whether to oppose it (for example, deny that the injury is compensable) or to question the determination of degree of disability. However, by pursuing this course of action, the employer incurs direct costs in the form of legal expenses as well as indirect costs in the form of damaged labor relations.

The market outcome in which we are ultimately interested is workplace safety. Typically, it is assessed by measures such as the injury rate or the workers' compensation claims rate. However, economic theory and empirical evidence predicts that injury rates will be affected by employer and worker behavior and that their behavior will be influenced by economic incentives. To accurately determine the effect of insurance arrangements on safety, it is necessary to control for these incentives.

INJURY RATE REGRESSION MODEL

There is substantial variation in the industrial and occupational composition of employment among states. Because some types of employment are more hazardous than others, this sectoral variation translates into heterogeneity with respect to the underlying risk of injury among states. To control for this variation, our analysis will use the lost-time injury rate measure that was introduced and used as an independent variable in Chapter 4. Here we use the lost-time injury rate as the dependent variable in equations examining workplace safety. Our construction of the injury rate variable controls for interstate variation in employment composition and thus for the underlying risk of injury by industrial sector. Specifically, this measure is a weighted average of industry-specific injury rates for each state, where weights are the proportion of national employment in the sector.

As indicated in the previous section, we may expect that the lost-time injury rate will be influenced by a number of factors affecting the worker's and employer's cost–benefit calculus, including the level or generosity of compensation benefits, the wage rate, the unemployment rate, and whether or not the employer is self-insured. Thus, it is important to control for these variables in our empirical work. In the remainder of this section, we discuss each of these factors in turn, indicating how it is measured and the expected relationship with the lost-time injury rate.

Workers' Compensation Benefits

Higher workers' compensation benefits reduce the expected costs of work accidents for injured workers. Economic theory predicts that benefit increases will thus induce workers to be less careful on the job, increase the probability that they will report a work-related injury, and extend the period of disability if they are injured. As a result, higher statutory benefits should be associated with higher injury rates. On the other hand, more generous benefits will also increase the expected accident costs of experience-rated employers. These firms will respond by improving workplace safety and by adopting more aggressive claims management policies, which should in turn lead to a reduction in injury frequency. Unfortunately, economic theory does not predict which of these opposing effects will dominate. Nevertheless, an extensive empirical literature has found a positive relationship between compensation benefits and injury or claims rates (see Thomason and Burton 1993; Burton and Chelius 1997; or Durbin and Butler 1998 for a review of this literature).

The cash benefit index regarding the relative generosity of workers' compensation statutes, which we discussed earlier and used in the employer cost models, is also used as a regressor in the injury rates model in order to control for interstate differences in benefit levels. We expect that this benefit variable will be positively related to injury rates.

Wages

The higher the wage rate, the greater the cost of a work accident for the injured worker, since the worker will not receive full replacement of wages while on disability, the cost is particularly high for those workers subject to the statutory maximum for weekly benefits. In addition, higher wages indicate higher-quality workers. Since high-quality employees typically embody greater human capital investment, firms will be more highly motivated to protect these employees from the risk of injury relative to low-wage, low-quality workers (Thomason and Pozzebon 1999). Thus, we expect the injury rate to be negatively related to wages.

Our wage measure is based on the statewide average wage of employees covered by the unemployment insurance program, after adjusting for interstate variation in industrial composition. Details of the methodology used to construct the wage measure are reported in Appendix D.

Unemployment Rate

Economic theory predicts that injury rates will be negatively related to unemployment levels for several reasons.[1] First, as the level of economic activity increases, firms will use the existing labor force more intensively, requiring workers to work more overtime. Increased overtime induces fatigue, which increases the probability of injury. Second, firms add new workers to the payroll as the economy expands, so the proportion of younger workers in the workforce thus increases. Because younger, inexperienced workers are more likely to suffer a workplace injury, a greater incidence of accidents will be associated with lower unemployment rates. Finally, these additional workers will initially be added to existing capital stock, which implies that workplaces will become more crowded and therefore more hazardous as the unemployment rate declines. For these reasons, we include a state-specific measure of the annual unemployment rate as a regressor in our model of the determination of injury rates. Data for this variable were obtained from various issues of the U.S. Department of Labor's *Employment and Earnings* series. We expect this variable to be negatively related to injury rates.

Self-Insurance

We also include as an independent variable in our injury-rate regressions a proxy measure for the proportion of the state's workforce that is employed by self-insured firms. This variable is a state-specific measure of the benefits paid by self-insured employers as a proportion of total benefits paid. However, Danzon and Harrington (1998) have demonstrated that these benefits data are highly correlated with employment of self-insureds. We obtained this variable from various issues of the Social Security Administration's *Social Security Bulletin* and from Schmulowitz (1997).

Since workers' compensation costs are tied to the accident experience of experience-rated employers, the injury rate should be lower for experience-rated firms than for comparable firms that are not experience-rated. Because self-insured employers are, in effect, perfectly experience-rated, we expect that the injury rate will be negatively related to the proportion of self-insured employment. However, this negative relationship is somewhat attenuated due to the fact that those firms that elect self-insurance will be large firms that are likely to be close to perfectly experience-rated by private carriers.

Other Variables and Hypotheses

The empirical specification of the injury rate model also includes the union density and coverage variables that we used in the cost regressions. There are competing hypotheses: union density could be either positively or negatively related to the injury rate for reasons we discussed previously, although existing empirical work suggests the former rather than the latter. We have no prior hypotheses regarding the impact of workers' compensation coverage on injury rates, but we expect that it will have the same sign as in the cost regressions. That is, if an increase in covered employment includes more workers in high-risk occupations, then we expect that both compensation costs and the injury rate will be positively related to covered employment. The opposite effect is expected if covered employment increases the number of workers in low-risk jobs. Lastly, all of our injury-rate regression equations include state and year dummies to control for unobserved state- and time-specific effects that could influence injury rates.

As with our cost and market structure regression equations, we modeled annual statewide injury rates as a function of a vector of control variables (specifically, the level of compensation benefits, the average wage, the unemployment rate, and the proportion of the state's workforce employed by self-insured firms); a set of insurance arrangement variables; and state and year dummies. Once again, comparisons of public versus private provision of workers' compensation insurance are made using dummy variables that indicate whether the state has a monopolistic or competitive state insurance fund.

The means and standard deviations of the control variables used in our injury rate analyses for 1975–1995, as well as predictions with respect to these variables and the regulatory environment variables, are presented in Table 8.1.

REGRESSION RESULTS: PUBLIC VERSUS PRIVATE PROVISION

As was the case with employer costs, it is difficult to establish *a priori* whether workplace safety should be better or worse where workers' compensation insurance is provided by a public agency rather than by a private insurance carrier. On the one hand, due to the profit motive, private carriers have an incentive to control losses and provide insureds with safety management services toward that end. Further, the lack of a profit motive for exclusive state funds may mean that their provision of safety management services is inefficient; that is, the profit motive ensures that private carriers will carefully monitor the outcome of safety management programs, whereas the state fund has no such incentive. As a result, we may expect that the improvement in workplace safety obtained by the private carrier for each dollar spent on loss control will be more than that obtained by the exclusive state fund for equivalent spending.

**Table 8.1 Means, Standard Deviations, and Predicted Signs
of Injury Rate Regressors**

Variable	Mean	Std. deviation	Prediction
Expected cash benefits ($)	9,449.89	4,795.78	+
Weekly wages ($)	527.87	49.71	−
Unemployment rate (%)	6.85	1.94	−
Union density (%)	18.75	8.01	+
Covered employment (%)	89.38	3.83	?
Proportion self-insured (%)	20.43	10.27	−

On the other hand, private carriers should only provide these services up to the point at which the additional dollar spent on loss control is equal to the additional dollar of losses saved. In contrast, motivated by broader political concerns, the state fund may choose to invest more than this profit-maximizing amount. If so, this should reduce the accident rate for exclusive-state-fund jurisdictions below the private market level. In addition, since there is a trade-off between accident prevention and claims adjustment efforts (Thomason and Pozzebon 1999), private carriers may choose to invest more resources in claims management and less in safety management than public state funds, increasing the private carrier injury rate, *ceteris paribus*.

Means and standard deviations of the injury rate variable, by insurance arrangement, are presented in Table 8.2. "Comparison A" provides injury rates in exclusive-state-fund jurisdictions versus injury rates in states where private insurance carriers offer workers' compensation coverage. "Comparison B" provides injury rates for states that have a competitive state fund with states that only have private carriers. Taken together, these comparisons suggest that injury rates are higher in states that have a public funding agency. They also suggest that injury rates are highest in exclusive-state-fund jurisdictions. However, these comparisons do not control for other factors that affect injury rates, such as the level of workers' compensation benefits.

Table 8.3 reports the results of regressions predicting annual statewide injury rates per 100 workers for a regression that includes an exclusive-state-fund dummy variable and for a regression that includes

Table 8.2 Comparisons of Injury Rates by Insurance Type

	Comparison A		Comparison B	
Variable	Exclusive state fund	Permits private insurance	Competitive state fund	Permits private insurance
Mean	9.1593	8.3079	8.3227	8.2973
Std. dev.	0.9834	1.3400	1.4955	1.2181
No. of observations	63	945	279	666

a competitive state fund dummy. The exclusive-state-fund regression does not include state dummies due to identification problems. Both regressions were estimated using weighted least squares to control for heteroscedasticity problems, with nonfarm employment serving as weights.

The results from these regressions generally conform to our prior expectations. The injury rate is positively related to benefit generosity. Specifically, a 10 percent increase in benefit levels appears to increase injury rates about 6 percent. This suggests that higher benefit levels reduce the cost of injury for workers, which results in a reduced level of care by workers or in a higher level of claims reporting. These results, including the elasticity estimates, are consistent with prior research investigating the relationship between benefit levels and the injury rate.

Similarly, wages are negatively related to the injury rate in the competitive-state-fund equation, as would be expected if higher wages increase the cost of injury for workers, although they are positively related to wages in the exclusive-state-fund equations. This latter result undoubtedly reflects omitted variable bias, since individual state dummies are not included in this equation. The negative relationship between the level of unemployment and the lost-time injury rate indicates that the injury rate is positively related to the state's economic activity. This could be due to the effects of increased levels of overtime; a higher labor-to-capital ratio; a younger, more inexperienced workforce; or a combination of any or all of the above.

Contrary to our expectations, the regression results indicate that union density is negatively related to the injury rate, suggesting that unions are successful in improving workplace safety. However, this is

Table 8.3 Regression Coefficients for Injury Rates as a Function of Insurance Arrangement[a]

Variable	Exclusive state fund	Competitive state fund
ln(Cash benefits)	0.0526***	0.0666***
	(4.46)	(4.06)
ln(Wages)	0.1304*	−0.2885***
	(1.87)	(3.86)
Unemployment	−0.0094***	−0.0107***
	(3.09)	(5.75)
Union density	−0.0084***	−0.0053***
	(9.22)	(3.68)
Covered employment	0.0230***	0.0059**
	(16.75)	(2.49)
Proportion self-insured	0.2698***	−0.0619
	(5.77)	(1.31)
Exclusive state fund	0.0842***	—[b]
	(4.89)	
Competitive state fund	—	−0.0461***
		(3.35)
State dummies	No	Yes
Year dummies	Yes	Yes
Adjusted R^2	0.3958	0.8589

[a] Coefficients are followed by t-ratios in parentheses. *** = significant at the 1% level; ** = significant at the 5% level; * = significant at the 10% level.
[b] A dash (—) = coefficient not estimated.

inconsistent with prior research (Schurman et al. 1998). The extent of covered employment is positively related to the injury rate, suggesting that increased coverage resulted in a greater proportion of workers employed in high-risk (as opposed to low-risk) occupations during this period. While we made no predictions concerning this variable, it is consistent with the cost equation results, i.e., insurance costs were also positively related to covered employment.

Self-insured employment, as a proportion of total employment, is positively and unexpectedly related to the injury rate in the exclusive state fund regression but negatively related to injury frequency in the competitive fund equation (although this latter relationship is not statistically significant at conventional levels). This unexpected result is possibly due to the fact that year dummies were not included in the exclusive-state-fund regression. As can be seen, omitting these dummies had a profound effect on the fit of the regression, as measured by the adjusted R^2.

The results for the exclusive- and competitive-state-fund dummies are contradictory. Exclusive-state-fund jurisdictions appear to have higher injury rates than states where private carriers provide compensation insurance, while states with competitive state funds appear to have lower injury rates than states with only private carriers. Thus, it appears that a competitive state fund may reduce the loss cost component of the workers' compensation premium at the same time that it increases the loading.[2] These results indicate, once again, that the effects of these two types of public insurance funds are substantially different.

THE DANZON–HARRINGTON HYPOTHESIS

The traditional economic theory of rate regulation (outlined in Chapter 6, pp. 159–172) assumes that deregulation only leads to lower costs if the regulatory agency had been captured by the insurance industry in the pre-deregulation period. Recently, Danzon and Harrington (1998) postulated that rate suppression by regulatory agencies can lead to increased costs in the regulatory period and to a reduction in costs following deregulation. Their argument focuses on certain institutional features in the insurance market and, in particular, on the residual (assigned-risk) market mechanism that insures firms that cannot obtain insurance directly from private carriers.

One of the consequences of rate suppression in the voluntary market is that insurers withdraw coverage from high-risk employers, who are then forced into the residual market. Since deficits in residual market accounts—which are common—are financed through a tax on insurers that varies according to the insurer's share of premiums in the voluntary market, voluntary market insureds effectively subsidize firms in the residual market. Danzon and Harrington argued that this subsidization encourages high-risk firms in the residual market to expand operations, which increases average losses experienced by all firms.

Danzon and Harrington also claimed that rate suppression in the voluntary market also results in cross-subsidies between high- and low-risk firms within the residual market. Specifically, they noted that:

> With higher rates for a given class in the residual market than the voluntary market . . . some employer with lower expected claim costs than other firms insured in the residual market will end up subsidizing these higher risk firms. The voluntary market for these employers is too low to induce voluntary supply; that is, it is less than the expected costs of providing coverage including the cost of the increased share of the expected residual market deficit that the insurer must pay if it provides coverage voluntarily. But the higher rate for the residual market may exceed the actuarial or expected cost, exclusive of any share of the deficit. Thus, these employers help subsidize the deficit caused by other residual market risks with higher expected costs. (P. 21)

Moreover, the extent of cross-subsidization within the residual market increases as the residual market differential increases. This within-market subsidization also encourages high-risk firms to expand operations.

Furthermore, institutional features of the labor market reduce insurer incentives for loss control. Since insurers share deficits for residual-market firms but solely bear the burden of loss control expenses for these firms, there is little incentive for insurance carriers to provide firms in the residual market with loss-control services, which results in higher costs due to a deterioration in accident experience. Additionally, state regulatory agencies are more likely to approve rate request increases based on higher pure premiums than on increased expense loadings, which further weakens insurer incentives for loss control.[3]

As the residual market expands, voluntary market costs increase to cover the increased subsidy for residual market insureds. Since voluntary market rates are suppressed by the regulatory agency according to the Danzon–Harrington hypothesis, these cost increases take the form of a reduction of experience rating or schedule rating credits and/or lower dividend payments. Consequently, employer loss control incentives in the voluntary market are reduced, resulting in lower levels of workplace safety and a deterioration of the employer's accident experience.

Specifically, Danzon and Harrington indicated that rate regulation constrains the incentive effects of experience rating in two ways. First, insurers can reduce experience-rating factors, i.e., credit modifiers (the amount, in percentage terms, by which the base rate is reduced or increased as a result of firm accident experience). Second, they can reduce the base rate to which the experience rating is applied. In either event, the credit or debit due to the employer's accident experience is reduced in absolute terms, which diminishes employer incentives for safety. Nevertheless, because the experience-rating program is uniform among most states and (until recently) has changed very little over time, Danzon and Harrington argued that the effect of lower base rates on experience-rating incentives is more significant than are changes in experience modification factors.

Prior Empirical Research

Danzon and Harrington (1998) used a three-pronged approach to test their hypotheses. First, they estimated a series of equations predicting loss-cost growth and the proportion of total payroll accounted for by self-insured employers, using data for 24 states for the period 1984–1990. Three measures of loss-cost growth were estimated: growth in cash benefit losses, medical benefit losses, and total losses.

They asserted that few states had truly deregulated their workers' compensation insurance market during this period and that *de facto* regulation could occur in a state that was nominally deregulated. They eschewed the dummy variable categorization of state statutes that is typically used in rate regulation studies. Instead, they used three continuous measures of regulatory stringency: the lagged value of the residual market share, the lagged value of the ratio of filed to approved rate increases, and the lagged statewide underwriting (profit) margin.

Danzon and Harrington found the hypothesized positive relationship between cost growth and residual market share in all equations, although it was only statistically significant in the total and indemnity loss growth regressions. The results for the other two regulation measures were mixed. Both the residual market share and the filed/

approved variables were significantly and positively related to the proportion of self-insured payroll, as expected, if rate regulation results in
rate suppression, which, in turn, increases the size of the residual market.

In the second component of their analysis, they estimated equations predicting several different measures of claims experience—
losses/payroll, losses/claim, claims/payroll, and premium/payroll—for
150 of the largest individual rate classes from eight states for the period
1987–1991. These data allowed them to distinguish between the experience of voluntary-market employers and that of their residual-market
counterparts. They found that the lagged residual market share was
positively related to each of these measures of claims experience for
both voluntary- and residual-market employers, but the magnitude of
this relationship was significantly greater for residual-market firms.
They attributed this result to greater moral hazard effects in the residual
market due to weaker incentives for loss control.

In the third section of their study, Danzon and Harrington used
class-level data described in the previous paragraph to test for the existence of cross-subsidies between classes and industries within a state.
They hypothesized that if rate suppression resulted in cross-subsidies
between rate groups or industries, there should be greater cross-class
variability in states with high loss ratios than in states with low ratios.
They tested this hypothesis by comparing the interquartile range of the
distribution of class-specific loss ratios in states with high loss ratios
with those in states with low loss ratios. They found evidence of
between-rate-group subsidies but not of between-industry subsidies.
This result was confirmed by their additional regression results, which
showed that both the extent of the subsidy (as measured by the residual
market share) and the loss ratio were related to variables measuring the
relative political influence of the beneficiaries of rate regulation.

Barkume and Ruser (1997) used workers' compensation cost and
injury rate data from two sample surveys of private industry establishments to test the Danzon–Harrington hypotheses. The cost data came
from a survey conducted by the U.S. Bureau of Labor Statistic (BLS)
for the Employment Cost Index program, with 115,709 observations on
private nonfarm jobs (of which 38,940 were distinct jobs) for the
period 1981–1996. The injury rate data were obtained from a nationally representative survey of 250,000 private establishments, which

was also conducted by the BLS and was based on injury logs mandated by the Occupational Safety and Health Act.

Barkume and Ruser used workers' compensation premiums as a percentage of gross earnings,[4] which they termed the *net workers' compensation cost for each job*, as a firm-specific measure of workers' compensation costs. The premiums were net after adjusting for experience modifiers, premium discounts, and expense constants applicable to the employer, but did not reflect dividends received by the employer. Data from all states except exclusive-state-fund jurisdictions were used. Their regression analyses included two alternative sets of dummy variables. The first approach utilized categorical variables for 9 industry categories, 11 occupational groups, collective bargaining status, and state; a set of year dummies was also included in order to capture national trends over time in workers' compensation costs. The second approach used only year dummies and dummy variables specific to distinct jobs (that is, 38,939 dummy variables) in order to control for cross-sectional variation in rates. Both sets of regressions also included a measure of benefits generosity (maximum benefit divided by the state average weekly wage).

State regulatory environments were categorized into three classes: states that had abandoned price setting by a rating bureau and prior approval of rates, states that had abandoned price setting by a rating bureau but not prior approval of rates, and states that had not abandoned either form of regulation. Different configurations of lagged dummy variables based on this categorization scheme were used to capture the effects of rate regulation.

Barkume and Ruser found that, in general, the elimination of rate bureau pricing resulted in a statistically significant reduction in workers' compensation premiums. However, the reduction was substantially larger when the state also eliminated the prior approval requirement. In addition, they failed to find these effects in some of their equations that did not control for fixed effects in which occupational dummies were used. With respect to the injury rate regressions, the elimination of rate-bureau pricing and prior approval was negatively related to their injury measures, but elimination of prior approval alone had no effect on the injury rate. In addition, elasticity estimates suggested that the effects of deregulation on injury rates were quite small, particularly when compared with its effect on compensation premiums. Barkume and Ruser concluded that their results offered only partial support for the Danzon–Harrington hypothesis that reduced incentives for loss control lead to higher injuries and premiums.

In summary, the Danzon–Harrington hypothesis predicts that rate suppression by regulatory agencies will result in higher employer costs of workers' compensation insurance. In particular, this theory postulates that rate regulation results in higher loss costs due to reduced incentives for loss control and the subsidization of high-risk employers by low-risk firms due to the nature of the residual market mechanisms in place in most states until the late 1980s. The Danzon–Harrington hypothesis differs from the traditional theory of rate regulation outlined in Chapter 6 in two ways. First, it unambiguously predicts that insurance deregulation will result in lower costs, while traditional theory fails to make an unambiguous prediction. Second, while Danzon and Harrington predicted higher employer costs due to a shift in the loss distribution, traditional rate regulation theory assumes that the loss distribution is unaffected by regulation; the impact of regulation on employer costs is thought to only affect insurer profit margins.

There is some evidence supporting this hypothesis. Danzon and Harrington found a positive relationship between various measures of regulatory rate suppression and workers' compensation loss costs. Notably, they did not examine the effect of the regulatory regime, as defined by statute, and loss costs. They also produced evidence of cross-subsidies between insurer rate groups. On the other hand, using dummy variables to measure the impact of the statutory regime, Barkume and Ruser only found partial support for the Danzon–Harrington hypothesis of a relationship between loss costs and the regulatory environment.

INJURY RATES AND RATE REGULATION

Danzon and Harrington (1998) predicted that if rates are suppressed, insurers will reduce the extent of loss-control services provided to employers. This occurs for two reasons. First, insurers have less incentive to offer loss-control services to employers in both the voluntary and residual markets. Second, rate suppression can lead to a reduction in experience-rating modification factors, schedule rating credits, or dividends, which will reduce employers' incentives to engage in loss-control activities. Consequently, they predict that rate regulation will result in an increase in the frequency and severity of occupational injuries. If so, workers' compensation insurance deregulation should be associated with a reduction in the frequency and severity of these injuries.

However, a contrary theory of the impact of deregulation on injury rates is also imaginable. It is possible that the regulatory agency sets rates at levels equal to or higher than those produced by a competitive market. If the underlying market structure is, in fact, competitive, insurers in this regulatory environment with market or above-market rates set by the regulatory agency will probably attempt to compete on the basis of product quality. Among other things, this could mean that insurers should increase the provision of loss-control services following deregulation. There may also be more extensive use of schedule rating credits, larger experience-rating modifications, and larger dividend payments. In any event, in this kind of an environment, regulation should be associated with lower injury rates than are found under deregulation. To examine this issue, we used regression analyses to determine the impact of rate regulation on statewide injury rates for the period from 1975–1995.

Table 8.4 reports injury rate means and standard deviations under different regulatory rules and regimes. The data provide only slight evidence that injury rates are higher under pure administered pricing than they are in deregulated market environments. However, there is no apparent relationship between the injury rate and the degree to which the insurance market has become deregulated. The lowest injury rates are found in states that allow variations from bureau rates subject to prior approval, which is the least deregulated of the deregulated regimes.

Injury Rates and Statutory Regimes

Of course, as we indicated earlier, a number of factors affect injury rates, and it is important to control for their extraneous influence. Once again, we employ multiple regression to isolate the effects of the regulatory environment. Table 8.5 reports the results of these analyses.

Table 8.4 Injury Rate Values by Regulatory Regime (per 100 workers)

Regulatory regime	Mean	Standard deviation	N
Pure admin. pricing	8.5635	1.3619	140
Var. from bureau rates w/prior appr.	8.1712	1.4272	635
Adv. rates w/o prior appr.	8.3142	1.3761	903
Loss costs w/prior appr.	8.3118	1.1686	71
Loss costs w/o prior appr.	8.3084	1.3622	888

The results reported in the model I column (which only include dummy variables indicating the nature of the statutory regulatory environment) suggest that there is little difference in injury rates between regulatory environments after controlling for the effects of other variables.[5]

The results of our previous analyses of employer costs imply that regulatory strategies vary across state insurance commissions. Failure to account for these differences in regulatory strategy may lead to the erroneous conclusion that rate regulation has no effect on injury rates. As before, we investigate this possibility by reestimating our regression equations, controlling for the degree to which the agency suppresses rates using the previously described measure of regulatory stringency.

The results of this regression analysis are reported in the model II column of Table 8.5. These results offer some evidence supporting the Danzon–Harrington hypothesis. While there is no apparent relationship between the lost-time injury rate and both regulatory stringency and the various partial deregulation dummies, injury rates are lower in the most deregulated environment (loss-cost systems that do not require prior approval) than in pure-administered-pricing jurisdictions after controlling for stringency. The interaction term for this regime is positively and significantly related to the injury rate, suggesting that the effects of deregulation are mitigated by the degree to which profit margins were reduced in the previous year. That is, the greater the degree of rate suppression in the previous year, the greater the injury rate in loss-cost regimes that do not require prior approval. This suggests that insurers may respond to declining profits by reducing loss-control services to employers. While this result is consistent with Danzon–Harrington hypothesis, it stands in contrast with other results that

Table 8.5 Regression Coefficients for Injury Rates as a Function of the Regulatory Environment[a]

	Model	
Variable	I	II
ln(Cash benefits)	0.0658***	0.0737***
	(3.89)	(4.29)
ln(Wages)	–0.2871***	–0.2744***
	(3.78)	(3.60)
Unemployment	–0.0135***	–0.0124***
	(6.99)	(6.01)
Union density	–0.0048***	–0.0045***
	(3.17)	(2.98)
Covered employment	0.0065**	0.0062**
	(2.22)	(2.12)
Proportion self-insured	–0.0557	–0.0711
	(1.14)	(1.44)
Competitive state fund	–0.0626***	–0.0737***
	(3.81)	(4.23)
Regulatory stringency	—[b]	–0.0211
		(0.65)
Admin. pricing w/dev. or sched. rating	0.0006	0.0153
	(0.05)	(0.38)
Admin. pricing w/dev. or sched. rating × loss ratio	—	–0.0141
		(0.39)
Adv. rates	0.0293*	0.0755
	(1.73)	(0.97)
Adv. rates × loss ratio	—	–0.0467
		(0.62)
Loss costs w/prior appr.	–0.0165	–0.0108
	(0.95)	(0.17)
Loss costs w/prior appr. × loss ratio	—	–0.0013
		(0.02)
Loss costs w/o prior appr.	0.0224	–0.1670***
	(1.43)	(2.82)
Loss costs w/o prior appr. × loss ratio	—	0.2052***
		(3.30)

Table 8.5 (continued)

	Model	
Variable	I	II
State dummies	Yes	Yes
Year dummies	Yes	Yes
Adjusted R^2	0.8652	0.8677

[a] Coefficients are followed by t-ratios in parentheses. *** = significant at the 1% level; ** = significant at the 5% level; * = significant at the 10% level.
[b] A dash (—) means the variable was not included in the regression specification.

are not, such as the fact that the injury rate is apparently unrelated to regulatory stringency in other regulatory environments.

Overall, these results provide little evidence for the Danzon–Harrington hypothesis that rate suppression in a regulated market results in greater claims experience and, consequently, higher loss costs. Not only is there little relationship between the statutory regulatory environment and the frequency of lost-time injuries, but injury incidence is apparently unrelated to the degree to which regulators suppress rates, a variable that is similar to that employed by Danzon and Harrington. Our findings indicate that workers' compensation insurance rate regulation has little, if any, effect on the injury rate.

THE EFFECT OF INSURANCE ARRANGEMENTS ON INJURY RATES

Two somewhat contradictory findings emerge from our analysis of the effect of insurance arrangements on injury rates. First, it does not appear that rate regulation has any substantial effect on the loss component of employer costs. On the other hand, results for state fund dummies imply that the public provision of workers' compensation insurance significantly affects employer accident experience. Specifically, the provision of insurance by an exclusive state fund appears to increase injury rates relative to states that permit private insurance, while the presence of a competitive state fund has the opposite effect.

Notes

1. A counterargument may be made. It is possible that recently unemployed workers may be more likely to file a workers' compensation claim in order to receive benefits that are more generous that those available through the unemployment insurance program. However, Fortin and Lanoie (1992), using data from Quebec, were unable to find evidence supporting this hypothesis.

2. Recall from Chapter 5 that the coefficient on the state fund dummies in the employer cost (adjusted manual rates or net weekly costs) equations is a measure of the loading factor. Further recall that the competitive-state-fund coefficient was positive and statistically significant, indicating that the loading factor was greater for competitive-state-fund jurisdictions.

3. Danzon and Harrington noted that their analysis was increasingly less applicable to workers' compensation as regulators and the NCCI began to address the problem of the residual market burden in the late 1980s. As noted in Chapter 2 and Appendix C, mechanisms that fund residual market benefits have changed substantially in many jurisdictions since that time. These reforms include two-tiered rate systems, assigned-risk rating plans that increase rates for firms with poor loss experience, and improved loss-control incentives for carriers. They have potentially increased employer and insurer incentives for loss control in the residual market and consequently reduced the extent of cross-subsidization and the adverse effects of rate regulation.

4. This was computed by multiplying, for each job, the workers' compensation costs per hour by the annual hours worked, and then dividing by annual gross earnings; the mean (for their full data set of 115,709) was 0.028.

5. It may argued that the Danzon–Harrington hypothesis implies that the injury rate response lags the change in the regulatory environment. To examine this issue, we also estimated the injury rate equation using lagged regulatory environment dummies; however, we failed to find evidence of a lagged response.

9
Conclusions

Workers' compensation provides cash benefits, medical care, and rehabilitation services to workers who experience work-related injuries and diseases. Workers' compensation programs in the United States were established by state statute and are modified by individual state's statutory revisions, workers' compensation agency regulations and decisions, and court opinions. These distinct, state-specific workers' compensation programs share some common features (such as similar legal rules for determining the compensability of an injury or illness, and similar types of medical and cash benefits).[1] However, there are also some significant differences among the states. For example, the level of cash benefits varies substantially among the state workers' compensation programs, with wide differences in maximum weekly benefits and, in some instances, the maximum durations of benefits.

One of the most important differences among state workers' compensation programs concerns the insurance arrangements for providing workers' compensation coverage. State laws prescribe workers' compensation benefits, but these laws assign to employers the responsibility for providing benefits. Employers in turn obtain workers' compensation coverage for the provision of these benefits by one of three mechanisms: they purchase insurance from 1) a private insurance carrier, 2) a competitive state workers' compensation fund, or 3) an exclusive (monopolistic) state workers' compensation fund. In addition, the self-insurance is available in almost every state (upon satisfying the requisite criteria).

In some states, such as New York, an employer may self-insure or may purchase insurance from either a private carrier or competitive state fund. Other states, such as Illinois or Wisconsin, restrict the employer's choice to private insurance carriers or self-insurance. A small number of jurisdictions, such as Ohio, restrict the employer's choice to an exclusive state fund or self-insurance.[2] This commingling of private (insurance carrier) and public (competitive or exclusive state fund) approaches to providing workers' compensation benefits is a distinctive feature of workers' compensation in the United States.[3]

Another important difference among state workers' compensation programs is the degree to which workers' compensation insurance pricing has been deregulated. The private provision of workers' compensation in the United States was highly regulated until recently. Carriers were subject to pure administered pricing, whereby maximum permissible rates were largely determined by state rating bureaus and the rates charged by carriers were subject to prior approval by state insurance commissions. However, most states in recent years have dismantled, in varying degrees, the system of rate regulation for workers' compensation insurance pricing. In fact, a deregulatory movement begun by just a few states in the early 1980s has become so widespread in recent years that only a few jurisdictions continue to use the pure-administered-pricing approach.

Increasingly, private carriers providing workers' compensation coverage are exposed to the vagaries of the competitive market (the extent of exposure varies, depending upon whether states have partially or largely deregulated workers' compensation insurance pricing). This raises questions as to whether the rationale that initially led to rate regulation still applies.[4] Alternatively stated, are different program outcomes with respect to the provision of workers' compensation insurance, such as employers' costs and program quality, affected by rate regulation?

There is substantial debate about the relative merits of public versus private provision of workers' compensation insurance and about the regulation of private-carrier-provided workers' compensation insurance. This debate has, for the most part, centered on questions concerning the availability and affordability of compensation insurance, since these two variables are relatively easy to measure. However, questions have also been raised regarding the quality of services provided to the parties to workers' compensation. Labor advocates, for example, have been particularly concerned that the profit motive causes insurers to unjustly deny claims or otherwise impede the delivery of benefits to workers, thus exacerbating the adverse consequences of workplace injuries or diseases.

Unfortunately, the existing theoretical and empirical literature on these topics is limited, inconsistent, and inconclusive. There are very few studies that explicitly examine the relative costs of public versus private provision of workers' compensation. Economic theory makes ambiguous predictions about insurance rate regulation's impact on most market outcomes, and the inconsistent findings of the little empirical research on this topic reflects this imprecision. These deficiencies in the literature were an important impetus for our study, which improves on previous research in a number of ways. However, empirical study of this topic presents very difficult challenges for the researcher, and it is likely that no empirical study will ever surmount all of these problems and completely dispose of the issue once and for all.

We were particularly concerned with the potentially important public policy implications of various insurance arrangements (the relative impact of public versus private provision of workers' compensation insurance, and the effect of insurance pricing deregulation), because the economic literature provides little guidance to public policymakers. As social scientists, we were intrigued by the prospect of being able to evaluate a social insurance program that varies, in least in certain dimensions, from state to state.

For all these reasons, we decided to empirically investigate the effect of insurance arrangements on interstate variations on system performance relative to the four objectives of the workers' compensation program outlined in Chapter 1: benefit adequacy, affordability, delivery system efficiency, and injury and disease prevention. In this chapter, we review evidence concerning system performance presented in preceding chapters. We conclude with a discussion of the public policy implications of our findings.

COST METHODOLOGY

Evaluation of system performance relative to two workers' compensation program objectives—affordability and delivery system efficiency—requires an analysis of workers' compensation costs. Unfortunately, it is difficult to measure the employers' costs of workers' compensation in multiple jurisdictions over extended periods because of a variety of factors that differ among those jurisdictions or that change over time. We have developed a sophisticated methodology that addresses many of these issues. Because it is central to our analyses and conclusions, it is appropriate to briefly review that methodology.

To calculate statewide average costs of workers' compensation insurance, we used 71 employer classification codes for insurance rates and the national distribution of national payroll among these classes to calculate the average cost in each state, which ensures that our measures of interstate cost differences represent a comparable set of employers and are not due to interstate variations in industry mix. We have carefully matched the National Council on Compensation Insurance classification codes for these employer classes to the unique insurance classification systems used by the three exclusive-state-fund jurisdictions in our study and to the classification systems used by other non-NCCI states in our study.

Furthermore, we have developed six different models that take into consideration myriad other factors in estimating the employers' costs of workers' compensation. Though only one model is used to compute employers' costs in a jurisdiction in a particular year, the appropriate model used for that jurisdiction varies across time. The choice of which models to use to compute employers' costs for a particular state and a particular year depends upon the nature of the workers' compensation insurance market. More specifically, it depends upon whether for any particular state and year 1) the state rating bureau publishes manual rates or pure premiums only, 2) rates in the assigned-risk (residual) market differ from those in the voluntary market, and 3) the state has an exclusive state fund or allows private carriers.

Our estimates of employers' costs thus take into consideration such things as premium discounts for quantity purchases, dividends received from insurance (mutual and participating stock) companies, manual rate modifications due to the employer's own compensable experience, and other variables. Our cost estimates also incorporate new competitive pricing arrangements that have become much more prevalent in recent years. Lastly, our estimates also reflect the provision of workers' compensation insurance to many employers in assigned-risk markets rather than in voluntary markets.

The end result of these cost computations is what we term adjusted manual rates, which represent the percentage of payroll expended by employers on workers' compensation insurance. Weekly insurance premiums per employee, which are calculated by multiplying a state's adjusted manual rate by the corresponding average weekly wage for that state, constitute another measure of employers' costs that is used for our study.

We have thus developed estimates for workers' compensation insurance costs for the period 1975–1995 and for 48 U.S. jurisdictions (because of data limitations, it was not possible to develop cost estimates for all 48 jurisdictions for all of the years from 1975 to 1995). Our data thus pertain to a relatively long period during which the insurance industry underwent several substantial changes. Since there is an important cyclical component to insurance pricing, estimates of the cost impact of deregulation or other public policies that use data from a short time period may be contaminated by other contemporaneous changes that also affect costs. The 21-year-period of our study spans at least one entire insurance cycle and thus avoids this problem.

BENEFIT ADEQUACY VERSUS AFFORDABILITY

As we noted in the first chapter, benefit adequacy was one of the five objectives of the workers' compensation program identified by the National Commission on State Workmen's Compensation Laws. Furthermore, the National Commission concluded that workers' compensation benefits in the vast majority of states were inadequate, in many respects, at the time of its report in 1972. The Commission made a number of recommendations with respect to benefit adequacy, and, under the threat of federal legislation, states initially responded by improving benefits. However, the political impetus for these reforms soon faded, and by the 1990s most states were still not in compliance with the National Commission's recommendations.

The reluctance of states to improve workers' compensation benefits can be explained by another objective of workers' compensation benefits: affordability. Since workers' compensation is a state rather than a federal program, lawmakers are concerned that generous compensation benefits will adversely affect employer costs, resulting in an exodus of firms (and jobs) to low-cost jurisdictions. Thus, there is a tension between these objectives and a perception that in order to improve performance with respect to benefit adequacy, the state must necessarily sacrifice the goal of affordability.

We examined this tradeoff by estimating equations predicting employer costs as a function of workers' compensation benefit levels while controlling for a number of other variables that are thought to influence costs (such as the injury rate, the proportion of benefits paid to permanent partial disability claims, union density, and the extent of workers' compensation coverage). We also included year and state dummy variables to control for unobserved time- and state-specific variation in costs. The results from these regressions were then used to simulate the effect of raising benefit levels to the adequacy standards contained in the Model Act of the Council of State Governments. The results of this simulation were compared with the results of a similar exercise conducted by Krueger and Burton (1990), who estimated the effect of the imposition of eight of the essential recommendations of the National Commission on employer costs. The most significant difference between the Model Act and the essential recommendations is that the Model Act sets standards for permanent partial disability benefits, while the National Commission does not.

Our regression results revealed that the measured effect of benefits on employer costs was substantially dependent on the regression specification. We also found evidence suggesting that our statutory benefit variable was significantly affected by measurement error. Consequently, we suggest that readers approach our findings cautiously.

Our simulation results were used to examine the impact of benefit adequacy on three measures of affordability: the average cost of workers' compensation nationally and two measures of cost dispersion, namely, the standard deviation of costs and the coefficient of variation. We found that higher benefit levels required by the Model Act increased average costs by 60–75 percent. Significantly, imposition of the Model Act also increases the cost differences among states. This latter result is particularly troubling due to its implications for firm location decisions. In other words, as a result of imposing federal standards, the gap between high- and low-cost states will grow, with adverse consequences for employment in those high-cost states. While the labor market may rectify these imbalances in the long run as unemployed workers migrate geographically or occupationally, in the short run the imposition of federal standards incorporating the Model Act could cause a severe economic dislocation of workers. This dislocation will particularly affect workers in high-risk industries that pay higher than average workers' compensation costs.[5]

On the other hand, the impact of the essential recommendations on employer costs estimated by Krueger and Burton was much smaller; they found that these recommendations were associated with a 15–20 percent increase in average costs in 1983. Significantly, they failed to find consistent evidence indicating whether the essential recommendations increased or decreased cost dispersion among states. This suggests that modest reforms to achieve benefit adequacy would have a much less substantial, although nontrivial, effect on affordability.

DELIVERY SYSTEM EFFICIENCY

Another objective of workers' compensation programs is that workers' compensation should be delivered to injured workers for the least possible administrative cost. While many factors influence performance on this objective, we are particularly interested in the effect of different insurance arrangements. Thus, a principal focus of our study was an investigation of the cost impact of public versus private provision of workers' compensation insurance, as well as the impact of deregulation. In this section, we first review our hypotheses and empirical findings regarding the public versus private comparison, which examined the influence of exclusive state funds and competitive state funds. We then present comparable information with respect to the cost impact of deregulation.

Public versus Private Provision

Advocates of public funding for workers' compensation insurance (that is, proponents of exclusive state funds) assert that employer costs are lower where compensation is exclusively funded through a state agency, because an exclusive state fund neither incurs marketing expenses nor needs to make a profit. Exclusive state funds are allegedly more efficient than private carriers, since they are able to capture economies of scale. Lastly, although market fluctuations cause periodic crises with respect to the availability of affordable workers' compensation insurance from private carriers (or from assigned-risk markets), this is not a problem in exclusive-state-fund jurisdictions.[6]

On the other hand, proponents of the private provision of workers' compensation insurance assert that the lack of a profit motive on the part of exclusive or competitive state funds creates administrative inefficiencies that increase costs. In addition, political factors allegedly cause state funds to create subsidies for one group of employers at the expense of another, either between different classes of employers at one point in time or between employers of different generations. In addition to creating obvious inequities, these state-fund subsidies also result in allocative inefficiencies that reduce social welfare. For similar reasons, it is also claimed that administrative determination by state funds of a claimant's benefit eligibility and duration of disability is less stringent than private carriers' determinations, thus exacerbating problems associated the worker's benefit utilization in response to higher benefits.

There is very little empirical evidence to substantiate the hypotheses concerning the relative merits of either the public or private provision of workers' compensation insurance, since very little research has been done in this area. The only recent interjurisdictional cost study involving exclusive state funds (Thomason and Burton 2000a) found that costs were somewhat lower, on average, in two Canadian monopolistic-state-fund provinces than in U.S. states with private carriers. However, several empirical analyses found that competitive-state-fund jurisdictions had higher costs than did states that relied solely on private carriers (Krueger and Burton 1990; Schmidle 1994).

Our study extends and improves upon this prior research in a number of ways. First, we used identical cost measures in all states to investigate the effects of public provision of insurance (by exclusive-state-fund jurisdictions and by competitive-state-fund jurisdictions that also allow private carriers) and the effects of private provision (in states that allow private carriers). Our examination of the cost impact of exclusive state funds is, to our knowledge, the first in recent decades to compare the relative cost of exclusive state funds in the United States with private-carrier states.

Second, we utilized a data set with a much longer time period (21 consecutive years) than that used in previous empirical studies of the cost impact of competitive state funds. Among other things, the length of this time series allowed us to examine relative costs at different stages of the insurance cycle. This is particularly important because the insurance cycle may have a different impact on private and public providers of workers' compensation insurance. In addition, data from a 21-year period allow us to compare states both before and after they adopted or abandoned a competitive state fund, so we were thus able to control for unobservable state-specific factors that influence compensation costs.

Empirical results: exclusive state funds

There are several interesting results from our analysis of exclusive state funds, although there are also several major caveats with respect to these findings. A simple comparison of average employer costs, which does not use a regression model to statistically control for the influence of other possible influences on costs (such as benefits or injury rates), indicated that employer costs were lower in exclusive-state-fund jurisdictions than in states where private carriers provide workers' compensation insurance. This pattern persists throughout the entire period of our analysis (1975–1995). These data also suggest that costs for exclusive state funds are much less cyclical than are costs for private-insurance jurisdictions. However, the cost differential between exclusive-state-fund jurisdictions and states with private carriers substantially disappears when we use a weighted least squares regression model that controls for other factors that influence costs.

There are compelling reasons to be circumspect in interpreting these results. We have data from only three (out of six) exclusive-state-fund jurisdictions, and data for two of these jurisdictions were limited to a subset of years in our study. Furthermore, controls for the difference between the statutory level of benefits and actual expenditures of cash benefits is particularly problematic for exclusive-state-fund jurisdictions.

In addition, there are important differences between exclusive state funds and private carriers that may not be fully reflected in our data. For example, our cost comparisons use the average cost of workers' compensation insurance paid by employers in a particular state and year. These employers' costs estimates in exclusive-state-fund jurisdictions and private-carrier states are not perfectly comparable. For example, private insurer costs incorporate both marketing expenses and taxes, as well as other fees or license costs. Exclusive state funds do not incur marketing expenses, and while they do pay some taxes (such as payroll taxes), they do not pay others such as income taxes, insurance department license fees, and state and local insurance taxes. As well, the employers' costs of workers' compensation insurance in private-carrier jurisdictions include a profit markup, which is also missing from exclusive-state-fund costs.

Thus, the problem is that some costs that appear in the private insurers' income statements are "hidden" in state insurance fund accounts. That is, these costs are incurred by exclusive state funds but are reflected neither in their accounts nor in the employers' workers' compensation premiums. For example, income taxes paid by private insurers necessarily relieve the tax burden of employers. Where there are no private workers' compensation insurers to pay income taxes, namely in exclusive-state-fund jurisdictions, the level of governmental services is reduced or the tax burden is spread over the remainder of the tax base, including employers who purchase insurance.[7]

The preceding discussion suggests that the problem of hidden costs is significant and that adjustments have to be made to ensure that the costs of workers' compensation insurance in exclusive-state-fund and private-insurance jurisdictions are comparable. Ideally, these adjustments should be made so that costs in both jurisdictions represent the real (including hidden) costs of compensation to employers. However, ascertaining the true extent of these hidden costs in the exclusive-fund jurisdictions in our study, both at one point in time and over time, is extremely problematic. While we conclude that the existence of hidden costs means that exclusive-state-fund rates are probably understated relative to private-carrier rates, we can not quantify the extent of this underestimate.

Our cost estimates for exclusive-state-fund jurisdictions may be understated for another reason: exclusive state funds are more likely than private carriers to incur deficits in the short and medium terms. Exclusive state funds can have artificially low rates because they can accumulate deficits without fearing the loss of policyholders when they ultimately have to raise rates. However, we have not made an effort to quantify the extent to which rates are artificially low, in part because of the difficulties in reconciling these underestimates through the use of actuarial evaluations of the exclusive state funds.

Nevertheless, despite (or perhaps because of) these data limitations, it is probably prudent to conclude that there is no clear difference in costs between exclusive-state-fund jurisdictions and private-carrier states.

Empirical results: competitive state funds

Our empirical results indicate that employers' costs are higher in jurisdictions with competitive state funds than in states with only private carriers. Specifically, we found that adjusted manual rates were 25 percent higher and net weekly costs were 24 percent higher in competitive-state-fund jurisdictions even after controlling for benefits, injury rates, and other factors that influence costs. The relatively higher costs associated with competitive state funds is consistent with earlier findings (Krueger and Burton 1990; Schmidle 1994) of inefficiencies associated with state funds.

However, once again, we are confronted by our results with respect to the costs in exclusive-state-fund jurisdictions relative to states with private carriers. If competitive state funds are inefficient due to the lack of a profit motive, why do we not find similar results for exclusive state funds? There are a number of possible explanations for this inconsistency. The lack of extensive data on exclusive-state-fund programs or any of the other problems discussed in the previous section could account for these results. In addition, it is possible that our results for competitive funds are due to uncontrolled endogeneity; that is, the causal arrow is reversed. Rather than competitive funds causing workers' compensation costs to soar, it is possible that high-cost states, such as Rhode Island, are more likely to establish competitive funds.

Deregulation

Historically, insurance rates were regulated due to a fear that property/casualty insurers would write policies at below-cost rates. In fact, the property/casualty insurance industry was subject to periodic waves of insolvency. This problem was in part due to a lack of accurate or complete actuarial data. As ratemaking organizations emerged to address this problem—in particular, the issue of inaccurate or incomplete actuarial data—policymakers became concerned about oligopolistic pricing. While other insurance lines were deregulated in response to these concerns, workers' compensation was treated as an exception because of its distinctive characteristic as a mandated social insurance program. In particular, policymakers believed that it was important to continue regulating workers' compensation insurance rates in order to ensure that workers' compensation insurance was both affordable and available.

Traditional economic theory of insurance rate regulation suggests that the impact of deregulation of insurance markets largely depends on the behavior or strategy of the regulatory agency. If, prior to deregulation, employers dominate the regulatory agency, then rate suppression by the regulatory agency should result in higher compensation costs following deregulation. On the other hand, if rate regulation permitted insurers to form a cartel, then deregulation could lead to lower prices, as the market forces prices down to competitive levels. Among other things, these competing theories mean that the effect of rate regulation can vary among jurisdictions and—if regulatory agency strategies change—over time.

This theory of rate regulation also predicts that regulation can affect other market outcomes, including the availability of insurance and market structure. Specifically, if regulatory agencies suppress rates, marginal insurers will quit the market, resulting in a reduction in the number of insurers underwriting policies and increased market shares for the survivors. In addition, the withdrawal of private carriers from the market can eventually lead to a reduction in the availability of insurance. In the extreme case of rate suppression, the market may eventually collapse, as occurred in Maine in the 1980s.

To determine the effects of insurance rate regulation on overall delivery system efficiency, we investigated its impact on two market outcomes: employer costs and market structure. In the process, we improved on the previous research of rate regulation in various property/casualty lines, which in large part used relatively simple measures of the regulatory environment. Often, states in these studies were categorized solely as regulated or deregulated jurisdictions. However, our detailed examination of the relevant workers' compensation legislation and the state regulatory practices revealed that rate regulation is better conceptualized along a continuum rather than as a simple dichotomy.

We used a more complex characterization of the regulatory environment than has most previous research in order to capture the actual practices of the state regulatory agency as well as interstate differences in statutory regimes.

Empirical results: employer costs

Our initial set of model specifications, which were discussed in Chapter 7, provided contradictory evidence concerning the impact of rate regulation (or deregulation) on workers' compensation costs. Our regression analyses, which control for interstate differences in benefits and a variety of other factors, show that the impact of regulation on compensation costs depends on the definition of the regulatory environment that is used. This may explain the lack of consistent results among previous studies examining this issue. In addition, our regression results suggest that insurance costs are higher under various forms of partial deregulation than under the most strict form of rate regulation (pure administered pricing). On the other hand, more comprehensive deregulation (where rating organizations file loss costs, rather than fully developed rates, that are not subject to prior approval by the state regulatory agency) results in a rate reduction of about 11 percent.

Other analyses, which controlled for the stage of the insurance cycle or the degree to which the regulatory agency suppressed rates, present an even more complicated picture of the effect of rate regulation on insurance costs. First, the data show a strong negative relationship between regulatory stringency (an index of state-to-national average loss ratios) and compensation costs under administered pricing. However, the relationship between regulatory stringency and employer costs either is not statistically different from zero or is significantly positive under other regulatory regimes. These findings are consistent with the "regulatory agency behavior" theory of rate regulation.[8] Second, our analyses of the cost effect of regulatory stringency under the hard and soft portions of the insurance cycle found that under administered pricing, rates fall during a hard market relative to their levels in a soft market, indicating increased rate suppression during a hard market, i.e., when insurance demand outstrips supply.

As indicated, the data show that partial deregulation of workers' compensation insurance rate-making has an impact on costs that is qualitatively different than the effect of more comprehensive deregulation. That is, costs under partial deregulation are higher than costs under administered pricing, while costs under more comprehensive deregulation are lower. Of all of the empirical findings in our study, this result is probably the most difficult one to explain.

One possible answer is provided by our findings regarding the relationship between regulatory stringency and compensation costs under partial versus comprehensive forms of deregulation. Specifically, these data suggest that under partial deregulation there is an asymmetric response to regulatory stringency. Under conditions of high stringency (rate suppression), partial deregulation leads to higher insurance prices as market forces push rates up to more competitive levels. However, partial deregulation under conditions of low stringency (where the rates are not being held below market levels) does not induce comparable rate reductions.

It is possible that because insurers have less latitude to adjust price under partially deregulated regimes relative to under complete deregulation, they are more reluctant to lower prices when market conditions become more favorable. They may view favorable market conditions as an opportunity to make up for losses incurred when the market was more adverse. Alternatively, it is possible that bureau rates under partial deregulation act as a pricing point for insurers when market conditions are more favorable for them; that is, the advisory bureau rates become the market price, even when they are above competitive market levels.

The preceding discussion was complex because it reflected the complexity in measuring the actual impact of deregulation. A variety of factors must be taken into consideration, such as 1) whether rates prior to deregulation were at, above, or below market rates, a situation that varies among jurisdictions and over time; 2) partially related to this first point, whether deregulation occurred during the hard market or soft market phase of the insurance cycle; and 3) the multiple forms of deregulation (for example, administered pricing with deviations or schedule ratings; advisory rates without prior approval; and loss costs with prior approval). Overall, after controlling for as many factors as possible that affect rates (such as benefits levels, injury rates, etc., and items 1 and 2 above), we find in general that partial deregulation appears to result in higher costs on average than would be found in administered pricing, while more comprehensive deregulation results in costs that are lower than those found in administered pricing.

Empirical results: market structure

For the most part, the results of our weighted least squares regression analyses concerning market structure support our interpretation of the cost findings. Concentration ratios are negatively related to all of the deregulation dummy variables, suggesting that markets are less concentrated in a deregulated environment relative to pure administered pricing. In addition, the regulatory stringency measure was associated with greater concentration ratios in non–loss cost regulatory environments but had no impact on concentration ratios in states that had partially or completed deregulated. All of these results are consistent with the hypothesis that state regulatory agencies suppress rates under pure administered pricing and that following deregulation, prices rise to competitive levels, which encourages private carriers to enter the market or otherwise compete for market share. With respect to partial deregulation, this explanation is also consistent with the cost findings.

On the other hand, this explanation is inconsistent with the cost results for more comprehensive regulation, which indicated that, if anything, state regulators pushed prices above competitive market levels under pure administered pricing. An explanation that could reconcile all of these disparate findings is that when states enact comprehensive deregulation, insurers cut prices dramatically—perhaps to (or below) pure premium levels—in order to gain market share. While this behavior is inconsistent with the economic assumption of rationality, it is consistent with anecdotal evidence from some states that have pursued comprehensive deregulation, including, most recently, California.

Taken together, these results lead us to conclude that the delivery system under comprehensive deregulation is more efficient than the delivery system either under partial deregulation or under pure administered pricing.

INJURY PREVENTION

The fourth objective of workers' compensation programs with which we are concerned is the encouragement of safety. As indicated in Chapter 1, by linking employer workers' compensation costs to the firm's claims experience, the compensation program strives to provide employers with incentives to reduce claim frequency and severity. In addition, market forces similarly encourage insurers to provide employers with safety management loss-control services as a part of the insurance product. We might expect that this is particularly likely in those states where, due to the regulatory environment, insurers are unable to compete on the basis of price. Furthermore, while state compensation funds lack a profit motive to improve their insurance "product" by offering safety management services, political pressures to provide such services could be equally, if not more, compelling.

Recently, Danzon and Harrington (1998) hypothesized that rate suppression in regulated markets results in reduced loss-control incentives for employers and insurers, which, in turn, increases the benefits paid and the cost of insurance. On the assumption that state regulatory agencies suppress rates below market levels, Danzon and Harrington argued that insurers respond to adverse market conditions by withdrawing insurance coverage in the voluntary market from riskier insureds, which are then forced into the residual market. They further claimed that there are substantial subsidies from the voluntary to the residual market, which reduces the loss-control incentives of employers in the residual market. In addition, when rates are suppressed, insurers reduce or eliminate loss-control incentives for employers in the voluntary market. Finally, if in the rate approval process the insurance commission is more likely to pass through loss costs than loss-control expenses, then insurers will have reduced loss-control incentives. Since the loss-control incentives of both insureds and insurers are thus reduced under rate regulation, Danzon and Harrington hypothesized that deregulation will result in lower loss costs. Among other things, they predicted that workplaces will be safer and the injury rate will be lower in an unregulated insurance market.

To investigate the relationship between insurance arrangements and performance on the prevention objective, we examined the effect of public provision of workers' compensation insurance (by exclusive and competitive state funds), as well as the effect of deregulation, on statewide injury rates. We found that injury rates were higher in exclusive-state-fund jurisdictions than in states that permit private insurers to underwrite workers' compensation insurance policies. There are at least three possible explanations for this result: state funds have more lenient eligibility criteria, lack incentives for loss control, and/or fail to provide insured employers with such incentives. Alternatively, private insurers may be relatively more aggressive in claims management.[9] However, without further investigation into the claims management issue, these data suggest that exclusive-state-fund jurisdictions have a record inferior to that of private insurance with respect to workplace health and safety.

Our findings also indicate that injury rates in jurisdictions with competitive fund states are lower than injury rates in states that only have private workers' compensation insurers. This result is difficult to reconcile with our finding that employers' costs are relatively higher in competitive-state-fund jurisdictions, as well as with our previously reported results concerning the relative costs and injury rates for exclusive state funds.

Lastly, with respect to deregulation, the results for our injury rate regressions provide only weak evidence supporting the Danzon–Harrington hypothesis that rate suppression increases the pure premium component of the adjusted manual rate. In this connection, it is important to recall that our cost regressions controlled for interstate difference in loss costs, so that our cost results only pertain to the effect of insurance arrangements on profit and expense loadings. While these cost components appear to be affected by rate regulation, the pure premium, as measured by work injury rates, does not.

POLICY IMPLICATIONS

There are three sets of policy implications that flow from the data that we have analyzed and discussed in preceding chapters of this book. These relate to 1) the effect of public versus private provision of workers' compensation insurance on delivery system efficiency and workplace safety; 2) the effect of deregulation of private insurance markets on delivery system efficiency and safety; and 3) the effect of federal standards with respect to benefit adequacy on the affordability objective of workers' compensation programs.

Public versus Private Provision of Workers' Compensation Insurance

Our analyses of the employers' cost of workers' compensation provide little, if any, evidence that either type of insurance arrangement is superior on the basis of delivery system efficiency. There is no measurable difference in costs between exclusive state funds and states with private insurance markets. While states with competitive state funds appear to be more costly than states without such funds, this result is likely to be due to factors other than the relative efficiency of the two types of insurance arrangements. State funds may be well or poorly administered; a well-run fund may be superior to a private insurance market, particularly a regulated market, while a poorly run fund may be inferior to the private market. Based on the limited data available to us, we have no reason to believe that either public or private provision of compensation insurance is inherently more efficient.

However, we again caution that our empirical results regarding state funds warrant a circumspect approach. Policymakers should be skeptical about claims that the "reform" of introducing private carriers into a market, or of establishing exclusive or competitive state funds, will reduce costs in a state. This is an important lesson from our research, especially since a number of states have introduced competitive state funds in the last two decades, generally because they thought that costs would be reduced. Based on our findings, we conclude that such a strategy is naive and misguided.

The results with respect to workplace safety are mixed. The injury rate is higher in exclusive-state-fund jurisdictions than in jurisdictions that have private workers' compensation insurance markets, but lower in those states with competitive funds than in those with private carriers only. While both results are statistically significant, together they are inexplicable, at least with respect to the question of the effectiveness of public versus private provision of workers' compensation insurance. We are reluctant to recommend policy on the basis of these contradictory findings.

Deregulation of Workers' Compensation Insurance Markets

On the other hand, the results of our study provide relatively strong evidence that comprehensive deregulation of the workers' compensation insurance markets results in significant gains in delivery system efficiency. Moving from pure administered pricing to comprehensive deregulation appears to be associated with an 11 percent reduction in employer costs. The cost reduction resulting from a move from some forms of partial deregulation to complete deregulation is even more impressive. Since our results with respect to the injury prevention objective do not show a clear advantage for regulation or deregulation, we conclude that states should comprehensively deregulate their workers' compensation insurance markets.

The impact of comprehensive deregulation relative to other changes in our regression model parameters is reported in Table 9.1 for adjusted manual rates and net weekly costs. This table shows that a one-standard-deviation reduction in only two of the control variables in our regression equation, medical benefits and the injury rate, has a cost effect similar to that associated with comprehensive deregulation of the workers' compensation market. Other policy changes, such as a reduction in cash benefits, have only a slight effect on costs. However, we note that more substantial changes in cash benefit generosity—such as the imposition of the provisions of the Model Act or the essential recommendations of the National Commission—have much greater effects on employer costs. As noted earlier in this chapter, we estimate that the essential recommendations would increase employer costs by 15–20 percent and that the Model Act would have increased costs by as much as 70 percent.

Aside from our findings with respect to employer costs, we note that there are several other compelling reasons to support a public policy of full deregulation. First, it eliminates the need to allocate resources to regulation rather than to other social purposes. Second, it avoids extreme distortions in the market, such as in Maine, where rate suppression caused the virtual collapse of the voluntary market, with enormous subsidies from carriers to employers in the residual market.

**Table 9.1 Predicted Effects of Selected Policy Changes on
Employer Costs**

	Mean ($)	Standard deviation ($)	Change from actual ($)	Change from actual (%)
Adjusted manual rates				
Actual costs	2.249	1.114		
Predicted costs following a one-standard-deviation reduction[a] in				
Cash benefits	2.140	1.015	−0.109	−4.85
Medical benefits	1.841	0.873	−0.408	−18.14
Injury rate	1.941	0.921	−0.308	−13.70
PPD proportion	2.030	0.963	−0.219	−9.73
Union density	2.220	1.053	−0.029	−1.29
Covered employment	2.186	1.037	−0.063	−2.79
Predicted costs following imposition of deregulation	1.924	0.937	−0.324	−14.42
Net weekly costs				
Actual costs	11.885	6.141		
Predicted costs following a one-standard-deviation reduction[a] in				
Cash benefits	11.172	5.619	−0.713	−6.00
Medical benefits	9.486	4.771	−2.400	−20.19
Injury rate	10.329	5.195	−1.556	−13.09
PPD proportion	10.758	5.411	−1.128	−9.49
Union density	11.441	5.755	−0.444	−3.74
Covered employment	11.447	5.758	−0.438	−3.69
Predicted costs following imposition of deregulation	10.199	5.306	−1.686	−14.19

[a] A one-standard-deviation change was chosen because it represents a substantial, yet plausible, departure from reality that is statistically identical for all control variables. The effects of a one-standard-deviation change were estimated by first determining the standard deviation of the variable. The standard deviation was then subtracted from the actual value of the variable for each observation in the sample. The resulting values for that variable, along with the actual values for every other variable in our model, were then substituted into the regression equation to compute predicted employer costs. These predicted costs were then averaged across the entire sample.

Third, it probably reduces the importance of residual markets in general, where incentives to safety are more muted (although we find little or no evidence for such an effect). Lastly, the results of our regressions predicting insurance market concentration indicate that deregulation increases the number of carriers in the market, which, in turn, increases options for employers and should ultimately hold down costs.

Importantly, while the evidence indicates that workers will pay for higher workers' compensation benefits (Moore and Viscusi 1990), it is unlikely that workers will pay for inefficient administration. Further, to the extent that insurance rate regulation (or deregulation) increases administrative costs without providing value in terms of greater equity or more generous benefits, these increased costs represent a deadweight loss to society.

There are several other reasons to exercise caution in interpreting the policy implications of our results. There were a number of major changes affecting workers' compensation between 1975 and 1995, such as business and underwriting cycles, increasing or decreasing cash and medical benefits in some states, and deregulation of private insurance markets in most states (with a considerable variation among states in the exact form of the deregulation). Disentangling the effects of particular policy changes is complicated, and we may not have isolated these effects, despite our best efforts and sophisticated methodology.

Furthermore, our findings were subject to limitations on data comparability among states and over time (for example, some states with private carriers do not have data on the share of benefits provided by voluntary and assigned-risk markets). Additionally, in an ideal situation, insurance premiums per $100 of payroll for a standardized set of classifications would be explained by a set of variables including benefits actually paid per $100 of payroll for the standardized set of classifications. We do not have such a benefits measure because, *inter alia*, data are not available for all jurisdictions in our study, and existing data do not control for variation in industrial composition (and therefore the injury rate) among states. Instead we use a benefits index, which is an actuarial evaluation of cash benefits that the average workers' compensation claimant could expect to receive in a particular jurisdiction. Since this benefit index does not account for administrative differences among states, there are likely discrepancies between our index measure of benefit generosity and actual benefits paid to injured workers. We partially control for these administrative differences by including the share of benefits accounted for by permanent partial disability cases (typically the most expensive category of cash benefits, and the category with the greatest opportunity for exercise of administrative discretion). Nonetheless, we may not completely control for all such differences affecting benefits paid.

Lastly, we only assessed the relative merits of public provision of workers' compensation insurance and of deregulation with respect to employers' costs, market structure, and injury rates. Our examination of market outcomes does not include all potential outcomes of regulation or deregulation. In particular, we ignore outcomes such as the effect of rate regulation on the probability and cost of insurer insolvency, which provided the initial rationale for insurance rate regulation. However, we hope that our analysis will at least help contribute to the ongoing discussion of the relative merits of deregulation and of state funds.

Benefit Adequacy and Affordability

The results of our analysis show that there is indeed a trade-off between benefit adequacy and affordability. Increasing workers' compensation benefits to the level prescribed by the Model Act increases the average cost of workers' compensation nationally by 60–75 percent and increases cost variation among states even more. This latter result was particularly troubling due to its implication for plant-location decisions, indicating that such a substantial increase in costs could adversely effect employment in high-cost states and have potentially severe consequences on workers at the bottom of the economic ladder. These results either support the advisability of a federal takeover of state workers' compensation programs or the abandonment of the adequacy objective, at least as defined by the Model Act.

On the other hand, Krueger and Burton (1990) reported that more modest reform, namely the essential recommendations of the National Commission on State Workmen's Compensation Laws, has a much less dramatic impact on affordability. They found that full implementation of the National Commission's essential recommendations are associated with a 10–15 percent cost increase and no evident change in cost variation. Recall that comprehensive deregulation of the private insurance market would reduce compensation costs by 11 percent, according to our results. Taken together, these two results suggest that state workers' compensation benefits could be improved to meet the National Commission's definition of adequacy without any overall cost increase (and the concomitant economic disruption) if the states were to simultaneously deregulate their workers' compensation insurance markets.

In the beginning of this book, we noted how policymakers in Rhode Island successfully repaired that state's broken workers' compensation system in the early 1990s, resolving conflicting interests of the different stakeholders in the system through compromise. These kinds of solutions are not always available to policymakers, but our results, in conjunction with those of Krueger and Burton, offer hope that the benefit adequacy objective can be realized, without sacrificing affordability, by improving delivery system efficiency.

Notes

1. We include the District of Columbia when we refer to "states." The federal government's involvement in workers' compensation is limited, for the most part, to administration of programs covering federal employees (per the Federal Employees' Compensation Act) and certain maritime employees (per the Longshore and Haborworkers' Compensation Act).
2. There are six exclusive-state-fund jurisdictions; two of these (North Dakota and Wyoming) do not permit self-insurance.
3. More specifically, workers' compensation in the United States uses private insurance carriers both as financial intermediaries and to administer claims (subject to oversight by state workers' compensation agencies) in all states, save for the exclusive-state-fund jurisdictions. Workers' compensation in the United States is distinctive among such programs worldwide because, with the exception of the exclusive-state-fund jurisdictions, it uses private carriers both to bear risk and to help administer the program.
4. Several decades ago, the rationale was questioned by a workers' compensation expert, though his call for additional research was in large part ignored during the intervening years (Williams 1969, p. 211):

    More research is needed on the feasibility and desirability of encouraging more price competition instead of the present, almost universal, practice of having all [workers' compensation] insurers use the same initial rates, these rates being subject to prior approval by the State insurance department. If this practice can be explained only in terms of historical precedent, it should be abandoned. However, the special characteristics of workmen's compensation insurance may make uniform initial pricing and positive rate regulation appropriate in this line.

5. We note that our estimate of the increasing gap between high- and low-cost states due to the imposition of federal standards is based on the assumption that the imposition of federal standards would not affect the behavior of the actors. However, there is evidence indicating that workers' compensation evaluations are influenced by the generosity (or penuriousness) of statutory benefits (Durbin and Kish 1997), so that adjudicators may evaluate claimants in states with low statutory benefits as being more severely disabled than claimants with comparable injuries in states with high statutory benefits. If true, this would imply that the gap between high and low costs may not increase as much as predicted by our models if federal standards are imposed.

6. Competitive state funds are thought to offer some of the advantages of exclusive state funds without the disadvantages. They provide workers' compensation insurance coverage to employers who are not able to obtain it from a private carrier in the context of a competitive market environment.

7. Profits may also represent another hidden cost for employers in exclusive-state-fund jurisdictions. Profits represent the private insurance carriers reward for risk; i.e., the reward that the insurer receives for risking their equity if losses exceed revenues. Similar risks exist for exclusive state funds, but these risks are borne by the employers themselves. That is, if losses exceed revenues, the exclusive state fund will replenish reserves by increasing premium rates in subsequent years. Thus, in a private insurance system, the employer is able to shift more risk to the carrier than is possible under an exclusive state fund. Of course, the preceding analysis assumes that competition causes insurer earnings to be limited to normal profits in the long run.

8. These results imply that regulators are able to suppress rates under pure administered pricing, but not after the rate-setting process has been deregulated.

9. However, it is important to recognize that aggressive claims management may increase costs. Aggressive claims management can result in a litigious atmosphere in which transaction costs are substantial and potentially overwhelm any savings accrued from denying invalid claims or from reducing claimant malingering.

Appendix A

Data on Workers' Compensation Costs, Benefits, and Insurance Arrangements

Table A.1 Workers' Compensation Costs and Benefits, 1960–98

Year	Col. 1 Benefits (as % of payroll)	2 Costs (as % of payroll)	3 Statutory cash benefits (average stated as % of Model Act)
1960	0.59	0.93	
1961	0.61	0.95	
1962	0.62	0.96	
1963	0.62	0.99	
1964	0.63	1.00	
1965	0.61	1.00	
1966	0.61	1.02	
1967	0.63	1.07	
1968	0.62	1.07	
1969	0.62	1.08	
1970	0.66	1.11	
1971	0.67	1.11	
1972	0.68	1.14	39.6
1973	0.70	1.17	44.3
1974	0.75	1.24	44.7
1975	0.83	1.32	45.4
1976	0.87	1.49	49.4
1977	0.92	1.71	49.6
1978	0.94	1.86	48.9
1979	1.01	1.95	50.4
1980	1.07	1.96	50.3
1981	1.08	1.85	49.3
1982	1.16	1.75	49.7
1983	1.17	1.67	50.7
1984	1.21	1.66	50.7
1985	1.30	1.82	50.5
1986	1.37	1.99	50.1
1987	1.43	2.07	50.6

Table A.1 (continued)

Year	Col. 1 Benefits (as % of payroll)	2 Costs (as % of payroll)	3 Statutory cash benefits (average stated as % of Model Act)
1988	1.49	2.16	50.1
1989	1.43[a]	2.04[a]	51.0
1990	1.49	2.13	50.1
1991	1.64	2.16	49.9
1992	1.66	2.13	48.9
1993	1.58	2.17	50.0
1994	1.52	2.05	49.3
1995	1.39	1.83	49.1
1996	1.28	1.67	50.1
1997	1.14	1.46	
1998	1.08	1.35	

SOURCE: Columns 1 and 2, 1960–88 data from Social Security Administration (1995), Table 9.B1; 1989–98 data from Mont, Burton, and Reno (2000), Table 10, col. 3. Column 3 data from Thomason and Burton (2000b).

[a] The drop in benefits and cash as a percentage of payroll between 1988 and 1989 is due at least in part to a change in methodology that increased the estimated coverage of the workers' compensation program.

Table A.2 Workers' Compensation Program Costs, 1960–98

Year	Amount ($, millions)	Annual rate of increase from previous year shown (%)
1960	2,055	—
1971	5,191	8.79
1979	20,330	18.61
1984	25,122	4.32
1991	55,216	11.91
1998	52,108	−0.82

SOURCE: 1960–84 data from Nelson (1992b), Table 7, p. 51; 1991 and 1998 data from Mont, Burton, and Reno (2000), Table 9, p. 16.

Table A.3 Benefit Payments by Regular Workers' Compensation Programs, by Type of Payment, 1960–98

Year	Total benefits		Medical and hospitalization payments			Cash benefits		
	Amount ($, millions)	Annual rate of increase from previous year shown (%)	Amount ($, millions)	Annual rate of increase from previous year shown (%)	Share of total (%)	Amount ($, millions)	Annual rate of increase from previous year shown (%)	Share of total (%)
1960	1,295	—	435	—	33.6	860	—	66.4
1971	3,184	8.5	1,130	9.1	35.5	2,054	8.2	64.5
1979	10,315	15.8	3,506	15.2	34.0	6,809	16.2	66.0
1984	18,044	11.8	6,315	12.5	35.0	11,728	11.5	65.0
1991	40,778	12.4	16,715	14.9	41.0	24,063	10.8	59.0
1998	40,657	0.0	15,802	−0.8	38.9	24,855	0.5	61.1

SOURCE: 1960 benefits data from Nelson (1992b), Table 2, p. 45; 1971–84 benefits data from Nelson (1992b), Table 3, p. 46; 1991 benefits data from Nelson (1993), Table 1, p. 4; 1998 data from Mont, Burton, and Reno (2000), Table 6, p. 13.

Table A.4 Workers' Compensation Insurance Underwriting Experience, 1973–99

Year	Col. 1[a] Losses incurred[b]	2 Loss adjustment expenses[b]	3 Losses and adjustment expenses incurred[b]	4 Underwriting expenses incurred[c]	5 Dividends to policyholders[b]	6 Combined ratio after dividends	7 Net inv. gain/loss and other income[b]	8 Overall operating ratio
1973	68.5	8.5	77.0	19.8				
1974	71.6	8.7	80.3	19.6				
1975	74.0	8.2	82.2	18.9	6.3	107.4		
1976	78.2	8.4	86.6	17.6	5.4	109.6	6.9	102.6
1977	78.0	8.9	86.9	16.7	5.1	108.6	7.4	101.2
1978	74.4	8.7	83.0	16.4	5.6	105.0	7.8	97.2
1979	70.4	9.2	79.6	16.8	6.5	103.0	9.2	93.7
1980	67.6	8.4	76.1	17.4	8.0	101.4	10.8	90.7
1981	66.1	9.0	75.1	19.0	8.7	102.8	13.0	89.8
1982	64.3	9.1	73.4	20.6	9.9	103.9	15.0	88.9
1983	70.6	9.2	79.9	22.0	10.6	112.5	16.2	96.3
1984	81.0	9.8	90.8	21.2	9.9	121.9	16.7	105.2
1985	81.0	9.5	90.5	19.0	9.3	118.8	15.0	103.8
1986	85.4	10.2	95.5	18.0	7.6	121.1	13.7	107.4
1987	82.2	10.9	93.1	18.0	6.4	117.6	12.8	104.8

	Col. 1	Col. 2	Col. 3	Col. 4	Col. 5	Col. 6	Col. 7	Col. 8
1988	83.4	10.8	94.2	17.8	6.4	118.4	12.7	105.7
1989	83.3	11.4	94.7	17.4	6.1	118.2	13.4	104.8
1990	83.8	10.7	94.6	17.6	5.1	117.4	13.0	104.4
1991	87.8	11.5	99.3	18.5	4.9	122.6	14.0	108.7
1992[d]	83.9	13.2	97.1	19.8	4.6	121.5	18.1	103.4
1993	71.6	12.4	84.0	20.4	4.7	109.1	16.7	92.4
1994	60.3	13.1	73.4	21.7	6.3	101.4	14.5	86.9
1995	55.2	12.5	67.7	23.3	6.0	97.0	16.8	80.2
1996	55.8	13.7	69.5	25.4	4.8	99.7	17.6	82.1
1997	55.6	13.8	69.4	25.9	5.4	100.7	20.4	80.3
1998	60.2	15.3	75.5	26.7	5.3	107.6	15.7	91.9
1999	65.9	15.8	81.7	28.0	5.6	115.3	20.5	94.8

SOURCE: From *Best's Aggregates and Averages, Property/Casualty*, 2000 edition and prior editions; copyright A.M. Best Company, used with permission.

[a] Losses incurred, also termed the pure less ratio, (Col. 1) plus loss adjustment expenses (Col. 2) equals losses and adjustment expenses incurred (Col. 3). Losses and adjustment expenses incurred (Col. 3) plus underwriting expenses incurred (Col. 4) plus dividends to policy holders (Col. 5) equals combined ratio after dividends (Col. 6). Combined ratio after dividends (Col. 6) minus net investment gain/loss and other income (Col. 7) equals overall operating ratio (Col. 8).

[b] As percentage of net premiums earned.

[c] As percentage of net premiums written.

[d] As of 1992, the methodology for allocating investment income changes slightly; as a result, 1992–99 numbers in the last two columns are not directly comparable with those for earlier years.

Table A.5 Nominal and Real Interest Rates, 1960–99 (%)

	Six-month Treasury bill rate	Year-to-year change in CPI	Real interest rate (Col. 1 – Col. 2)
1960	3.247	1.7	1.547
1961	2.605	1.0	1.605
1962	2.908	1.0	1.908
1963	3.253	1.3	1.953
1964	3.686	1.3	2.386
1965	4.055	1.6	2.455
1966	5.082	2.9	2.182
1967	4.630	3.1	1.530
1968	5.470	4.2	1.270
1969	6.853	5.5	1.353
1970	6.562	5.7	0.862
1971	4.511	4.4	0.111
1972	4.466	3.2	1.266
1973	7.178	6.2	0.978
1974	7.926	11.0	−3.074
1975	6.122	9.1	−2.978
1976	5.266	5.8	−0.534
1977	5.510	6.5	−0.990
1978	7.572	7.6	−0.028
1979	10.017	11.3	−1.283
1980	11.374	13.5	−2.126
1981	13.776	10.3	3.476
1982	11.084	6.2	4.884
1983	8.750	3.2	5.550
1984	9.800	4.3	5.500
1985	7.660	3.6	4.060
1986	6.030	1.9	4.130
1987	6.050	3.6	2.450
1988	6.920	4.1	2.820
1989	8.040	4.8	3.240

Table A.5 (continued)

	Six-month Treasury bill rate	Year-to-year change in CPI	Real interest rate (Col. 1 – Col. 2)
1990	7.470	5.4	2.070
1991	5.490	4.2	1.290
1992	3.570	3.0	0.570
1993	3.140	3.0	0.140
1994	4.660	2.6	2.060
1995	5.590	2.8	2.790
1996	5.090	3.0	2.090
1997	5.180	2.3	2.880
1998	4.850	1.6	3.250
1999	4.760	2.2	2.560

SOURCE: Council of Economic Advisers (2000): T-bill rate from Table B-73, p. 412; changes in CPI from Table B-62, p. 378.

**Table A.6 Work-Related Injury and Illness Incidence Rates, 1972–98
(per 100 full-time private sector workers)**

Year	Total cases	Lost workday cases	Lost workdays
1972	10.9	3.3	47.9
1973	11.0	3.4	53.3
1974	10.4	3.5	54.6
1975	9.1	3.3	56.1
1976	9.2	3.5	60.5
1977	9.3	3.8	61.6
1978	9.4	4.1	63.5
1979	9.5	4.3	67.7
1980	8.7	4.0	65.2
1981	8.3	3.8	61.7
1982	7.7	3.5	58.7
1983	7.6	3.4	58.5
1984	8.0	3.7	63.4
1985	7.9	3.6	64.9
1986	7.9	3.6	65.8
1987	8.3	3.8	69.9
1988	8.6	4.0	76.1
1989	8.6	4.0	78.7
1990	8.8	4.1	84.0
1991	8.4	3.9	86.5
1992	8.9	3.9	93.8
1993	8.5	3.8	ND[a]
1994	8.4	3.8	ND
1995	8.1	3.6	ND
1996	7.4	3.4	ND
1997	7.1	3.3	ND
1998	6.7	3.1	ND

SOURCE: 1972–1993 data from Burton and Schmidle (1995), Table III.B.11, p. III-25; 1994–1998 data from *Monthly Labor Review*, Vol. 123, No. 3, March 2000, Table 46, p. 103.
[a] ND = no data available.

Table A.7 Benefits Paid by Regular Workers' Compensation Programs, by type of insurance, 1960–98

Year	303 Amount ($, millions)	Private carriers Amount ($, millions)	%	State and federal funds Amount ($, millions)	%	Self-insuring employers Amount ($, millions)	%
1960	1,295	810	62.5	325	25.1	160	12.4
1970	2,921	1,843	63.1	645	22.1	432	14.8
1980	11,879	7,029	59.2	2,591	21.8	2,259	19.0
1990	36,803	22,222	60.4	7,332	19.9	7,249	19.7
1998	39,483	20,617	52.2	8,994	22.8	9,872	25.0

SOURCE: 1960 data from Nelson (1992b), Table 5, p. 48; 1970–80 data from Nelson (1992b), Table 3 for total and Table 5 for private carriers and self-insuring employers, with state and federal funds (excluding the black-lung program) calculated by Schmidle; 1990 data from Nelson (1993), Table 3, for all except state and federal funds (excluding the black-lung program), which were calculated by Schmidle; 1998 data from Mont, Burton, and Reno (2000), Table 5, pp. 10–11, for all except state and federal funds (excluding the black-lung program), which were calculated by Burton.

Table A.8 State Workers' Compensation Insurance Funds[a]

Funds in operation as of 1960

Exclusive:	Competitive:	
Nevada	Arizona	New York
North Dakota	California	Oklahoma
Ohio	Colorado	Pennsylvania
Oregon	Idaho	Utah
Washington	Maryland	
West Virginia	Michigan	
Wyoming	Montana	

Developments since 1960[b]

Competitive funds that were privatized: Michigan, December 28, 1994

Exclusive funds that became competitive: Nevada, July 1, 1999

New competitive funds:

Oregon[c]	January 1, 1966
Minnesota	April 1, 1984
New Mexico	December 31, 1991
Texas	January 1, 1992
Louisiana	October 1, 1992
Rhode Island	October 1, 1992
Maine	January 1, 1993
Missouri	March 1, 1995
Kentucky	September 1, 1995
Hawaii	July 20, 1997

[a] Exclusive state funds are state-operated insurance funds that provide workers' compensation insurance policies to employers in the public and private sectors. States with exclusive state funds do not permit private insurance companies to provide workers' compensation insurance policies to employers in the state. Some (but not all) of the states with exclusive state funds permit employers who meet specified criteria to self-insure their workers' compensation risks.

Competitive state funds are 1) state-operated insurance funds that provide workers' compensation insurance policies to employers in the public and private sector, and 2) private mutual companies that provide workers' compensation insurance policies to employers in the public and private sectors and that are exempt from federal income taxes under the Internal Revenue Code because, *inter alia*, the state had a financial commitment during the organization of the fund and the majority of the members of the board of directors or oversight body of the fund are appointed by state officials. States with competitive state funds permit private insurance companies to provide workers' compensation insurance policies to employers in the state. Also, as of 2000, all of the states with competitive state funds permit employers who meet specified criteria to self-insure their workers' compensation risks.

[b] Dates indicate when funds began or ceased operation.

[c] Converted from an exclusive state fund.

Table A.9 States with Open Competition in the Workers' Compensation Insurance Market

State	Effective date[a]
Arkansas	July 17, 1981
Oregon	July 1, 1982
Kentucky	July 15, 1982
Illinois	August 18, 1982
Rhode Island	September 1, 1982
Michigan	January 1, 1983
Georgia	January 1, 1984
Minnesota	January 1, 1984
Vermont	July 1, 1984
Maine[b]	January 1, 1986 – November 19, 1987
New Mexico	October 1, 1987
Maryland	January 1, 1988
Louisiana	September 1, 1988
Indiana	September 1, 1989
Connecticut	October 1, 1989
Hawaii	June 25, 1990
South Carolina	July 1, 1990
District of Columbia	January 1, 1991
Colorado	March 1, 1991
Alabama	November 1, 1991
Texas	March 1, 1992
Utah	May 20, 1992
Maine	January 1, 1993
South Dakota	July 1, 1993
Nebraska	September 1, 1993
Pennsylvania	December 1, 1993
Missouri	January 1, 1994
New Hampshire	January 1, 1994
Oklahoma	January 1, 1994
Virginia	January 1, 1994

Table A.9 (continued)

State	Effective date[a]
Kansas	July 1, 1994
Delaware	August 1, 1994
California	January 1, 1995
North Carolina	July 28, 1995
Montana	October 1, 1995
Mississippi	January 1, 1996
Tennessee	January 1, 1997
Alaska	January 1, 1998

SOURCE: NCCI (1995, 2000), Exhibit II, "Premiums Level Changes by State ("Competitive Rate Law Effective" entries). Delaware and Pennsylvania dates are from rating bureaus for those states.

[a] Unless otherwise indicated, open competition is still in effect.

[b] Almost all of the Maine premiums in 1986–87 were in the residual market, and so Maine may be treated as if the open competition law were not in effect.

Table A.10 Workers' Compensation Insurance Residual Market Share[a]

Year	Share (%)
1975	4.6
1976	7.7
1977	11.8
1978	12.7
1979	12.7
1980	12.0
1981	10.2
1982	8.0
1983	6.2
1984	5.5
1985	9.7
1986	16.3
1987	19.0
1988	19.6
1989	22.0
1990	24.1
1991	25.8
1992	28.5
1993	27.8
1994	24.1
1995	17.3
1996	10.3
1997	7.7
1998	3.9

SOURCE: NCCI (1993) for 1975–87 data; NCCI (1993) for 1988 data; NCCI (1995) for 1989–93 data; and NCCI (2000) for 1994–98 data. The NCCI tables report data for 33 jurisdictions (including the District of Columbia) for 1975–90, for 34 jurisdictions for 1991–92, for 31 jurisdictions for 1993, for 29 jurisdictions for 1994–95, and for 27 jurisdictions for 1996–98.

[a] National average for NCCI states.

Appendix B

Insurance Terminology

This appendix reviews the terminology used in the workers' compensation insurance field. These terms are adapted from the definitions in several publications of the National Council on Compensation Insurance, including *Loss Development Exhibits: Sample State Report Evaluated as of 12/94* (NCCI 1996); *Annual Statistical Bulletin, 2000 Edition* (NCCI 2000); and *Reporting Guidebook for the Annual Calls for Experience* (NCCI 1997).

MATRIX FOR TIME PERIODS AND MEASURES OF LOSSES

An understanding of workers' compensation insurance terminology is facilitated by use of a two-by-four matrix (Table B.1). There are four alternative time periods for reporting results and two particularly important alternative measures of losses (or benefit costs), which means that conceptually there are eight different ways to measure losses. Fortunately, only a subset of these methods of measuring losses is typically used in practice. Other important measures of workers' compensation insurance performance, such as premiums and expenses, can also be measured using the four alternative time periods for presenting results, although again only a subset of these alternatives is used in practice.

Table B.1 Insurance Terminology: Alternative Characterizations

Alternative measures of losses	Alternative time periods			
	Calendar year	Accident year	Policy year	Policy period
Paid losses	X	X	X	X
Incurred losses	X	X	X	X

ALTERNATIVE TIME PERIODS FOR REPORTING RESULTS

Calendar Year

A method of reporting or accounting for all financial transactions (e.g., premiums and losses [benefit costs]) occurring during a specific year, regardless of the years in which the accidents occur or policies are written. (Dividends are only reported on a calendar-year basis.)

Accident Year (also known as calendar-accident year)

A method of reporting or accounting for losses for all accidents occurring during a calendar year, regardless of the years in which the losses for those accidents are paid. (The premium associated with accident-year losses is normally a calendar-year premium.)

Policy Year

A method of reporting or accounting for all financial transactions (e.g., premiums and benefit costs) for all policies with coverage beginning during a given calendar year. The policy year always corresponds with the calendar year. For example, the 1994 policy year for Florida includes all policies with initial effective dates between January 1, 1994, and December 31, 1994. The experience in a single policy year occurs over a 24-month time span because a policy may be initially effective on any date during the calendar year and does not expire until 12 months later. Thus, the 1994 policy-year experience for Florida includes those accidents that occurred between January 1, 1994, and December 31, 1995, and that were covered by policies sold during policy year 1994.

Policy Period

A method of reporting or accounting for all financial transactions (e.g., premiums and benefit costs) for all policies with coverage beginning during the policy period used in a state. The policy period typically is a 12-month period. In many states, the policy period begins on January 1, and thus the policy year and the policy period correspond. (For example, the 1996 policy period for Alabama began on January 1, 1996, and ended on December 31, 1996.) However, the policy period in many states begins on a date other than January 1, and thus the policy year and the policy period do not correspond. (For example, the 1993–1994 policy period for Florida began on October 1, 1993, and ended on September 30, 1994). The experience in a single policy period occurs over a 24-month time span because a policy may be effective on any date during the policy period and does not expire until 12 months later. Thus the 1993–1994 policy-year experience for Florida includes those accidents that occurred between October 1, 1993, and September 30, 1995, and that were covered by policies sold during the 1993–1994 policy period.

DATES FOR REPORTING RESULTS

Valuation Date

A specific time at which data are evaluated in order to determine the losses (or benefits) paid and reserves as of that date.

Reports

A report contains the evaluation of a particular policy year or accident year at a specific point in time (valuation date). The valuation date for the first report is the last date on which accidents can occur in the policy year or accident year. For example, accident year 1988 evaluated as of December 31, 1988, is a first report and accident year 1988 evaluated as of December 31, 1995, is an eighth report. Likewise, policy year 1985 evaluated as of December 31, 1986, is a 1st report and policy year 1985 evaluated as of December 31, 1995, is an 11th report.

ALTERNATIVE MEASURES OF LOSSES (OR BENEFITS)

Paid Losses

The losses (or benefits) that an insurance company has paid as of a valuation date. The paid losses normally refer to the cumulative payments as of the valuation date (e.g., accident year 1994 losses paid as of December 31, 1996). Alternatively, the paid losses can refer to the incremental losses paid during a specific time period (e.g., accident year 1995 losses paid during 1997).

Case Reserves

The reserves that an insurance company establishes to pay losses that are anticipated subsequent to the valuation date for specific claims that are known as of that date.

Bulk Reserves

Additional reserves that an insurance company establishes for an entire state to pay losses that are anticipated subsequent to the valuation date. The NCCI definition is "those reserves for general case reserve inadequacy, supplemental case reserves, cases that may reopen, or other reserves not associated to specific cases."

IBNR Reserves

The "pure" definition of IBNR (incurred but not reported) reserves includes those reserves that an insurance company establishes to pay losses that (based on prior experience) are anticipated subsequent to the valuation date for claims that have not yet been reported as of the valuation date, even though the claims occurred in the specified period (i.e., during the specified accident year). The NCCI reporting guidelines permit carriers to include bulk reserves with their IBNR reserves.

Incurred Excluding IBNR Losses

The sum of paid losses, case reserves, and bulk reserves. (For those carriers that include bulk reserves with their IBNR reserves, "incurred excluding IBNR losses" is the sum of paid losses and case reserves.)

Incurred Including IBNR Losses

The sum of paid losses, case reserves, bulk reserves, and IBNR reserves. This measure is what the NCCI refers to as "incurred losses."

Loss Development Factor

The incurred loss development factor is the relation (or ratio) between 1) incurred losses for a particular accident year (or policy year) at a particular valuation date and 2) comparable estimates at a later valuation date. An incurred loss development factor of 1.200 for first to second means that a 20 percent growth is expected in incurred losses between the first report and the second report. This definition assumes that the loss measure is "incurred including IBNR losses." Loss development factors can be derived for other loss measures, such as paid losses, paid losses plus case reserves, or incurred excluding IBNR losses.

Nth to Ultimate Loss Development Factor

A particularly important loss development factor is the Nth to ultimate loss development factor, which is the ratio of 1) the eventual or ultimate cost of claims to 2) the estimate of the cost of claims at an Nth report for a particular accident year (or policy year). For example, an eighth-to-ultimate factor applied to 1988 accident year losses valued as of December 31, 1995, (eighth report) would represent the estimate of what the ultimate total losses will be for accident year 1988.

Ultimate Losses

Losses for a particular accident year (or policy year) developed to an ultimate reporting basis.

OTHER FACTORS THAT AFFECT UNDERWRITING RESULTS

Loss Adjustment Expenses

Loss adjustment expenses include salaries for staff claims adjusters, fees to independent adjusters, and other expenses involved in adjusting claims.

Underwriting Expenses

Underwriting expenses include commissions and brokerage expenses; other acquisition expenses; general expenses, including salaries and costs of office space; and taxes, licenses, and fees.

Dividends

Mutual insurers and participating stock insurers pay dividends to policyholders. Data are available on a calendar year basis from the National Association of Insurance Commissioners (NAIC) or A.M. Best.

ALTERNATIVE MEASURES OF PREMIUMS

Standard Earned Premium at Designated Statistical Reporting (DSR) Level

There are two possibilities for the voluntary market.

1. In those states using manual rates that include expense allowances, the premium is calculated by the multiplication of manual rates by the exposure base (typically, total payroll of the insured enterprise). In these states, the standard earned premium at DSR level includes experience rating plan adjustments, expenses constants, and loss constants.

2. In those states using pure premiums that exclude expense allowances, the premium is calculated by the multiplication of pure premiums by the exposure base. In these states, the standard earned premium at DSR level includes experience-rating plan adjustments (except in Michigan), but in the voluntary market excludes expense constants and loss constants.

All assigned-risk policies must be written at approved assigned-risk rates. For such policies, standard earned premium at DSR level (as well as the standard earned premium at company level) will reflect those approved rates along with approved experience-rating plan adjustments, expense constants, and loss constants.

Standard Earned Premium at Company Level

In those states using manual rates that include expense allowances, the premium is calculated by adjusting the standard earned premium at DSR level for the effect of deviations from manual rates. In those states using pure premiums that exclude expense allowances, the premium is calculated by adjusting the standard earned premium at DSR level for the effects of deviations from pure premiums, carrier-charged expense constants, and carrier-charged loss constants.

Net Earned Premium

The premium is calculated by adjusting the standard earned premium at company level for the effects of 1) deviations from NCCI experience rating modification factors; 2) retrospective rating plan adjustments; 3) other individual risk rating plan adjustments, such as schedule rating; 4) premium discounts; 5) premium credits for small deductible coverage; and 6) adjustments for certain assigned-risk market programs.

ALTERNATIVE MEASURES OF UNDERWRITING EXPERIENCE

There are several ways to utilize the measures of losses, expenses, dividends and premiums defined in the previous paragraphs in order to measure underwriting experience in workers' compensation. Table 2.1 [p. 25] illustrates one use of the measurements: all of the entries are 1999 calendar year data stated as a percentage of net premiums. Losses incurred (line 1, also known as the pure loss ratio) is incurred losses for cash and medical benefits. The sum of losses incurred and loss adjustment expenses (line 2) equals line 3, the losses and adjustment expenses incurred. In turn, the sum of line 3 plus line 4 (underwriting expenses incurred, including state and local insurance taxes) plus line 5 (dividends to policyholders) is line 6, the combined ratio after dividends. Subtracting net investment gain (loss) and other income (line 7) from line 6 produces line 8, the overall operating ratio, which is prior to state and federal income taxes.

When the combined ratio after dividends exceeds 100, insurers lose money on their underwriting experience because premiums are not adequate to cover losses and expenses. When the overall operating ratio exceeds 100, insurers lose money on the combination of their underwriting experience, taxes, and other income. There are years when the combined ratio is in excess of 100, which means that carriers lose money on their underwriting experience, but the net tax gain plus earnings on reserves are large enough to produce an overall operating ratio that is less than 100, which means that the workers' compensation insurance line is profitable. This happened, for example, in 1999, when the combined ratio was 115.3 but the overall operating ratio was 94.8.

Appendix C

Detailed Methodology for Measuring Employers' Costs of Workers' Compensation Insurance

Chapter 3 described several methods of measuring interstate differences in workers' compensation costs and provided a brief explanation of the methodology we used to measure interstate differences in the costs of workers' compensation insurance. This appendix provides additional discussion of the methodology, together with estimates of workers' compensation costs based on this procedure.[1]

INSURANCE CLASSIFICATIONS

The Standard Set of Classifications

The cost methodology for this study utilized a standard set of 71 insurance classes for all states and all years in our sample. We selected these 71 classes from among more than 500 active classifications in the National Council on Compensation Insurance classification system. These particular classes were chosen because they are commonly used by state workers' compensation programs; they account for a large proportion of total payroll nationally; and they are representative of each of the five divisions of workers' compensation insurance classifications: manufacturing, contracting, office and clerical, goods and services, and "miscellaneous."

Table C.1 briefly describes these classifications and shows the aggregate percentage of total payroll accounted for by each class in the 36 National Council states for which payroll information was available for selected policy years. We used this aggregate payroll data to calculate a weighted average insurance rate for each state. Specifically, the greater the proportion of payroll associated with a particular classification, the greater the influence that classification had on the calculation of the statewide average rate. The same distribution of payroll was used for all states and for all years, so that interstate and intertemporal differences in workers' compensation costs are due to factors other than differences in industry mix.

Modifications in the Standard Set of Classifications

The NCCI's classification scheme is used in 42 of the states included in our study.[2] Insurance categories in states using other classification systems were

Table C.1 Insurance Classification and Distribution of Payroll

Code no. and classification description[a]	% of covered payroll[b]
Manufacturing classes	
2003 Bakeries	0.335
2039 Ice cream	0.026
2070 Creameries	0.189
2157 Bottling N.O.C.[c]	0.186
2220 Yarn or thread-cotton	0.395
2361 Hosiery manufacturing	0.115
2501 Clothing	1.097
2585 Laundries N.O.C.	0.122
2586 Cleaning or dyeing	0.072
2660 Boot or shoe manufacturing N.O.C.	0.159
2802 Carpentry—shop only	0.195
2883 Wood furniture N.O.C.	0.280
3066 Sheet metal work-shop	0.196
3076 Fireproof equipment	0.319
3081 Foundries—iron N.O.C.	0.116
3082 Foundries—steel castings	0.037
3085 Foundries—nonferrous metals N.O.C.	0.055
3113 Tool N.O.C.	0.282
3179 Electrical apparatus N.O.C.	0.460
3400 Metal goods N.O.C.	0.228
3507 Agricultural machinery	0.394
3612 Pump and engine N.O.C.	0.159
3632 Machine shops N.O.C.	0.981
3643 Electrical power equipment	0.401
3681 Telephone apparatus	0.549
4034 Concrete products	0.117
4299 Printing	0.668
4304 Newspaper publishing	0.121
4484 Plastics—molded products manufacturing N.O.C.	0.358
Percentage for 29 manufacturing classes	8.612

Code no. and classification description[a]	% of covered payroll[b]
Contracting classes	
3724 Millwright work N.O.C.	0.427
5022 Masonry N.O.C.	0.349
5183 Plumbing N.O.C.	0.879
5190 Electrical wiring—within building	0.742
5213 Concrete construction N.O.C.	0.457
5215 Concrete work	0.049
5221 Concrete work—floors, sidewalks, etc.	0.289
5403 Carpentry N.O.C.	0.500
5506 Street or road construction	0.389
5538 Sheet metal work erection N.O.C.	0.429
5606 Contractors—executive supervisors	0.433
5645 Carpentry—detached private residences	0.547
6217 Excavation N.O.C.	0.330
Percentage for 13 contacting classes	5.820
Office and clerical classes	
8742 Salesmen, collectors, or messengers–outside	6.418
8748 Automobile sales or service agencies	0.534
8810 Clerical office employees N.O.C.	25.425
8833 Hospitals—professional employees	2.765
8868 Colleges or schools—professional employees	6.361
Percentage for 5 office and clerical classes	41.503
Goods and services classes	
8006 Retail grocery stores—no fresh meats	0.240
8008 Retail clothing or dry goods stores	0.790
8010 Hardware stores—wholesale or retail	0.515
8017 Retail stores N.O.C.	1.402
8018 Wholesale or combined wholesale—retail N.O.C.	0.631
8033 Meat, grocery, and provision stores—retail	1.236
8039 Retail department stores	0.710

(continued)

320

Table C.1 (continued)

Code no. and classification description[a]	% of covered payroll[b]
8044 Wholesale or retail furniture stores	0.329
8232 Lumber yards	0.444
8292 General merchandise warehouses N.O.C.	0.104
8293 Furniture storage warehouses	0.073
8350 Gasoline or oil dealers	0.217
8387 Gasoline stations—accessories stations	0.677
8391 Automobile garages	1.194
8829 Convalescent or nursing homes	0.849
9015 Buildings operation N.O.C.	0.544
9040 Hospitals—all other employees	0.565
9052 Hotels	0.468
9079 Restaurant N.O.C.	2.566
9101 Colleges or schools—all other employees	0.901
Percentage for 20 goods and services classes	14.455
Miscellaneous classes	
7219 Truckmen N.O.C.	1.278
7380 Chauffeurs, drivers, helpers N.O.C.	0.910
7539 Electric light or power companies N.O.C.—all operations	0.158
7720 Policemen	0.615
Percentage for 4 miscellaneous classes	2.961
Percentage for 71 classes	73.351

[a] Code number and classification description taken from the classification code of the National Council on Compensation Insurance.
[b] The percentage of covered payroll in 36 selected states is based on 1978–79, 1979–80, or 1980–81 policy year data.
[c] N.O.C. means "not otherwise classified."

converted to NCCI classification by selecting the category in the state's system that was most nearly analogous to each of the 71 NCCI classes.[3]

OVERVIEW OF THE SIX BASIC MODELS FOR CALCULATING COSTS

Table C.2 presents our six basic models for calculating adjusted manual rates. There are two variants of Models III, IV, and V (e.g., Models III and IIIa), depending on the type of assigned-risk program used in the state on the comparison date; thus, in effect, we used nine models to calculate adjusted manual rates. The models are mutually exclusive; that is, for each state, only one of the nine models was applicable for any single year.[4]

Three Categories of States

Three decision rules were used to assign the states to one of the six basic models: 1) whether the state had an exclusive state fund or a private insurance market; 2) whether the state's rating bureau promulgated fully developed manual rates or loss costs only; and 3) whether the state's rating bureau published different rates (or loss costs) for the voluntary and assigned-risk (residual) markets.

Exclusive-fund states versus other states

Three states in our study have exclusive state insurance funds: Ohio, Washington, and West Virginia. We used Model VI to calculate statewide employ-

Table C.2 Six Basic Models Used to Calculate Employers' Costs

	States using manual rates in the voluntary market	States using pure premiums in the voluntary market
States with private carriers		
States with voluntary market only	Model I	Model II
States with identical rates in voluntary and residual market	Model III	Note a
States with different rates in voluntary and residual market	Model IV	Model V
States with exclusive state funds		
States with voluntary market only	Model VI	Note a

[a] There are no states in this category.

er costs for these states; variations within Model VI are discussed later in this appendix.

Manual rates versus pure premiums

In some states, the rating bureau publishes *manual rates* (rates per $100 of payroll that represent expected losses plus an allowance for expenses and profit). In other states, the rating bureau publishes *pure premiums* (rates per $100 of payroll that represent expected losses plus loss adjustment expenses, but no other element of expense or profit). In still other states, the rating bureau may simultaneously publish both manual rates and pure premiums.

Voluntary markets versus assigned-risk markets

Most workers' compensation insurance policies are purchased in the voluntary market, which means that the insurance carrier and employer are voluntary parties to the workers' compensation insurance contract. In some instances, an employer is unable to find an insurer who is willing to provide coverage. This may occur for a number of reasons. For example, a firm that is too small to be experience-rated may have a record of loss experience that is much worse than that of the average risk in the firm's classification. Alternatively, the insurer may believe that the manual rate applicable to an employer is so low that, even if the employer has average loss experience, losses plus expenses will exceed premiums paid.

An employer who is unable to purchase an insurance policy in the voluntary market is nonetheless required, in most states, to obtain workers' compensation insurance coverage. Most states have an assigned-risk plan or a similar arrangement that provides policies to employers who cannot find insurance in the voluntary market; typically, those employers are assigned to the carriers who participate in the voluntary workers' compensation insurance market in the state.

Five Basic Models in States with Private Carriers

Here we describe the five basic models that we used to calculate rates for states that permit private carriers to provide workers' compensation insurance coverage. Most states historically relied exclusively on the voluntary market and published manual rates as opposed to pure premiums. Also, until recently, states with voluntary and assigned-risk (residual) markets used manual rates that were identical in the two markets. Employers assigned to the residual market might not be eligible for certain discounts or dividends that are available in the voluntary market, but the starting point for determining policy premiums—the manual rate—was identical to the starting point in the voluntary market.

We used Model I to calculate rates for those states in which the rating bureau published one set of manual rates for the both voluntary and residual markets. The "adjusted" manual rates charged employers in the two markets may have differed because premium discounts or other modifying factors may not have been applicable in the residual market. However, the data we use on the effect of modifying factors encompasses both markets, and so the adjusted manual rates we calculate pertain to the entire market.

Model III was used for those states in which the rating bureau published separate manual rates for voluntary and residual markets, although the manual rates were in fact identical. The adjusted manual rates paid by residual market employers may have been different than the rates paid by voluntary market employers. Again, the data on the effect of the modifying factors we used encompass all policies in the state, and so the adjusted manual rates we calculated pertain to the entire market. In recent years, various states have authorized carriers to charge different manual rates for the voluntary and assigned-risk markets. Model IV was used to calculate rates for these states.

There are now some states that rely exclusively on the voluntary market and utilize pure premiums, in which case we used Model II. Model V was used to calculate rates in states that use pure premiums in the voluntary market and manual rates in the residual market.

There were additional variations of these models that depended on the pricing mechanisms used in the residual market. In some states, the effects of residual market programs are reflected in normal insurance industry data, but in others it was necessary to further adjust rates using supplemental NCCI data to account for the rate impact of these residual market programs. Models IIIa, IVa, and Va utilized this supplemental data to calculate statewide average rates for these jurisdictions.

Table C.3 lists the model(s) used to calculate the employers' costs of workers' compensation insurance for each state and year from 1975 to 1995. The next several sections illustrate the specific procedure used to calculate adjusted manual rates.

The entries for the District of Columbia, Hawaii, Kentucky, Nebraska, Oklahoma, Rhode Island, and South Dakota contain a notation that particular manual rates or pure premiums were the Designated Statistical Reporting (DSR) level for the Annual Calls for Experience for certain years. This typically occurred when the states were in transition from administered pricing to a more deregulated approach to insurance pricing. Kentucky provides an example. The competitive law was effective July 15, 1982, and pure premiums were issued with that effective date. However, the Annual Calls for Experience from carriers for 1983 were based on the manual rates that were effective July 15, 1981. Thus, Model I was appropriate for the purposes of calculating

Table C.3 The Basic Models Used for the 48 Jurisdictions, 1975–95

Jurisdiction	Model and years applied
Alabama	I (1975–91), V (1992–95)
Alaska	I (1975–83), IV (1984–88), IIIa (1989–95)
Arizona	I (1975–86), IV (1987–95)
Arkansas	I (1975–90), IIIa (1991–92), IVa (1993–95)
California	ND[a] (1975–85), I (1986–94), II (1995)
Colorado	I (1975–91), II (1992–95)
Connecticut	I (1975–89), V (1990–92), Va (1993–95)
Delaware	ND (1975–85), I (1986–94), V (1995)
District of Columbia	I (1975–87), IV (1988–92), V (1993–95) [4/1/91 manual rates were the DSR level in 1992]
Florida	I (1975–87), III (1988–89), IIIa (1990–93), IVa (1994–95)
Georgia	I (1975–81), IV (1982–95)
Hawaii	I (1975–92), Va (1993–95) [10/1/89 manual rates were the DSR level in 1992]
Idaho	I (1975–91), IIIa (1992–95)
Illinois	I (1975–82), IV (1983–93), IVa (1994–95)
Indiana	I (1975–89), IIIa (1990–95)
Iowa	I (1975–88), IV (1989–92), IVa (1993–95)
Kansas	I (1975–90), IIIa (1991–95)
Kentucky	I (1975–83), V (1984–95) [7/15/81 manual rates were the DSR level in 1983]
Louisiana	I (1975–88), V (1989), Va (1990–92), II (1993–95 [state fund data unavailable])
Maine	I (1975–87), IV (1988–92), I (1993), II (1994–95 [Maine Employers Mutual Insurance Co. data unavailable])
Maryland	I (1975–87), II (1988–95)
Massachusetts	I (1975–95)
Michigan	I (1975–82), V (1983–95)
Minnesota	I (1975–83), V (1984–95)
Mississippi	I (1975–90), IIIa (1991–92), IV (1993–95)
Missouri	I (1975–89), III (1990), IIIa (1991–93), V (1994–95)
Montana	I (1975–95)

Jurisdiction	Model and years applied
Nebraska	I (1975–89), IV (1990), IVa (1991–94), Va (1995) [9/1/93 manual rates were the DSR level in 1994]
New Hampshire	I (1975–90), III (1991–92), IIIa (1993), Va (1994–95)
New Jersey	I (1975–95)
New Mexico	I (1975–89), V (1990), Va (1991–95)
New York	I (1975–95)
North Carolina	IIIa (1975–95)
Ohio	ND (1975–82, 1985–86), VI (1983–84, 1987–95)
Oklahoma	I (1975–94), II (1995) [7/1/93 manual rates were the DSR level in 1994]
Oregon	I (1975–82), V (1983–92), Va (1993–95)
Pennsylvania	ND (1975–85), I (1986–93), II (1994–95)
Rhode Island	I (1975–82), III (1983–89), IV (1990–92), I (1993–95 [state fund data unavailable]) [6/22/89 manual rates were the DSR level in 1990–95]
South Carolina	I (1975–90), Va (1991–95)
South Dakota	I (1975–88), IIIa (1989–94), Va (1995) [6/1/93 manual rates were the DSR level in 1994]
Tennessee	I (1975–88), III (1989), IIIa (1990–95)
Texas	I (1975–91), ND (1992–95)
Utah	I (1975–92), II (1993–95 [state fund data unavailable])
Vermont	I (1975–85), III (1986–92), IIIa (1993–94), Va (1995)
Virginia	I (1975–91), IIIa (1992), IVa (1993), Va (1994–95)
Washington	ND (1975–84), VI (1985–95)
West Virginia	VI (1975–95)
Wisconsin	I (1975–95)

[a] ND = no data available.

adjusted manual rates in Kentucky in 1983, even though in terms of public policy the state no longer relied on administered pricing.

Three states (Louisiana, Maine, and Rhode Island) recently established state funds, which took over the function of the residual market and for which we do not have data. Thus, as shown in Table C.3, for Louisiana we used Model V in 1989 and Model Va in 1990–1992 because the state used pure premiums in the voluntary market and manual rates in the assigned-risk market. The total market adjusted manual rates we calculated for Louisiana for these years were a blend of the adjusted manual rates for the voluntary and assigned-risk markets, using the procedures described in the next two sections. In 1993, a state fund took over the function of the assigned-risk market. However, we only have data on the insurance policies in the voluntary market, and so of necessity we relied on Model II for 1993–1995. To the extent that the policies sold in the voluntary market are not representative of the total insurance market in Louisiana in 1993–1995, the adjusted manual rates we calculated for Louisiana for those years are biased. A similar bias may exist for Maine's adjusted manual rates for 1994–1995 and for Rhode Island's adjusted manual rates for 1993–1995. This means that eight of our observations may be biased because we were not able to include data on state funds that took over the residual market functions in these three states.

We have examined the sensitivity of our empirical results in subsequent chapters by recalculating various regressions omitting the eight observations. Fortunately, the effects on the regression results were trivial.[5] As a result, we treat the eight potentially biased observations as comparable to our other observations for purposes of all additional analyses.[6]

CALCULATION OF WORKERS' COMPENSATION COSTS IN STATES WITH PRIVATE CARRIERS

Types of Data Used to Produce Adjusted Manual Rates

We used 13 types of data as inputs to produce, as outputs, three variants of the adjusted manual rates with the five basic models that pertain to states with private carriers. As shown in Table C.4, these include four types of insurance rates (the starting point for the calculations), seven types of adjustment factors, and two measures of market shares for the voluntary and residual markets. These 16 variables (13 types of data as inputs and 3 variants of adjusted manual rates as outputs) were defined in Appendix B and this appendix, and their uses are illustrated in this appendix.

Table C.4 Compendium of Variables with Data for the Five Basic Models for States with Private Carriers

Insurance rates	
IR1	Manual rates in voluntary market
IR2	Manual rates in residual market
IR3	Pure premiums in voluntary market
IR4	Manual rates for total market
Adjustment factors[a]	
AF1	Experience-rating adjustment (standard premium ÷ manual premium)
AF2	Expense-constant adjustment
AF3	Standard earned premium at company level ÷ standard earned premium at DSR
AF4	Net earned premium ÷ standard earned premium at company level
AF5	Dividend adjustment
AF6	RM impact (residual market impact)
AF7	Net earned premium ÷ standard premium at DSR $[AF7 = AF3 - AF4]$
Market shares	
MS1	Voluntary market share
MS2	Residual market share
Adjusted manual rates	
AMR1	Voluntary market adjusted manual rates
AMR2	Residual market adjusted manual rates
AMR3	Total market adjusted manual rates

[a] Policy-year data for variables AF3, AF4, and AF7 were used whenever possible; otherwise, calendar-year data were used.

Calculation of Adjusted Manual Rates for Markets in Which the Starting Point Is Manual Rates

Manual rates have two components: pure premiums and an expense loading. The pure premiums cover expected payments for cash benefits, medical care, and (in most jurisdictions) loss-adjustment expenses. The expense-loading factor provides an allowance for other insurance carrier expenses, such as general administrative expenses, commissions, profits, and contingencies. In most states using manual rates, the loading factor historically has been 35–40 percent of the manual rates. The general procedure used to calculate adjusted manual rates when the starting point is manual rates is summarized in Table C.5.[7]

Manual rates (line 1) are stated as dollars per $100 of payroll. The employer's total *payroll* (line 2) falling within the payroll limit[8] multiplied by the appropriate manual rate equals *manual premium without constants* (line 3). In practice, few employers pay such a premium because of several modifications.

The first modification arises from the experience rating that is permitted for medium and large firms. In simple terms, experience rating uses the employer's own past record of benefit payments to modify published manual rates that would otherwise apply. If the employer's record is worse than the experience of the average employer in its classification, then its actual premium for the current policy period is larger than its manual premium.[9]

Table C.5 Calculation of Adjusted Manual Rates from Manual Rates

1.	Manual rates (MR)
2.	× Payroll
3.	= Manual premium without constants
4.	× Experience-rating modification
5.	= Standard earned premium excluding constants
6.	÷ Adjustment for expense constants (and loss constants)
7.	= Standard earned premium at bureau rates (DSR)
8.	× Adjustment for deviations
9.	= Standard earned premium at company level
10.	× Adjustment for premium discounts, retrospective rating, and schedule rating
11.	= Net earned premium
12.	× Dividends adjustment
13.	= Net cost to policyholders
14.	÷ Payroll
15.	= Adjusted manual rates (AMR)

The same experience-rating formula is used in all the NCCI states, but the experience-rating modification differs among these states and therefore must be taken into account in determining the actual costs of workers' compensation insurance in each state. Moreover, it is necessary to determine the effects of experience rating in the NCCI jurisdictions in order to compare their insurance costs with those in other states that have their own experience-rating plans.[10] The product of the manual premium without constants (line 3) and the *experience-rating modification* (line 4) is line 5, *the standard earned premium excluding constants.*

The standard earned premium excluding constants also is modified for most employers, although the form of this modification depends on the size of the employer's premium. Employers in almost every state are assessed a flat charge, termed an "expense constant," to cover the minimum costs of issuing and servicing a policy. In addition, employers in some states are assessed another flat charge, termed a "loss constant," because of the generally inferior safety record of small businesses. When the standard earned premium excluding constants (line 5) is divided by line 6, the *adjustment for the expense constants (and loss constants)*, the result is the *standard earned premium at bureau rates (DSR)* (line 7), also termed the "standard earned premium at the designated statistical reporting (DSR) level."

The standard earned premium at bureau rates is further adjusted for many employers. Deviations are a competitive pricing device that have been available in over 30 states since 1975, but they have only been in active use in many jurisdictions since approximately 1980. In a state allowing deviations, individual carriers may use the manual rates promulgated by the rating organization or may deviate from those rates. The carrier might, for example, use manual rates that are 10 percent less than those issued by the rating organization. The deviations offered by a particular carrier must be uniform for all policyholders in the state in a particular insurance class (although different deviations for different classes are sometimes possible). If the standard earned premium at bureau rates (line 7) is multiplied by the *adjustment for deviations* (line 8), the result is the *standard earned premium at company level* (line 9).[11]

There are several additional factors that may reduce workers' compensation insurance premiums. Premium discounts apply to employers with annual premiums in excess of $5,000, which basically reflect reductions in carrier expenses for larger policies because of economies of scale. The discounts based on a specified schedule are compulsory in the NCCI states, unless both the insurance carrier and the employer agree to substitute "retrospective rating" for the premium discounts. Though these retrospective rating plans vary among the NCCI states, they are basically similar in that they allow the employer to increase the effect of its own claims experience on the published manual rates.

The main difference between experience rating and retrospective rating is that the former uses the employer's experience from previous periods to modify the premium for the current policy period rate, whereas the retrospective plan uses experience from the current policy period to determine the current premium on an *ex post facto* basis. The same expense retention (reduction in premiums for the employer) provided by the premium discounts is built into the retrospective rating plans. Identical discount schedules and retrospective plans are used in virtually all NCCI jurisdictions; however, because states differ in matters such as the distribution of the size of workers' compensation insurance policies, the schedules and plans nonetheless have different effects on rates in different states and therefore are measured with state-specific data.

Schedule-rating plans have also been actively used in many jurisdictions since the 1980s. Under these plans, insurers can change (usually decrease) the insurance rate the employer would otherwise pay through debits or credits based on a subjective evaluation of factors such as the employer's loss-control program. There are two types of schedule rating. In states with uniform schedule-rating plans, regulators authorize all carriers to use identical schedule-rating plans. If all carriers are not given this permission, then individual carriers can apply for approval of their own schedule-rating plans.

The result of multiplying the standard earned premium at company level (line 9) by the *adjustment for premium discounts, retrospective rating, and schedule rating* (line 10) is the *net earned premium* (line 11).

One final adjustment factor, a *dividends adjustment* (line 12), needs to be used to compute the premiums actually paid by employers.[12] Mutual companies or stock companies with participating policies write a substantial portion of the workers' compensation insurance. While these companies normally use a quantity discount schedule less steeply graded than that of the nonparticipating stock companies, they pay dividends that usually decrease policyholders' net costs to levels below that charged by nonparticipating stock companies, especially for large employers. The product of the net earned premium (line 11) and the dividends adjustment is the *net cost to policyholders* (line 13), which is the premium actually paid by employers purchasing workers' compensation insurance.

The final modification shown in Table C.5 is to divide the net cost to policyholders by *payroll* (line 14) in order to produce *adjusted manual rates* (line 15) that can be used to provide meaningful comparisons among firms. Adjusted manual rates are measured as dollars of premium per $100 of payroll, which can be interpreted as the percentage of payroll actually expended by employers on workers' compensation insurance.

The astute reader will note that payroll is included at steps 2 and 14 in adjustments that are exactly offsetting. This was done to facilitate understanding of insurance terminology and our procedure. In our actual calculations, discussed below, we skip steps 2 and 14 without affecting the relationship between manual rates and adjusted manual rates.

Use of State-Level Data for the Modification Factors

Our calculations involving the modifying factors shown in Table C.5 (and the subsequent tables in this appendix) rely on state-level data (or separate state-level data for the voluntary market and for the residual market), rather than on data for each of the 71 insurance classes included in our study. There are three reasons we used aggregated data. First, most of the adjustment factors are only available at an aggregate level, including the adjustments for deviations and dividends. Second, the data for experience-rating modifications at the individual classification level are available from the NCCI, but only at considerable expense that exceeded our budget. Third, because we are using 71 insurance classifications in this study, which accounted for more than 70 percent of all payroll covered by the workers' compensation program nationally (see Table C.1), we expect that our procedure of relying on state-level experience-rating modification factors will not produce results that would significantly differ from using individual modification factors for the 71 classes and then averaging the results.

We recognize, of course, that comparisons of workers' compensation insurance costs among states for individual insurance classes will be more accurate if modifying factors (such as the experience-rating modification factor) at the classification level are used. However, we confine ourselves in this study to interstate comparisons of the weighted averages of the adjusted manual rates for 71 insurance classifications, and we therefore are confident that the use of state-level data for adjustment factors is appropriate.

Calculation of Adjusted Manual Rates for Markets in Which the Starting Point Is Pure Premium Rates

The general procedure used to calculate adjusted manual rates in workers' compensation markets in which the starting point is pure premium rates (or loss costs) is summarized in Table C.6.[13] The pure premiums cover expected payments for cash benefits, medical care, and (in most jurisdictions) loss-adjustment expenses.

The *pure premium rates* (line 1) are stated as dollars per $100 of payroll. The employer's total *payroll* (line 2) falling within the payroll limit multiplied by the appropriate pure premium rates is *pure premium* (line 3). In practice, no employer pays such an amount.

Table C.6 Calculation of Adjusted Manual Rates from Pure Premiums

1.	Pure premium rates
2.	× Payroll
3.	= Pure premium
4.	× Experience-rating modification
5.	= Standard earned premium at bureau rates (DSR)
6.	× Adjustment for deviations, expense constants (and loss constants), and expense loadings
7.	= Standard earned premium at company level
8.	× Adjustment for premium discounts, retrospective rating, and schedule rating
9.	= Net earned premium
10.	× Dividends adjustment
11.	= Net cost to policyholders
12.	÷ Payroll
13.	= Adjusted manual rates (AMR)

The first modification in calculating employers' premiums arises from experience rating. The product of the pure premium and the *experience-rating modification* (line 4) is line 5, the *standard earned premium at bureau rates (DSR)*, or "standard earned premium at DSR."

The standard earned premium at bureau rates (DSR) is modified for most employers. Carriers will add their own expense loadings to cover expenses such as general administrative expenses and commissions. Employers may also be assessed a flat charge, termed an expense constant, to cover the minimum costs of issuing and servicing a policy. In addition, some employers are assessed another flat charge, a loss constant, to compensate for the generally inferior safety record of small businesses.

The standard earned premium at bureau rates is further adjusted for many employers by the use of deviations. Individual carriers may use the pure premium rates promulgated by the rating organization or may deviate from those rates. If the standard earned premium at bureau rates (DSR) is multiplied by line 6, the *adjustment for deviations, expense constants (and loss constants), and expense loadings*, the result is line 7, the *standard earned premium at company level*.

There are additional factors that reduce workers' compensation insurance premiums for many employers. Premium discounts may apply to employers with significant annual premiums (in excess of $5,000), reflecting the reductions in carrier expenses for larger policies because of economies of scale. Alternatively, the insurance carrier and the employer may agree to substitute "retrospective rating" for the premium discounts

Schedule-rating plans have also been introduced in many jurisdictions in recent years. Under these plans, insurers can change (usually decrease) the insurance rate the employer would otherwise pay through debits or credits based on a subjective evaluation of factors such as the employer's loss-control program.

The result of multiplying the standard earned premium at company level by line 8, the *adjustment for premium discounts, retrospective rating, and schedule rating* is the *net earned premium* (line 9).

One final adjustment factor, a *dividends adjustment* (line 10), needs to be used in the order to compute the premiums actually paid by employers. The product of the net earned premium and the dividends adjustment is the *net cost to policyholders* (line 11), which is the premium actually paid by employers purchasing workers' compensation insurance.

The final modification shown in Table C.6 is to divide the net cost to policyholders by *payroll* (line 12) in order to produce *adjusted manual rates* (line 13) that can be used to provide meaningful comparisons among firms. Adjusted manual rates are measured as dollars of premium per $100 of payroll, which can be interpreted as the percentage of payroll actually expended by employers on workers' compensation insurance.

In our actual calculations, discussed below, we skip steps 2 and 12 without affecting the relationship between manual rates and adjusted manual rates.

Calculation of Adjusted Manual Rates When There Is an Assigned-Risk Market

Most workers' compensation insurance is provided in the voluntary insurance market. However, because the employers whose applications for insurance are rejected in the voluntary market still must have insurance, all states that do not have state funds that are obligated to accept all employers have established assigned-risk plans. The national average for this assigned-risk (residual) market share in NCCI states ranged between 4.6 percent and 28.5 percent between 1975 and 1996 (see Figure 2.13 and Table A.8). Residual market shares for most of the states with private carriers are available for 1980–1995.

The residual market share data in Table C.7 indicate that there are considerable variations among states and years in the importance of residual markets. Arkansas, for example, had only 2.8 percent of private insurance in the residual market in 1983, but its share reached 51.4 percent in 1993. And in 1992, for example, when the national average share peaked at 28.5 percent,

Table C.7 State Residual Market Shares, 1980–95 (%)

	Ala.	Alaska	Ariz.	Ark.	Calif.	Colo.	Conn.	Del.	D.C.	Fla.	Ga.	Hawaii
1980	12.0	9.1	0.2	10.1	—a	—	11.7	5.1	12.7	15.7	9.7	5.8
1981	10.4	8.6	0.1	6.7	—	—	8.3	3.4	9.8	11.3	6.7	3.9
1982	8.1	6.1	0.2	4.0	—	—	6.0	2.4	7.9	8.0	3.7	4.0
1983	5.5	4.9	0.4	2.8	—	—	4.1	1.5	5.5	6.6	3.0	3.9
1984	5.9	4.0	0.3	3.4	—	—	3.4	1.8	3.6	6.2	3.0	3.6
1985	10.8	8.0	0.7	11.6	—	—	5.3	—	6.8	10.4	8.3	5.7
1986	18.4	15.9	2.2	24.4	—	—	9.8	5.5	9.8	17.7	16.7	7.8
1987	21.6	13.9	2.4	26.5	—	—	12.0	6.7	10.1	22.2	19.5	8.9
1988	22.5	15.1	1.7	34.7	—	—	11.1	6.7	9.7	21.0	16.2	9.5
1989	23.5	13.3	2.2	34.7	—	—	12.7	7.3	10.3	22.9	18.7	10.4
1990	30.6	15.0	3.1	35.7	—	—	12.0	9.6	13.2	23.4	19.5	10.1
1991	36.3	13.1	3.3	41.8	—	—	13.0	—	16.0	21.5	20.6	11.4
1992	42.1	17.0	3.3	50.9	—	—	13.9	—	16.4	27.9	24.5	12.5
1993	40.9	16.3	3.3	51.4	—	—	11.6	—	18.6	34.2	28.7	20.3
1994	39.4	16.4	1.3	39.2	—	—	11.4	—	14.5	4.0	30.7	35.3
1995	30.7	15.0	0.5	26.2	—	—	9.3	12.2	12.6	3.0	21.4	47.5

335

	Idaho	Ill.	Ind.	Iowa	Kans.	Ky.	La.	Maine	Md.	Mass.	Mich.	Minn.
1980	—	16.2	8.8	6.3	10.0	22.3	17.8	25.7	—	21.7	7.0	—
1981	—	11.7	7.6	4.4	10.5	27.3	15.1	22.7	—	20.5	5.0	—
1982	—	7.1	5.6	2.8	8.4	22.8	11.0	20.1	—	17.2	3.7	—
1983	—	5.1	3.5	2.2	6.5	17.2	8.8	18.8	—	12.4	2.9	—
1984	—	5.3	4.8	2.7	7.1	8.1	8.0	20.4	—	10.4	3.5	4.8
1985	—	11.6	9.9	8.6	12.9	10.7	16.4	30.2	—	14.7	6.8	8.5
1986	—	17.4	20.0	14.5	21.7	15.4	33.2	54.6	—	20.4	10.5	14.1
1987	—	17.8	22.6	16.5	24.5	20.9	36.5	67.2	—	25.0	11.7	16.7
1988	—	15.2	20.3	17.2	21.7	21.1	43.9	82.3	—	29.5	10.6	16.9
1989	—	15.1	20.0	17.2	24.1	23.7	56.7	90.6	—	40.1	10.1	14.5
1990	—	14.9	20.5	17.0	27.7	25.3	65.8	87.8	—	46.3	10.7	15.1
1991	2.3	15.3	17.6	17.6	30.0	29.3	79.9	78.2	—	50.7	10.7	15.5
1992	2.9	13.5	17.3	17.4	35.2	42.1	78.5	82.4	—	64.7	13.1	18.3
1993	2.6	12.6	14.7	18.6	38.6	44.1	—	—	—	61.0	14.4	20.8
1994	2.6	10.8	11.6	13.9	35.4	49.1	—	—	—	47.0	10.4	20.5
1995	2.3	7.8	6.4	938	24.9	34.9	—	—	—	27.8	8.7	15.5

(continued)

336

Table C.7 (continued)

	Miss.	Mo.	Mont.	Nebr.	N.H.	N.J.	N.Mex.	N.Y.	N.C.	Ohio	Okla.	Oreg.
1980	11.0	14.4	—	6.0	27.2	13.1	10.8	—	12.1	—	—	0.1
1981	6.6	14.3	—	6.4	23.0	8.3	4.8	—	10.0	—	—	0.2
1982	6.8	9.4	—	3.2	19.3	5.5	3.3	—	7.0	—	—	0.3
1983	6.2	7.2	—	2.7	12.7	3.0	2.3	—	5.3	—	—	0.2
1984	5.5	7.6	—	2.7	12.2	2.0	2.0	—	5.0	—	—	0.5
1985	10.5	15.1	—	7.6	14.9	4.0	7.3	—	8.1	—	—	2.0
1986	18.3	23.9	—	16.0	24.6	8.1	20.1	—	12.6	—	—	3.6
1987	25.7	25.1	—	17.2	30.3	9.2	30.2	—	15.4	—	—	3.4
1988	28.2	25.2	—	17.9	26.4	9.6	31.3	—	16.2	—	—	3.3
1989	28.0	26.5	—	23.4	30.3	7.9	34.4	—	18.2	—	—	4.2
1990	36.2	28.8	—	23.3	30.8	10.0	40.7	—	19.4	—	—	9.8
1991	40.3	33.1	—	25.2	30.1	—	46.4	—	21.2	—	—	11.4
1992	51.6	32.5	—	20.5	39.8	—	51.8	—	24.1	—	—	7.7
1993	41.6	35.0	—	19.7	38.4	—	46.9	—	28.4	—	—	8.0
1994	38.6	37.0	—	15.6	41.8	—	3.5	—	23.7	—	—	8.7
1995	25.0	17.3	—	11.0	27.1	—	21.4	—	18.2	—	—	7.9

	Pa.	R.I.	S.C.	S.Dak.	Tenn.	Texas	Utah	Vt.	Va.	Wash.	W.Va.	Wisc.
1980	—	21.8	11.7	9.5	11.0	—	—	24.6	16.5	—	—	—
1981	—	20.8	9.7	9.1	8.8	—	—	20.5	13.4	—	—	—
1982	—	20.7	8.1	6.6	6.4	—	—	20.0	13.1	—	—	—
1983	—	18.1	7.4	5.4	5.1	—	—	19.3	8.9	—	—	—
1984	—	14.4	5.7	4.8	5.7	—	—	14.8	3.7	—	—	—
1985	—	22.8	8.7	11.0	11.0	—	—	17.3	4.8	—	—	—
1986	—	36.8	16.5	28.0	19.2	—	—	26.8	9.6	—	—	—
1987	—	44.4	19.2	25.2	22.2	—	—	29.8	11.6	—	—	—
1988	—	51.5	20.9	27.4	23.3	—	—	27.2	12.4	—	—	—
1989	—	66.8	23.6	30.2	22.3	—	—	34.0	14.3	—	—	—
1990	—	79.5	25.6	23.2	27.2	—	—	35.8	17.8	—	—	—
1991	—	85.2	34.5	23.9	32.3	—	—	32.4	19.2	—	—	—
1992	—	88.6	41.0	24.2	41.4	—	—	40.7	26.9	—	—	—
1993	—	—	46.2	23.5	55.0	—	—	41.8	32.6	—	—	—
1994	—	—	42.7	20.4	52.3	—	—	36.4	29.1	—	—	—
1995	—	—	26.3	15.4	42.7	—	—	24.9	24.3	—	—	—

[a] A dash (—) indicates either that the state has no residual market or that no data are available for that market.

the shares in individual states ranged from 2.9 percent in Idaho to 88.6 percent in Rhode Island.

Six models are used to calculate the employers' costs of workers' compensation insurance, as previously discussed in conjunction with Table C.2. The first two models are used when the only data for a state pertain to the voluntary market. Model III is used when the states use identical manual rates in the voluntary and residual market. Model IV is used when the state uses one set of manual rates in the voluntary market and another set of manual rates in the residual market. Model V applies if the state uses pure premiums in the voluntary market and manual rates in the residual market. Model VI is applicable if the state has an exclusive state fund which uses the same set of manual rates for all employers.

A further distinction must be drawn for Models III, IV, and V, depending on the type of residual market pricing program used in the state. There are six types of residual market programs, which we label RMP1 to RMP6:

RMP1: different manual rates (or loss costs) are used in the voluntary and residual markets;

RMP2: premium discounts are eliminated or modified in the residual market for large policyholders, who would qualify for the discounts in the voluntary market;

RMP3: loss-sensitive rating plans (LSRP)—including the Assigned Risk Rating Program (ARRP), which is a type of retrospective rating plan—are used in the residual market, which increase the effect of an employer's own experience on the premiums paid by the employer;

RMP4: premium surcharges are added in the residual market to the premiums the employer would otherwise pay;

RMP5: the Assigned Risk Adjustment Program (ARAP); and

RMP6: other experience-rating adjustment programs that are applicable to firms in the residual market.

The calculations for the residual market adjusted manual rates depend on which of these six residual market programs is used. The crucial distinction is whether the state relies solely on programs RMP1, RMP2, and RMP3. If so, then the standard adjustment factors (shown in Tables C.5 and C.6) used to calculate adjusted manual rates will capture the effects of the residual market programs as well as the effects of the various adjustment factors in the voluntary market. Depending on the combination of manual rates and/or pure premiums used in the voluntary and residual markets, Model III, IV, or V will pertain to a state that uses only RMP1, RMP2, and RMP3.

If, however, the state relies on residual market programs RMP4, RMP5, or RMP6, then the "normal" adjustment factors used to calculate adjusted manual rates in Tables C.5 and C.6 will not capture the effects of these residual market programs. Rather, the adjusted manual rates in the residual market have to be computed by using an additional factor measuring the residual market program impact on rates. These effects were calculated for us by the NCCI and are shown in the "Impact" column of Table C.8. Depending on the combination of manual rates and/or pure premiums in the voluntary and residual markets, the state using RMP4, RMP5, or RMP6 will be classified as Model IIIa, IVa, or Va.

Florida provides an illustration of the choice of model depending on the type of residual market program used in the state. Between 1975 and 1987, Florida only used the voluntary market to provide workers' compensation insurance, and thus Model I was applicable (see Table C.3). In 1988, Florida established a residual market, which used the same manual rates in the voluntary and residual markets but eliminated the premium discount in the residual market (RMP2), which made Model III applicable. In 1989, the state continued to use the same manual rates in the voluntary and residual markets and implemented an ARRP program (RMP3), which meant that Florida was still a Model III jurisdiction in our classification scheme. In 1990, Florida continued the ARRP program (RMP3), but it also established a $267 flat charge plus a 15 percent surcharge for all policies in the residual market (RMP4); because Florida continued to use the same manual rates in the voluntary and residual markets in 1990, Model IIIa was applicable. The latest change occurred in 1994, when Florida relied on manual rates in the residual market that were 26 percent higher than the manual rates in the voluntary market. Florida also relied on the ARAP program (RMP5) as well as surcharges (RMP4) in the residual market in 1994, which meant that Model IVa was applicable. The next section provides numerical examples of the calculation of adjusted manual rates for all of the models used for states with private insurance carriers.

THE FIVE BASIC MODELS IN STATES WITH PRIVATE CARRIERS

Model I: Voluntary Market Only with Manual Rates

This model is used when 1) the voluntary market relies on manual rates and 2) there are no separate rates or data for the assigned-risk market. The manual rates for the voluntary market can be mandatory or advisory.

A complete description of the procedure for moving from manual rates to adjusted manual rates with this model was provided in the previous section

Table C.8 Adjustments for Residual Market Pricing Programs

Comparison dates	Residual program Rates used[a]	Adjustments[b]	Impact	Rates used in vol. market[c]	Model[d]
Alabama					
1/1/92	AR			PP	V
1/1/93	AR			PP	V
1/1/94	AR			PP	V
1/1/95	AR			PP	V
Alaska					
1/1/84	VM × 1.1			MR	IV
1/1/85	VM × 1.1			MR	IV
1/1/86	VM × 1.1			MR	IV
1/1/87	VM × 1.2			MR	IV
1/1/88	VM × 1.2			MR	IV
1/1/89	VM	25% Surcharge	1.161	MR	IIIa
1/1/90	VM	25% Surcharge	1.161	MR	IIIa
1/1/91	VM	25% Surcharge	1.161	MR	IIIa
1/1/92	VM	25% Surcharge	1.161	MR	IIIa
1/1/93	VM	25% Surcharge	1.161	MR	IIIa
1/1/94	VM	25% Surcharge	1.161	MR	IIIa
1/1/95	VM	25% Surcharge	1.161	MR	IIIa
Arizona					
1/1/87 (through 1/1/95)	VM × 1.2			MR	IV
Arkansas					
1/1/91	VM	ARAP	1.120	MR	IIIa
1/1/92	VM	ARAP	1.120	MR	IIIa
1/1/93	AR	ARAP	1.088	MR	IVa
1/1/94	AR	ARAP	1.088	MR	IVa
1/1/95	AR	Merit rating, etc.	1.088	MR	IVa
Connecticut					
1/1/90	AR			PP	V
1/1/91	AR			PP	V
1/1/92	AR			PP	V
1/1/93	AR	ARAP	1.099	PP	Va

Comparison dates	Rates used[a]	Residual program Adjustments[b]	Impact	Rates used in vol. market[c]	Model[d]
1/1/94	AR	ARAP	1.099	PP	Va
1/1/95	AR	ARAP	1.099	PP	Va
District of Columbia					
1/1/88 (through 1/1/92)	AR			MR	IV
1/1/93	AR			PP	V
1/1/94	AR			PP	V
1/1/95	AR			PP	V
Florida					
1/1/88	VM	[Removal of discounts]		MR	III
1/1/89	VM	[ARRP]		MR	III
1/1/90	VM	ARRP $(1.0) \times$ \$267 flat charge $(1.067) \times 15\%$ surcharge (1.110)	1.184	MR	IIIa
1/1/91	VM	ARRP $(1.065) \times$ \$267 flat charge $(1.067) \times 15\%$ surcharge (1.110)	1.184	MR	IIIa
1/1/92	VM	ARRP $(1.129) \times$ \$475 flat charge $(1.086) \times 26\%$ surcharge (1.162)	1.425	MR	IIIa
1/1/93	VM	ARRP $(1.120) \times$ \$475 flat charge $(0.152) \times 26\%$ surcharge (0.260)	1.532	MR	IIIa
1/1/94	VM $\times 1.26$	ARRP $(0.151) \times$ \$475 flat charge $(0.117) \times$ surcharge (0.826)	$2.354 \times$ VM rates or $1.868 \times$ AR rates	MR	IVa
1/1/95	VM $\times 1.26$	ARRP $(0.151) \times$ \$475 flat charge $(0.117) \times$ surcharge (1.826)	$2.354 \times$ VM rates or $1.868 \times$ AR rates	MR	IVa
Georgia					
1/1/82 (through 1/1/86)	VM $\times 1.2$			MR	IV

(continued)

Table C.8 (continued)

	Residual program			Rates used	
Comparison dates	Rates used[a]	Adjustments[b]	Impact	in vol. market[c]	Model[d]
Georgia (cont.)					
1/1/87	VM × 1.145			MR	IV
1/1/88 (through 1/1/91)	VM × 1.221			MR	IV
1/1/92	VM × 1.25			MR	IV
1/1/93	VM × 1.25			MR	IV
1/1/94	VM × 1.25	ARRP (= LSRP)		MR	IV
1/1/95	VM × 1.25	ARRP (= LSRP)		MR	IV
Hawaii					
1/1/93	AR	ARAP	1.115	PP	Va
1/1/94	AR	ARAP	1.115	PP	Va
1/1/95	AR	ARAP	1.115	PP	Va
Idaho					
1/1/92 (through 1/1/95)	VM	20% Surcharge	1.2	MR	IIIa
Illinois					
Pre 1/1/88		Not in 10/20/97 table			
1/1/88	VM × 1.038			MR	IV
1/1/89	VM × 1.038			MR	IV
1/1/90 (through 1/1/93)	VM × 1.2			MR	IV
1/1/94	VM × 1.2	ARAP	1.09	MR	IVa
1/1/95	VM × 1.2	ARAP	1.09	MR	IVa
Indiana					
1/1/90 (through 1/1/94)	VM	25% Surcharge	1.224	MR	IIIa
1/1/95	VM	25% Surcharge/offset	1.189	MR	IIIa
Iowa					
1/1/89	VM × 1.09			MR	IV
1/1/90	VM × 1.2			MR	IV
1/1/91	VM × 1.2	ARRP (= LSRP)		MR	IV

Comparison dates	Rates used[a]	Residual program Adjustments[b]	Impact	Rates used in vol. market[c]	Model[d]
1/1/92	VM × 1.2	ARRP (= LSRP)		MR	IV
1/1/93	VM × 1.2	ARAP	1.108	MR	IVa
1/1/94	VM × 1.2	ARAP	1.098	MR	IVa
1/1/95	VM × 1.2	ARAP	1.073	MR	IVa
Kansas					
1/1/91	VM	ARAP	1.075	MR	IIIa
1/1/92	VM	ARAP	1.075	MR	IIIa
1/1/93	VM	ARAP	1.062	MR	IIIa
1/1/94	VM	ARAP (1.080) × surcharge (1.116)	1.205	MR	IIIa
1/1/95	VM	ARAP (1.080) × surcharge (1.116)	1.205	MR	IIIa
Louisiana					
1/1/90	AR	20% Surcharge	1.144	PP	Va
1/1/91	AR	25% Surcharge	1.138	PP	Va
1/1/92	AR	25% Surcharge	1.138	PP	Va
Mississippi					
1/1/91	VM	20% Surcharge	1.2	MR	IIIa
1/1/92	VM	20% Surcharge	1.2	MR	IIIa
1/1/93	AR			MR	IV
1/1/94	AR			MR	IV
1/1/95	AR			MR	IV
Missouri					
1/1/90	VM	[Removal of discounts]		MR	III
1/1/91	VM	ARAP	1.086	MR	IIIa
1/1/92	VM	ARAP (1.087) × 20% surcharge (1.2)	1.304	MR	IIIa
1/1/93	VM	ARAP (1.087) × 20% surcharge (1.2)	1.304	MR	IIIa
1/1/94	AR			PP	V
1/1/95	AR			PP	V

(continued)

Table C.8 (continued)

Comparison dates	Residual program			Rates used in vol. market[c]	Model[d]
	Rates used[a]	Adjustments[b]	Impact		
Nebraska					
1/1/90	AR			MR	IV
1/1/91	AR	ARAP	1.067	MR	IVa
1/1/92	AR	ARAP	1.067	MR	IVa
1/1/93	AR	ARAP	1.107	MR	IVa
1/1/94	AR	ARAP	1.107	MR	IVa
1/1/95	AR	ARAP	1.107	PP	Va
New Hampshire					
1/1/91	VM	[Removal of discounts]		MR	III
1/1/92	VM	[Removal of discounts]		MR	III
1/1/93	VM	10% Surcharge	1.1	MR	IIIa
1/1/94	AR	10% Surcharge	1.1	PP	Va
1/1/95	AR	10% Surcharge	1.1	PP	Va
New Mexico					
1/1/90	AR			PP	V
1/1/91	AR	10% Surcharge	1.1	PP	Va
1/1/92	AR	10% Surcharge (1.1) × ARAP (1.103)	1.213	PP	Va
1/1/93	AR	10% Surcharge (1.1) × ARAP (1.103)	1.213	PP	Va
1/1/94	AR	10% Surcharge (1.1) × ARAP (1.103)	1.213	PP	Va
1/1/95	AR	10% Surcharge (1.1) × ARAP (1.074)	1.181	PP	Va
North Carolina					
1/1/75 (through 1/1/90)	VM	8% Surcharge	1.08	MR	IIIa
1/1/91	VM	8% Surcharge (1.08) × ARAP (1.061)	1.146	MR	IIIa
1/1/92	VM	8% Surcharge (1.08) × ARAP (1.061)	1.146	MR	IIIa
1/1/93	VM	14% Surcharge (1.14) × ARAP (1.068)	1.218	MR	IIIa

Comparison dates	Rates used[a]	Residual program			Rates used in vol. market[c]	Model[d]
		Adjustments[b]	Impact			
1/1/94	VM	14% Surcharge (1.14) × ARAP (1.062)	1.211		MR	IIIa
1/1/95	VM	14% Surcharge (1.14) × ARAP (1.062)	1.211		MR	IIIa
Oregon						
1/1/83 (through 1/1/89)	AR	[AR Rates = VM 1.1]			PP	V
1/1/90 (through 1/1/92)	AR	[AR Rates = VM 1.15]			PP	V
1/1/93	AR	ARAP	1.148		PP	Va
1/1/94	AR	ARAP	1.133		PP	Va
1/1/95	AR	ARAP	1.116		PP	Va
South Carolina						
1/1/91	AR	ARAP	1.087		PP	Va
1/1/92	AR	ARAP	1.087		PP	Va
1/1/93	AR	ARAP	1.087		PP	Va
1/1/94	AR	ARAP	1.076		PP	Va
1/1/95	AR	ARAP	1.076		PP	Va
South Dakota						
1/1/89	VM	15% Surcharge to premium in excess of $500	1.079		MR	IIIa
1/1/90	VM	15% Surcharge	1.079		MR	IIIa
1/1/91	VM	15% Surcharge	1.079		MR	IIIa
1/1/92	VM	15% Surcharge	1.079		MR	IIIa
1/1/93	VM	15% Surcharge	1.079		MR	IIIa
1/1/94	VM	15% Surcharge to premium in excess of $3750	1.122		MR	IIIa
1/1/95	AR	15% Surcharge	1.122		PP	Va

(continued)

Table C.8 (continued)

Comparison dates	Residual program Rates used[a]	Adjustments[b]	Impact	Rates used in vol. market[c]	Model[d]
Tennessee					
1/1/89	VM			MR	III
1/1/90	VM	10% Surcharge, selective	1.0585	MR	IIIa
1/1/91	VM	10% Surcharge, selective	1.0585	MR	IIIa
1/1/92	VM	Tabular surcharge	1.112	MR	IIIa
1/1/93	VM	Tabular surcharge	1.112	MR	IIIa
1/1/94	VM	Tabular surcharge	1.112	MR	IIIa
1/1/95	VM	Tabular surcharge	1.112	MR	IIIa
Vermont					
1/1/86 (through 1/1/92)	VM			MR	III
1/1/93	VM	ARAP	1.082	MR	IIIa
1/1/94	VM	ARAP	1.076	MR	IIIa
1/1/95	AR	ARAP	1.076	PP	Va
Virginia					
1/1/92	VM	ARAP	1.098	MR	IIIa
1/1/93	AR	ARAP	1.101	MR	IVa
1/1/94	AR	ARAP	1.094	PP	Va
1/1/95	AR	ARAP	1.094	PP	Va

SOURCE: The information in this table was provided by Barry I. Llewellyn of the National Council on Compensation Insurance.

[a] AR = assigned-risk market rates.
VM = aoluntary market rates.
[b] ARAP = Assigned Risk Adjustment Program.
ARRP = Assigned Risk Rating Program.
LSRP = Loss-sensitive rating plan.
[c] PP = pure premium.
MR = manual rate.
[d] "Model" refers to those listed in Table C.3.

(see Table C.5). A simplified illustration of the procedure used to derive adjusted manual rates for Colorado for January 1, 1981, is shown in Table C.9; this table uses the variables described in Table C.4.

The starting point for the calculations is the variable IR1, the average of the 71 manual rates, which was $1.416 per $100 of payroll in Colorado in 1981.[14] This rate was multiplied by adjustment factor AF1, the experience-rating adjustment, which was 0.984, indicating that experience rating was reducing the workers' compensation premiums paid by Colorado employers. The expense constant was $35 in Colorado in 1981, which, based on actuarial data on the effect of this constant on the amount of premium paid by employers, meant that AF2, the expense constant adjustment factor, was 0.993. The ratio of standard earned premium at company level to standard earned premium at DSB (AF3) was 0.779, which indicates that substantial deviations were being offered by carriers in Colorado. The ratio of net earned premium to standard earned premium at company level (AF4) was 0.961, indicating that some additional reductions in premiums were occurring due to factors such as retrospective rating. The final adjustment factor, the dividend adjustment (AF5), was 0.934, indicating that dividends were 6.6 percent of net premium in Colorado in 1981.

For Colorado, we thus started with the average manual rates of $1.416 and computed an average adjusted manual rate (AMR3) of $0.982 per $100 of payroll for the 71 types of Colorado employers in 1981 (Table C.9). The average of adjusted manual rates was 30.6 percent less than the average of the manual rates, indicating that the adjustment factors used by carriers in Colorado in 1981 had a dramatic effect in lowering the premiums actually paid by

Table C.9 Sample Calculation of Adjusted Manual Rates for Model I, for Colorado on January 1, 1981

IR1	Manual rates (averages for 71 classes)		$1.416
AF1	Experience rating adjustment	×	0.984
AF2	Expense-constant adjustment	÷	0.993
AF3	Standard earned premium at company level ÷ standard earned premium at DSR	×	0.779
AF4	Net earned premium ÷ standard earned premium at company level	×	0.961
AF5	Dividend adjustment	×	0.934
AMR3	Total market adjusted manual rates	=	$0.982

employers. Similar calculations were performed for all of the states and years for which Model I applies (as shown in Table C.3).

Model II: Voluntary Market Only with Pure Premium Rates

This model is used when 1) the rates for the voluntary market are pure premium rates (loss costs) and 2) there are no separate rates or calculations for the assigned-risk market.

A complete description of the general procedure of moving from pure premium rates to adjusted manual rates was provided in the previous section (see Table C.6). A simplified illustration of the procedure used to derive adjusted manual rates for Colorado for January 1, 1995, is shown in Table C.10, using the variables included in Table C.4.

The average pure premium rate for the 71 insurance classes (IR3) was $2.857 per $100 of payroll in Colorado in 1995. The experience-rating adjustment (AF1) is 0.969; the ratio of standard earned premium at the company level to standard earned premium at the DSR level (AF3) is 1.341; the ratio of net earned premium to standard earned premium at the company level (AF4) is 0.797; and the dividend adjustment (AF5) is 0.942. The result of multiplying the average pure premium rate (for the 71 classes) by these adjustment factors is a total market adjusted manual rate (AMR3) of $2.788 per $100 of payroll. It is of interest that the adjusted manual rates were actually less than the pure premiums in Colorado in 1995 as a result of these adjustments. As a result, Colorado employers in 1995 expended, on average, 2.788 percent of payroll on workers' compensation insurance.

Table C.10 Sample Calculation of Adjusted Manual Rates for Model II, for Colorado on January 1, 1995

IR3	Pure premiums (loss costs)		$2.857
AF1	Experience-rating adjustment	×	0.969
AF3	Standard earned premium at company level ÷ standard earned premium at DSR	×	1.341
AF4	Net earned premium ÷ standard earned premium at company level	×	0.797
AF5	Dividend adjustment	×	0.942
AMR3	Total market adjusted manual rates	=	$2.788

Model III: Voluntary and Residual Markets with Identical Manual Rates

This model is used when 1) the rates for the voluntary market contain expense loadings (and thus are manual rates) and 2) there are manual rates for the assigned-risk market that are identical to the manual rates in the voluntary market. The manual rates for the voluntary market can be mandatory or advisory. There are two variants, Model III and Model IIIa, depending on the nature of the adjustments to premiums in the residual markets.

Model III

Various adjustments are made to the manual rates in the assigned-risk market that are not made in the voluntary market. Specifically, the assigned-risk market may 1) eliminate or modify premium discounts or 2) use loss-sensitive rating plans. The effect of these adjustments will be reflected in the adjustment factors data that are applicable to the entire market (voluntary plus assigned-risk), such as the experience-rating adjustment, the net earned premium/standard earned premium ratio, or the dividends adjustments. As a result, the calculation of adjusted manual rates for Model III is straightforward and, in essence, is identical to the procedure used for Model I.

An illustration of the procedure used to derive adjusted manual rates for Model III is provided in Table C.11 for Florida for January 1, 1988. The illustration uses the variables included in Table C.4. The only difference from the Model I calculation is that here the procedure starts with the IR4 manual rates.

Table C.11 Sample Calculation of Adjusted Manual Rates for Model III, for Florida on January 1, 1988

IR4	Manual rates		$3.484
AF1	Experience-rating adjustment	×	0.988
AF2	Expense-constant adjustment	÷	0.989
AF3	Standard earned premium at company level ÷ standard earned premium at DSR	×	0.989
AF4	Net earned premium ÷ standard earned premium at company level	×	1.015
AF5	Dividend adjustment	×	0.964
AMR3	Total market adjusted manual rates	=	$3.366

Model IIIa

Model IIIa is applicable when the residual (assigned-risk) market 1) relies on premium surcharges, or 2) uses an Assigned Risk Rating Program (ARRP), or 3) uses some other type of experience rating adjustment program, or any combination of the three. The effect of these factors <u>will not</u> be reflected in the adjustment factors applicable to the entire workers' compensation market (voluntary plus residual markets), such as experience rating adjustment, the net earned premium/standard earned premium ratio, and the dividends adjustment. The effect of these factors <u>will</u> be reflected, however, in the residual market impact (RM impact) figures that have been provided by the NCCI (see Table C.8).

Model IIIa involves three sets of calculations (Table C.12). Adjusted manual rates are calculated for the voluntary market, separate calculations are required for the adjusted manual rates in the residual market, and then the adjusted manual rates from the voluntary and residual markets are blended as the "total market."

The voluntary market. The starting point for the calculations is the variable IR1, the average of the 71 manual rates in the voluntary market, which was $5.875 per $100 of payroll in Florida in 1993. This rate was multiplied by the experience-rating adjustment (AF1), which was 0.991, indicating that experience rating was reducing the workers' compensation premiums paid by Florida employers. The expense constant was $140 in Florida in 1993, which meant that the expense constant adjustment factor (AF2) was 0.989. The ratio of standard earned premium at company level to standard earned premium at bureau rates (AF3) was 1.000, which indicates that Florida carriers were not offering deviations. The ratio of net earned premium to standard earned premium at company level (AF4) was 0.928, indicating that reductions in premiums were occurring due to factors such as retrospective rating. The final adjustment factor, the dividend adjustment (AF5), was 0.980, indicating that dividends were 2.0 percent of net premium in Florida in 1993.

Starting with the average manual rates of $5.875, the calculations produced an average adjusted manual rate in the voluntary market (AMR1) of $5.354 per $100 of payroll for the 71 types of Florida employers in 1993. Adjusted manual rates were 8.9 percent less than manual rates, indicating the relatively modest effect of the adjustment factors in the Florida voluntary market in 1993.

The residual market. The calculations for the adjusted manual rates in the residual market in Florida in 1993 start at the same point as those for the voluntary market, with average manual rates of $5.875 per $100 of payroll. In addition, the first four steps of moving from manual rates to adjusted manual rates are identical to those for the voluntary market. Where the markets differ is the final adjustment factor for the residual market. The residual market im-

Table C.12 Sample Calculations of Adjusted Manual Rates for Model IIIa, for Florida on January 1, 1993

The voluntary market

IR1	Manual rates for the voluntary market		$5.875
AF1	Experience-rating adjustment	×	0.991
AF2	Expense-constant adjustment	÷	0.989
AF3	Standard earned premium at company level ÷ standard earned premium at DSR	×	1.000
AF4	Net earned premium ÷ standard earned premium at company level	×	0.928
AF5	Dividend adjustment	×	0.980
AMR1	Adjusted manual rates for the voluntary market	=	$5.354

The residual market

IR2	Manual rates for the residual market		5.875
AF1	Experience-rating adjustment	×	0.991
AF2	Expense-constant adjustment	×	0.989
AF3	Standard earned premium at company level ÷ standard earned premium at DSR	×	1.000
AF4	Net earned premium ÷ standard earned premium at company level	×	0.928
AF5	Dividend adjustment	×	0.980
AF6	RM impact	×	1.532
AMR2	Adjusted manual rates for the residual market	=	$8.202

The total market

AMR1	Adjusted manual rates for the voluntary market		5.354
MS1	Share of total market accounted for by voluntary market	×	0.658 +
AMR2	Adjusted manual rates for the residual market		8.202
MS2	Share of total market accounted for by residual market	×	0.342
AMR3	Adjusted manual rates for the total market	=	$6.328

pact (AF6) is 1.532, reflecting the combined effect shown in Table C.8 of the use of the ARRP plus a $475 flat charge plus a 26 percent surcharge for policies sold in the residual market. The result of these residual market programs is that the average adjusted manual rates for the 71 insurance classes in the residual market were $8.202 per $100 of payroll, which is 53.2 percent higher than the average adjusted manual rates in the voluntary market.

The total market. The adjusted manual rates for the voluntary market (AMR1) and the adjusted manual rates for the residual market (AMR2) are multiplied by their respective shares of the total market to produce an adjusted manual rate for the total market (AMR3) of $6.328 per $100 of payroll. Similar calculations were performed for all of the states and years for which Model IIIa applies (as shown in Table C.3).

Model IV: Voluntary and Residual Markets with Different Manual Rates

This model is used when 1) the rates for the voluntary market contain expense loadings (and thus are manual rates) and 2) there are also manual rates for the residual market, but the rates are different than the manual rates in the voluntary market. The manual rates for the voluntary market can be mandatory or advisory. There are two variants: Model IV and Model IVa, depending on the nature of the adjustments to premiums in the residual markets.

Model IV

Model IV is used in states when the residual market has different manual rates than the voluntary market, and when it may also have various additional adjustments made to the manual rates that are not made in the voluntary market. Specifically, Model IV is applicable if the adjustments in the residual market 1) eliminate or modify premium discounts and/or 2) use loss-sensitive rating plans. The effects of these two factors are reflected in the adjustment factors, such as the experience-rating adjustment (AF1) or the ratio of net earned premium to standard earned premium at the company level (AF4), which are applicable to the entire market (voluntary plus residual).

One way to compute total market manual rates in this situation is shown in Table C.13. First, adjusted manual rates are computed for the voluntary market, then residual market adjusted manual rates are computed, and finally the adjusted manual rates for the respective markets are blended together in order to estimate adjusted manual rates for the total market. The alternative calculation method presents a simplified way to actually compute the adjusted manual rates for the total market.

Table C.13 Sample Calculations of Adjusted Manual Rates for Model IV, for Arizona on January 1, 1995

The voluntary market			
IR1	Manual rates for the voluntary market		$3.992
AF1	Experience-rating adjustment	×	0.948
AF2	Expense-constant adjustment	÷	0.996
AF3	Standard earned premium at company level ÷ standard earned premium at DSR	×	0.964
AF4	Net earned premium ÷ standard earned premium at company level	×	0.786
AF5	Dividend adjustment	×	0.912
AMR1	Adjusted manual rates for the voluntary market	=	$2.628
The residual market			
IR2	Manual rates for the residual market		4.790
AF1	Experience-rating adjustment	×	0.948
AF2	Expense-constant adjustment	÷	0.996
AF3	Standard earned premium at company level ÷ standard earned premium at DSR	×	0.964
AF4	Net earned premium ÷ standard earned premium at company level	×	0.786
AF5	Dividend adjustment	×	0.912
AMR2	Adjusted manual rates for the residual market	=	$3.153
The total market			
AMR1	Adjusted manual rates for the voluntary market		2.628
MS1	Share of total market accounted for by voluntary market	×	0.995 +
AMR2	Adjusted manual rates for the residual market		3.153
MS2	Share of total market accounted for by residual market	×	0.005
AMR3	Adjusted manual rates for the total market	=	$2.630

(continued)

Table C.13 (continued)

Alternative calculation
method for the
total market

AMR1	Manual rates for voluntary market		3.992
MS1	Share of total market accounted for by voluntary market	×	0.995 +
AMR2	Manual rates for the residual market		4.790
MS2	Share of total market accounted for by residual market	×	0.005
IR4	Average manual rates for the total market	=	$3.996
AF1	Experience-rating adjustment (standard premium ÷ manual premium)	×	0.948
AF2	Expense-constant adjustment	÷	0.996
AF3	Standard earned premium at company level ÷ standard earned premium at DSR	×	0.964
AF4	Net earned premium ÷ standard earned premium at company level	×	0.786
AF5	Dividend adjustment	×	0.912
AMR3	Adjusted manual rates for the entire market	=	$2.630

Model IVa

Model IVa applies when there are different manual rates in the voluntary and residual markets <u>and</u> the residual market 1) relies on premium surcharges, or 2) uses an Assigned Risk Adjustment Program (ARAP), or 3) uses some other type of experience-rating adjustment program, or any combination of the three. The effect of these factors will <u>not</u> be reflected in the adjustments factors such as the experience-rating adjustment (AF1) and the net earned premium/standard earned premium at company level ratio (AF4), which are applicable to the total market (voluntary plus residual). The effect of these factors is reflected in residual market impact (RM impact) data provided by the NCCI.

The procedure for calculating adjusted manual rates for Model IVa (Table C.14) is similar to the procedure used for Model IIIa (see Table C.12), except that for Model IVa, the manual rates in the voluntary market (IR1) are different from the manual rates in the residual market (IR2).

Table C.14 Sample Calculation of Adjusted Manual Rates for Model IVa, for Arkansas on January 1, 1995

	The voluntary market		
IR1	Manual rates for the voluntary market		$3.217
AF1	Experience-rating adjustment	×	0.945
AF2	Expense-constant adjustment	÷	0.990
AF3	Standard earned premium at company level ÷ standard earned premium at DSR	×	1.006
AF4	Net earned premium ÷ standard earned premium at company level	×	0.911
AF5	Dividend adjustment	×	0.971
AMR1	Adjusted manual rates for the voluntary market	=	$2.734
	The residual market		
IR2	Manual rates for the residual market		4.025
AF1	Experience-rating adjustment	×	0.945
AF2	Expense-constant adjustment	÷	0.990
AF3	Standard earned premium at company level ÷ standard earned premium at DSR	×	1.006
AF4	Net earned premium ÷ standard earned premium at company level	×	0.911
AF5	Dividend adjustment	×	0.971
AF6	RM impact	×	1.088
AMR2	Adjusted manual rates for the residual market	=	$3.722
	The total market		
AMR1	Adjusted manual rates for the voluntary market		2.734
MS1	Share of total market accounted for by voluntary market	×	0.738 +
AMR2	Adjusted manual rates for the residual market		3.722
MS2	Share of total market accounted for by residual market	×	0.262
AMR3	Adjusted manual rates for the total market	=	$2.993

Model V: Voluntary Market with Pure Premiums and Residual Market with Manual Rates

This model is used when 1) the rates for the voluntary market are pure premiums (loss costs) and 2) there are separate rates for the residual market.

Model V

This model is applicable when the residual market has manual rates. The residual market can also have various additional adjustments that are not made in the voluntary market. Specifically, Model V is applicable when the residual market 1) eliminates or modifies premium discounts and/or 2) uses loss-sensitive rating plans. The effect of these two programs will be reflected in adjustment factors such as the experience-rating adjustment (AF1) and the net earned premium/standard earned premium at company level ratio (AF4), which are applicable to the total market (voluntary plus residual).

The method used to calculate adjusted manual rates for Model V is illustrated in Table C.15. The procedure for the Model V voluntary market is identical to that used for the voluntary market in Model II (see Table C.10). The procedure for the Model V residual market is identical to that for the residual market in Model IV (see Table C.13). The procedure used to calculate adjusted manual rates for the total market for Model V is identical to the procedure used for Model IV (see Table C.13).

Model Va

This model is used when the residual market has various adjustments made to the manual rates that are not made for the pure premiums in the voluntary market. Specifically, Model Va is applicable when there are pure premiums in the voluntary market and manual rates in the residual markets, and the residual market 1) relies on premium surcharges, or 2) uses an Assigned Risk Adjustment Program (ARAP), or 3) uses some other type of experience-rating adjustment program, or any combination of the three. The effect of these programs will not be reflected in adjustment factors applicable to the total market such as the experience rating adjustment (AF1) or the net earned premium/ standard earned premium at company ratio (AF4). The effect of these programs is reflected in the residual market impact (RM impact) data provided by the NCCI.

The method used to calculate adjusted manual rates for Model Va is illustrated in Table C.16. The procedure for the Model Va voluntary market is identical to that used for the voluntary market in Model II (see Table C.10). The procedure for the residual market is identical to that used for the residual

Table C.15 Sample Calculation of Adjusted Manual Rates for Model V, for Alabama on January 1, 1995

The voluntary market			
IR3	Pure premiums (loss costs)		$2.714
AF1	Experience-rating adjustment	×	0.924
AF3	Standard earned premium at company level ÷ standard earned premium at DSR	×	1.267
AF4	Net earned premium ÷ standard earned premium at company level	×	0.926
AF5	Dividend adjustment	×	0.976
AMR1	Adjusted manual rates for the voluntary market	=	$2.869
The residual market			
IR2	Manual rates for the residual market		4.866
AF1	Experience-rating adjustment	×	0.924
AF2	Expense-constant adjustment	÷	0.989
AF3	Standard earned premium at company level ÷ standard earned premium at DSR	×	1.267
AF4	Net earned premium ÷ standard earned premium at company level	×	0.926
AF5	Dividend adjustment	×	0.976
AMR2	Adjusted manual rates for the residual market	=	$5.202
The total market			
AMR1	Adjusted manual rates for the voluntary market		2.869
MS1	Share of total market accounted for by voluntary market	×	0.693 +
AMR2	Adjusted manual rates for the residual market		5.202
MS2	Share of total market accounted for by residual market	×	0.307
AMR3	Adjusted manual rates for the total market	=	$3.585

**Table C.16 Sample Calculation of Adjusted Manual Rates for Model Va,
for Connecticut on January 1, 1995**

The voluntary market

IR3	Pure premiums (loss costs)		$3.275
AF1	Experience-rating adjustment	×	0.959
AF3	Standard earned premium at company level ÷ standard earned premium at DSR	×	1.151
AF4	Net earned premium ÷ standard earned premium at company level	×	0.884
AF5	Dividend adjustment	×	0.944
AMR1	Adjusted manual rates for the voluntary market	=	$3.018

The residual market

IR2	Manual rates for the residual market		4.505
AF1	Experience-rating adjustment	×	0.959
AF2	Expense-constant adjustment	÷	0.989
AF3	Standard earned premium at company level ÷ standard earned premium at DSR	×	1.151
AF4	Net earned premium ÷ standard earned premium at company level	×	0.884
AF5	Dividend adjustment	×	0.944
AF6	RM impact	×	1.099
AMR2	Adjusted manual rates for the residual market	=	$4.614

The total market

AMR1	Adjusted manual rates for the voluntary market		3.018
MS1	Share of total market accounted for by voluntary market	×	0.907 +
ADM2	Adjusted manual rates for the residual market		4.614
MS2	Share of total market accounted for by residual market	×	0.093
AMR3	Adjusted manual rates for the total market	=	$3.167

market in Model IVa (see Table C.14). The procedure used to calculate adjusted manual rates for the total market for Model Va is also identical to the procedure used for Model IVa.

SPECIAL PROCEDURES FOR SEVERAL STATES WITH PRIVATE CARRIERS

Most states with private insurance carriers rely upon the National Council on Compensation Insurance for the preparation of rate filings with proposed manual rates or with pure premiums. There are, however, 12 states with private carriers that currently rely upon local rating organizations to prepare rate filings. Three of these states (Indiana, North Carolina, and Wisconsin) use classifications similar to those in NCCI states, use modification factors that correspond to those previously discussed in conjunction with Models I to V, and provide data to the NCCI, which in turn we obtained and used to calculate adjusted manual rates. We therefore do not further discuss these states. There are also nine states with local rating organizations (California, Delaware, Massachusetts, Michigan, Minnesota, New Jersey, New York, Pennsylvania, and Texas) from which we had to obtain data directly from the states. We describe in this section the nature of the data obtained and any special procedures that were needed to use the data. We also discuss the special procedures that were necessary in Kentucky, Oregon, and South Dakota, which are NCCI states.

California

California uses a classification system that is significantly different than the NCCI's system. We converted the NCCI classification codes shown in Table C.1 to the equivalent California codes.

We were unable to obtain appropriate data to calculate adjusted manual rates for 1975–1985. From 1986 until 1994, California published manual rates and did not have separate rates for the residual market, and so Model I was applicable. However, the general procedure shown in Table C.5 had to be modified, because California did not rely on loss or expense constants, nor did the state allow any form of premium discounts. California made limited use of retrospective-rating plans; however, we do not have data on the effect of these plans on premiums. California did have an experience-rating plan, which was reflected in the off-balance factor included in the manual rates. We divided the manual rates by the off-balance factor to capture the effect of experience rating. California also relied on dividends, which we measured by using the dividends adjustment factor.

In 1995, California began to use pure premiums, and so Model II was applicable. The Workers' Compensation Insurance Rating Bureau has reported that for policy year 1995, the average "charged" rate was 104 percent of the pure premium rates. The differential reflects all individual pricing adjustments exclusive of deductibles, retrospective rating adjustments, or dividends. We reduced the charged rates by the dividends adjustment factor to obtain adjusted manual rates for California in 1995.

Delaware

Delaware uses a classification system that is significantly different than the NCCI's system. We converted the NCCI classification codes shown in Table C.1 to the equivalent Delaware codes with the assistance of the Delaware Compensation Rating Bureau.

We were unable to obtain appropriate data to calculate adjusted manual rates for 1975–1985. From 1986 until 1994, Delaware published manual rates and did not have separate rates for the residual market, so Model I was applicable. In 1995, Delaware began to use pure premiums in the voluntary market and manual rates in the residual market, so Model V was applicable. The Rating Bureau provided us the data necessary to calculate adjusted manual rates for 1986 through 1995, including the share of the total market accounted for by the residual market in 1995.

Kentucky

Kentucky relies on the NCCI for rate-making assistance. Kentucky used the same manual rates for the voluntary and residual markets from 1975 to 1982, so Model I was applicable. Kentucky adopted a competitive law that was effective July 15, 1982, and thus it was not an administered-pricing state in 1983. However, the July 15, 1981, manual rates were the designated statistical reporting (DSR) level of rates in 1983, and so for purposes of calculating adjusted manual rates, Model I was also used for 1983. For 1984 to 1995, Kentucky used pure premiums in the voluntary market and manual rates in the residual market, and so Model V was applicable.

The procedures used to calculate adjusted manual rates in Kentucky contain an additional step not used in other Model I or Model V states. There is an assessment for the Kentucky special fund that is not included in the manual rates or pure premiums (as in most states); it is a separate charge. In 1987, for example, the assessment was 41.5 percent of premium. We have adjusted the Kentucky rates to include this assessment for all years between 1975 and 1995.

Massachusetts

Massachusetts uses a classification system that is similar to the NCCI's system. For a limited number of classes, we converted the NCCI classification codes shown in Table C.1 into equivalent Massachusetts codes. From 1975 to 1995, the same manual rates were used in the voluntary and residual markets, so Model I was applicable. The Workers' Compensation Rating and Inspection Bureau of Massachusetts provided most of the data necessary to calculate adjusted manual rates for 1975 to 1995. (Calendar-year premium data provided by the NCCI were used for several steps of the calculations of the 1975 to 1977 adjusted manual rates.)

Michigan

Michigan uses a classification system that is similar to the NCCI's system. For a limited number of classes, we converted the NCCI classification codes shown in Table C.1 into equivalent Michigan codes. From 1975 to 1982, the same manual rates were used in the voluntary and residual markets, so Model I was applicable.

Open competition became effective in Michigan on January 1, 1983, and thereafter pure premiums were used in the voluntary market and manual rates were used in the assigned-risk market. The Compensation Advisory Organization of Michigan (CAOM) provided information used to calculate adjusted manual rates since 1983. Every carrier must file an "information page" with the CAOM for each workers' compensation policy sold to Michigan employers. The information page contains data on the insurance classification(s) used; the annual payroll; manual premiums; and total estimated annual premium after application of premium discounts, experience rating, and other factors affecting premiums actually paid. Total estimated annual premium divided by annual payroll is termed *average charged rates in actual transactions* (or *average charged rates*). The only factors affecting costs that are not included in average charged rates in actual transactions are retrospective rating and dividends. We assume that the overall impact of retrospective rating on the rates that employers would otherwise pay is zero, and we adjust for dividends by multiplying the average charged rates by the dividend adjustment factor.

For 1983 to 1987, average charged rates are available only for the voluntary market. However, data are available for those years that permit us to calculate the ratio of average charged rates in the residual market to average charged rates in the voluntary market, and use of this ratio permitted us to estimate average charged rates for the total market. These average charged rates for the total market times the dividend adjustment factor produced average adjusted manual rates for the total market in Michigan for 1983 to 1987.

For 1988 to 1995, average charged rates are available for both the voluntary market and the residual market, and we combined the data to determine the average charged rates for the total market. These average charged rates for the total market times the dividend adjustment factor produced average adjusted manual rates for the total market for 1988 to 1995.

Minnesota

Minnesota uses a classification system similar to the NCCI's system. For a limited number of classes, we converted the NCCI classification codes shown in Table C.1 into equivalent Minnesota codes. From 1975 to 1983, the same manual rates were used in the voluntary and residual markets, so Model I was applicable. From 1984 to 1995, pure premiums were used in the voluntary market and manual rates were used in the residual market, so Model V was used. The Minnesota Workers' Compensation Insurers Association, Inc., provided the data needed to calculate adjusted manual rates from 1975 to 1995, including the share of the total market accounted for by the residual market from 1984 to 1995.

Minnesota warrants special consideration because its workers' compensation program, unlike those in most other jurisdictions, excludes all payments for vacations, holidays, and sick leave from the payroll base. This exclusionary rule has been in effect since June 1, 1981, and so the 1982 to 1995 Minnesota rates were affected by this adjustment. Minnesota employers are permitted to pay premiums based on the published manual rates times this truncated version of the payroll base. Alternatively, if Minnesota employers select the option of multiplying manual rates times the full payroll base (comparable to the base used in other states), their premium is 90 percent of this product. In this study, we have reduced all average adjusted manual rates for Minnesota between 1982 and 1995 by 10 percent in order to make their rates comparable to those elsewhere.

New Jersey

New Jersey uses a classification system that is similar to the NCCI's system. For a limited number of classes, we converted the NCCI classification codes shown in Table C.1 into equivalent New Jersey codes. From 1975 to 1995, the same manual rates were used in the voluntary and residual markets, so Model I was applicable. The Compensation Rating and Inspection Bureau provided most of the data necessary to calculate adjusted manual rates for 1975 to 1995. (Calendar-year premium data provided by the NCCI were used for several steps of the calculations of the adjusted manual rates from 1975 to 1985.)

New York

New York uses a classification system that is similar to the NCCI's system. For a limited number of classes, we converted the NCCI classification codes shown in Table C.1 into equivalent New York codes. From 1975 to 1995, the same manual rates were used in the voluntary and residual markets, so Model I was applicable. The New York Compensation Insurance Rating Bureau provided most of the data necessary to calculate adjusted manual rates for 1975 to 1995. (Calendar-year premium data provided by the NCCI were used for several steps of the calculations of the adjusted manual rates from 1975 to 1980.)

Oregon

The state of Oregon relies on the NCCI for rate-making assistance. Oregon Rule V B (3)-(e), which has been in effect since November 1, 1981, excludes payments for vacations and for bonuses from the payroll base unless they are part of a contract-for-hire. In order to make the Oregon rates comparable to those elsewhere, we have reduced the adjusted manual rates from 1982 to 1995 by 5.1 percent.

Pennsylvania

Pennsylvania uses a classification system that is significantly different than the NCCI's system. We converted the NCCI classification codes shown in Table C.1 to the equivalent Pennsylvania codes with the assistance of the Pennsylvania Compensation Rating Bureau.

We were unable to obtain appropriate data to calculate adjusted manual rates for 1975–1985. From 1986 until 1993, Pennsylvania published manual rates and did not have a residual market, and so Model I was applicable. In 1994 and 1995, Pennsylvania used pure premiums in the voluntary market and did not have a residual market, so Model II was applicable. The Rating Bureau provided us with the data necessary to calculate adjusted manual rates for 1986 to 1995.

South Dakota

South Dakota relies on the NCCI for rate-making assistance. South Dakota has a payroll limitation (in effect as of July 1, 1983) that is similar to Minnesota's, and so all adjusted manual rates for South Dakota between 1984 and 1995 have been reduced by 10 percent.

364

Texas

Data were available from the NCCI to calculate adjusted manual rates for Texas from 1975 to 1991. During these years, manual rates were published that were applicable to the entire market, and so Model I was used. Efforts to obtain comparable data for 1992 to 1995 from the NCCI and the Texas Department of Insurance have been unsuccessful, so Texas adjusted manual rates are unavailable for those years.

ELABORATIONS OF BASIC MODEL VI IN STATES WITH EXCLUSIVE STATE FUNDS

Ohio

We discuss in this subsection the methodology used to estimate the adjusted manual rates for Ohio employers for January 1 comparison dates for 1983 and 1984 and for 1987 to 1995. Lack of data on the effects of experience rating precluded us from computing employer cost measures for 1975 to 1982 and for 1985 and 1986.

We initially matched the classification codes for Ohio with those for NCCI states using an updated version of a conversion chart that Burton developed for earlier interstate cost studies.[15] We then calculated average manual rates for the 71 Ohio classes comparable to those shown in Table C.1 using national payroll weights to calculate the averages. We then applied various adjustment factors to compute adjusted manual rates.

The experience-rating plan in Ohio is complex and as sophisticated as the method used in NCCI states. The influence of Ohio's experience-rating plan can be estimated with precision. When an Ohio employer is experience-rated, the employer's actual losses and expected losses during the experience period are compared (the experience period is the oldest four of the latest five calendar years prior to the date when the employer's current rate is determined).

Thus, the experience-rating modification for the manual rates in effect as of July 1, 1994 (that is, the rates used for the January 1, 1995, comparison date in our study) is based on data on actual and expected losses during calendar years 1989 to 1992. During that four-year period, the overall effect of experience rating for all private employers in Ohio was to reduce the employers' insurance costs by 22.59 percent.[16] In this study, we assume that the 22.59 percent influence of experience rating for 1989 to 1992 is applicable to all the manual rates that took effect on July 1, 1994. A similar procedure was used to determine the effect of experience rating on the manual rates in effect from 1987 to 1994.

Ohio's workers' compensation program also assesses employers for administrative costs and for the Disabled Workers' Relief Fund. As of our January 1, 1995, comparison date (using rates that took effect on July 1, 1994), these assessments for private employers were $0.411 per $100 of payroll for administrative costs and $0.10 per $100 of payroll for the Disabled Workers' Relief Fund. There is yet another set of assessments, which are related to the base rate. An assessment of 0.1 percent for rates that took effect on July 1, 1994, provides additional funding for the Disabled Workers' Relief Fund. For six of the comparison dates in our study (January 1, 1987, to January 1, 1992), there was also an intentional tort assessment; this varied between 0.10 and 0.75 percent of the base rate.

Data from Ohio classification code 2501 (the clothing manufacturing industry) will be used to illustrate how, in computing Ohio workers' compensation costs, we took into consideration these various assessments. As of July 1, 1994, the published base rate for classification code 2501 was $5.610 per $100 of payroll; after the assessments are added (0.1 percent of the base rate, plus $0.511), the total becomes a manual rate of $6.127 per $100 of payroll.

Ohio's manual rates were then modified by an adjustment factor for experience rating to compute adjusted manual rates. For example, after the $6.127 manual rate we calculated for classification code 2501 was reduced by the experience-rating modification (0.2259 percent of the base rate), the resultant adjusted manual rate for this classification code was $4.860 per $100 of payroll. This value was one of the adjusted manual rates used to calculate the average adjusted manual rates for Ohio.

Adjusted manual rates in Ohio (which has an exclusive state fund) may thus be compared to workers' compensation costs in states with private carriers, but there is one major qualification. Because of inadequate reserves in the Ohio state fund during most or all of the years encompassed by our study, the Ohio employers' costs reported in our study are artificially low compared with those in most states. An example of the inadequate reserves was provided in the *Actuarial Audit of the State Insurance Fund as of December 31, 1985* (completed in January 1987), which reported that the state fund's liabilities exceeded assets by about one billion dollars. The audit concluded, ". . . very substantial rate increases are needed if the goal is to have current premiums cover present and future costs of claims currently being incurred. These increases are about 50% for private employers, and about 30% for public employers."[17]

A recent publication by the Ohio Bureau of Workers' Compensation (BWC) suggests that the deficit has been eliminated in recent years. According to that source, after legislative reforms supported by Governor Voinovich were passed by the Ohio Legislature in 1993 and 1995, the BWC turned a $2.4 billion deficit into a $3.6 billion surplus and saved Ohio employers $4.6 billion.[18] Obviously, the impact of the legislative changes occurred in large part after the data period used for our study. As a result, the Ohio employers' costs reported by us for 1987 to 1995 are probably artificially low for most of the period.

Washington

The calculation of average adjusted manual rates for Washington state that are comparable to those used in other jurisdictions is complicated by two factors: 1) like Ohio and West Virginia, Washington uses a rate classification scheme that is different from that used in NCCI states and 2) premiums in Washington are based on hours worked rather than payroll.

The first step in the procedure used to calculate Washington manual rates was to identify the Washington industrial insurance risk classifications that most closely matched the 71 NCCI classes used to calculate average rates in other jurisdictions. The manual rate for each class was then obtained by calculating two values: 1) the total number of hours worked and 2) the average wage.[19] Payroll was estimated by multiplying hours worked by the average wage. Total premiums were obtained by multiplying the manual rate (per hour) for the class by the number of hours. Finally, the manual rate (per $100 of payroll) for each class was estimated by dividing total premiums by payroll, divided by $100. Actuaries at the Department of Labor and Industries of the state of Washington performed all of these tasks. Once again, a weighted average manual rate for each of the years for which we had data (1985–1995) was calculated using national payroll for the 71 NCCI classes as weights.

Washington employers are subject to both retrospective and prospective experience rating. To account for these modifications to the manual rate, we obtained data on two variables: the average retrospective rating refund discount factor and the average experience-rating discount factor.[20] The retrospective rating factor is equal to 1 minus (total net retrospective rating refund ÷ total standard premium), while the targeted average experience modification was used for the experience-rating factor.[21] The Department of Labor and Industries supplied data for both factors.

Adjusted manual rates were obtained by multiplying the average manual rate for each year by the applicable retrospective rating and experience modification discount factors. For example, as of January 1, 1995, the weighted average manual rate was equal to $2.74, the experience-rating modification factor was 0.91, and the retrospective refund factor was 0.89. Thus, the adjusted manual rate for 1995 is equal to $2.74 × 0.91 × 0.89, or $2.22.

West Virginia

We estimated adjusted manual rates and net weekly costs for West Virginia for comparison dates from January 1, 1975, to January 1, 1995. We discuss in this section the methodology used to compute employers' costs in West Virginia.

We initially matched the classification codes for West Virginia rates with those for NCCI states, using a conversion table developed by Burton for this analysis. We then calculated average manual rates for the 42 West Virginia classifications corresponding to the 71 NCCI classes shown in Table C.1, using national payroll as weights. In recent years, West Virginia has used an experience-rating plan that, like Ohio's, is as sophisticated as the plan used in NCCI states. The influence of West Virginia's experience-rating plan can also be also be rather precisely determined. Manual rates are promulgated yearly on July 1 and remain in effect until the following June 30. For the same 12-month period, data arrayed by insurance classification are available on payroll and the premiums actually collected after the application of any experience-rating modification.

For example, for West Virginia classification J-2 (textile and garment manufacturing), the manual rate effective July 1, 1994—which is a rate was used for our January 1, 1995, comparison date—was $2.55 per $100 of payroll. Because the payroll between July 1994 and June 1995 for this class was $49,241,852, the simulated manual premium (i.e., what employers in this class would expect to pay if no further adjustments were made) was $1,255,667. (The simulated manual premium was computed by multiplying payroll by the corresponding manual rate.) The gross premium actually collected for the class during this period was $1,148,499, which suggests that experience rating resulted in actual premiums for classification J-2 that were 8.5 percent less than what employers would have otherwise paid (i.e., less than the simulated manual premium).

Simulated manual premiums for the 42 West Virginia classifications used for the January 1, 1995, comparison date totaled $163,499,456. Gross premiums actually collected for these classifications totaled $166,103,183. Thus, in the July–June period for 1994–1995, the actual collected premium was greater than the simulated manual premium, indicating that, in general, experience rating increased the employers' costs of workers' compensation in West Virginia. For the combined 1994–1995 experience, actual collected premiums were 2.0 percent greater than simulated manual premiums, indicating that experience rating for this combination of classifications increased manual premiums by 2.0 percent.

In this study, we used the 2.0 percent influence of experience rating for 1994–1995 to adjust the manual rates used in this study that were in effect on July 1, 1994, in West Virginia. Thus, the average adjusted manual rates for West Virginia as of January 1, 1995, are 2.0 percent higher than West Virginia's average manual rates.

In West Virginia's workers' compensation program, assessments for administrative expenses and for the catastrophe and second-injury accounts are included in the base or manual rates. Therefore, the rates as published in the annual reports of the West Virginia Workers' Compensation Division were used to calculate average manual rates. Likewise, the simulated manual premiums and premiums actually collected include the charges for these accounts and for administrative expenses. Thus, no additional adjustments were necessary, and the experience-rating adjustment of 2.0 percent could be applied to base rates (average manual rates) to compute West Virginia adjusted manual rates for the January 1, 1995, comparison date.

The funding status of West Virginia's exclusive state fund, like that in Ohio, warrants caution in making interstate comparisons of workers' compensation costs that include West Virginia. For example, a newspaper article suggested that the July 1, 1987, rates used in this study are artificially low because of inadequate reserves of the state fund.[22] In July 1985, Governor Arch Moore cut rates by 30 percent in order to bring new business to the state. According to the press account, "Moore said the rate cut was intended to put the fund on a pay-as-you-go basis. Under that arrangement, the fund would take in enough money each year to cover the benefits and administrative expenses paid out during that year. But the fund would no longer set aside reserves to cover the future costs of that year's injuries, as required."

Although the fund's independent actuary had calculated that a 30 percent increase would allow the fund to operate on a pay-as-you-go basis, even that assumption was optimistic; the fund actually paid out $20 million more than it took in during fiscal year 1987. If the reserves necessary to cover future payments for the injuries that occurred during fiscal year 1987 were included, the deficit for the fiscal year was more than $90 million.

There apparently was some underfunding even before 1985. However, the financial difficulties of the fund worsened between 1985 and 1988 because rates were frozen at the 1985 level. The total amount of underfunding by 1988 was more than $300 million. According to the independent actuary for the state fund, West Virginia "would have needed a 50 percent increase just to operate soundly for 1987." Even an increase of that magnitude would not have addressed the $300 million deficit; "it would merely keep the deficit from growing." In order to temporarily cover the deficit, "fund officials took the unprecedented step of raiding the $800 million in reserves that had been set aside [prior to 1985] to cover future payments . . ."

As of 1995, West Virginia's state fund had a deficit of $2.2 billion. Employers who moved to West Virginia because of the attractive workers' compensation insurance rates presumably had a short time horizon or inadequate information. News coverage of West Virginia's workers' compensation program can be found in Nyden (1997a, 1997b, 1998a, 1998b).

ADJUSTED MANUAL RATES: 1975–1995

In the previous sections of this appendix, we have explained the procedures for calculating the adjusted manual rates for the states in our study. The procedures are obviously complex and vary among jurisdictions, depending on matters such as the type of rates promulgated in the states (manual rates or pure premiums), the use of special pricing programs in the residual market that are not applicable to the voluntary market, and whether the state has private carriers or relies on an exclusive state fund.

Adjusted manual rates for the 48 jurisdictions in our study for as many years for which we have data between 1975 and 1995 are presented in Table C.17. The only missing jurisdictions are Nevada, North Dakota, and Wyoming, which are states with exclusive state funds relying on insurance classifications that are not comparable with those in the states with private carriers. There are also six states for which data are not available for all 21 years encompassed by our study: these include two of the states with exclusive state funds (Ohio and Washington), for which comparable data are only available since 1983, as well as four states with independent rating bureaus (California, Delaware, Pennsylvania, and Texas), for which data could not be obtained for all years.

The rates in dollars shown in Table C.17 can also be interpreted as the percentage of payroll expended on workers' compensation insurance by employers in 71 insurance classifications in each of the 48 jurisdictions as of January 1 for each of the years between 1975 and 1995. The results indicate, for example, that as of January 1, 1975, in Alabama, the employers in the 71 classes expended, on average, $0.579 per $100 of payroll, which can be restated as 0.579 percent of payroll on workers' compensation premiums. By January 1, 1995, these same employers expended, on average, 3.585 per $100 of payroll (i.e., 3.585 percent of payroll) on workers' compensation premiums, which means that workers' compensation costs as a percentage of payroll had increased for Alabama employers more than sixfold over the 21-year period included in Table C.17.

Table C.17 Adjusted Manual Rates, 1975–95[a] ($)

	Ala.	Alaska	Ariz.	Ark.	Calif.	Colo.	Conn.	Del.	D.C.	Fla.	Ga.	Hawaii
1975	0.579	1.030	1.594	1.025	ND[b]	0.535	0.835	ND	1.396	1.939	0.678	1.484
1976	0.767	1.586	1.758	1.103	ND	0.653	0.953	ND	1.797	2.027	0.879	1.849
1977	0.753	1.786	1.989	1.205	ND	0.919	1.025	ND	2.398	2.523	0.973	2.001
1978	0.927	1.668	2.189	1.264	ND	1.086	1.286	ND	3.356	2.853	1.070	2.094
1979	1.013	1.905	2.606	1.291	ND	1.106	1.465	ND	4.257	2.642	1.262	2.476
1980	1.022	1.996	2.426	1.486	ND	0.878	2.019	ND	4.931	2.208	1.201	2.569
1981	1.044	2.360	1.924	1.535	ND	0.982	1.966	ND	4.541	2.006	1.185	3.372
1982	1.048	2.475	1.443	1.402	ND	1.209	2.143	ND	3.968	1.483	1.165	3.715
1983	1.068	2.128	1.281	1.325	ND	1.366	2.019	ND	2.591	1.708	1.044	4.456
1984	1.039	2.100	1.265	1.338	ND	1.361	1.984	ND	2.214	1.721	1.049	4.179
1985	1.270	2.273	1.778	1.334	ND	1.770	2.080	ND	2.292	2.341	1.324	4.366
1986	1.482	2.584	2.118	1.511	3.017	1.881	2.265	1.885	2.783	2.786	1.576	4.748
1987	1.738	3.040	2.088	1.861	3.449	2.332	2.567	1.978	2.950	2.909	1.865	4.176
1988	1.961	3.289	2.122	1.904	3.836	2.682	2.896	2.119	2.737	3.366	1.978	3.448
1989	2.120	2.932	2.510	2.018	3.876	3.193	3.154	2.081	2.773	4.063	2.422	3.362
1990	2.246	3.147	2.634	2.051	3.954	3.166	3.383	2.096	2.754	5.329	2.636	3.395
1991	2.433	2.989	2.662	2.215	4.244	3.531	3.544	2.044	2.981	4.172	2.988	3.468
1992	3.382	2.807	2.899	2.648	4.744	3.342	3.582	2.192	3.159	5.480	3.478	3.557
1993	3.525	2.440	2.865	3.519	4.856	3.236	3.961	2.341	3.494	6.328	3.558	3.715
1994	3.436	2.567	2.744	3.249	3.805	3.107	3.336	2.423	3.234	4.330	3.555	3.610
1995	3.585	2.400	2.630	2.993	3.150	2.788	3.167	2.288	3.341	4.366	3.370	4.867

	Idaho	Ill.	Ind.	Iowa	Kans.	Ky.	La.	Maine	Md.	Mass.	Mich.	Minn.
1975	1.122	0.664	0.398	0.603	0.788	1.077	1.487	0.914	0.864	1.073	1.174	1.141
1976	1.320	1.119	0.451	0.681	0.856	1.306	2.404	1.093	1.143	1.228	1.363	1.301
1977	1.373	1.513	0.449	0.820	1.015	1.296	1.710	1.138	1.430	1.278	1.627	1.538
1978	1.285	1.380	0.568	0.899	1.055	1.732	1.757	1.216	1.447	1.465	2.112	1.821
1979	1.413	1.430	0.533	1.172	0.941	1.698	1.698	1.588	1.819	1.691	2.126	1.955
1980	1.347	1.682	0.593	1.345	0.949	1.708	1.893	2.096	1.726	1.783	2.570	2.016
1981	1.606	1.606	0.486	1.280	0.968	1.263	1.928	2.172	2.047	1.831	2.472	1.931
1982	1.455	1.495	0.419	1.245	1.134	1.200	1.683	2.589	2.102	1.808	1.864	1.759
1983	1.452	1.341	0.430	1.063	1.049	1.173	1.845	2.579	2.029	2.059	1.770	1.614
1984	1.467	1.348	0.453	1.010	1.006	1.245	1.382	2.665	1.882	2.079	1.650	1.792
1985	1.551	1.623	0.517	1.072	1.109	1.571	1.463	2.681	2.002	2.043	1.938	2.415
1986	1.666	1.927	0.610	1.118	1.288	1.665	1.967	2.327	2.208	2.064	2.316	2.769
1987	2.064	1.989	0.684	1.472	1.342	2.075	1.925	2.295	2.020	2.138	2.639	2.793
1988	2.315	2.162	0.775	1.478	1.631	2.083	2.312	2.562	2.047	2.689	2.565	3.049
1989	2.198	2.451	1.025	1.839	1.680	2.472	2.586	3.324	1.932	3.008	2.581	3.207
1990	2.428	2.646	1.260	1.793	1.761	2.604	3.088	3.946	1.843	3.772	3.493	3.533
1991	2.409	2.806	1.374	1.990	1.985	2.636	3.188	4.552	1.830	4.516	3.649	3.563
1992	2.663	2.905	1.457	2.226	2.411	3.030	4.424	4.484	1.928	4.408	3.806	3.736
1993	2.838	2.949	1.519	2.393	2.873	3.610	4.220	4.275	1.835	4.486	3.135	3.079
1994	2.633	3.037	1.473	2.306	2.837	3.718	4.299	3.908	2.006	4.120	2.945	2.925
1995	2.394	2.803	1.397	1.946	2.673	3.650	4.059	3.373	1.891	3.207	2.689	2.782

(continued)

Table C.17 (continued)

	Miss.	Mo.	Mont.	Nebr.	N.H.	N.J.	N.Mex.	N.Y.	N.C.	Ohio	Okla.	Oreg.
1975	0.887	0.755	1.410	0.678	0.702	1.035	1.030	0.914	0.432	ND	1.030	1.666
1976	0.874	0.803	1.489	0.866	1.029	1.128	1.145	1.123	0.459	ND	1.223	2.136
1977	0.894	0.863	1.678	0.733	1.117	1.223	1.235	1.318	0.486	ND	1.425	2.694
1978	0.929	0.839	2.234	0.739	1.449	1.398	1.286	1.683	0.508	ND	1.434	2.801
1979	0.866	0.897	1.477	0.754	1.513	1.422	1.524	2.119	0.614	ND	1.585	2.756
1980	0.937	0.882	1.642	0.845	1.731	1.781	1.678	2.129	0.701	ND	1.489	2.564
1981	0.917	0.822	1.611	0.870	1.519	1.859	2.010	1.844	0.838	ND	1.764	2.135
1982	1.016	0.865	1.899	0.876	1.584	1.758	2.050	1.500	0.878	ND	1.740	2.151
1983	0.999	0.759	2.150	0.983	1.693	1.506	2.211	1.355	0.811	1.602	1.691	1.544
1984	1.073	0.875	2.189	0.967	2.023	1.517	2.396	1.348	0.651	1.758	1.836	1.724
1985	1.137	1.027	2.672	1.048	2.092	1.197	2.706	1.620	0.721	ND	1.802	2.171
1986	1.296	1.238	2.918	1.068	2.273	1.242	2.843	1.777	0.920	ND	2.189	2.831
1987	1.589	1.415	3.825	1.195	2.344	1.391	2.804	1.771	1.025	1.960	2.246	3.034
1988	1.558	1.563	3.465	1.290	2.518	1.478	3.276	1.779	1.191	2.517	2.359	2.911
1989	1.966	1.626	4.084	1.437	2.710	1.386	3.382	1.903	1.262	2.855	2.760	2.924
1990	2.005	1.744	4.733	1.671	2.790	1.470	3.563	2.282	1.383	3.312	2.639	3.171
1991	2.472	2.028	4.109	1.932	3.089	1.535	3.552	2.832	1.709	3.318	2.666	3.023
1992	2.916	2.533	4.544	2.095	3.277	1.750	4.322	3.117	1.870	3.547	3.328	2.802
1993	3.309	2.856	4.578	2.409	3.870	1.918	4.488	3.788	2.441	3.618	3.893	2.497
1994	3.174	2.634	5.074	2.618	4.426	1.832	3.516	4.169	2.426	3.503	3.855	2.331
1995	2.750	2.463	4.937	2.338	3.757	1.777	3.713	3.883	2.316	3.358	3.456	2.275

	Pa.	R.I.	S.C.	S.Dak.	Tenn.	Texas	Utah	Vt.	Va.	Wash.	W.Va.	Wisc.
1975	ND	0.838	0.542	0.509	0.714	1.424	0.585	0.608	0.489	ND	0.618	0.567
1976	ND	1.104	0.645	0.683	0.804	1.488	0.776	0.595	0.571	ND	0.686	0.665
1977	ND	1.370	0.684	0.619	0.820	1.806	0.767	0.738	0.722	ND	0.830	0.650
1978	ND	1.435	0.699	0.720	1.063	1.909	0.828	0.935	0.895	ND	0.925	0.769
1979	ND	1.543	0.954	0.915	1.038	1.896	0.956	0.935	1.122	ND	1.085	0.825
1980	ND	1.578	0.975	0.814	0.935	1.803	0.796	1.056	1.204	ND	1.113	0.907
1981	ND	1.847	1.010	0.847	0.956	1.884	0.822	1.076	1.340	ND	1.285	0.949
1982	ND	1.820	0.996	0.909	0.981	1.947	0.845	0.983	1.312	ND	1.454	1.008
1983	ND	1.936	1.051	0.938	0.949	2.204	0.871	0.946	1.206	1.652	1.465	1.001
1984	ND	1.906	1.123	0.885	0.966	2.321	0.916	0.974	0.994	1.958	1.855	1.142
1985	ND	2.045	1.146	1.038	1.023	1.765	0.915	1.153	1.109	1.652	1.737	1.072
1986	1.960	2.532	1.353	1.087	1.148	2.685	1.169	1.357	1.340	1.958	1.737	1.290
1987	2.222	2.649	1.529	1.328	1.318	3.072	1.189	1.465	1.272	1.879	1.380	1.439
1988	2.315	2.540	1.650	1.388	1.560	3.990	1.231	1.550	1.245	1.839	1.399	1.677
1989	2.624	2.977	1.883	1.661	1.735	4.675	1.542	1.754	1.350	1.838	1.642	1.836
1990	2.573	3.675	1.931	1.806	2.054	5.291	1.640	1.962	1.333	1.941	1.831	2.025
1991	3.387	3.888	2.085	2.054	2.116	5.089	1.738	2.142	1.472	2.001	2.016	1.951
1992	3.509	3.803	2.314	2.219	2.453	ND	1.826	2.160	1.540	2.031	2.300	2.115
1993	4.222	3.761	2.723	2.324	2.680	ND	2.069	2.656	1.765	2.053	2.389	2.289
1994	3.332	3.635	2.689	2.741	2.870	ND	1.931	3.083	2.009	2.086	2.562	2.305
1995	3.340	3.448	2.445	2.425	3.071	ND	2.186	3.171	1.907	1.981	2.540	2.044

[a] "As of" date is January 1 of each year.
[b] ND = no data available.

Table C.17 is valuable for tracing changes in workers' compensation costs over time in a particular state, but the volume of information makes it difficult to identify general developments. Table C.18 provides a more compact summary of these data, which more readily permits an evaluation of temporal trends, showing unweighted observations for each state as well as observations weighted by each state's employment.

The first two data columns in Table C.18 present the average (mean) and standard deviation for all 48 states in our study, which is the most comprehensive set of data for any year. In some years, there are fewer than 48 observations and the statistics pertain to only those states with available data. The means of the weighted averages are consistently higher than the means of the unweighted averages, indicating that larger states tend to have higher workers' compensation costs. Both the weighted and unweighted means show a significant increase in costs between 1975 (when the costs of workers' compensation insurance in all states averaged less than 1.0 percent of payroll) and 1993 (when costs averaged over 3.0 percent of payroll), followed by a decline that brought both the weighted and unweighted averages below 3.0 percent of payroll in 1995.

The data for all 48 states indicate that the variation in costs among jurisdictions (as measured by the standard deviation) increased from 1975 until 1990. During the 1990s, the variation among states has fluctuated from year to year, but both the weighted and unweighted data show less variation among the states in 1995 than in 1990.

There are data available for all years for 42 states, and the means and standard deviations for these states are shown in the third and fourth data columns of Table C.18. The results for the 42 states are very similar to the results for all 48 states. The mean costs were less than 1.0 percent of payroll in 1975, peaked in 1993 in excess of 3.0 percent of payroll, and declined to less than 3.0 percent of payroll in 1995. Likewise, the standard deviation increased from 1975 to 1990 and then fluctuated during the 1990s; it ended up smaller in 1995 than in 1990.

Workers' compensation costs in a third combination of states, those 45 with private carriers, are shown in the right-most two columns of Table C.18. (The states with exclusive state funds—for which we have data that are omitted from these two columns—are Ohio, Washington, and West Virginia). Again the pattern is the same for the 45 states as for the full set of 48. The mean costs were less than 1.0 percent of payroll in 1975, peaked in 1993 in excess of 3.0 percent of payroll, and declined to less than 3.0 percent of payroll in 1995. Likewise, the standard deviation increased from 1975 to 1990 and then fluctuated during the 1990s; it ended up smaller in 1995 than in 1990.

Table C.18 Adjusted Manual Rates, Means and Standard Deviations, 1975–95 ($)

Year	All 48 states in study		42 States with no missing data		45 States with private carriers	
	Mean	Std. dev.	Mean	Std. dev.	Mean	Std. dev.
Unweighted observations						
1975	0.926	0.372	0.915	0.368	0.934	0.373
1976	1.115	0.463	1.106	0.465	1.125	0.463
1977	1.243	0.540	1.229	0.540	1.252	0.543
1978	1.396	0.634	1.383	0.637	1.407	0.637
1979	1.509	0.697	1.500	0.703	1.519	0.702
1980	1.582	0.763	1.576	0.771	1.593	0.768
1981	1.598	0.737	1.591	0.744	1.605	0.744
1982	1.567	0.699	1.558	0.705	1.570	0.707
1983	1.531	0.672	1.511	0.687	1.528	0.696
1984	1.510	0.685	1.474	0.693	1.485	0.703
1985	1.674	0.691	1.673	0.707	1.673	0.707
1986	1.882	0.770	1.833	0.785	1.884	0.787
1987	2.078	0.747	2.028	0.751	2.100	0.763
1988	2.214	0.758	2.135	0.711	2.234	0.770
1989	2.430	0.822	2.349	0.760	2.451	0.834
1990	2.662	0.986	2.586	0.932	2.682	1.001
1991	2.791	0.913	2.712	0.851	2.814	0.925
1992	3.002	0.938	2.978	0.927	3.028	0.948
1993	3.184	0.960	3.156	0.942	3.218	0.968
1994	3.072	0.778	3.077	0.791	3.097	0.784
1995	2.923	0.784	2.935	0.805	2.943	0.793

Table C.18 (continued)

Year	All 48 states in study		42 States with no missing data		45 States with private carriers	
	Mean	Std. dev.	Mean	Std. dev.	Mean	Std. dev.
Weighted observations						
1975	0.949	0.387	0.910	0.377	0.952	0.388
1976	1.130	0.441	1.100	0.446	1.134	0.441
1977	1.294	0.528	1.251	0.527	1.299	0.529
1978	1.466	0.608	1.428	0.618	1.471	0.608
1979	1.582	0.628	1.554	0.648	1.587	0.630
1980	1.645	0.640	1.631	0.667	1.650	0.641
1981	1.613	0.584	1.587	0.605	1.616	0.586
1982	1.511	0.511	1.467	0.516	1.511	0.514
1983	1.490	0.510	1.408	0.500	1.480	0.532
1984	1.466	0.561	1.351	0.524	1.434	0.574
1985	1.599	0.529	1.581	0.558	1.596	0.538
1986	1.977	0.718	1.744	0.645	1.979	0.727
1987	2.189	0.756	1.924	0.630	2.211	0.779
1988	2.420	0.901	2.067	0.674	2.433	0.927
1989	2.653	0.997	2.286	0.790	2.666	1.023
1990	2.951	1.181	2.604	1.061	2.962	1.211
1991	3.096	1.054	2.721	0.886	3.116	1.078
1992	3.267	1.091	3.037	1.053	3.289	1.115
1993	3.478	1.166	3.252	1.157	3.512	1.189
1994	3.188	0.791	3.100	0.842	3.202	0.800
1995	2.973	0.747	2.929	0.823	2.979	0.756

NET WEEKLY COSTS: 1975–1995

Adjusted manual rates, which represent the percentage of payroll expended on workers' compensation premiums, do not represent the only way to measure the employers' costs of workers' compensation. An alternative measure of workers' compensation costs is the weekly premium per worker in constant dollars. The rationale for developing this measure of workers' compensation costs is presented in the "Cost Methodology" section of Chapter 3 (pp. 58–64).

The weekly workers' compensation premium per worker is the product of the adjusted manual rates per $100 of payroll (shown in Table C.17) multiplied by the U.S. average weekly wage in 1995 dollars for the appropriate year (Table C.19), multiplied by the state weekly earnings index (Table C.20), and divided by 100 to convert the result to a weekly dollar amount of premium per worker, which is shown in Table C.21. An example using Alabama for 1975 is an adjusted manual rate of $0.579 per $100 of payroll, multiplied by the U.S. average real wage of $538.66, multiplied by the Alabama weekly earnings index of 0.8708, divided by 100, which results in a weekly premium of $2.72 per employee in constant 1995 dollars (Table C.21). By January 1, 1995, these same employers expended, on average, $17.19 per employee per week on workers' compensation premiums, which means that workers' compensation weekly premiums in real terms had increased in Alabama more than sixfold over the 21-year period.

Table C.21 is valuable for tracing changes in workers' compensation weekly premiums over time in a particular state, but the volume of information makes it difficult to identify general developments. Table C.22 provides a more compact summary of these data, more readily permitting evaluation of temporal trends; it shows unweighted observations for each state as well as observations weighted by each state's employment.

The first two data columns in Table C.22 present the means and standard deviations for all 48 states in our study, which is the most comprehensive set of data for any one year. For some years, there are fewer than 48 observations and the statistics pertain to only those states with available data. The unweighted means show a significant increase in costs between 1975 (when the weekly costs of workers' compensation insurance in all states measured in 1995 dollars averaged less than $5.00 per employee) and 1993 (when weekly costs averaged over $16.00 per worker), followed by a decline that brought the unweighted average weekly premiums below $16.00 per worker in 1995. The means of the weighted averages are higher in most years than the means of the unweighted averages, indicating that larger states tend to have higher

Table C.19 U.S. Average Weekly Wages, 1975–95

Year	Nominal wage ($)	Real wage (1995 $)
1975	190.28	538.66
1976	203.88	545.71
1977	217.63	546.95
1978	232.90	544.03
1979	252.82	530.36
1980	276.89	511.78
1981	301.89	505.81
1982	321.95	508.11
1983	335.68	513.29
1984	350.04	513.59
1985	365.38	517.17
1986	380.00	527.57
1987	396.77	531.47
1988	416.47	535.71
1989	428.03	525.72
1990	446.68	520.90
1991	464.08	519.32
1992	489.97	532.26
1993	497.21	524.78
1994	507.77	522.17
1995	525.91	525.91

Table C.20 State Weekly Earnings Indexes, 1975–95

	Ala.	Alaska	Ariz.	Ark.	Calif.	Colo.	Conn.	Del.	D.C.	Fla.	Ga.	Hawaii
1975	0.8708	1.7777	1.0344	0.7710	1.0905	1.0029	0.9799	0.9923	1.2170	0.8763	0.8737	0.9855
1976	0.8853	1.7781	1.0151	0.7790	1.0793	1.0063	0.9716	1.0023	1.1061	0.8624	0.8431	0.9886
1977	0.8761	1.8728	1.0109	0.7816	1.0825	1.0070	0.9784	0.9412	1.0543	0.8524	0.8613	0.9655
1978	0.8805	1.5828	1.0160	0.7768	1.0742	0.9888	0.9812	0.9669	1.2813	0.8577	0.8606	0.9641
1979	0.9020	1.5478	1.0206	0.7913	1.0814	1.0249	0.9800	0.9490	1.3123	0.8456	0.8630	0.9530
1980	0.9423	1.5808	1.0248	0.8017	1.0921	1.0563	0.9831	0.9506	1.2720	0.8561	0.8621	0.9431
1981	0.9257	1.5481	1.0199	0.8072	1.0967	1.0373	0.9613	0.9302	1.3071	0.8472	0.8829	0.9577
1982	0.9139	1.4914	1.0374	0.8105	1.1163	1.0443	0.9631	0.9341	1.2824	0.8591	0.8498	0.9614
1983	0.9166	1.4154	1.0280	0.8191	1.1055	1.0362	0.9769	0.9190	1.3161	0.8566	0.8854	0.9626
1984	0.9282	1.4332	0.9896	0.8152	1.0919	1.0300	1.0020	0.9000	1.3127	0.8537	0.8888	0.9319
1985	0.9526	1.4503	0.9982	0.8197	1.0956	0.9941	1.0025	0.9136	1.3489	0.8516	0.8995	0.9274
1986	0.9613	1.3853	1.0161	0.8265	1.1443	0.9838	1.0118	0.9811	1.2076	0.8514	0.9223	0.9610
1987	0.9618	1.3487	0.9900	0.8298	1.1249	0.9882	1.0273	0.9948	1.1944	0.8520	0.9210	0.9867
1988	0.9475	1.3322	0.9591	0.8255	1.1126	0.9873	1.0222	0.9278	1.2485	0.8529	0.9094	1.0134
1989	0.9302	1.3687	0.9317	0.8154	1.1123	0.9703	1.0303	0.9817	1.2492	0.8596	0.8970	1.0393
1990	0.9280	1.4389	0.9245	0.8236	1.1157	1.0059	1.0267	0.9623	1.2505	0.8716	0.8919	1.0678
1991	0.9259	1.3753	0.9367	0.8385	1.1171	0.9978	1.0294	0.9976	1.2524	0.8824	0.9016	0.9927
1992	0.9335	1.3161	0.9262	0.8344	1.1091	0.9816	1.0363	0.9499	1.2550	0.8843	0.9099	1.0497
1993	0.9394	1.3246	0.9006	0.8331	1.1087	1.0103	1.0595	1.0198	1.2585	0.8761	0.9010	1.0656
1994	0.9565	1.3327	0.9125	0.8355	1.1026	0.9947	1.0831	1.0376	1.2628	0.8691	0.9016	1.0445
1995	0.9119	1.4730	0.9726	0.7998	1.0906	0.9954	1.0240	0.9813	1.2682	0.8489	0.8743	0.9761

(continued)

Table C.20 (continued)

	Idaho	Ill.	Ind.	Iowa	Kans.	Ky.	La.	Maine	Md.	Mass.	Mich.	Minn.
1975	0.8979	1.1147	1.0330	1.0083	0.8940	0.9861	0.9663	0.8657	0.9816	0.9500	1.1270	0.9797
1976	0.9229	1.1361	1.0387	1.0011	0.8971	0.9935	0.9533	0.8787	0.9860	0.9306	1.1652	0.9911
1977	0.9487	1.1107	1.0574	1.0107	0.8995	1.0058	0.9464	0.8809	0.9926	0.9252	1.1914	0.9823
1978	0.9676	1.0879	1.0554	1.0159	0.9012	1.0140	0.9682	0.8917	0.9782	0.9171	1.1831	0.9825
1979	0.9602	1.0902	1.0549	1.0382	0.9304	1.0020	0.9615	0.9099	0.9962	0.9331	1.1584	0.9845
1980	0.9602	1.0673	1.0512	1.0572	0.9545	0.9986	0.9889	0.9121	0.9848	0.9248	1.1426	0.9915
1981	0.9890	1.0636	1.0523	1.0692	0.9423	0.9804	0.9918	0.9329	0.9930	0.9079	1.1534	0.9874
1982	0.9868	1.0712	1.0483	1.0710	0.9587	0.9759	0.9796	0.9369	0.9880	0.9239	1.1616	1.0121
1983	0.9895	1.0830	1.0496	1.0601	0.9007	0.9666	0.9562	0.9110	0.9819	0.9273	1.1717	1.0172
1984	1.0008	1.0696	1.0564	1.0319	0.8887	0.9782	0.9635	0.9139	1.0138	0.9245	1.1854	1.0148
1985	0.9931	1.0869	1.0252	1.0053	0.8463	0.9801	0.9878	0.9268	0.9869	0.9666	1.1799	1.0202
1986	0.9874	1.0896	1.0350	1.0050	0.8627	0.9959	0.9651	0.9268	0.9917	0.9824	1.1658	1.0293
1987	0.9691	1.0915	1.0454	1.0209	0.8903	1.0125	0.9540	0.9386	1.0023	0.9946	1.1593	1.0214
1988	0.9648	1.0872	1.0435	0.9939	0.8793	0.9840	0.9838	0.8958	1.0321	1.0302	1.1182	0.9958
1989	0.9561	1.0704	1.0411	0.9771	0.8746	0.9685	0.9776	0.9335	1.0384	1.0460	1.0928	1.0141
1990	0.9652	1.0556	1.0403	0.9861	0.8951	0.9726	1.0160	0.9545	1.0331	1.0677	1.0697	1.0129
1991	0.9588	1.0559	1.0486	0.9947	0.8962	0.9753	1.0019	0.9315	1.0426	1.0799	1.0761	1.0319
1992	0.9666	1.0320	0.9724	1.0003	0.9180	0.9661	0.9935	0.9495	1.0618	1.0748	1.0678	1.0546
1993	0.9785	1.0259	0.9960	1.0039	0.9297	0.9561	1.0078	0.9611	1.0671	1.0615	1.0715	1.0596
1994	0.9537	1.0300	0.9960	1.0058	0.9112	0.9531	1.0440	0.9373	1.0543	1.0515	1.0894	1.0634
1995	0.9538	1.0947	1.0557	1.0365	0.9222	0.9713	0.9683	0.9382	1.0290	0.9997	1.1552	1.0310

	Miss.	Mo.	Mont.	Nebr.	N.H.	N.J.	N.Mex.	N.Y.	N.C.	Ohio	Okla.	Oreg.
1975	0.7755	0.9947	1.1229	1.0089	0.8938	1.0420	0.7747	1.0517	0.7939	1.0655	0.8874	1.0580
1976	0.7747	0.9936	1.1365	0.9950	0.8952	1.0348	0.8022	1.0460	0.7982	1.0787	0.8893	1.0413
1977	0.7653	1.0020	1.1930	0.9755	0.8765	1.0450	0.7829	1.0431	0.8004	1.0900	0.8904	1.0390
1978	0.7663	0.9872	1.3552	0.9991	0.8761	1.0245	0.7854	1.0249	0.8052	1.0912	0.8947	1.0320
1979	0.7689	0.9889	1.3473	1.0238	0.8783	1.0366	0.8011	1.0234	0.8089	1.0953	0.9092	1.0395
1980	0.7862	1.0003	1.3064	1.0475	0.8794	1.0400	0.8119	1.0282	0.8203	1.0903	0.9493	1.0474
1981	0.7963	0.9963	1.1770	1.0121	0.8741	1.0386	0.8184	1.0207	0.8232	1.0959	0.9526	1.0498
1982	0.7957	0.9844	1.1660	1.0203	0.9192	1.0419	0.8422	1.0305	0.8153	1.0861	0.9577	1.0792
1983	0.8058	1.0027	1.1317	0.9841	0.9268	1.0413	0.8397	1.0349	0.8330	1.0877	0.9506	1.0553
1984	0.8186	1.0035	1.0846	0.9302	0.9169	1.0469	0.8428	1.0425	0.8342	1.0801	0.9684	1.0383
1985	0.8143	0.9864	1.0881	0.9203	0.9221	1.0459	0.9612	1.0505	0.8402	1.0722	0.9656	1.0106
1986	0.8120	0.9995	1.0819	0.9248	0.9548	1.0484	0.9639	1.0493	0.8529	1.0771	0.9388	1.0062
1987	0.8054	1.0028	1.0162	0.8899	0.9996	1.0496	0.9506	1.0375	0.8695	1.0838	0.9439	1.0014
1988	0.8288	0.9902	1.0006	0.8190	1.0273	1.0692	0.9183	1.0783	0.8713	1.0725	0.9627	0.9741
1989	0.8097	0.9823	1.0281	0.7998	1.0509	1.0598	0.8962	1.0615	0.8735	1.0199	0.9750	0.9837
1990	0.8053	0.9714	1.0224	0.8019	1.0427	1.0926	0.8893	1.0705	0.8865	1.0253	0.9569	0.9955
1991	0.8201	0.9550	1.0017	0.8221	1.0233	1.0994	0.8806	1.0787	0.9011	1.0257	0.9530	1.0093
1992	0.8315	0.9540	1.0195	0.8390	1.0275	1.1102	0.8763	1.0679	0.9063	1.0234	0.9329	1.0102
1993	0.8369	0.9650	0.9942	0.8519	1.0423	1.1125	0.8746	1.0684	0.9010	1.0325	0.9460	0.9887
1994	0.8375	0.9560	0.9864	0.8640	1.0305	1.1082	0.8618	1.0582	0.9062	1.0359	0.9270	0.8593
1995	0.7907	1.0045	1.1010	0.9452	0.9716	1.0781	0.8467	1.0670	0.8350	1.0851	0.9256	1.0103

(continued)

Table C.20 (continued)

	Pa.	R.I.	S.C.	S.Dak.	Tenn.	Texas	Utah	Vt.	Va.	Wash.	W.Va.	Wisc.
1975	1.0105	0.8891	0.8116	0.8825	0.9133	0.9616	0.9205	0.9027	0.8508	1.1187	0.9027	1.0522
1976	0.9942	0.8809	0.8205	0.8567	0.9057	0.9327	0.9374	0.8866	0.8563	1.1196	0.8866	1.0481
1977	1.0039	0.8615	0.8201	0.8261	0.9234	0.9378	0.9453	0.9021	0.8626	1.1202	0.9021	1.0456
1978	1.0050	0.8628	0.8211	0.8708	0.9161	0.9378	0.9300	0.9190	0.8570	1.1191	0.9190	1.0509
1979	1.0074	0.8503	0.8338	0.8843	0.9170	0.9465	0.9503	0.9352	0.8743	1.1045	0.9352	1.0550
1980	0.9978	0.8610	0.8421	0.9170	0.9329	0.9767	0.9725	0.9467	0.8811	1.1289	0.9467	1.0674
1981	1.0011	0.8392	0.8398	0.9295	0.9327	0.9781	0.9867	0.9369	0.8878	1.1471	0.9369	1.0619
1982	0.9968	0.8583	0.8263	0.9090	0.9326	0.9794	0.9767	0.9414	0.8817	1.1855	0.9414	1.0813
1983	1.0027	0.8370	0.8597	0.8495	0.9387	0.9753	0.9792	0.9722	0.8906	1.1447	0.9722	1.0848
1984	1.0214	0.8778	0.8692	0.8106	0.9466	0.9683	0.9681	0.9717	0.8903	1.1139	0.9717	1.0655
1985	1.0136	0.8784	0.8667	0.8093	0.9546	0.9717	1.0149	0.8705	0.8990	1.0935	0.9733	1.0575
1986	1.0140	0.8944	0.8785	0.7716	0.9567	0.9816	1.0353	0.8782	0.9233	1.0792	0.9783	1.0433
1987	1.0233	0.9059	0.8837	0.7712	0.9647	0.9778	1.0229	0.8800	0.9388	1.0835	0.9638	1.0304
1988	1.0313	0.9031	0.8683	0.7616	0.9619	0.9696	0.9326	0.8905	0.9229	1.0615	0.8747	1.0187
1989	1.0300	0.9139	0.8722	0.7574	0.9566	0.9776	0.8511	0.9058	0.9278	1.0306	0.8697	1.0051
1990	1.0324	0.9294	0.8632	0.7535	0.9278	0.9737	0.8430	0.9366	0.9238	1.0696	0.8880	1.0075
1991	1.0341	0.9232	0.8658	0.7648	0.9404	0.9827	0.8818	0.9769	0.9263	1.0514	0.9153	1.0163
1992	1.0365	0.9111	0.8761	0.9031	0.9075	0.9778	0.9031	0.9954	0.9253	1.0525	0.9201	1.0277
1993	1.0358	0.9096	0.8723	0.8822	0.9018	0.9635	0.8822	0.9901	0.9254	1.0474	0.9155	1.0290
1994	0.7507	0.8860	0.9509	0.9546	0.9707	0.9277	1.0164	0.9023	1.0292	0.9303	0.9023	1.0292
1995	1.0351	0.9028	0.8405	0.9324	0.9188	0.9540	0.9324	0.9114	0.9173	1.0824	0.9138	1.0626

Table C.21 Net Weekly Costs, 1975–95[a] ($)

	Ala.	Alaska	Ariz.	Ark.	Calif.[b]	Colo.	Conn.	Del.	D.C.	Fla.	Ga.	Hawaii
1975	2.717	9.864	8.879	4.255	ND[b]	2.889	4.408	ND	9.149	9.154	3.192	7.880
1976	3.703	15.391	9.739	4.689	ND	3.584	5.054	ND	10.847	9.541	4.044	9.976
1977	3.606	18.298	10.999	5.151	ND	5.060	5.487	ND	13.827	11.763	4.585	10.567
1978	4.439	14.366	12.101	5.342	ND	5.845	6.864	ND	23.395	13.315	5.007	10.981
1979	4.845	15.637	14.108	5.416	ND	6.013	7.615	ND	29.632	11.849	5.775	12.513
1980	4.929	16.145	12.721	6.095	ND	4.747	10.159	ND	32.102	9.675	5.300	12.402
1981	4.888	18.481	9.924	6.267	ND	5.150	9.558	ND	30.024	8.596	5.291	16.333
1982	4.869	18.758	7.609	5.773	ND	6.415	10.488	ND	25.854	6.472	5.031	18.147
1983	5.023	15.457	6.761	5.569	ND	7.263	10.125	ND	17.503	7.509	4.744	22.017
1984	4.952	15.457	6.428	5.601	ND	7.202	10.211	ND	14.924	7.545	4.786	20.004
1985	6.257	17.053	9.181	5.657	ND	9.099	10.786	ND	15.987	10.311	6.162	20.941
1986	7.516	18.886	11.352	6.589	18.215	9.763	12.092	9.756	17.730	12.514	7.670	24.073
1987	8.884	21.794	10.985	8.205	20.620	12.246	14.015	10.456	18.725	13.173	9.129	21.900
1988	9.952	23.475	10.902	8.420	22.861	14.187	15.856	10.531	18.303	15.378	9.634	18.720
1989	10.367	21.099	12.292	8.649	22.665	16.286	17.082	10.741	18.210	18.362	11.423	18.369
1990	10.855	23.592	12.685	8.801	22.980	16.589	18.094	10.505	17.939	24.193	12.249	18.884
1991	11.702	21.346	12.951	9.647	24.620	18.295	18.945	10.591	19.390	19.117	13.990	17.881
1992	16.803	19.665	14.293	11.759	28.005	17.459	19.755	11.083	21.100	25.793	16.843	19.871
1993	17.379	16.957	13.543	15.384	28.256	17.155	22.022	12.529	23.075	29.095	16.825	20.777
1994	17.160	17.863	13.075	14.172	21.905	16.139	18.867	13.126	21.323	19.652	16.736	19.687
1995	17.195	18.591	13.455	12.589	18.067	14.596	17.055	11.808	22.283	19.490	15.494	24.981

(continued)

Table C.21 (continued)

	Idaho	Ill.	Ind.	Iowa	Kans.	Ky.	La.	Maine	Md.	Mass.	Mich.	Minn.
1975	5.428	3.986	2.216	3.278	3.793	5.723	7.738	4.263	4.570	5.491	7.126	6.022
1976	6.647	6.939	2.558	3.722	4.190	7.080	12.505	5.243	6.150	6.237	8.668	7.036
1977	7.125	9.191	2.597	4.534	4.995	7.128	8.853	5.485	7.766	6.466	10.603	8.263
1978	6.765	8.168	3.262	4.966	5.173	9.556	9.256	5.899	7.703	7.310	13.591	9.736
1979	7.198	8.269	2.979	6.455	4.643	9.022	8.657	7.662	9.613	8.368	13.064	10.206
1980	6.619	9.187	3.187	7.278	4.638	8.728	9.580	9.785	8.697	8.440	15.027	10.229
1981	8.035	8.640	2.584	6.920	4.614	6.261	9.670	10.251	10.279	8.409	14.424	9.646
1982	7.294	8.140	2.234	6.775	5.525	5.951	8.379	12.326	10.552	8.490	11.000	9.045
1983	7.376	7.455	2.315	5.784	4.850	5.818	9.057	12.059	10.226	9.800	10.647	8.427
1984	7.542	7.407	2.455	5.354	4.590	6.254	6.838	12.509	9.799	9.870	10.048	9.132
1985	7.966	9.122	2.739	5.572	4.855	7.964	7.472	12.853	10.215	10.211	11.827	12.741
1986	8.676	11.080	3.333	5.926	5.863	8.746	10.015	11.377	11.550	10.696	14.247	15.014
1987	10.630	11.540	3.803	7.987	6.347	11.164	9.763	11.446	10.761	11.300	16.262	15.162
1988	11.967	12.590	4.333	7.870	7.683	10.981	12.187	12.297	11.320	14.840	15.366	16.266
1989	11.049	13.793	5.612	9.449	7.726	12.588	13.290	16.312	10.545	16.543	14.829	17.099
1990	12.210	14.552	6.826	9.210	8.211	13.192	16.344	19.618	9.917	20.976	19.463	18.642
1991	11.996	15.387	7.484	10.279	9.238	13.354	16.588	22.020	9.907	25.329	20.389	19.091
1992	13.699	15.954	7.543	11.851	11.778	15.582	23.396	22.660	10.896	25.216	21.633	20.969
1993	14.576	15.874	7.939	12.609	14.020	18.112	22.320	21.560	10.274	24.991	17.627	17.123
1994	13.111	16.334	7.662	12.111	13.500	18.505	23.434	19.126	11.044	22.623	16.751	16.243
1995	12.008	16.137	7.759	10.607	12.962	18.645	20.672	16.640	10.235	16.860	16.335	15.084

	Miss.	Mo.	Mont.	Nebr.	N.H.	N.J.	N.Mex.	N.Y.	N.C.	Ohio	Okla.	Oreg.
1975	3.706	4.045	8.527	3.686	3.381	5.809	4.297	5.175	1.847	ND	4.924	9.496
1976	3.695	4.352	9.234	4.700	5.025	6.367	5.012	6.411	2.001	ND	5.935	12.138
1977	3.742	4.730	10.951	3.909	5.353	6.993	5.290	7.517	2.125	ND	6.941	15.311
1978	3.871	4.508	16.470	4.017	6.905	7.792	5.494	9.382	2.227	ND	6.982	15.725
1979	3.530	4.707	10.554	4.095	7.047	7.818	6.475	11.503	2.632	ND	7.644	15.195
1980	3.770	4.517	10.979	4.531	7.790	9.479	6.972	11.206	2.943	ND	7.232	13.745
1981	3.692	4.141	9.589	4.452	6.717	9.764	8.319	9.521	3.490	ND	8.501	11.336
1982	4.108	4.326	11.251	4.543	7.399	9.308	8.773	7.852	3.637	ND	8.467	11.796
1983	4.131	3.908	12.491	4.964	8.053	8.047	9.531	7.197	3.466	8.944	8.249	8.364
1984	4.511	4.511	12.196	4.621	9.527	8.156	10.371	7.217	2.788	9.752	9.134	9.191
1985	4.790	5.239	15.037	4.987	9.978	6.475	13.451	8.803	3.134	ND	9.001	11.349
1986	5.551	6.529	16.657	5.210	11.451	6.870	14.459	9.837	4.138	ND	10.842	15.028
1987	6.801	7.542	20.658	5.653	12.451	7.762	14.166	9.768	4.736	11.286	11.266	16.149
1988	6.915	8.289	18.575	5.661	13.857	8.468	16.115	10.277	5.557	14.464	12.168	15.190
1989	8.368	8.399	22.076	6.044	14.973	7.723	15.936	10.619	5.797	15.307	14.148	15.122
1990	8.409	8.827	25.209	6.982	15.155	8.365	16.506	12.724	6.385	17.688	13.156	16.442
1991	10.528	10.058	21.377	8.247	16.414	8.764	16.246	15.863	7.997	17.674	13.195	15.844
1992	12.907	12.863	24.656	9.354	17.924	10.339	20.159	17.718	9.018	19.319	16.525	15.067
1993	14.533	14.464	23.885	10.770	21.170	11.196	20.599	21.238	11.540	19.602	19.326	12.955
1994	13.880	13.148	26.133	11.812	23.815	10.601	15.820	23.035	11.480	18.947	18.660	12.021
1995	11.434	13.011	28.587	11.622	19.194	10.076	16.535	21.790	10.173	19.166	16.823	12.086

(continued)

	Pa.	R.I.	S.C.	S.Dak.	Tenn.	Texas	Utah	Vt.	Va.	Wash.	W.Va.	Wisc.
1975	ND	4.011	2.371	2.419	3.514	7.376	2.899	2.859	2.243	ND	3.006	3.212
1976	ND	5.309	2.889	3.192	3.976	7.572	3.969	2.819	2.667	ND	3.320	3.805
1977	ND	6.453	3.067	2.795	4.139	9.265	3.963	3.439	3.405	ND	4.098	3.717
1978	ND	6.736	3.124	3.411	5.298	9.737	4.188	4.386	4.172	ND	4.623	4.399
1979	ND	6.960	4.220	4.291	5.047	9.517	4.817	4.279	5.205	ND	5.380	4.615
1980	ND	6.952	4.203	3.821	4.465	9.010	3.962	4.622	5.427	ND	5.393	4.956
1981	ND	7.838	4.291	3.984	4.510	9.319	4.102	4.616	6.017	ND	6.088	5.096
1982	ND	7.939	4.182	4.199	4.650	9.690	4.194	4.247	5.877	ND	6.955	5.536
1983	ND	8.317	4.637	4.092	4.572	11.034	4.375	4.095	5.514	9.704	7.313	5.576
1984	ND	8.591	5.014	3.683	4.699	11.541	4.554	4.223	4.545	11.203	9.258	6.248
1985	ND	9.292	5.139	4.344	5.051	8.871	4.804	5.191	5.158	9.340	8.745	5.861
1986	10.485	11.946	6.269	4.425	5.792	13.904	6.384	6.285	6.526	11.149	8.967	7.098
1987	12.084	12.756	7.180	5.442	6.756	15.966	6.463	6.854	6.348	10.820	7.066	7.880
1988	12.788	12.287	7.676	5.662	8.039	20.726	6.148	7.397	6.155	10.457	6.555	9.149
1989	14.210	14.304	8.634	6.616	8.727	24.026	6.902	8.351	6.582	9.958	7.506	9.704
1990	13.838	17.792	8.684	7.089	9.928	26.836	7.200	9.572	6.413	10.814	8.470	10.627
1991	18.189	18.640	9.375	8.159	10.332	25.969	7.959	10.869	7.082	10.927	9.584	10.298
1992	19.358	18.440	10.792	8.880	11.846	ND	8.779	11.444	7.583	11.376	11.266	11.571
1993	22.950	17.953	12.464	9.034	12.685	ND	9.580	13.797	8.570	11.285	11.479	12.363
1994	18.024	16.980	12.064	10.744	13.276	ND	9.627	15.626	9.733	11.071	12.072	12.386
1995	18.179	16.370	10.807	10.676	14.837	ND	10.718	15.196	9.198	11.278	12.205	11.425

[a] Weekly premium per worker in constant 1995 dollars for employers in 71 classes in each of the 48 jurisdictions in the study. "As of" date is January 1 of each year.
[b] ND = no data available.

Table C.22 Net Weekly Costs, 1975–95 ($)

Year	All 48 states in study		43 States with no missing data		45 States with private carriers	
	Mean	Std. dev.	Mean	Std. dev.	Mean	Std. dev
Unweighted observations						
1975	4.903	2.287	4.844	2.282	4.948	2.296
1976	5.998	3.022	5.961	3.048	6.062	3.029
1977	6.734	3.604	6.674	3.625	6.797	3.623
1978	7.593	4.329	7.542	4.368	7.663	4.356
1979	8.025	4.726	7.989	4.777	8.088	4.765
1980	8.178	4.991	8.158	5.049	8.244	5.032
1981	8.131	4.818	8.103	4.872	8.180	4.865
1982	8.001	4.430	7.961	4.476	8.026	4.481
1983	7.830	3.802	7.683	3.889	7.771	3.923
1984	7.688	3.742	7.463	3.769	7.517	3.812
1985	8.614	3.902	8.590	3.994	8.593	3.994
1986	9.916	4.481	9.584	4.505	9.909	4.575
1987	11.045	4.537	10.689	4.539	11.133	4.649
1988	11.760	4.660	11.254	4.403	11.845	4.730
1989	12.592	4.798	12.083	4.468	12.703	4.865
1990	13.742	5.565	13.261	5.306	13.837	5.647
1991	14.357	5.214	13.837	4.875	14.465	5.290
1992	15.761	5.332	15.515	5.153	15.882	5.403
1993	16.457	5.206	16.163	4.962	16.616	5.247
1994	15.768	4.359	15.667	4.395	15.887	4.387
1995	15.126	4.361	15.058	4.457	15.188	4.406

(continued)

Table C.22 (continued)

Year	All 48 states in study		43 States with no missing data		45 States with private carriers	
	Mean	Std. dev.	Mean	Std. dev.	Mean	Std. dev
Weighted observations						
1975	5.029	2.079	4.837	2.045	5.049	2.080
1976	6.073	2.484	5.948	2.545	6.100	2.481
1977	6.986	3.006	6.794	3.052	7.014	3.007
1978	7.875	3.618	7.715	3.727	7.906	3.622
1979	8.306	3.782	8.199	3.929	8.334	3.790
1980	8.409	3.898	8.354	4.071	8.438	3.906
1981	8.109	3.562	7.992	3.711	8.128	3.574
1982	7.631	3.076	7.425	3.152	7.637	3.089
1983	7.634	2.789	7.164	2.765	7.511	2.877
1984	7.504	2.988	6.872	2.809	7.272	3.007
1985	8.222	2.880	8.131	3.040	8.192	2.920
1986	10.655	4.310	9.143	3.520	10.667	4.365
1987	11.901	4.590	10.171	3.547	11.983	4.470
1988	13.184	5.265	10.970	3.635	13.218	5.414
1989	14.058	5.527	11.799	4.004	14.122	5.673
1990	15.500	6.230	13.353	5.267	15.538	6.387
1991	16.339	5.956	14.036	4.826	16.436	6.099
1992	17.602	6.259	15.922	5.442	17.706	6.410
1993	18.401	6.328	16.730	5.610	18.556	6.461
1994	16.741	4.502	15.914	4.517	16.793	4.559
1995	15.691	3.980	15.095	4.215	15.636	3.997

workers' compensation costs. However, the patterns over time are similar; weekly premiums increased yearly with minor exceptions from 1975 to 1993 and then declined by 1995. The data for all 48 states indicate that the variation in costs (as measured by the standard deviation) among jurisdictions increased from 1975 until 1990. However, both the weighted and unweighted data show less variation among the states in 1995 than in 1990.

There are data available for all years for 42 states, and the means and standard deviations for these states are shown in the third and fourth data columns of Table C.22. The results for the 42 states are very similar to the results for the 48 states. For example, the unweighted mean weekly premiums were less than $5.00 per worker in 1975, peaked in 1993 in excess of $16.00 per worker, and declined to less than $16.00 per worker in 1995. Likewise, the standard deviation increased from 1975 to 1990 and then declined between 1990 and 1995.

Workers' compensation costs in a third combination of states, those 45 with private carriers, is shown in the right-most two columns of Table C.22. Again the pattern is the same as for the full set of 48 states: average weekly premiums were less than $5.00 per worker in 1975, peaked in 1993 in excess of $16.00 per worker, and declined to less than $16.00 per worker per week in 1995. Likewise, the standard deviation increased from 1975 to 1990, but ended up smaller in 1995 than in 1990.

Notes

1. We attempt to thoroughly explain our methodology and to provide comprehensive state-level data on the outcome of methodology in this appendix. We do not include all the data we have used, such as manual rates or pure premiums for individual workers' compensation insurance classes. The data set of 71 classes times 21 years times 42 to 48 states (depending on the year) plus, for some years, separate rates for both the voluntary and assigned-risk markets, is too large to include as an appendix. We will share our data with researchers and will post additional data on a Web site as soon as the Upjohn Institute publishes the study.

2. Three of the jurisdictions included in our study (Ohio, Washington, and West Virginia) have exclusive state funds; each uses its own classification system. Though 13 of the remaining states in our study (as of 1995) had their own rate-making organizations, the NCCI's classification codes were usually applicable. We used a substantial number of non-NCCI classification codes only for California, Delaware, and Pennsylvania.

3. Most of the conversions were fairly obvious from the classification descriptions in the NCCI's classification codes and the "deviant" state's classification manual. When ambiguities existed, the NCCI class descriptions were sent to the appropriate official in the non-Council state and he or she chose the most nearly analogous

390

class in that state, or the staff of the National Council selected the most nearly analogous class.

4. The rate-setting regime in effect on January 1 was used to categorize the model for the year.

5. Examples of the regression coefficients predicting adjusted manual rates with our basic model of explanatory variables and our preferred characterization of the regulatory environment, with the eight observations included and then with the eight observations deleted, are as follows: ln benefits, 0.066273 and 0.068766; administered pricing with deviations, 0.051339 and 0.051962; advisory rates, 0.126207 and 0.128325; loss costs with prior approval, 0.027508 and 0.024408; and loss costs without prior approval, –0.019338 and –0.187916. The differences in these coefficients do not pass the heuristic "wow" test.

6. Maryland has relied on a residual market for many years, but data on the shares accounted for by the voluntary and residual markets are unavailable. As a result, we use Model I for 1975–1987 and Model II for 1988–1995 for Maryland.

7. This procedure pertains to Models I, III, and IV, which are listed in Table C.2.

8. One factor that formerly hindered interstate workers' compensation cost comparisons was the use of different payroll limitations among the states. A payroll limitation is a figure that determines the maximum amount of an employee's weekly earnings that will be used in calculating insurance premiums. For many years, the normal payroll limitation was $100, which meant that the manual rate was multiplied by an employee's weekly earning or $100, whichever was less, to determine the weekly benefit.

Most state workers' compensation programs affiliated with the NCCI converted from a $100 payroll limitation to a $300 limitation circa 1957, and to no limit (which means that the manual rates were charged against the whole payroll) during 1974–1975. However, four states (Florida, Louisiana, Missouri, and Texas) still had weekly payroll limits of $200 or less as of July 1, 1975. By July 1, 1978, these four states either had payroll limits of $300 or had eliminated the payroll limitation. As late as January 1, 1984, only Texas still had a payroll limit ($300), which was subsequently removed.

Although payroll limitations have been eliminated, their operation is important to explain because they mean that the historical record for these four states is somewhat misleading. To illustrate the significance of the payroll limitation, assume that the insurance premium for a worker earning $300 per week was identical in two states, one of which had a $3.00 manual rate and a $100 payroll limitation, and the other of which had a $1.00 manual rate and a $300 per week payroll limit. Obviously, it is incorrect to say that the state with the $3.00 manual rate (and resultant higher adjusted manual rate) had a higher cost of workers' compensation than the other jurisdiction.

Fortunately, the problem of the payroll limits is confined to only four states in our study, and then only for a limited number of years before the payroll limits reached at least $300 per week. However, for those four states there are several years in which the costs of workers' compensation as we measure those costs are overstated, because we ignore the effects of the payroll limits.

9. Because the firm's workers' compensation insurance premium is adjusted based on its loss experience relative to the experience of the average firm in its insurance classification, one might expect that these firm adjustments would sum to zero over all firms in the state. If so, there should be no need to adjust state-wide average manual rates. However, in practice, the predominant effect of experience rating is to reduce the employers' costs of workers' compensation insurance.

10. For the experience rating adjustment, we used manual premium and standard earned premium data from the NCCI and comparable data from non-NCCI states that have their own rate-making organizations (including California, Delaware, Massachusetts, Minnesota, New Jersey, New York, and Pennsylvania).

11. In states that do not permit deviations, standard earned premium at bureau rates and standard earned premium at the company level are identical.

12. The dividend adjustment factor was computed from data published by A.M. Best and was calculated by subtracting from 1 the ratio of direct dividends to direct premium earned for the same calendar year.

13. This procedure applies to Models II and V, which are listed in Table C.2.

14. In Model I (and also in Model III), the manual rates for the total market (IR4) are the same as the manual rates in the voluntary market (IR1).

15. The Ohio Bureau of Workers' Compensation is converting its classification codes to those used by the NCCI over a four-year phase-in period starting July 1, 1998. The Bureau will discontinue its classification code system upon completion of the conversion. See Ohio Bureau of Workers' Compensation, *Understanding Conversion of Industry Classifications*, BWC Fact Sheet (FactSheets Online) v. 1.1 (no date). This document was accessed by the authors in July 1999 at the web site http://www.bwc.state.oh.us/resource/library/brochure/convind.pdf.

16. The "base rate calculation" for rate date July 1, 1994, which is based on data from January 1, 1989, to January 1, 1992, for private employers, shows an adjustment for the off-balance factor due to experience rating of 1.2259. This indicates that experience rating was reducing insurance premiums by 22.59 percent during the base period. This information was provided in correspondence from the Actuarial Section of the Ohio Bureau of Workers' Compensation (William E. Darlage to John F. Burton, Jr., July 15, 1997).

17. The quotation is from the January 20, 1987, cover letter by Frederick W. Kilbourne that constitutes part of the *Actuarial Audit of the State Insurance Fund As of December 31, 1985*. Future Cost Analysts of Ohio prepared the audit for the Ohio Industrial Commission.

18. Ohio Bureau of Workers' Compensation, *BWC online*: "Mail doesn't get any better than this." Accessed by the authors in July 1999 at the Web site http://www.bwc.state.oh.us/FEATURE/rebate/rebate.htm

19. Data for these two variables were available only for the years 1985, 1990, and 1995. Values for other years were interpolated.

20. The factors were averaged over all rate classes.

21. Actuaries in the Washington Department of Labor and Industry indicated that the actual experience modification factor tends to vary only slightly from the targeted modification.
22. Unless otherwise noted, all quotations and data in the balance of the discussion of West Virginia are from Geiger (1988).

Appendix D

Benefit Index Methodology

Workers' compensation programs provide workers who have experienced a work-related injury or illness with a variety of benefits. These include reimbursement for medical and other expenses related to the rehabilitation of the claimant. They also include two types of cash benefits: disability compensation, which is paid to injured workers to compensate for lost wage income resulting from disability, and death (fatality) compensation, which is paid to surviving dependents of workers who have died as the result of an occupationally related injury or disease.

While all states pay some form of both types of cash benefits, there are substantial differences among states with respect to their structure and form as well as generosity. Within jurisdictions, benefits can vary significantly among claimants, depending on factors such as the claimant's wage, age, extent and type of disability, and family status. These complexities in benefit structure among states make interjurisdictional comparisons difficult.

In this appendix, we describe a cash benefits index used in the regression analyses reported in Chapters 4 through 8. The remainder of the appendix is divided into seven sections. The first section describes the calculation of a state-specific wage index that is independent of the state's industrial composition. The next outlines a fourfold classification scheme that characterizes the workers' compensation benefit structure. In the following four sections, the methodology used to calculate benefits for each of these categories is described.[1] In the final section, we describe the calculation of the overall cash benefit index.

WAGE INDEX

With few exceptions, compensation benefits for all benefit categories are paid in the form of weekly or monthly payments made to claimants. The amount of these periodic payments is typically based on the claimant's pre-injury weekly or monthly wage. As a result, to calculate the benefit index, it was first necessary to estimate the average weekly or monthly wage for each jurisdiction. While statewide average wage measures are readily available from a number of sources, these are problematic. Since states are heterogeneous with respect to industrial mix and since wages vary substantially across industries, the statewide average wage reflects differences in sectoral composition.

To control for these differences in industrial mix, we used average wages for one- and two-digit industries from the U.S. Bureau of Labor Statistics (BLS) to calculate a weighted statewide wage index for each year and state in the sample. Specifically, this index, designated as I_{Wst}, is equal to

$$I_{Wst} = \Sigma \left[(w_{ist}/W_{it}) \times n_{it}\right]/\Sigma n_{it}$$

where

w_{ist} = the average wage for the ith industry in the sth state in the tth year,

W_{it} = the national average wage for the ith industry in the tth year, and

n_{it} = national employment in the ith industry in the tth year.

Two indices are calculated for each state and year, a one-digit index and a two-digit index. Unfortunately, data for the same set of one- or two-digit industries were unavailable for every state for every year. As a result, different sets of industries were used to calculate the average wage for different states.

The wage adjusted for industrial mix was obtained by multiplying the state average weekly wage in employment covered by the unemployment insurance program by either the one-or two-digit wage index described in the previous paragraph. If the number of one-digit industries for which data are available for a particular state and year exceed the number of two-digit industries for which data are available for that state and year, then the one-digit index was employed; otherwise, the two-digit index was used.

BENEFIT STRUCTURE

As previously indicated, cash benefits paid by workers' compensation programs fall into two primary types: *fatality benefits*, which are paid to the surviving dependents of workers who have been killed as the result of an occupational injury or disease, and *disability benefits*, which are paid to workers who are unable to work as the result of a workplace injury or disease. Disability benefits may be further categorized, according to a threefold scheme based on the severity and permanency of the compensation claimant's injury.

Workers who experience disabling injuries will, if they satisfy eligibility criteria, receive temporary total disability (TTD) benefits until they return to work or until the date of maximum medical improvement (MMI), that is, the date at which their condition is not expected to further improve.[2] At this point, the overwhelming majority of workers will have recovered and returned to work with no further lost wages. However, some workers will continue to experience permanent consequences of the injury, e.g., a worker whose arm has been amputated. If so, the severity of these consequences is evaluated at this point. Those workers who are judged to be totally unable to work will receive permanent total disability (PTD) benefits. Workers who continue to experience permanent consequences but retain some wage-earning capacity are considered to be partially disabled and receive permanent partial disability (PPD) benefits.

With few exceptions, compensation benefits for all benefit categories are paid in the form of weekly or monthly payments made to claimants for a period that varies according to the duration or severity of disability (in the case of disability benefits) or according to the duration of dependency (in the case of fatality benefits). Consequently, we calculate the expected award for each benefit category by separately estimating the weekly payment and benefit duration for the average claimant in each benefit category in a particular jurisdiction and in a particular year.

TEMPORARY TOTAL DISABILITY BENEFITS

Weekly Benefits

Typically, weekly benefits for TTD claims are equal to a proportion of the injured worker's pre-injury wages, subject to a maximum and minimum. For example, in 1995, TTD claimants in Alabama received benefits equal to 66.67 percent of preinjury wages up to a maximum weekly benefit of $427. In addition, Alabama TTD claimants in 1995 did not receive less than $118 unless their actual wages were less than $118, in which case they received their actual preinjury wages as benefits. However, in other jurisdictions the minimum is absolute, so claimants may not receive less than the statutory minimum even if their pre-injury wage was less than the minimum.

To compute average weekly benefits, it is necessary to construct a representative wage distribution for each jurisdiction to account for the proportion of workers who are earning wages above the maximum and below the minimum, as well as the average wage paid to workers between these two points. We use a national wage distribution supplied by the National Council of Compensation Insurance and centered on the state average weekly wage, the calculation of which was described in the previous section.[3] It is important to note that since the average wage varies among states, the wage distribution will similarly vary, so that the average weekly benefit will differ from state to state even though statutory benefit parameters are identical. This distribution permits us to compute benefits for each claimant in this distribution and use this benefit distribution to obtain a representative average weekly benefit for all workers' compensation claimants in the state.

In several jurisdictions, weekly benefits vary according to the claimant's family status. For example, both the replacement rate and the benefit minimum vary according to the claimant's marital status and the number of dependent children in Washington. In other jurisdictions, claimants receive an additional flat rate amount for a dependent spouse or child, so that claimants with dependents in Arizona receive an additional $25 per month per dependent. Unfortunately, we lack information concerning the distribution of TTD claimants by family status, so we are forced to rely on a fatal injury distribution that provides such data. For those states in which benefits vary by family status, we first calculated an average benefit for each household type and then computed a single average weekly benefit for all TTD claimants using the family status proportions as weights.[4]

In a handful of states, benefits are computed as a proportion of spendable earnings (as opposed to gross earnings), so that it was necessary to calculate after-tax wages. This was done by determining the amount of state and federal income tax withholding as well as FICA for each claimant in our wage distribution and then subtracting this amount from the gross wage. Since income tax withholding varies by the number of claimed exemptions, it was necessary to derive a distribution of compensation claims that vary by the number of income tax exemptions. Once again, we used the family status distribution for fatal injuries and assumed that the number of dependent exemptions was equal to the number of minor children in the household. Based on these assumptions, we calculated spendable earnings and the weekly benefit amount for each claimant in the wage distribution for each family status category. An overall average weekly TTD benefit was computed using frequencies from the family status and wage distributions as weights.

Benefit Duration

The principal parameters affecting TTD benefit duration are the waiting and retroactive periods. In all jurisdictions, the claimant must experience a minimum duration of lost-time disability before he or she becomes eligible for benefits. This eligibility criterion is known as a *waiting period*. Furthermore, in most jurisdictions, the claimant then receives benefits for the waiting period if his or her disability exceeds the *retroactive period*, at which time these benefits are paid retroactively. In addition, a few states limit the duration of TTD, in the form of a maximum number of weeks (or months) of benefit payments, an aggregate dollar award, or a maximum age.

To account for differences in limits across jurisdictions, we employ a distribution of the duration of TTD, in days, obtained from the NCCI. However, since a very few TTD claims have a duration in excess of 100 weeks, we ignore TTD limits greater than this.

PERMANENT TOTAL DISABILITY BENEFITS

Weekly Benefits

In most states, the weekly permanent total disability benefit is identical to that paid to TTD claims. In only a few jurisdictions (California, Illinois, Massachusetts, Minnesota, Ohio, Texas, Utah, and Wyoming) are there any differences between the TTD and PTD weekly benefit formulae. However, in those states, the method used to compute the weekly PTD benefit is substantially the same as that used to calculate TTD claim benefits described previously.

There are two differences between the weekly benefit calculations for TTD and PTD benefits. Both relate to the nature and size of the claimant's household and both require the use of the family status distribution for fatal injuries, which was described previously. As noted earlier, a few jurisdictions pay differential benefits to claimants with dependents; that is, claimants with dependent children receive higher weekly benefits than claimants without children. Once the children reach the age of majority, as defined in the statute, benefits are reduced. Since PTD claimants in some jurisdictions can receive benefits for life, it is necessary to compute two weekly benefit amounts, one that is a measure of the benefit the claimant receives while his or her children are still minors (as defined by the workers' compensation statute) and a second that is a measure of the weekly benefits due after the children have reached the age of majority.[5]

Additionally, in several jurisdictions, PTD benefits are offset by Social Security disability or retirement benefits.[6] To calculate these benefits, we make a number of simplifying assumptions. First, we assumed that all claimants had earned a sufficient number of quarters of coverage to satisfy Social Security eligibility requirements. We further assume that the claimant's wages on the date of injury are an accurate reflection of his or her earnings over the course of the working life (adjusted for inflation), so that the weekly wage rate in the wage distribution can act as a proxy for the Average Indexed Monthly Earnings (AIME). Because Social Security benefits vary by family status, we made separate calculations for each family status category, using the household distribution described previously. Using this information, we calculated the Social Security benefits received by each claimant in our sample. These benefits were subtracted from the weekly workers' compensation PTD benefit according to the particular offset provisions in effect in the state.[7] Because the timing of Social Security benefits typically differs from the workers' compensation PTD benefit, it was necessary to compute two or more weekly benefit amounts, including a weekly PTD benefit offset by Social Security benefits and a monthly amount that is not offset.[8]

Benefit Duration

In most states, permanent total disability benefits are paid for the duration of disability or for the remainder of the claimant's life. To simplify calculations, we are assuming that these two periods are identical. Since the payment period is over the course of the claimant's life, it is necessary to incorporate assumptions about claimant life expectancy, which requires an age distribution for PTD claims. An age distribution, supplied by the NCCI, was used to compute the average PTD duration. Because money has a time value, it was also necessary to discount future benefit payments in order to obtain an appropriate present value for a PTD claim. To calculate PTD duration, we used standard actuarial techniques to calculate the present value of a one-dollar annuity paid for life, using the 1979–1981 Decennial Census Life Table for the Total Population (U.S. Department of Health and Human Services 1985) and assuming a 3.5 percent discount rate. Where statutory limitations on the duration or total amount of PTD benefits apply, these were incorporated into our annuity calculations.

Where more than one weekly benefit applies to a claimant, either due to Social Security offsets or differential benefits for dependents, we calculated a different duration for each weekly amount using actuarial techniques.

PERMANENT PARTIAL DISABILITY BENEFITS

Weekly Benefits

There is considerably greater interstate variation in the structure of weekly benefits for permanent partial disability claims than in the structure of PTD or TTD weekly benefits. In some states, the PPD benefit formula is substantially the same as the PTD and TTD formula, although specifics such as the replacement rate, the benefit minimum, or the maximum may be different. In other states, the replacement rate may vary according to the extent of the claimant's functional impairment, while in still others, benefits are expressed as a proportion of the claimant's wage loss or loss of earning capacity. Some states do not pay PPD claimants a weekly or monthly benefit but instead provide compensation in the form of a lump-sum payment.

Where weekly benefits vary by functional impairment, it is necessary to account for this by using a national distribution of PPD claim severity supplied by the NCCI. This distribution contains information on a set of PPD claims that vary by body part.[9] For each type of PPD, these data indicate the average extent of functional impairment, the average claimant age, the average duration of temporary total disability that preceded the attainment of maximum medical improvement, and the relative frequency of occurrence.[10] Where benefits vary by lost earning capacity, we assume that lost wage-earning capacity is equivalent to functional impairment, so that the same distribution was used for these jurisdictions. In a handful of states (such as California, Montana, and New Mexico), the functional impairment rating is translated into a disability rating using modifying factors like claimant age, occupation, etc. For these states, data from distributions with respect to each modifying factor were combined, based on the statutory formula, to produce a disability rating distribution.[11] Finally, an actual wage-loss distribution was constructed combining actual wage-loss data from Florida, California, and Wisconsin with the NCCI PPD distribution.[12]

In all cases, information from the appropriate impairment, disability, or wage-loss distribution was combined with the wage distribution data so that an average benefit was first calculated for each category of PPD claim. These individual claim averages were then combined, based on the relative frequency of the PPD claim category, to produce a single PPD weekly benefit for each state and year. Once again, benefits in some states may vary due to the family status of the claimant, either because benefits are computed as a proportion of spendable earnings, or because there is a Social Security retirement offset, or because differential benefits are paid to claimants with a dependent spouse or children. In these instances, an algorithm similar to that described for TTD and PTD claims was used; i.e., an average weekly benefit is determined for each type of household, and the results are aggregated using the fatal injury family status distribution.

Benefit Duration

In general, the rules applying to PPD duration differ for what are termed "scheduled" and "nonscheduled" injuries. Most state statutes provide a schedule of injuries, which lists various members or sensory organs (i.e., arm, leg, hand, foot, fingers, toes, eye, ears) with a corresponding maximum benefit duration (in weeks or months) for each.[13] Benefit duration for a particular injury to one of these members or sensory organs is obtained by multiplying the scheduled maximum duration by the extent of functional impairment for that member or organ. For example, a claimant who experienced a 50 percent loss of the arm in New York would receive benefits for 50% × 312 = 156 weeks. The duration of PPD benefits for injuries that are not on this schedule ("nonscheduled injuries") is usually determined in one of two ways. In many states, there is a specified duration for injuries that are not included in the schedule, in which case the determination of benefit duration is identical to that used for scheduled claims. In other jurisdictions, PPD benefits are paid for the duration of wage loss, the duration of lost earning capacity, or the duration of disability. In these instances, we assumed lifetime benefits unless there was a statutory age limit.

Since PPD benefits may extend over a lengthy period, we made an actuarial determination of PPD duration similar to that for PTD claims, assuming that benefits cease upon the death of the claimant. In other words, we estimate the present discounted value of an annuity paid for the statutory duration or until death, whichever comes first, assuming a 3.5 percent discount rate and life expectancies as estimated from the 1979–1981 U.S. Decennial Census. As indicated, the PPD distribution contains information on average age for each PPD type, which was used in these calculations.

Because TTD benefits are paid to PPD claims, it was necessary to calculate the average healing period as well. Healing-period data from the PPD distribution of the NCCI were used to compute a weighted average for the state and year, where the relative frequency of the PPD claim types served as weights. Some states limit healing-period duration, so that it was necessary to recalculate the average healing period. That is, if the average healing period for a particular type of PPD claim when there are no restrictions on the duration of the healing period is, for example, 52 weeks, and if the healing period for a particular state is limited to 52 weeks, then we may expect that the average healing period in this state will be less than 52 weeks.[14]

To obtain an estimate of the total benefits paid to PPD claims, we added 1) the product of the average PPD duration and the average weekly PPD benefit and 2) the product of the average healing period and the average weekly TTD benefit. In some states, benefits are paid in the form of a lump sum; for these jurisdictions, the NCCI PPD distribution was used to obtain estimates of the average lump-sum amount. Finally, some states pay more than one benefit, sometimes concurrently and sometimes consecutively. In these instances, we calculate each benefit separately and combine the results to obtain an overall average benefit for PPD claims.

FATALITY BENEFITS

Weekly Benefits

In general, the fatal-injury weekly benefit is calculated in a manner similar to that used to calculate the TTD or PTD weekly benefit: that is, weekly benefits are equal to a proportion of the deceased worker's pre-injury wage, subject to a minimum and maximum. Weekly fatality benefits depend on the characteristics of the deceased worker's family situation to a greater extent than was the case for TTD, PTD, and PPD claims. As before, we account for these differences among states by calculating average benefits for each household type in the fatal-injury family status distribution and then taking a weighted average. Similarly, we also account for variation due to Social Security survivor benefit offsets and taxes in states that use spendable earnings as a basis for benefits. The fact that the weekly benefit could change as children reach the age of majority required the computation of two or more weekly benefit figures.

Benefit Duration

In most jurisdictions, benefits are paid for the period of dependency, which is assumed to be until death or remarriage.[15] Thus, our duration calculation is similar to that used to calculate PTD or PPD duration; that is, we use actuarial techniques to account for life expectancy and the probability of remarriage.[16] Where applicable, statutory limitations with respect to benefit duration were factored into our calculations.

Since many states provide claimants who remarry with a lump-sum payment—typically 104 weeks of benefits—it was also necessary to compute this amount. In addition, all states with the exception of Oklahoma pay funeral expenses up to a maximum. To account for this we assumed that the maximum amount was paid in every case. Finally, a few states pay a lump sum in addition to other benefits. To obtain an average benefit for the state, we take the sum of each, including the periodic pension.

TOTAL BENEFITS

To obtain an overall measure of benefit generosity, the separate components described above were combined using the relative frequency of each type of benefit as weights. A national injury distribution was used for this purpose. The results of this exercise for the jurisdictions used in this study for the years 1975 to 1995 are reported in Table D.1

Table D.1 Real Expected Benefits, 1975–95 ($)

	Ala.	Alaska	Ariz.	Ark.	Calif.	Colo.	Conn.	Del.	D.C.	Fla.	Ga.	Hawaii
1975	1,817	5,217	5,451	2,060	1,997	1,598	4,050	3,003	7,400	2,214	1,909	3,462
1976	2,418	13,106	5,632	2,099	2,026	2,054	4,302	3,750	8,051	2,435	2,343	3,689
1977	2,598	12,873	5,853	2,404	2,255	2,129	4,620	3,907	8,558	2,568	2,406	3,905
1978	2,822	8,917	6,639	2,589	2,300	2,213	5,415	4,049	9,184	2,682	2,464	4,175
1979	3,038	8,950	7,050	2,752	2,354	2,346	6,591	5,736	9,865	2,796	3,735	4,472
1980	3,265	9,426	7,453	3,384	2,407	2,657	7,669	6,217	10,784	2,669	3,913	4,833
1981	3,543	9,877	8,023	3,776	2,600	2,853	8,363	6,624	11,821	3,670	4,062	5,216
1982	3,801	10,395	8,199	4,128	2,641	3,061	9,043	7,274	12,928	3,907	4,273	5,518
1983	4,046	10,484	8,350	4,468	3,531	3,116	9,566	7,678	12,943	4,636	4,825	5,801
1984	4,247	10,436	8,492	4,530	3,871	3,206	10,133	8,061	13,550	4,793	4,922	6,065
1985	4,447	10,309	8,617	4,577	3,917	3,325	10,853	8,328	14,061	5,349	5,013	6,289
1986	5,391	10,162	8,767	4,632	3,980	3,442	11,460	8,481	14,790	5,549	5,544	6,512
1987	5,631	10,177	8,887	4,884	4,000	3,526	12,195	8,853	16,218	5,807	6,055	6,933
1988	5,851	10,222	10,284	5,021	4,032	3,600	14,257	9,176	17,558	6,043	6,174	7,411
1989	6,032	9,671	10,369	5,196	4,053	4,240	14,829	9,718	18,610	6,211	6,246	7,967
1990	6,280	9,694	11,019	5,495	4,382	4,366	15,631	10,246	19,511	6,090	6,363	8,482
1991	6,499	9,765	11,235	5,642	4,922	4,479	16,445	10,825	20,532	4,185	7,460	8,947
1992	6,823	9,853	12,409	5,893	5,071	6,663	15,480	11,374	21,936	4,388	7,675	11,729
1993	6,224	9,918	12,536	6,040	5,105	6,829	15,851	11,699	23,534	4,438	8,183	13,010
1994	6,386	9,941	12,750	6,290	5,105	6,974	11,297	12,090	24,129	5,464	8,247	13,503
1995	6,527	9,950	12,995	6,413	5,589	7,303	11,636	12,442	25,157	5,630	8,806	13,750

	Idaho	Ill.	Ind.	Iowa	Kans.	Ky.	La.	Maine	Md.	Mass.	Mich.	Minn.
1975	2,957	3,007	1,494	2,580	3,875	6,329	1,324	19,329	2,123	6,201	2,884	2,697
1976	3,385	4,517	1,499	3,382	4,054	6,795	1,943	21,145	3,004	6,315	3,357	3,245
1977	3,708	4,928	1,597	3,729	4,262	7,843	2,180	22,176	3,362	7,539	3,701	3,271
1978	4,086	5,275	1,908	4,233	4,677	8,425	2,666	23,977	3,600	7,992	4,120	4,580
1979	4,298	5,583	1,918	4,614	4,863	9,135	2,856	25,900	3,898	9,020	4,521	4,965
1980	4,533	6,116	2,096	5,046	5,647	9,952	3,122	28,886	4,268	9,478	4,951	5,340
1981	4,939	6,472	2,181	5,348	6,209	4,862	3,452	31,152	4,479	9,943	5,288	5,758
1982	5,387	6,821	2,193	5,557	6,585	5,188	3,770	33,365	4,848	11,757	5,765	6,139
1983	5,850	7,086	2,199	5,758	6,860	5,442	3,970	35,020	5,143	12,521	6,028	6,423
1984	6,103	7,370	2,325	5,982	5,568	5,682	2,755	36,733	5,450	13,775	6,325	7,852
1985	6,373	7,405	2,403	6,120	5,746	5,802	2,799	38,042	5,717	14,561	6,634	8,072
1986	6,553	7,636	2,490	6,289	5,954	5,971	3,141	20,186	6,017	15,090	6,909	8,283
1987	6,764	7,892	2,579	6,678	6,107	6,147	3,206	21,270	6,385	16,100	7,224	8,524
1988	6,898	8,297	2,595	6,900	5,916	6,313	3,293	10,097	6,526	17,177	7,558	8,827
1989	7,094	8,546	3,369	7,065	6,020	6,482	3,344	10,506	6,843	17,920	7,724	8,996
1990	7,348	8,938	3,621	7,336	6,166	6,758	3,481	11,017	7,197	18,868	7,907	9,260
1991	7,569	9,213	3,874	7,546	6,297	6,970	3,595	11,360	7,481	19,637	8,085	9,479
1992	7,978	9,728	4,752	7,995	6,487	7,348	3,729	10,691	7,829	12,524	8,450	9,848
1993	8,254	9,950	5,412	8,270	6,372	7,503	3,796	10,721	8,129	12,835	8,755	9,844
1994	8,618	10,237	5,969	8,558	11,536	7,765	3,901	10,910	8,316	13,197	9,136	10,079
1995	8,889	10,582	6,118	8,811	11,689	7,978	4,008	11,193	8,522	13,731	9,535	10,350

(continued)

Table D.1 (continued)

	Miss.	Mo.	Mont.	N.H.	N.J.	N.Mex.	N.Y.	N.C.	N. Dak.	Ohio	Okla.	Oreg.
1975	2,441	2,164	1,816	3,958	2,203	2,675	4,859	1,548	3,303	2,153	1,526	2,199
1976	2,489	2,198	2,094	4,530	2,292	3,228	5,070	2,195	3,509	2,808	1,535	2,398
1977	3,202	2,226	2,306	4,834	2,389	3,838	5,285	2,339	3,608	2,993	1,543	2,493
1978	3,448	2,252	2,458	5,206	2,478	4,427	5,694	2,506	3,542	3,225	1,549	2,700
1979	3,545	2,656	2,671	5,667	2,593	5,066	6,466	2,692	3,743	3,636	2,733	2,929
1980	3,825	2,756	2,830	6,216	3,349	5,576	6,928	2,932	3,795	3,940	3,081	3,211
1981	3,926	3,009	3,122	6,767	3,520	6,135	7,393	3,175	3,946	4,228	3,495	3,344
1982	4,399	3,421	3,385	7,406	4,000	6,606	7,852	3,444	4,053	4,525	4,409	3,549
1983	4,437	3,643	3,619	7,931	4,311	6,921	8,187	3,678	4,206	4,817	4,821	3,635
1984	4,468	4,530	3,764	8,828	4,629	7,203	8,879	3,855	5,360	5,030	5,120	3,715
1985	4,913	4,748	3,866	9,167	4,898	7,437	9,443	4,045	5,392	5,261	5,256	3,769
1986	5,144	4,952	3,935	9,754	5,172	7,587	10,095	4,224	5,569	5,405	5,255	4,124
1987	5,383	5,237	4,016	10,393	5,481	7,659	10,561	4,422	5,617	6,942	5,221	4,199
1988	5,429	5,413	7,271	11,124	5,848	6,945	11,128	4,721	5,696	7,177	5,489	4,477
1989	6,932	5,590	7,342	11,512	6,205	7,108	11,349	4,897	5,740	7,912	5,524	4,576
1990	7,172	5,791	7,499	12,081	6,734	7,330	11,796	5,085	8,343	8,262	5,588	4,719
1991	7,407	6,587	7,671	12,623	6,989	10,112	13,414	5,288	8,571	8,461	5,899	6,261
1992	7,731	7,004	4,441	13,258	7,441	10,478	14,798	5,580	8,890	8,765	5,959	6,459
1993	7,962	7,343	4,592	13,401	7,758	10,871	15,444	5,723	9,122	9,087	6,212	6,656
1994	8,222	7,619	4,708	13,754	8,193	11,200	15,554	5,923	9,484	9,479	6,678	7,049
1995	8,501	7,844	4,818	11,919	8,367	11,496	16,108	6,148	9,722	9,711	6,504	7,269

	Pa.	R.I.	S.C.	S.Dak.	Tenn.	Texas	Utah	Vt.	Va.	Wash.	W.Va.	Wisc.
1975	5,592	7,050	2,038	1,740	1,681	2,224	2,810	1,765	3,414	2,607	2,852	2,895
1976	7,241	7,727	2,210	2,067	1,978	2,274	3,379	1,883	4,495	3,547	3,364	3,428
1977	7,724	8,023	2,712	2,370	2,012	2,491	3,556	2,335	4,830	3,717	3,711	3,539
1978	6,603	8,547	2,968	2,650	2,309	2,884	3,525	4,295	5,121	3,879	3,958	3,925
1979	8,867	9,249	3,301	3,070	2,362	3,284	4,069	4,639	5,598	4,092	4,424	4,078
1980	9,602	10,081	3,592	3,394	2,542	3,703	4,213	4,986	6,068	5,650	4,731	4,343
1981	10,423	10,838	3,913	3,696	2,813	4,232	4,560	5,381	6,586	5,921	5,181	4,539
1982	11,047	11,563	4,160	3,922	2,981	4,778	4,865	5,853	7,089	6,126	5,477	5,407
1983	11,611	12,868	4,494	4,146	3,201	5,380	5,132	6,277	7,609	6,259	5,746	5,448
1984	12,137	13,421	4,693	4,275	3,233	5,579	5,335	6,612	8,106	6,334	6,030	5,871
1985	12,650	13,933	4,901	4,412	3,261	5,907	5,447	6,961	8,503	6,389	6,106	6,224
1986	13,128	14,643	5,075	4,555	3,862	6,181	5,545	7,322	8,963	6,495	6,274	6,451
1987	13,746	15,806	5,291	4,690	4,251	6,364	5,657	8,261	9,432	7,972	6,433	6,709
1988	14,463	16,863	5,497	4,856	4,607	6,570	5,805	8,658	9,966	8,117	6,603	6,957
1989	15,062	17,641	5,831	5,270	4,935	6,763	5,850	9,050	10,369	8,766	6,747	7,158
1990	15,797	18,482	6,111	5,450	5,278	6,897	6,024	9,517	10,793	9,076	6,967	7,481
1991	16,382	20,015	6,337	5,630	5,634	6,760	6,199	9,827	11,313	9,333	7,121	7,767
1992	17,245	21,006	6,662	5,896	6,038	7,033	6,471	10,367	11,869	9,540	7,416	8,264
1993	17,656	9,208	6,832	5,657	6,507	7,224	6,641	10,453	12,145	9,617	7,516	8,578
1994	18,104	9,391	7,048	5,892	6,964	7,341	6,795	10,694	12,473	11,197	7,655	8,886
1995	18,750	9,619	7,836	6,664	7,353	7,553	6,955	12,482	12,915	11,659	7,755	9,198

Notes

1. States also pay cash benefits for temporary partial disability and for disfigurement, as well as benefits to claimants who are undergoing a vocational rehabilitation program. We do not consider these types of benefits in our analysis.

2. Workers' compensation programs also pay temporary partial benefits to workers who retain some earning capacity prior to the point of MMI. However, these benefits represent a tiny fraction of total benefits paid.

3. This is done by normalizing the wage distribution (which is, as indicated, a national wage distribution) by dividing each wage in the distribution by the mean. This normalized distribution is then multiplied by the average weekly wage for the state to obtain an appropriate wage distribution for each state.

4. We assume that the wage distribution is identical for each family type.

5. Several simplifying assumptions are relied upon in these calculations. First, we assume that the only change in family status occurs when dependent children reach the age of majority. In other words, we do not attempt to account for divorce, widowhood, remarriage, etc. Second, based on NCCI data, we assume that all children were 10 years of age on the date of injury. Third, in most states, children who are deemed to be mentally or physically incapacitated are considered to be dependent children for the purpose of compensation past the age of majority for the period of their incapacity. Similarly, in many states the period of dependency for students enrolled in an approved educational program is extended beyond the normal majority age. We ignore these provisions and assume that for all children, benefits terminate on the age of majority.

6. It is also possible that Social Security offsets apply to TTD or PPD benefits. However, to simplify calculations, we arbitrarily assume that no Social Security offsets apply to TTD benefits and that PPD benefits are only offset by retirement benefits.

7. In addition to Social Security benefits, several states offset workers' compensation payments by benefit payments from other social insurance programs, including unemployment insurance, as well as employer-provided disability or pension benefits. Because we lack data on the size or distribution of these other types of offsets, we ignore them in our calculations.

8. For example, Social Security disability benefits do not begin until at least five months after the onset of disability and terminate at age 62. Normal retirement benefits begin at age 65. (We assume that all claimants opt for normal-age retirement benefits.)

9. In addition to data on a set of specific body parts, such as the arm, leg, eye, etc., the distribution contained two unspecified or "nonscheduled" categories designed to capture variation in PPD severity that is not attributable to the specific or "scheduled" types of injuries.

10. Except for nonscheduled injuries, the PPD distribution from the NCCI provided data on the average extent of impairment for the specific body part. It was sometimes necessary to translate this into "whole-person" impairment. This was done using the AMA *Guides to the Evaluation of Permanent Impairment* (American

Medical Association 1984), which provide data relating the loss of the entire body part to "whole-person" impairment.

11. An age distribution was obtained by centering the NCCI's age distribution for PTDs on the age according to the PPD distribution. An occupation distribution was constructed from Current Population Survey (CPS) data. Occupationally related information—the amount of general education, specific vocational training, or physical effort required by the job—was obtained from the *Dictionary of Occupational Titles* (U.S. Department of Labor 1991) based on CPS three-digit occupation codes.

12. These wage-loss data were taken from a study by Berkowitz, Burton, and Vroman (1979), as reported in Berkowitz and Burton (1987), that examined the extent of actual wage loss among workers suffering permanent partial disability due to an occupational industry in these three states (California, Florida, and Wisconsin). This study tracked workers who had suffered injuries in 1968 for a period of six years after the injury. The authors reported post-injury wage-earnings relative to pre-injury earnings for claimant with different degrees of functional impairment. We collapsed the data into five functional impairment categories: 1) claimants who suffered an impairment between 1 and 5 percent of the whole person, 2) between 6 and 10 percent, 3) between 11 and 15 percent, 4) between 16 and 50 percent, and 5) between 51 and 100 percent. Based on functional impairment ratings, these wage-loss data were matched with the PPD distribution from the NCCI, to establish a wage-loss distribution comparable to the functional impairment or disability distributions used in other states.

13. Some schedules go beyond these members or organs and list other body parts, e.g., testicles. Since these parts are not included in the NCCI PPD distribution, they were ignored, as were scheduled amounts for injuries to multiple body parts (such as two fingers) and distinctions between left and right members.

14. This recalculation of the average healing period was done by assuming that the healing period distribution had the same shape as the distribution of TTD duration except that it is centered on the healing-period average. In other words, first the TTD distribution was first normalized on the mean. This distribution was then converted to a healing-period distribution for a particular PPD type by multiplying the normalized scores by the average healing period for that type. Any duration greater than the maximum was then assigned the maximum value, and a new average healing period was calculated.

15. Dependent beneficiaries under most state statutes include a surviving spouse and children, but also other family relationships (such as parents, siblings, grandparents, and grandchildren) where a demonstrable dependency existed upon the deceased worker. Our calculations ignore benefits to persons (including orphan children) other than the surviving spouse and his or her minor children. According to NCCI data, the beneficiaries we include in our calculations account for nearly 93 percent of actual fatality benefit recipients.

16. Once again, we assume a 3.5 percent discount rate. Remarriage probabilities were derived from a 1979 NCCI study.

Appendix E

The Insurance Cycle

Historical data show that various measures of prices, profitability, and availability of policies for property and liability insurance (such as premium growth and the combined ratio) exhibit a distinct and fairly regular cycle that is approximately six years in length (Venezian 1985). Butler and Worrall (1990) found state-specific cycles in premiums and losses for workers' compensation insurance over the period 1954–1983; these varied substantially among states, from about 4 to 40 years for losses and from about 7 to 124 years for premiums.[1] Evidence regarding the existence and length of workers' compensation insurance cycles is also provided by data from our study period (see Chapter 2, Figure 2.5, and Chapter 3, Figures 3.2 and 3.4, which depict movement in the cost of workers' compensation and underwriting results).

An understanding of the dynamic nature of insurance pricing is important for two reasons. First, it points out the need to control for cycle effects in empirical research. If deregulation occurs concurrent with a cyclical decline in prices, an investigator could misinterpret this price change as the effect of deregulation. Alternatively, a cyclical increase in insurance prices could mask the impact of deregulation on costs. Fortunately, the data set employed in our analysis is sufficiently long to permit us to control for the effects of the insurance cycle. Second, an understanding of the dynamic of insurance pricing can shed light on the market effects of various insurance arrangements.

In this appendix, we briefly examine theories of the insurance cycle. As will be seen, several of these theories postulate a relationship between interest rates and insurer pricing decisions.

INSURANCE CYCLE THEORIES

There are several explanations for the existence and length of insurance cycles; these explanations fall into two categories. Theories in the first category are based on the assumption of irrationality on the part of insurers; theories in the second category attribute the cycle to rational responses to external shocks such as interest-rate changes or changes in the loss or injury distribution, or to institutional interventions such as the actions of the regulatory agency or other aspects of the rate-setting process. In this section, we summarize both theories and discuss their implications for our empirical analyses.

Models that Assume Irrationality

Cash-flow underwriting

One of the earliest hypotheses explaining the existence of insurance cycles assumes that insurers' underwriting decisions are based on interest-rate fluctuations. Since interest income represents a substantial portion of the insurers' total income, insurers' profit expectations are partially based on the interest rate. According to this theory, higher interest rates cause insurers to unduly revise upward their profit expectations for new business, leading to lower premium rates and increased insurance coverage. In other words, insurers lower premiums (to below the point at which costs may be recovered) in order to increase premiums and thereby take advantage of higher investment income on loss reserves.

Some versions of the cash-flow underwriting theory assert that insurers deliberately underestimate loss reserves when interest rates are high in order to circumvent regulatory concerns that the insurers are risking insolvency by pricing below cost. Then, as interest rates drop, insurers revise their reserves upward, resulting in lower profit expectations and constrained supply, leading to higher premium rates and reduced availability of workers' compensation coverage. (The threat of financial insolvency due to inadequate loss reserves also causes insurers to constrain supply in order to restore the surplus.)

The cost-flow underwriting hypothesis regarding the existence of insurance cycles is criticized by many economists as an unsatisfactory explanation because it postulates that insurers irrationally write policies at below-cost rates. However, Harrington and Danzon (1994) revived this model, postulating that insurers are heterogeneous in two respects. First, insurers have different incentives for solvency. A moral hazard to risk insolvency by underpricing exists due to limited-liability, risk-insensitive guaranty programs and uninformed or unconcerned consumers who cannot or do not bother to investigate the financial solvency of insurers. Second, insurers are heterogeneous with respect to their information on the nature of the loss distribution. Variation among insurers with respect to this information results in differences in loss forecasts. In either event, some insurers set rates at levels that are profitable when real interest rate are high but that cannot be sustained when interest rates fall. Competition induces excessive price-cutting that affects the entire industry.

Moral hazard

Harrington and Danzon speculated that some insurers have a weak incentive to avoid the risk of insolvency, so they set prices too low (i.e., below expected costs). This heterogeneity among insurers is due to differences among carriers with respect to the value of intangible assets (including reputation and quasi-rents on renewal business attributable to private information on insureds) and with respect to the value of nontransferable tangible assets (including the costs of attracting and screening new policyholders). Private carriers with substantial nontransferable assets have more to lose from insolvency, and they will be reluctant to risk those assets by engaging in below-cost pricing. However, firms without substantial nontransferable assets have incentives to engage in aggressive marketing efforts if there are limits on downside risks. Harrington and Danzon suggest that a number of institutional features of the property/casualty insurance market (including government-mandated guarantees of insurer obligations, long-tailed payout lags, losses that fall on third-party claimants if the insurer defaults, and regulatory detection problems) make liability insurers particularly susceptible to these moral hazard problems.

Heterogeneous information

Insurance carriers base loss-cost forecasts on both public and private information, so forecasts vary among insurers. Firms whose forecasts are low may be subject to the "winner's curse"; that is, by underbidding, low-price insurers are able to increase market share. Harrington and Danzon hypothesized that new carriers are more likely to underbid than more-experienced, established firms that have "learned to adjust their forecasts to avoid the curse."

Harrington and Danzon examined insurers' revisions of claim-cost forecasts and premium growth rates to determine the relative contribution of 1) moral hazard and 2) information heterogeneity to underpricing in general liability insurance in 1980–1982 (the period immediately prior to the liability crisis of the mid 1980s). If insurers underprice, then forecast revisions and premium growth are both expected to be inversely related to price; that is, lower insurance prices should result in larger subsequent revisions to initial loss forecasts, since insurers are more likely to underprice when prices are low. In addition, underpricing will induce increased demand and, consequently, greater premium growth. Furthermore, forecast revisions and premium growth should be positively related to one another, indicating that insurers expand business by underpricing

Harrington and Danzon found, consistent with the moral hazard hypothesis, that premium growth and forecast revisions were positively and significantly related to the amount of liabilities ceded to reinsurers. This result is expected if reinsurance induces carriers to take greater insolvency risks. Furthermore, they found that mutual companies had smaller forecast revisions and lower premium growth than stock companies, a result that is also expected if mutual insurance policyholders have less incentive to risk insolvency. On the other hand, they failed to find a relationship between insurer underpricing and measures of insurer experience, contrary to the heterogeneous information hypothesis.

Models that Assume Rational Behavior in the Face of External Shocks

Institutional lags

Another theory attributes insurance cycles to lags inherent in the rate-making and regulatory process. Unlike the cash-flow underwriting hypothesis, this theory (or, more accurately, set of theories) assumes that insurers do not deliberately underprice, but are induced to do so by inherent delays in the rate-making process or delays associated with the institutional "stickiness" of rate regulation. For example, Venezian (1985) argued that insurance bureaus forecast future loss costs on the basis of past experience and these forecasts are erroneous to the extent that they do not reflect changed conditions. Venezian's model assumed irrationality on the part of insurers who routinely fail to adjust their loss-cost predictions to account for systematic forecast error.[2]

However, Cummins and Outreville (1987) hypothesized that several institutional features—data collection lags, regulatory lags, policy renewal lags, and statutory accounting rules—are responsible for the profit cycles in insurer markets in spite of rational expectations by insurers. First, ratemaking is based on incurred loss data, although in many insurance lines (including workers' compensation), policyholder claims do not fully mature until years after the policy has expired, so that the data may not reflect all of the losses on claims occurring in a particular year. This means that cost forecasts are necessarily based on data that are incomplete and therefore inaccurate, so that these forecasts are likewise inaccurate.

Second, the administrative process involved in rate regulation creates delays between the experience and forecast periods; in other words, current rates are based on loss-cost information that is older than would be used by insurers in an unregulated market. In addition, due to administrative costs associated with the regulatory process, rates are revised less often than would be the case in an unregulated, competitive market. Third, insurance policies typically have a term of one year; instantaneous price adjustments are thus not possible because prices are "locked in" for a year at a time. Cummins and Outreville provided evidence suggesting that these lags introduce systematic error into the rate-making process. [3]

Other studies have examined the relationship between institutional lags and the variability (rather than the existence) of insurance cycles. These studies have hypothesized that regulatory lag exacerbates cycles (as measured by insurer loss ratios) by delaying rate increases in hard markets and delaying rate reductions in soft markets. As we noted in Chapter 6, some empirical research suggests that regulation increases price volatility, as measured by the loss ratio. In addition, the insurance cycle appears to have a longer period in a regulated market environment.

Capacity constraints

The capacity constraint models hypothesize that insurer underwriting capacity is constrained by information deficiencies and other imperfections in capital markets. There are several parts to this argument.

First, regulatory financial requirements, as well as consumers' desires for security and fears of insurer insolvency, limit insurers' discretion as to how extensively they may deplete surplus relative to loss reserves. Second, the cost of internal equity is less than the cost of external equity due to agency costs and dividend taxation. Agency costs in this context are the costs associated with investor (or potential investor) monitoring of insurer behavior. They arise due to informational asymmetries between insurers and potential investors (investors interpret the willingness to share profits as a signal that profits are low). Corporate taxes trap equity because the transfer of wealth from stockholders to the firm is not taxed, although dividends, which represent the transfer of wealth from firm to shareholders, are taxed.

These characteristics imply that the supply price for insurance is perfectly elastic up to the point at which insurers can no longer replace surplus from internal equity (retained earnings). (In addition, since raising new equity internally is less costly than raising it externally, insurers will prefer to keep excess capital on hand in a "soft" market to ameliorate the consequences of a future "hard" market.) However, at some point the "limited liability" constraint—where *limited liability* refers to the fact that under bankruptcy law, an incorporated insurer's liability to policyholders is limited to the corporation's net worth—becomes binding on the insurers' ability to supply coverage. That is, the maximum possible payout by the insurer is reached and the supply curve assumes an upward sloping shape, reflecting the additional cost of raising new equity in financial markets. The capacity constraint theory hypothesizes that a shock that depletes insurer surplus, such as a catastrophic loss or a change in the loss distribution, creates the insurance cycle. When capital is depleted beyond the limited liability constraint, the price of insurance rises and availability (relative to demand) declines. As the surplus is replenished and capacity restored, the price declines once again.

Cummins and Danzon (1997) extended the capacity constraint model by hypothesizing that insurers are heterogeneous with respect to insolvency risk and that insureds and insurers sort themselves according to risk and price preferences. More specifically, they postulated that insurers have different target leverage ratios (or safety levels; i.e., the ratio of equity or surplus to debt or liability) and that carriers with high surplus relative to reserves are able to charge higher prices than highly leveraged firms. Insurance carriers attempt to maintain these ratios at all times, so an external shock that depletes surplus will require the insurer to raise new equity in order to remain in its preferred quality classification. However, because new capital is used to pay old liabilities, the insurer must raise prices above the competitive equilibrium that existed before the shock in order to attract investment.[4] Individual insurers are able to do this because they possess private information about their policyholders (i.e., information about risk) that is not shared by other insurers.

Cummins and Danzon (1997) asserted that there are two reasons why prices may not immediately and fully respond to a shock that depletes surplus. First, raising prices may exacerbate adverse selection by policyholders; that is, good risks will drop insurance coverage (e.g., by self-insuring) following a price hike, while bad risks will continue to insure. As a result, price increases could cause a decline in net revenue. In response to this potential problem, insurers will ration supply by implementing (or reducing) the upper limit of coverage.[5] Availability may thus become a problem.

Cummins and Danzon offered another reason why prices may not rise immediately following a shock that depletes surplus. They claim that the entry of new carriers into the insurance market will also prevent market prices from rising to market-clearing levels, because these new firms have not incurred a shock to surplus. Since new carriers do not bear the burden of old liabilities that have increased in value for old carriers (i.e., prior reserves that were inadequate are now restated), they can charge prices that are below those charged by existing insurers. However, the ability of new entrants to attract customers is also limited by information asymmetries. New entrants are more likely than existing insurers to be uncertain about the prospective loss distribution and may face relatively greater adverse selection. Greater adverse selection is due to the risk-reduction strategies of existing carriers, who may be expected to impose or lower upper limits on coverage rather than raising prices, thus retaining low-risk insureds and losing high-risk insureds.[6]

Interest rate changes

Doherty and Kang (1988) noted that the insurance contract is a contingent promise to pay over a period of time, where insurers hold policyholder assets for a period equal, on average, to one-half the policy period. Since prices should reflect the interest earnings on the funds held by the insurer during this period, insurance prices should be expected to fall as interest rates rise and vice versa. (A corollary of this hypothesis is that long-tailed lines [that is, those with long payout periods for individual policies] should be more sensitive to interest rate changes than shorter-tailed lines.)

Doherty and Garven (1995) combined the capacity constraint model and the Doherty and Kang interest rate model. They provided evidence that rising interest rates lead to a drop in the value of the insurer's equity and thus decrease the leverage ratio. As the value of surplus declines, insurers attempt to restore the surplus/liability ratio for reasons explained by the capacity constraint model. (In other words, an interest rate increase is tantamount to a shock in the capacity constraint model.) Doherty and Garven further postulated that insurers respond to interest-rate changes by adjusting capital structure, increasing equity when interest rates fall and decreasing equity when interest rates increase. However, the response to falling or rising interest rates is asymmetrical because it is easier to pay dividends when equity is too great than to raise new capital when the surplus has been depleted.

Doherty and Garven presented evidence of capacity constraints in insurance markets. Among other things, they showed that there is an asymmetrical response to falling and rising interest rates; as predicted, underwriting profits are more responsive to falling than to rising interest rates. They also showed that firms with more costly access to new capital are more sensitive to interest rate changes. As was noted by Cummins, Harrington, and Klein (1991, p. 70) ". . . the Doherty-Garven results imply that interest rates changes may be the triggering mechanism shifting the market between hard and soft periods."

CONCLUSIONS

Insurance pricing has a dynamic quality. Specifically, time-series data show a cyclical regularity for various insurance market outcomes, including prices. The explanations offered to account for this regularity can be grouped into two categories: theories assuming insurer irrationality and theories assuming rational behavior in the face of external shocks. One "irrationality" hypothesis posits that insurers cut prices excessively when real interest rates are high. Another suggests that imperfections in financial markets, such as agency costs and dividend taxation, prevent funds from freely flowing into insurance markets, so that an external shock that depletes capital (such as falling interest rates) results in a price increase. Yet another theory postulates that institutional delays (and, in particular, delays in the regulatory process) are responsible for price fluctuations. It is important to note that these different theories are not mutually exclusive and that each explanation may have some validity.

Among other things, these hypotheses all suggest the importance of controlling for these cyclical changes in our empirical work. They also provide some clues that will aid our understanding of the results of our analyses, which are discussed in Chapters 5 through 8.

Notes

1. However, Butler and Worrall (1990) were unable to detect a cycle using a data set that pooled observations for and imposed an identical autoregressive structure on all states in their sample.
2. Venezian hypothesized that this systematic error is due to autocorrelation in the time-series data used to predict loss costs, i.e., the fact that the error term in the current period is systematically related to past error.
3. Specifically, Cummins and Outreville concluded that these lags introduced first- or second-order autocorrelation into insurance forecasts.
4. Cummins and Danzon hypothesized that there are three sources of risk for the potential investor: 1) inadequacy of prior loss reserves, 2) parameter uncertainty for the prospective loss distribution and nonindependence of risks, and 3) sampling or selection risk. Risk-averse potential investors will be reluctant to invest when prices are at competitive levels because "normal" profits do not compensate these new investors for their increased risk.
5. Cummins and Danzon claimed that lowering coverage limits—as opposed to increasing deductibles—is an optimal strategy if policyholders are heterogeneous and this heterogeneity takes the form of a "mean-preserving" spread. That is, expected loss is identical across policyholders but varies with respect to the dispersion: high-risk insureds have a loss distribution with a greater variance than low-risk insureds, although the means of these two distributions are equal. In such a world, deductibles create an adverse selection for insurers, as low-risk insureds will choose to decline coverage and high-risk insureds will choose to accept coverage; upper limits on coverage would create a positive selection, i.e., upper coverage limits would induce low-risk insureds to seek coverage and high-risk insureds to decline it. In fact, Danzon and Cummins predicted that in the face of heterogeneous risks of this type, insurers are likely to offer two types of policies that force high-risk insureds to reveal themselves: high premium coverage without an upper limit and a low premium coverage with an upper limit.
6. By imposing or lowering coverage, the insurer increases the expected losses for all insureds. High-risk insureds exit the market when coverage limits are imposed or lowered, because their expected losses if insured are now greater than their expected losses if uninsured.

Appendix F

Insurance Commission Survey

The regulatory environment for workers' compensation insurance is complex. Unfortunately, there is no single source that authoritatively defines the dimensions of compensation insurance rate regulation or comprehensively identifies the regulatory rules in effect in specific states. Consequently, specific indices of the regulatory environment were developed for this study after a review of the rate regulation literature.

State-specific values for these indices were determined through a survey of state insurance commissioners. The following survey instrument and accompanying cover letter were sent to insurance commissioners in all 45 jurisdictions that regulate private workers' compensation insurance. Responses were received from 41 of these state insurance commissions. In some instances, follow-up phone calls were made to survey respondents for clarification.

Exhibit F.1 Cover Letter

[date]

Marianne K. Burke
Director
Dept. of Commerce & Economic Development
Alaska Division of Insurance
P. O. Box 110805
Juneau, Alaska
99811-0805

Dear Director Burke:

I am writing to request your assistance in a study that Terry Thomason of McGill University, Tim Schmidle of Cornell University, and I are conducting of interstate differences in workers' compensation costs sponsored by the W.E. Upjohn Institute for Employment Research. Since the regulatory environment of the workers' compensation insurance market is an important variable explaining compensation costs, we are interested in constructing measures of this environment for each state for the period contemplated by the study, i.e., 1975-1995. (Other explanatory variables, such as the level of cash and medical benefits, will also be included in our analyses.)

It is important to have accurate data on these regulatory environment variables. Thus, we are asking for your assistance in verifying our understanding of the nature of the regulation of workers' compensation insurance markets in your state.

We would very much appreciate a response by December 31, 1997. If you have any questions, you may contact Terry Thomason at his **home (xxx) xxx-xxxx** or **office (514) xxx-xxxx**. He may also be reached via e-mail at

thomason@management.mcgill.ca.

In return for your assistance, we will be happy to share our results with you once the study is completed.

Thanks for your assistance.

Sincerely

John F. Burton, Jr.

Exhibit F.2 Survey Instrument

We use five variables to classify the regulatory environment for workers' compensation insurers: (1) prior approval, (2) adherence, (3) the role of the regulatory agency, (4) deviations, and (5) schedule rating. A detailed description of each of these variables is provided below. For each, we are interested in the actual practice in your state's workers' compensation market during the year in question. That is, we are interested in implementation -- *in the policies that were actually implemented by the regulatory agency* -- as opposed to what may be contained in the statute or in agency regulations. In addition, since the regulatory practice may have changed during the year, we have arbitrarily categorized a state based on our understanding of the practice *in effect at the beginning of the year, that is, on January 1.*

1. **Prior approval:** We classify states into one of three categories: prior approval required (PRIOR), file and use (FILE), and use and file (USE). A state is assigned to the PRIOR category if it requires that rates must be approved by the regulatory agency before the insurer is allowed to use them. This category would include states that have deemer provisions whereby the rates are deemed to be approved if they are not denied within a specified number of days. FILE states require insurers to file their rates with the regulatory agency on or before they come into effect; no specific approval is required but the agency retains the right to disapprove the rates at a later date. In USE states, while the insurer must still file rates, the insurer may begin using those rates before they are filed with the regulatory agency.

2. **Adherence:** We classify states into two categories: advisory (ADV) or required (REQ). States that require that member insurers adhere to the full manual rates or loss costs filed by the rating/advisory organization are classified as REQ, while states that do not have such a requirement are classified as ADV.

3. **Role of the regulatory agency:** We classify states into two categories: lost costs (LOSS) or full manual rates (RATES). In LOSS states the rating/advisory organization may only file lost costs (or pure premiums) with the state regulatory agency, and individual insurers are responsible for developing their own expense provisions – which normally include acquisition costs, general overhead expenses, premium taxes, other fees and assessments, plus a profit and contingency margin. In RATES states, the rating/advisory organization either files full manual rates, including expense loadings, instead of loss costs or the rating/advisory organization separately files expense and profit factors.

4. **Deviations:** We classify states into two categories: deviation (DEV) or no deviation (NODEV). States that allow member insurers to deviate from the rating/advisory organization rates – upon receiving permission from the state regulatory agency are classified as DEV. States that do not permit deviations are classified as NODEV. If the state files loss costs, it is classified as NA.

5. **Schedule rating:** We classify states into two categories: schedule rating (SCHED) or no schedule rating (NOSCHD). States that allow insurers to modify the premium of an individual risk to reflect characteristics of the risk – such as the condition of the premises, the rigor of the employer's selection, training and supervision policies, and/or the provision of safety equipment or medical facilities -- that are not reflected in its experience are classified as SCHED. States that do not permit insurers to modify the premiums of individual risks are classified as NOSCHD states.

On the following page, we have reproduced our understanding of the regulatory environment in effect in your state from 1975 to 1995, according to variable definitions provided above.

1. Please indicate whether we have miscategorized the regulatory environment for workers' compensation in your state. You may do so by correcting the table we have provided by writing the appropriate category in the space below our category label. If none of our categories is appropriate (see question #2 below), write "OTHER".

   For example, assume that for 1985 we classified your state's regulatory environment as requiring prior approval when in fact your state was a "file and use" state that year. You would change our table, as follows:

1985	PRIOR *file & use*	REQ	RATES	DEV	NOSCHD

2. If you believe that one or more of our variables and/or our categories is inappropriate for your state, please describe in detail why and how you would change the variable or category definition so that it is more suitable.

_____

_____

_____

_____

3. Please provide any other comments that you think may be relevant concerning the regulatory environment in your state.

_____

_____

_____

4. Please provide your name, title, and phone number so that we may able to reach you should we have any questions concerning your response to this survey.

Name: _____

Title: _____

Phone: _____

Please return to: Dean John F. Burton, Jr.
School of Management and Labor Relations
Rutgers University
P.O. Box 10480
New Brunswick, NJ 08906-0480
Fax: (732) 445-5188

Alaska

Year	Prior Approval	Adherence	Role of the Regulatory Agency	Deviations	Schedule Rating
1975	PRIOR	REQ	RATES	DEV	N0SCHD
1976	PRIOR	REQ	RATES	DEV	N0SCHD
1977	PRIOR	REQ	RATES	DEV	N0SCHD
1978	PRIOR	REQ	RATES	DEV	N0SCHD
1979	PRIOR	REQ	RATES	DEV	N0SCHD
1980	PRIOR	REQ	RATES	DEV	N0SCHD
1981	PRIOR	REQ	RATES	DEV	N0SCHD
1982	PRIOR	REQ	RATES	DEV	N0SCHD
1983	PRIOR	REQ	RATES	DEV	N0SCHD
1984	PRIOR	REQ	RATES	DEV	SCHED
1985	PRIOR	REQ	RATES	DEV	SCHED
1986	PRIOR	REQ	RATES	DEV	SCHED
1987	PRIOR	REQ	RATES	DEV	SCHED
1988	PRIOR	REQ	RATES	DEV	SCHED
1989	PRIOR	REQ	RATES	DEV	SCHED
1990	PRIOR	REQ	RATES	DEV	SCHED
1991	PRIOR	REQ	RATES	DEV	SCHED
1992	PRIOR	REQ	RATES	DEV	SCHED
1993	PRIOR	REQ	RATES	DEV	SCHED
1994	PRIOR	REQ	RATES	DEV	SCHED
1995	PRIOR	REQ	RATES	DEV	SCHED

Appendix G

Supplemental Regression Results

The following tables contain the full set of coefficients for some of the regression equations predicting costs reported in Chapter 7. Unlike the data reported in that chapter, which are elasticity estimates, the coefficients contained in these tables have not been transformed into elasticities and represent the unit change in log costs (adjusted manual rates or net weekly costs) given a unit change in the corresponding independent variable.

Table G.1 Regression Equations Predicting Adjusted Manual Rates

Variable	Model 1	Model 2	Model 3	Model 4	Model 5	Model 6	Model 7	Model 8
ln(Cash benefits)	0.1165*** (2.77)	0.1079*** (2.56)	0.1057** (2.54)	0.1071** (2.53)	0.1145*** (2.73)	0.1032** (2.48)	0.1098*** (2.58)	0.1041** (2.44)
Medical benefits	0.0001*** (4.91)	0.0001*** (5.06)	0.0001*** (4.82)	0.0001*** (4.83)	0.0001*** (5.11)	0.0001*** (5.04)	0.0001*** (4.76)	0.0001*** (4.79)
ln(Injury)	0.8369*** (8.82)	0.9140*** (9.58)	0.9087*** (9.77)	0.8870*** (9.40)	0.8580*** (9.03)	0.9222*** (9.96)	0.8996*** (9.38)	0.8612*** (8.89)
Union density	0.0013 (0.32)	−0.0009 (0.21)	−0.0020 (0.49)	0.0017 (0.41)	0.0009 (0.22)	−0.0013 (0.31)	0.0021 (0.50)	0.0012 (0.29)
PPD percentage	0.0096*** (5.85)	0.0096*** (5.90)	0.0097*** (5.96)	0.0103*** (6.23)	0.0101*** (6.20)	0.0097*** (6.00)	0.0104*** (6.31)	0.0105*** (6.35)
Covered employment	0.0198*** (2.86)	0.0129* (1.85)	0.0140** (2.16)	0.0146** (2.15)	0.0160** (2.33)	0.0114* (1.71)	0.0159** (2.29)	0.0148** (2.10)
Competitive state fund	0.1883*** (3.71)	0.2123*** (4.24)	0.2252*** (4.53)	0.1761*** (3.50)	0.1958*** (3.89)	0.2133*** (4.30)	0.1636*** (3.23)	0.1709*** (3.38)
Without prior appr.	−0.0535* (1.71)	—	—	—				
Adv. rates	0.0351 (1.18)	—	—	—				
Loss costs	−0.1179*** (3.83)	—	—	—				
Var. from bureau rates w/prior appr.					0.0402 (1.38)	—	—	—
Admin. pricing w/ dev. or sched.					—	0.0690** (2.44)	0.0422 (1.43)	—
Admin. pricing w/ dev.					—	—	—	0.0461 (1.48)

Variable	(1)	(2)	(3)	(4)
Deviations	-0.0022 (0.11)	—	—	—
Schedule rating	0.0760*** (2.89)	—	—	—
Admin. pricing w/dev.	—	0.0590*** (1.90)	—	—
Admin. pricing w/sched. rating	—	0.0794** (2.05)	—	—
Adv. rates w/prior appr.	—	0.0825** (2.22)	—	—
Adv. rates w/o prior appr.	—	0.1676*** (3.23)	—	—
Loss costs w/prior appr.	—	0.0537 (1.26)	-0.0195 (0.59)	—
Loss costs w/o prior appr.	—	-0.1099*** (2.82)	-0.1796*** (5.75)	—
Partial competition	—	—	—	-0.0070 (0.20)
Open competition	—	—	—	0.0432 (1.51)
Adj. R^2	0.9167	0.9180	0.9168	0.9142

Variable	(5)	(6)	(7)	(8)
Admin. pricing w/ sched. rating	—	—	—	0.0101 (0.27)
Adv. rates or loss costs	—	—	0.0231 (0.71)	—
Adv. rates	—	0.1533*** (3.25)	—	—
Adv. rates w/prior app.	—	—	—	0.0657* (1.74)
Adv. rates w/o prior appr.	—	—	—	—
Loss costs/adv. rates w/o prior appr.	0.0975*** (2.74)	—	—	-0.0088 (0.25)
Loss costs	-0.0463 (1.32)	—	—	—
Loss costs w/prior appr.	—	0.0541 (1.27)	—	—
Loss costs w/o prior appr.	—	-0.1144*** (2.98)	—	—
Adj. R^2	0.9161	0.9179	0.9137	0.9144

Table G.2 Regression Equations Predicting Net Weekly Costs

Variable	1	2	3	4	Variable	5	6	7	8
			Model					Model	
ln(Cash benefits)	0.1450*** (3.40)	0.1375*** (3.22)	0.1370*** (3.25)	0.1363*** (3.18)	ln(Cash benefits)	0.1424*** (3.34)	0.1317*** (3.12)	0.1380*** (3.20)	0.1342*** (3.10)
Medical benefits	0.0001*** (5.30)	0.0001*** (5.49)	0.0001*** (5.18)	0.0001*** (5.24)	Medical benefits	0.0001*** (5.50)	0.0001*** (5.44)	0.0001*** (5.17)	0.0001*** (5.21)
ln(Injury)	0.7963*** (8.29)	0.8826*** (9.14)	0.8625*** (9.15)	0.8423*** (8.82)	ln(Injury)	0.8227*** (8.54)	0.8779*** (9.36)	0.8620*** (8.88)	0.8284*** (8.45)
Union density	0.0042 (1.01)	0.0022 (0.53)	0.0008 (0.19)	0.0047 (1.12)	Union density	0.0039 (0.93)	0.0018 (0.42)	0.0050 (1.19)	0.0044 (1.04)
PPD percentage	0.0094*** (5.63)	0.0093*** (5.68)	0.0096*** (5.82)	0.0101*** (6.08)	PPD percentage	0.0100*** (6.03)	0.0096*** (5.85)	0.0103*** (6.15)	0.0103*** (6.14)
Covered employment	0.0232*** (3.31)	0.0158** (2.24)	0.0184*** (2.80)	0.0179*** (2.60)	Covered employment	0.0186*** (2.67)	0.0146** (2.15)	0.0185*** (2.64)	0.0178** (2.51)
Competitive state fund	0.1931*** (3.76)	0.2205*** (4.35)	0.2322*** (4.61)	0.1814*** (3.56)	Competitive state fund	0.2024*** (3.97)	0.2178*** (4.33)	0.1720*** (3.36)	0.1786*** (3.49)
Without prior appr.	-0.0573* (1.81)	—	—	—	Variation from bureau rates w/prior appr.	0.0605** (2.05)	—	—	—
Adv. rates	0.0194 (0.65)	—	—	—	Admin. pricing w/dev. or sched.	—	0.0860*** (3.01)	0.0624** (2.08)	—

Loss costs	-0.1053*** (3.38)	—	—	—
Deviations	0.0093 (0.45)	—	—	—
Sched. rating	0.0864*** (3.25)	—	—	—
Admin. pricing w/dev.	—	0.0766** (2.44)	—	—
Admim. pricing w/sched. rating	—	0.1102*** (2.81)	—	—
Adv. rates w/prior appr.	—	0.0886** (2.36)	—	—
Adv. rates w/o prior appr.	—	0.1816*** (3.46)	—	—
Loss costs w/prior appr.	—	0.0713* (1.65)	-0.0169 (0.51)	—
Loss costs w/o prior appr.	—	-0.0990** (2.51)	-0.1790*** (5.66)	—
Open competition	—	—	—	0.0065 (0.19)
Partial competition	—	—	—	0.0602 (2.09)
Adj. R^2	0.9227	0.9239	0.9226	0.9205

Admin. pricing w/dev.	—	—	—	0.0628** (1.99)
Admin. pricing w/sched. rating	—	—	—	0.0405 (1.08)
Adv. rates or loss costs	—	—	0.0324 (0.99)	—
Adv. rates	—	0.1610*** (3.37)	—	—
Adv. rates w/prior appr.	—	—	—	0.0718* (1.88)
Advisory rates w/o prior appr.	0.1028*** (2.85)	—	—	—
Loss costs/adv. rates w/o prior	—	—	—	0.0049 (0.14)
Loss costs	-0.0331 (0.93)	—	—	—
Loss costs w/prior appr.	—	0.0725* (1.68)	—	—
Loss costs w/o prior appr.	—	-0.1017*** (2.61)	—	—
Adj. R^2	0.9220	0.9238	0.9201	0.9206

**Table G.3 Regression Equations Predicting Costs as a Function
of the Regulatory Regime, Regulatory Stringency, and the
Insurance Cycle**

Variable	Adjusted manual rates	Net weekly costs
ln(Cash benefits)	0.2381***	0.2678***
	(5.06)	(5.67)
Medical benefits	0.0003***	0.0003***
	(17.72)	(18.62)
ln(Injury)	0.8379***	0.8733***
	(10.27)	(10.67)
Union density	–0.0392***	–0.0358***
	(11.83)	(10.74)
PPD percentage	0.0118***	0.0113***
	(6.88)	(6.59)
Covered employment	0.0129*	0.0178**
	(1.71)	(2.35)
Competitive state fund	0.1490**	0.1639***
	(2.44)	(2.68)
Regul. stringency	–0.4789***	–0.4756***
	(3.96)	(3.92)
Hard market	–0.2493	–0.2866*
	(1.57)	(1.80)
Regul. stringency × hard market	0.1749	0.2417
	(1.10)	(1.52)
Var. from bureau rates w/prior appr.	–0.2168	–0.2059
	(1.43)	(1.36)
Var. from bureau rates w/prior appr. × hard market	–0.0160	0.0305
	(0.08)	(0.16)
Var. from bureau rates w/prior appr. × regul. stringency	0.3688***	0.3747***
	(2.64)	(2.67)
Var. from bureau rates w/prior appr. × hard market × regul. stringency	–0.1032	–0.1566
	(0.54)	(0.82)
Adv. rates w/o prior appr.	–0.1916	–0.4513
	(0.36)	(0.84)
Adv. rates w/o prior appr. × hard market	0.8238	1.1204*
	(1.38)	(1.87)

Table G.3 (continued)

Variable	Adjusted manual rates	Net weekly costs
Adv. rates w/o prior appr. × regul. stringency	0.3674 (0.67)	0.6435 (1.16)
Adv. rates w/o prior appr. × hard market × regul. stringency	−0.7562 (1.23)	−1.0597* (1.72)
Loss costs w/prior appr.	−0.2076 (0.93)	−0.1784 (0.80)
Loss costs w/prior appr. × hard market	0.1959 (0.56)	0.2059 (0.59)
Loss costs w/prior appr. × regul. stringency	0.2368 (1.17)	0.2365 (1.16)
Loss costs w/prior appr. × hard market × regul. stringency	−0.1103 (0.34)	−0.1456 (0.44)
Loss costs w/o prior appr.	−1.1623*** (4.56)	−1.1827*** (4.63)
Loss costs w/o prior appr. × hard market	0.8016** (2.35)	0.9571*** (2.79)
Loss costs w/prior appr. × regul. stringency	0.9796*** (4.08)	1.0179*** (4.22)
Loss costs w/prior appr. × hard market × regul. stringency	−0.5925* (1.80)	−0.7651** (2.31)
State dummies	Yes	Yes
Year dummies	No	No
Adj. R^2	0.8939	0.9033

References

Allen, Robert F. 1974. "Cross-Sectional Estimates of Cost Economies in Stock Property-Liability Companies." *Review of Economics and Statistics* 56: 100–103.

American Medical Association. 1984. *Guides to the Evaluation of Permanent Impairment.* 2nd edition. Chicago: AMA.

Appel, David, and Philip S. Borba. 1988. "Costs and Prices of Workers' Compensation Insurance." In *Workers' Compensation Insurance Pricing: Current Programs and Proposed Reforms,* Philip S. Borba and David Appel, eds. Boston, Massachusetts: Kluwer Academic, pp. 5–9.

Appel, David, and James Gerofsky. 1985. "Regulating Competition: The Case of Workers' Compensation Insurance." *Journal of Insurance Regulation* 3: 408–425.

Appel, David, Michael McMurray, and Mark Mulvaney. 1992. "An Analysis of the Net Costs of Workers' Compensation Insurance." Photocopy, Milliman & Robertson, Inc., New York, New York.

Barth, Peter S. 1987. *The Tragedy of Black Lung: Federal Compensation for Occupational Disease.* Kalamazoo, Michigan: W.E. Upjohn Institute for Employment Research.

Barkume, Anthony J., and John W. Ruser. 1997. "Open Competition, Workers' Compensation Costs, and Injury Rates." Photocopy, Bureau of Labor Statistics, Washington, D.C.

Berkowitz, Monroe, and John F. Burton, Jr. 1987. *Permanent Disability Benefits in Workers' Compensation.* Kalamazoo, Michigan: W.E. Upjohn Institute for Employment Research.

Berkowitz, Monroe, John F. Burton, Jr., and Wayne Vroman. 1979. *Permanent Disability Benefits in the Workers' Compensation Program.* Final Report for a project supported by the National Science Foundation.

Berreth, Charles A. 1992. "Workers' Compensation: State Enactments in 1991." *Monthly Labor Review* 115(1): 56–63.

———. 1994. "Workers' Compensation Laws: Significant Changes in 1993." *Monthly Labor Review* 117(1): 53–64.

———. 1996. "Workers' Compensation Laws Enacted in 1995." *Monthly Labor Review* 119(1): 59–72.

———. 1997. "State Workers' Compensation Legislation Enacted in 1996." *Monthly Labor Review* 120(1): 43–50.

Best. 2000. *Best's Aggregate & Averages Property/Casualty.* Oldwick, New Jersey: A.M. Best Company.

Blackmon, B. Glenn, Jr., and Richard Zeckhauser. 1991. "Mispriced Equity: Regulated Rates for Auto Insurance in Massachusetts." *American Economic Review* 81(2): 65–69.

Bouzouita, Raja, and Vickie L. Bajtelsmit. 1997. "The Impact of Rate Regulation on the Residual Market for Automobile Insurance." *Journal of Insurance Regulation* 16(1): 61–72.

Brown, Ruth A. 1993. "Workers' Compensation: State Enactments in 1992." *Monthly Labor Review* 116(1): 50–55.

———. 1995. "Workers' Compensation Laws: Enactments in 1994." *Monthly Labor Review* 117(1): 53–59.

Burton, John F., Jr. 1965. "The Significance and Causes of the Interstate Variations in the Employer's Costs of Workmen's Compensation." Ph.D. dissertation, University of Michigan.

———. 1979. "Workers' Compensation Costs for Employers." In *Research Report of the Interdepartmental Workers' Compensation Task Force*, Volume III, Employment Standards Administration, U.S. Department of Labor, pp. 9–32.

———. 1992. "Workers' Compensation Costs in 1991." *Workers' Compensation Monitor* 5(3): 1–3, 18.

———. 1997. "Workers' Compensation, Twenty-Four-Hour Coverage, and Managed Care." In *Disability: Challenges for Social Insurance, Health Care Financing, and Labor Market Policy*, Virginia P. Reno, Jerry L. Mashaw, and Bill Gradison, eds. Washington, D.C.: National Academy of Social Insurance, pp. 129–149.

Burton, John F., Jr., and James R. Chelius. 1997. "Workplace Safety and Health Regulations: Rationale and Results." In *Government Regulation of the Employment Relationship*, Bruce E. Kaufman, ed. Madison, Wisconsin: Industrial Relations Research Association, pp. 253–293.

Burton, John F., Jr., H. Allan Hunt, and Alan B. Krueger. 1985. *Interstate Variations in the Employers' Cost of Workers' Compensation, with Particular Reference to Michigan and the Other Great Lake States*. Ithaca, New York: Workers' Disability Income Systems, Inc.

Burton, John F., Jr., and Timothy B. Schmidle. 1991. *The Employers' Cost of Workers' Compensation in Michigan and the Nation*. Watchung, New Jersey: Workers' Disability Income Systems, Inc.

———. 1992. "Workers' Compensation Insurance Rates: National Averages Up, Interstate Differences Widen." *Workers' Compensation Monitor* 5(1): 1–14.

Burton, John F., Jr., and Timothy P. Schmidle, eds. 1995. *1996 Workers' Compensation Year Book*. Horsham, Pennsylvania: LRP Publications.

Butler, Richard J. 1994. "Economic Determinants of Workers' Compensation Trends." *Journal of Risk and Insurance* 61(3): 383–401.

Butler, Richard J., and John D. Worrall. 1986. "The Costs of Workers' Compensation Insurance: Private versus Public." *Journal of Law and Economics* 29(2): 329–356.

_____. 1990. "Premium and Loss Cycles in Workers' Compensation." In *Benefits, Costs, and Cycles in Workers' Compensation*, Philip S. Borba and David Appel, eds. New York: Kluwer Academic, pp. 129–162.

Carroll, Anne M., and Robert Kaestner. 1995. "The Relationship between Regulation and Prices in the Workers' Compensation Insurance Market." *Journal of Regulatory Economics* 8(2): 149–166.

Chelius, James R. 1977. *Workplace Safety and Health*. Washington, D.C.: American Enterprise Institute.

Chelius, James R., and John F. Burton, Jr. 1994. "Who Actually Pays for Workers' Compensation? The Empirical Evidence." In *1995 Workers' Compensation Year Book*, John F. Burton, Jr. and Timothy P. Schmidle, eds. Horsham, Pennsylvania: LRP Publications.

Chidambaran, N.K., Thomas A. Pugel, and Anthony Saunders. 1997. "An Investigation of the Performance of the U.S. Property-Liability Insurance Industry." *The Journal of Risk and Insurance* 64(2): 371–381.

Cho, Dongsae. 1988. "Some Evidence of Scale Economies in Workers' Compensation Insurance." *Journal of Risk and Insurance* 55: 324–330.

Council of Economic Advisers. 2000. *Economic Report of the President*. Washington D.C.: U.S. Government Printing Office.

Council of State Governments. 1974. *Workmen's Compensation and Rehabilitation Law* (Revised). Lexington, Kentucky: Council of State Governments.

Cummins, J. David, and Patricia M. Danzon. 1997. "Price, Financial Quality, and Capital Flows in Insurance Markets." *Journal of Financial Intermediation* 6: 3–38.

Cummins, J. David, and Scott E. Harrington. 1987. "The Impact of Rate Regulation in U.S. Property-Liability Insurance Markets: A Cross-Sectional Analysis of Individual Firm Loss Ratios." *Geneva Papers on Risk and Insurance* 12(42): 51.

Cummins, J. David, Scott E. Harrington, and Robert W. Klein. 1991. "Cycles and Crises in Property/Casualty Insurance: Causes and Implications." *Journal of Insurance Regulation* 11: 50–93.

Cummins, J. David, and J. Francois Outreville. 1987. "An International Analysis of Underwriting Cycles in Property-Liability Insurance." *Journal of Risk and Insurance* 54: 246–262.

434

Cummins, J. David, and Mary A. Weiss. 1993. "Measuring Cost Efficiency in the Property-Liability Insurance Industry." *Journal of Banking and Finance* 17: 463–481.

Danzon, Patricia Munch. 1983. "Rating Bureaus in U.S. Property Liability Insurance Markets: Anti or Pro-competitive?" *Geneva Papers on Risk and Insurance* 8(29): 371–402.

Danzon, Patricia M., and Scott E. Harrington. 1998. *Rate Regulation of Workers' Compensation Insurance: How Price Controls Increase Costs.* Washington, D.C.: American Enterprise Institute.

Doherty, Neil A. 1981. "The Measurement of Output and Economies of Scale in Property-Liability Insurance." *Journal of Risk and Insurance* 48(3): 390–402.

Doherty, Neil A., and James R. Garven. 1995. "Insurance Cycles: Interest Rates and the Capacity Constraint Model." *Journal of Business* 68(3): 383–404.

Doherty, Neil A., and Han Bin Kang. 1988. "Interest Rates and Insurance Price Cycles." *Journal of Banking and Finance* 12(June): 199–214.

Durbin, David, and Richard J. Butler. 1998. "Prevention of Disability from Private Work-Related Sources: The Roles of Risk Management, Government Intervention, and Insurance." In *New Approaches to Disability in the Workplace*, Terry Thomason, John F. Burton, Jr., and Douglas Hyatt, eds. Madison, Wisconsin: Industrial Relations Research Association, pp. 63–86.

Durbin, David L., and Jennifer Kish. 1998. "Factors Affecting Permanent Partial Disability Ratings in Workers' Compensation." *Journal of Risk and Insurance* 65(1): 81–99.

Elson, Martin W., and John F. Burton, Jr. 1981. "Workers' Compensation Insurance: Recent Trends in Employer Costs." *Monthly Labor Review* 104(3): 45–50.

Fishback, Price V., and Shawn Everett Kantor. 1996. "The Durable Experiment: State Insurance of Workers' Compensation Risk in the Early Twentieth Century." *Journal of Economic History* 56(4): 809–836.

Fortin, Bernard, and Paul Lanoie. 1992. "Substitution between Unemployment Insurance and Workers' Compensation: An Analysis Applied to the Risk of Workplace Accidents." *Journal of Public Economics* 49(3): 287–312.

Frech, H.E., and Joseph C. Samprone, Jr. 1980. "The Welfare Loss of Excess Nonprice Competition: The Case of Property-Liability Insurance Regulation." *Journal of Law and Economics* 23(2): 429–440.

GAO. 1986. *Auto Insurance: State Regulation Affects Cost and Availability.* U.S. General Accounting Office Report GAO/OCE-86-2, Washington, D.C.: U.S. Government Printing Office.

Geiger, Bob. 1988. "Workers' Compensation: Should Present Trends Continue, Fund May Face Difficulties." *Charleston Sunday Gazette-Mail*, February 7.

Grabowski, Henry, W. Kip Viscusi, and William N. Evans. 1989. "Price and Availability Tradeoffs of Automobile Insurance Regulation." *Journal of Risk and Insurance* 56(2): 275–299.

Greene, William H. 1993. *Econometric Analysis*. Second edition. New York: Macmillan.

Hammond, J.D., E.R. Melander, and N. Shilling. 1971. "Economies of Scale in the Property and Liability Insurance Industry." *Journal of Risk and Insurance* 28(2): 181–191.

Hanweck, Gerald A., and Arthur M.B. Hogan. 1996. "The Structure of the Property/Casualty Insurance Industry." *Journal of Economics and Business* 48(2): 141–155.

Harrington, Scott E. 1984. "The Impact of Rate Regulation on Prices and Underwriting Results in the Property-Liability Insurance Industry: A Survey." *Journal of Risk and Insurance* 51(4): 579–580.

———. 1987. "A Note on the Impact of Auto Insurance Rate Regulation." *Review of Economics and Statistics* 69(1): 167.

———. 1992. "Rate Suppression." *Journal of Risk and Insurance* 59: 185–202.

Harrington, Scott E., and Patricia M. Danzon. 1994. "Price Cutting in Liability Insurance Markets." *Journal of Business* 67(4): 511–538.

Hirsch, Barry T., and David A. Macpherson. 1996. *Union Membership and Earnings Data Book: Compilations from the Current Population Survey.* 1996 edition. Washington, D.C.: Bureau of National Affairs.

Hirsch, Barry T., David A. Macpherson, and J. Michael Dumond. 1997. "Workers' Compensation Recipiency in Union and Nonunion Workplaces." *Industrial and Labor Relations Review* 50(2): 213–236.

Huebner, S.S., Kenneth Black, Jr., and Robert S. Cline. 1982. *Property and Liability Insurance.* Third edition. Englewood Cliffs, New Jersey: Prentice-Hall, pp. 575–592.

Johnson, Joseph E., George B. Flanigan, and Steven N. Weisbart. 1981. "Returns to Scale in the Property and Liability Insurance Industry." *Journal of Risk and Insurance* 48(1): 18–45.

Joskow, Paul L. 1973. "Cartels, Competition and Regulation in the Property-Liability Insurance Industry." *The Bell Journal of Economics and Management Science* 4(2): 375–427.

Kallop, Roy H. 1976. "A Current Look at Workers' Compensation Ratemaking." In *Proceedings of the Casualty Actuarial Society,* Volume 62. Boston: Sperry Rand, pp. 62–176.

Kimball, Spencer L., and Ronald N. Boyce. 1958. "The Adequacy of State Insurance Rate Regulation: The McCarran-Ferguson Act in Historical Perspective." *Michigan Law Review* 56: 545–578.

Klein, Robert W. 1995. "Insurance Regulation in Transition." *Journal of Risk and Insurance* 62(3): 363–404.

Klein, Robert W., Eric C. Nordman, and Julienne L. Fritz. 1993. *Market Conditions in Workers' Compensation Insurance*. Photocopy, National Association of Insurance Commissioners, Workers' Compensation Task Force.

Kokkelenberg, Edward C., and Donna R. Sockell. 1985. "Union Membership in the United States, 1973–1981." *Industrial and Labor Relations Review* 38(4): 497–543.

Krueger, Alan B., and John F. Burton, Jr. 1990. "The Employers' Costs of Workers' Compensation Insurance: Magnitudes, Determinants, and Public Policy." *Review of Economics and Statistics* 72(2): 228–240.

Larson, Arthur, and Lex K. Larson. 1999. *Larson's Workers' Compensation: Desk Edition*. Through release no. 43. New York: Matthew Bender.

Meier, Kenneth J. 1988. *The Political Economy of Regulation: The Case of Insurance*. Albany, New York: SUNY Press.

Mont, Daniel, John F. Burton, Jr., and Virginia Reno. 2000. *Workers' Compensation: Benefits, Coverage, and Costs, 1997–1998: New Estimates*. Washington, D.C.: National Academy of Social Insurance.

Moore, Michael J., and W. Kip Viscusi. 1990. *Compensation Mechanisms for Job Risks: Wages, Workers' Compensation, and Product Liability*. Princeton, New Jersey: Princeton University Press.

National Commission. 1972. *The Report of the National Commission on State Workmen's Compensation Laws*. Washington, D.C.: U.S. Government Printing Office.

NCCI. 1981. *Ratemaking: The Pricing of Workers' Compensation Insurance*. New York: National Council on Compensation Insurance.

_____. 1993. *Annual Statistical Bulletin*. 1993 edition, Boca Raton, Florida: National Council on Compensation Insurance.

_____. 1994. *Annual Statistical Bulletin*. 1994 edition, Boca Raton, Florida: National Council on Compensation Insurance.

_____. 1995. *Annual Statistical Bulletin*. 1995 edition, Boca Raton, Florida: National Council on Compensation Insurance.

_____. 1996. *Loss Development Exhibits: Sample State Report Evaluated as of 12/94*. Boca Raton, Florida: National Council on Compensation Insurance.

_____. 1997. *Reporting Guidebook for the Annual Calls for Experience*. Sixth reprint, Boca Raton, Florida: National Council on Compensation Insurance.

———. 1998. *Annual Statistical Bulletin.* 1998 edition, Boca Raton, Florida: National Council on Compensation Insurance.

———. 2000. *Annual Statistical Bulletin.* 2000 edition, Boca Raton, Florida: National Council on Compensation Insurance.

National Foundation. 1997. "Fiscal Data for State Workers' Compensation System[s], 1986–95." *Research Bulletin* issue '97 W.C.-2, National Foundation for Unemployment Compensation and Workers Compensation, Washington, D.C.

Nelson, William J., Jr. 1988. "Workers' Compensation: 1980–84 Benchmark Revisions." *Social Security Bulletin* 51(7): 4–21.

———. 1992a. "Workers' Compensation: Coverage, Benefits, and Costs, 1989." *Social Security Bulletin* 55(1): 51–56.

———. 1992b. "Workers' Compensation: 1984–1988 Benchmark Revisions." *Social Security Bulletin* 55(3): 41–58.

———. 1993. "Workers' Compensation: Coverage, Benefits, and Costs, 1990–91." *Social Security Bulletin* 56(3): 2–8.

Nyden, Paul. 1997a. "Giveaway Viewed Hurting Fund." *Charleston Gazette*, October 28.

———. 1997b. "The Making of a Deficit: Moore's Actions Put Fund on Brink of Insolvency." *Charleston Sunday Gazette-Mail*, December 21.

———. 1998a. "West Virginia Workers' Compensation Rates to Remain Fairly Steady." *Charleston Gazette*, April 29.

———. 1998b. "Large Workers Comp Surplus Predicted." *Charleston Gazette*, August 27.

Pauly, Mark, Howard Kunreuther, and Paul Kleindorfer. 1986. "Regulation and Quality Competition in the U.S. Insurance Industry." In *The Economics of Insurance Regulation: A Cross-National Study*, Jorg Finsinger and Mark V. Pauly, eds. New York: St. Martin's, pp. 65–107.

Peltzman, Sam. 1976. "Toward a More General Theory of Regulation." *Journal of Law and Economics* 8(2): 211–240.

Price, Daniel N. 1979. "Workers' Compensation: Coverage, Payments, and Costs, 1977." *Social Security Bulletin* 42(10): 18–22.

———. 1983. "Workers' Compensation: Coverage, Benefits, and Costs, 1980." *Social Security Bulletin* 46(5): 14–19.

Samprone, Joseph C., Jr. 1979. "Rate Regulation and Nonprice Competition in the Property and Liability Insurance Industry." *Journal of Risk and Insurance* 46: 683–696.

Schmidle, Timothy P. 1994. "The Impact of Insurance Pricing on the Employers' Costs of Workers' Compensation Insurance." Ph.D. dissertation, Cornell University.

Schmulowitz, Jack. 1997. *Workers' Compensation: Benefits, Coverage, and Costs, 1994–95*. Washington, D.C.: National Academy of Social Insurance.

Schurman, Susan J., David Weil, Paul Landsbergis, and Barbara A. Israel. 1998. "The Role of Unions and Collective Bargaining in Preventing Work-Related Disability." In *New Approaches to Disability in the Workplace*, Terry Thomason, John F. Burton, Jr. and Douglas Hyatt, eds. Madison, Wisconsin: Industrial Relations Research Association, pp. 121–155.

Skogh, Goran. 1982. "Returns to Scale in the Swedish Property-Liability Insurance Industry." *Journal of Risk and Insurance* 49(2): 218–228.

Smallwood, Dennis E. 1975. "Competition, Regulation, and Product Quality in the Automobile Insurance Industry." In *Promoting Competition in Regulated Markets*, Almarin Phillips, ed. Washington, D.C.: The Brookings Institution.

Smith, Robert S. 1992. "Have OSHA and Workers' Compensation Made the Workplace Safer?" In *Research Frontiers in Industrial Relations and Human Resources*. Madison, Wisconsin: Industrial Relations Research Association, pp. 557–586.

Social Security Administration. 1995. *Annual Statistical Supplement, 1995*. Washington, D.C.: U.S. Government Printing Office.

Spieler, Emily A., and John F. Burton, Jr. 1998. "Compensation for Disabled Workers: Workers' Compensation." In *New Approaches to Disability in the Workplace*, Terry Thomason, John F. Burton, Jr., and Douglas E. Hyatt, eds. Madison, Wisconsin: Industrial Relations Research Association, pp. 205–244.

Stigler, George. 1971. "The Theory of Economic Regulation." *Bell Journal of Economics and Management Science* 2: 3–21.

Suponcic, Susan J., and Sharon Tennyson. 1995. "Rate Regulation and the Industrial Organization of Automobile Insurance." Working paper no. 5275, National Bureau of Economic Research.

Tennyson, Sharon. 1991. "The Effect of Rate Regulation on Underwriting Cycles." *CPCU Journal* 44(1): 34.

———. 1997. "The Impact of Rate Regulation on State Automobile Insurance Markets." *Journal of Insurance Regulation* 15(4): 502–523.

Thomason, Terry, and John F. Burton, Jr. 1993. "Economic Effects of Workers' Compensation in the United States: Private Insurance and the Administration of Compensation Claims." *Journal of Labor Economics* 11(1), Part 2: S1–S37.

———. 2000a. "The Cost of Workers' Compensation in Ontario." In *New Perspectives in Workers' Compensation Policy*, Morley Gunderson and

Douglas E. Hyatt, eds. Toronto, Ontario: University of Toronto Press, pp. 261–298.

_____. 2000b. "Statutory Workers' Compensation Benefits, 1972 to 1978." In *The Adequacy of Workers' Compensation Cash Benefits*, H. Allan Hunt, ed. Preliminary unpublished edition. Washington, D.C.: National Academy of Social Insurance.

Thomason, Terry, and Douglas Hyatt. 1997. "Workers' Compensation Costs in Canada, 1961–1993." In *Transition and Structural Change in the North American Labour Market*, Michael Abbott, Charles Beach, and Richard Chaykowski, eds. Kingston, Ontario: Industrial Relations Centre and John Deutsch Institute, Queen's University, pp. 235–255.

Thomason, Terry, Douglas Hyatt, and Karen Roberts. 1998. "Disputes and Dispute Resolution." In *New Approaches to Disability in the Workplace*, Terry Thomason, John F. Burton, Jr., and Douglas E. Hyatt, eds. Madison, Wisconsin: Industrial Relations Research Association, pp. 269–298.

Thomason, Terry, and Silvana Pozzebon. 1999. "Determinants of Firm Workplace Health and Safety and Claims Management Practices." Unpublished manuscript, Labor Research Center, University of Rhode Island.

Thompson, Roger. 1992. "Workers' Comp Costs: Out of Control." *Nation's Business* 80(7): 22–25, 28, and 30.

Tinsley, LaVerne C. 1990. "State Workers' Compensation: Significant Legislation in 1989." *Monthly Labor Review* 113(1): 57–63.

———. 1991. "State Workers' Compensation: Legislation Enacted in 1990." *Monthly Labor Review* 114(1): 57–62.

U.S. Department of Health and Human Services. 1985. *U.S. Decennial Life Tables for 1979–81*. Vol. 1, No. 1, DHHS Publication no. (PHS) 85-1150-1. U.S. Department of Health and Human Services, Public Health Service, National Center for Health Statistics, Hyattsville, Maryland, August.

U.S. Department of Justice. 1977. *The Pricing and Marketing of Insurance*. A report of the U.S. Department of Justice to the Task Group on Antitrust Immunities. Washington, D.C.: U.S. Government Printing Office.

U.S. Department of Labor. 1977. *Employment and Wages, Annual Averages*. Bureau of Labor Statistics, Washington, D.C.: U.S. Government Printing Office.

———. 1980. *Employment and Wages, Annual Averages*. Bureau of Labor Statistics, Washington, D.C.: U.S. Government Printing Office.

———. 1981. *Employment and Wages, Annual Averages*. Bureau of Labor Statistics, Washington, D.C.: U.S. Government Printing Office.

———. 1984. *Employment and Wages, Annual Averages*. Bureau of Labor Statistics, Washington, D.C.: U.S. Government Printing Office.

440

———. 1989. *Employment and Wages, Annual Averages.* Bureau of Labor Statistics, Washington, D.C.: U.S. Government Printing Office.

———. 1991. *Dictionary of Occupational Titles.* Employment and Training Administration, U.S. Employment Service. Indianapolis: JIST Works.

———. 1998a. *State Workers' Compensation Laws in Effect on January 1, 1998 Compared with the 19 Essential Recommendations of the National Commission on State Workmen's Compensation Laws.* Washington, D.C.: U.S. Department of Labor, Employment Standards Administration, Office of Workers' Compensation Programs.

———. 1998b. *State Workers' Compensation Laws.* Washington, D.C.: U.S. Department of Labor, Employment Standards Administration, Office of Workers' Compensation Programs.

Venezian, Emilio C. 1985. "Ratemaking Methods and Profit Cycles in Property and Liability Insurance." *Journal of Risk and Insurance* 52: 477–500.

Virginia Bureau of Insurance. 1978. *Competition in the Property and Casualty Insurance Industry: An Evaluation of Alternative Methods of Rate Regulation.* Richmond, Virginia: State Corporation Commission.

Webb, Bernard L., J.J. Launie, Willis Park Rokes, and Norman A. Baglini. 1984. *Insurance Company Operations.* Volume II, third edition. Malvern, Pennsylvania: American Institute for Property and Liability Underwriters.

Weil, David. 1991. "Enforcing OSHA: The Role of Labor Unions." *Industrial Relations* 30(1): 20–36.

White, Lawrence J. 1996. "Competition versus Harmonization: An Overview of International Financial Services." In *International Regulation of Financial Services: Harmonization versus Competition,* Claude R. Barfield, ed. Washington, D.C.: AEI Press.

Williams, C. Arthur, Jr. 1969. *Insurance Arrangements under Workmen's Compensation.* Washington, D.C.: U.S. Department of Labor, Wage and Labor Standards Administration, Bureau of Labor Standards.

———. 1986. "Workers' Compensation Insurance Rates: Their Determination and Regulation." In *Current Issues in Workers' Compensation,* James Chelius, ed. Kalamazoo, Michigan: W.E. Upjohn Institute for Employment Research, pp. 209–235.

Williams, C. Arthur, Jr., and Peter S. Barth. 1973. *Compendium on Workmen's Compensation.* Washington, D.C.: National Commission on State Workmen's Compensation Laws.

Williams, C. Arthur, Jr., and Andrew F. Whitman. 1973. "Open Competition Rating Laws and Price Competition." *Journal of Risk and Insurance* 40(4): 490.

Witt, Robert C., and Harry Miller. 1980. "A Comparative Analysis of Relative Costs under Competitive and Non-Competitive Rate Regulatory Laws." *CPCU Journal* 33(4): 174–189.

_____. 1981. "Rate Regulation, Competition, and Underwriting Risk in Automobile Insurance Markets." *CPCU Journal* 34(4): 202–220.

Witt, Robert C., and Jorge Urrutia. 1983. "Price Competition, Regulation, and Systematic Underwriting Risk in Automobile Insurance." *Geneva Papers on Risk and Insurance* 8(29): 403–429.

Cited Author Index

The italic letters *f*, *n*, and *t* following a page number indicate that the cited name is within a figure, note, or table, respectively, on that page.

444

Subject Index

The italic letters *f*, *n*, and *t* following a page number indicate that the subject information is within a figure, note, or table, respectively, on that page.

452

About the Institute

The W.E. Upjohn Institute for Employment Research is a nonprofit research organization devoted to finding and promoting solutions to employment-related problems at the national, state, and local levels. It is an activity of the W.E. Upjohn Unemployment Trustee Corporation, which was established in 1932 to administer a fund set aside by the late Dr. W.E. Upjohn, founder of The Upjohn Company, to seek ways to counteract the loss of employment income during economic downturns.

The Institute is funded largely by income from the W.E. Upjohn Unemployment Trust, supplemented by outside grants, contracts, and sales of publications. Activities of the Institute comprise the following elements: 1) a research program conducted by a resident staff of professional social scientists; 2) a competitive grant program, which expands and complements the internal research program by providing financial support to researchers outside the Institute; 3) a publications program, which provides the major vehicle for disseminating the research of staff and grantees, as well as other selected works in the field; and 4) an Employment Management Services division, which manages most of the publicly funded employment and training programs in the local area.

The broad objectives of the Institute's research, grant, and publication programs are to 1) promote scholarship and experimentation on issues of public and private employment and unemployment policy, and 2) make knowledge and scholarship relevant and useful to policymakers in their pursuit of solutions to employment and unemployment problems.

Current areas of concentration for these programs include causes, consequences, and measures to alleviate unemployment; social insurance and income maintenance programs; compensation; workforce quality; work arrangements; family labor issues; labor-management relations; and regional economic development and local labor markets.

457